W9-DJG-821

TALLER THAN
BANDAI MOUNTAIN

Illustrated by Fred Banbery

TALLER THAN
BANDAI MOUNTAIN

The Story of Hideyo Noguchi

DAN D'AMELIO

THE VIKING PRESS   NEW YORK

To my wife, Fanny,
whose loyalty
is exceeded only by her love

Contents

TALLER THAN
BANDAI MOUNTAIN

His Left Hand

The sun was low, its rays reflecting off the shallow water in the rice paddy. In the water, a woman was bent over from the waist, her hands swiftly pulling up weeds.

She straightened up now and wiped a strand of hair from her face. She closed her eyes and arched her back. A sigh escaped her lips.

Her gaze fixed on something in the distance. A boy in a black uniform trudged along the dirt road. He carried books in one hand. Using this hand, he waved.

The two met on the dirt road, near the rice paddy. The woman bowed. The boy returned the bow. She smiled.

"The day went so fast," she said. "Here, let me carry your books."

The boy shook his head. "No, Mother."

They walked together, her bare feet keeping in step with his rice-straw sandals. She took off her straw hat and shook her head so that her thick black hair fell back over her shoulders. She was young, yet there were deep lines in her forehead and her eyes were puffed from lack of sleep.

"I will change into my work clothes and help you in the paddy," the boy said.

"It will not be necessary," she said. "Inu will help me."

The boy did not answer. He held his small body very straight and cocked his head to one side. His father had had the same habit. It was a sign that Hideyo had made up his mind. There would be no use in arguing.

The house stood on wooden piers, several feet above the ground. Bamboo frames supported the sides and the thatched roof. A narrow porch extended before the doorway.

Inside the house rectangular mats were laid on the floor. In the center of the room was a fire pit, and in a corner, on a low shelf, was the family shrine.

Hideyo stepped behind a paper partition and began to disrobe. His mother put some *o-mugi*—porridge—in a bowl. "What did Hideyo study today?" she asked.

"We studied other people, other lands," he said.

"Is their world like ours?"

"They live in big houses, they have warm clothes for winter, and their bellies are always full," he said.

"Are they all lords?"

"No, they are common people. Even farmers."

His mother shook her head. She had never gone beyond Wakamatsu, twenty miles to the west.

Hideyo stepped from behind the partition. He was barefoot. His coarse robe, tied around the waist with a strand of rope, reached to his knees. He knelt down by the bowl. Using two long sticks, which he held in his right hand, he ate silently. The bowl rested on his left forearm and against his chest. The fingers of the left hand were gnarled stumps.

His mother did not eat. She tucked several bamboo shoots into the sash around her waist. These she would eat later as she worked in the rice paddy.

When Hideyo stepped outside, his mother was already in the paddy. Her bent figure looked tiny in the wide, flooded field. Beyond their paddy stretched a checkerboard of flooded paddies belonging to other farmers. Towering in the distance was Bandai Mountain.

The soil under his feet was like dust. It was the month of September and it had not rained for weeks. He looked up at the sky. There were only a few puffs of clouds. It would not rain this day, and that was good. Rain would hinder their work in the paddy, and a heavy rain would raise the water to a dangerous level. It was backbreaking work, but the weeding had to be finished as soon as possible. Other farmers had finished long ago and some had already begun the harvest. But there was only his mother, his sister Inu, and himself to work the paddy. His father had left them and gone to Hokkaido years ago.

Hideyo stepped down into the water. The cool mud under his feet felt good. He was careful not to step on the delicate green rice shoots that rose above the water in neat rows. Already he was surrounded by swarms of mosquitoes. It was useless to swat at them. He had learned to endure their stings.

Together they worked, side by side, the mother and the boy reaching down into the water between the shoots to pull up the weeds. When the water chilled the mother's hand so that she could no longer feel anything, she used the other hand. Hideyo used only his right hand. Whenever he felt it becoming numb he would raise it from the water and shake it back and forth for a moment, letting the quickened circulation restore feeling.

At dusk Inu joined them. She was several years older than Hideyo. When he was small, she had been a little mother to him. She was a fragile-looking girl with long black hair like her mother's. This day she was proud because she had caught two fish at Lake Inawashiro.

The day changed to night, but they continued to work. It was difficult to see now, but in a while the moon would rise. When the moon was full over the trees, they worked quickly, the only sound that of their feet moving through the water. Once Inu sneezed and her mother ordered her to rest. The girl sat on the dike, knees drawn up under her chin, shivering in the moonlight, watching her mother and brother work.

Hideyo could no longer feel anything with his right hand, it was so numb. He plunged his left hand into the water and felt around for weeds with the stumps. Then, using his left arm to guide him, he moved his right hand down to grasp the weeds. When his mother saw this, she stopped working. She straightened up and called his name. Hideyo followed her out of the paddy.

Walking home he did not notice the chill air; his thoughts centered on his stomach. He told himself, unconvincingly, that he had eaten well that day: he had had a handful of rice for lunch at school, and the bowl of o-mugi that afternoon. Perhaps tonight, before going to bed, they would have the fish Inu had caught. That and the tender bamboo shoots would make a good meal.

In the house Inu and her mother cleaned and sliced the fish. "And what did Hideyo learn today at school?" Inu asked.

Hideyo smiled at his sister. "I learned that foreigners prefer their fish cooked."

"Oh, no?"

"Yes, it is true," said Hideyo.

The mother served Hideyo first, placing the *sashimi* —sliced raw fish—before him. When he had eaten it she gave him several bamboo shoots. Only when he had finished did she and Inu begin to eat.

Mother and daughter ate in silence, each immersed in her own thoughts. Inu could not go to school, even though she was the oldest. Boys were given preference in all things. She understood well that her mother could not afford to send them both to school. She did not mind. She was glad to be at home to help. But she wished her mother did not have to work so hard. Work had withered her hands like those of an old woman.

The mother promised herself that she would say a prayer of thanks that night. Her children were safe and fed. Maybe things would be better now. Like winter, the past chilled her memory. There had been times when she'd had to leave Inu and the infant Hideyo alone in the house while she worked in the fields. Her neighbors had been kind. Etsu had looked in on the children occasionally, and she had even given them scrapings when they cried in hunger. And the time Hideyo had been burned, Kaiten had lent her money for drugs.

It pained her even now to think about her son's injury. If she had been with him, instead of in the fields, it would not have happened. Inu had come outside to help her, leaving Hideyo asleep. The infant had awakened, then crawled into the fire pit. His screams had raised the whole village.

She could still hear those screams. The infant was in

the fire pit when she reached him. His animal-like screams changed to yelps as she placed him on the mat, and his whole body was convulsed in the effort to breathe. Kaiten had rushed in, taken one look at the child, and darted out again. In a moment he was back with a bowl of fat. Hurriedly they rubbed the fat over the child's body. His breathing was soft and choked. The whole left side of his body was severely burned. Etsu had come with a blanket and they had wrapped the child in it.

There was no doctor in the small village of Okinajima. The blisters on Hideyo's foot, knee, shoulder, and forearm had swelled to silk-cocoon size and burst, and then infection had set in. For three weeks the baby sweated in high fever. The mother never left his side. She fought back sleep with all the strength in her. With the yen that Kaiten lent her she was able to get some drugs, and they had helped keep the infection down. But there was nothing that could be done for the left hand. Most of the fingers were burned away.

The mother looked at her own hands now. She had labored hard to feed her family, working longer hours than other women because her husband had left her. He had been a good man but a poor father. He had left for the northern island of Hokkaido not long after Hideyo was born. That was twelve years ago. Though he had returned once several years later, they had not heard from him since.

Tembo

It rained the next morning. Hideyo carried his sandals, for the water would ruin them. He held a burlap sack over his head and shoulders. Since it was only a light rain, the sack kept some of his black uniform dry. The rain had stopped by the time he reached the school, but the sky was still dark.

The school was one of the largest buildings in the village, and was used also as a community center for public meetings. It was a tall building with a pitched, thatched roof. The sides, with their several tiny windows, were of unpainted wood. A tall pine tree grew near the entrance.

In front of the building Hideyo neatly folded the burlap sack and placed it under the stairs, together with his sandals, and went up the steps. He bowed before the large picture of the Emperor over the threshold, then stepped inside.

There was a map of Asia across the front of the

classroom. Above the map was the Japanese flag. On either side of a center aisle there were tables and benches. Boys sat on one side, girls on the other.

Hideyo walked to the first bench and sat down, near the window. The seats were filling quickly. The children's voices and laughter rose in shrill crescendo. Suddenly there was silence.

Kobayashi-san entered, walking with firm steps to his desk. All the students stood and bowed. Kobayashi-san returned the bow.

Turning to the flag, the teacher and students burst into a song about their "beautiful" national flag with the red sun on it. When the song ended, they all recited:

"The Emperor is the head; we are the body. He depends on us as his arms and legs. The supreme good is to live in honor: to fulfill one's obligation to the Emperor, the nation, the family, and to one's own name."

The students sat down. The school day had begun.

During the writing lesson, the usual happened. Writing with his right hand, Hideyo held the paper steady with his left hand. He had pulled the sleeve down, as he always did, to cover that hand, but as he wrote some of its ugliness peeked through. As usual, someone nearby began to snicker. This time it was Yoshio, his round face split in a wide grin.

"Tembo," Yoshio whispered.

Hideyo did not answer. He was used to being called *tembo*—hand-boy.

When the history lesson began, the students tensed. There was to be a review today.

"For how long was our nation under military rule?" Kobayashi-san asked. There was no response.

"Hideyo."

Hideyo came to his feet. "From 1192 to 1868," he answered.

"During this time what group held local power?"

A girl in the corner stood. "The feudal lords," she replied.

"When did our national policy of isolationism end?" Again there was no response. Kobayashi-san looked about the room. Yoshio was glancing at a companion.

"Yoshio."

The boy slowly came to his feet. "Er . . . 1889," he said. The class laughed.

"I did not ask you what year it is. Sit down."

When Kobayashi went on to geography, the class relaxed. Kobayashi, speaking about Japan, used a pointer:

"Nippon consists of a series of over three thousand islands. The four main islands from north to south are Hokkaido . . . Honshu . . . Shikoku . . . and Kyushu. Nippon is a mountainous country with less than fifteen per cent of its area suitable for farming . . ."

Something hit Hideyo in the neck. It was a piece of

rice paper rolled into a tiny ball. He turned and saw Inazo about to hurl another at him and he ducked. Inazo withdrew his arm and waited, his flat face pale and tense.

"Hideyo," Kobayashi said, interrupting his lecture. Hideyo stood.

"You were not paying attention," Kobayashi said. "As the head of the class, is that the way you set an example? I am disappointed in you. Be seated."

Kobayashi turned back to the map. In a moment another rice-paper ball hit Hideyo. Several students giggled. Kobayashi faced the class and instantly there was silence. His sad, intelligent eyes searched every face; then slowly he turned to the map again. Placing the pointer on the map, Kobayashi cleared his throat, then suddenly wheeled about. Inazo was about to hurl another rice-paper ball.

"Inazo." Kobayashi's voice was calm. "Come here." The boy walked to the front of the room and stood before the teacher. "Put out your hand." The boy bit his lip but did as he was told. A loud smack resounded as the stick struck the boy's palm. Inazo did not flinch; to show pain would have been shameful.

Kobayashi's voice was still calm. "If you dare to act again as a fool, your parents will be notified." The boy bowed his head. This was a frightening prospect, for every child knew that a bad report would bring disgrace to his family, and the culprit would have to un-

dergo *kinshin*—repentance—by either living in the outhouse or being confined to the house.

Inazo bowed and returned to his seat. There were no further disturbances.

At recess Hideyo went outside with the other children, but he did not join them as they ran, shouting and laughing, to the recreation field behind the school. He went directly to his favorite place, the village cemetery beside the school. The other children had already eaten in the school, but he had waited, as he always did, so that he would be alone. He had learned long ago that it would save him torment if he ate apart from the others, for then no one could see his hand.

Leaning against a gravestone, Hideyo opened the tiny bundle of straw; inside was his lunch, a handful of rice. He ate absent-mindedly, grateful for the few moments of peace. In the distance loomed Bandai, its

conical peak jutting up into the gray clouds. Slowly
the clouds drifted over the peak. He wished he were
older than twelve, for Bandai was very high. It would
be good to climb the mountain, to be far away, above
everything.

Suddenly he tensed. He could hear voices and they
were near. Hideyo crouched behind the gravestone.

"Hey, Tembo." It was Yoshio. "Where are you?"

He did not answer. Instead, he looked about, planning his escape. A small grove of pines stood just beyond the cemetery. Maybe he could get to it without
being seen.

He darted in the direction of the grove. For a moment he thought he would be free of them.

"Hey, there he is!"

Hideyo ducked behind a large gravestone. Quickly
he gathered up several stones.

He did not have to wait long. A rock struck the edge of the gravestone, chipping off a piece. Hideyo held one of the stones tightly in his hand, poised to throw. When Yoshio's face appeared around the side of another gravestone, Hideyo hurled the stone.

Yoshio laughed. "You missed, Tembo. Come on, boys. Let's go."

Four of them charged Hideyo. In rapid succession he hurled the remaining stones, then retreated. He ran in a crouch, flitting behind the gravestones. In a moment he would be in the school area. Suddenly he felt a sharp pain in his shoulder; then he tripped and fell.

"I got him!" shouted one of the boys. "I got him!"

Quickly Hideyo picked himself up. He had to get to the schoolyard. He almost fell again before he reached it. When he glanced back, Yoshio was shaking his fist at him.

"There is always tomorrow," he yelled.

But Hideyo was not worried. There had always been "tomorrow." He had learned to live with it. He was their favorite target, and so it had been from the beginning. He was glad to have escaped this day. He had been lucky, too. The rock that had struck him had not been large.

The Prettiest Smile

On his way home from school it rained again. Hideyo took off his sandals and placed the burlap sack over his head. The rain began to fall heavily. In a moment the sack was wet through and his uniform was getting drenched. Hideyo ran for a maple tree. There he found some protection from the heavy sheets of water.

A figure with an umbrella came into shadowy view and stopped. It was Kobayashi-san's wife, Takike.

"And who is this here, crouched beneath the tree—a toad?" She smiled. She had the prettiest smile he had ever seen. Hideyo stood and bowed.

"Your name is Hideyo Noguchi, is it not?"

"Yes," he managed.

"Come. Come under this umbrella before you get drowned. Do not be afraid. Dear me, look at that rain." She shook her head. "I will never get used to Honshu, I'm afraid. The weather changes so quickly here." She looked at Hideyo. He was timidly standing beside her, afraid even to look at her. "You and I are together until the rain lets up. You will not let me chatter on by myself, will you?" She smiled prettily and Hideyo felt ashamed.

"I am sorry," he said. "Where do you come from?"

"Kyushu," she said. "It is very far away. Someday, I hope, the government will transfer my husband there. My family—all my friends—are there."

"It must be lonely for you here in Okinajima."

"I keep busy, very busy," she said. "It makes the days go by quickly and leaves little time for thoughts of the past. It is funny that it came to mind now. I had not thought of home in a long while."

"It was my fault for mentioning it," said Hideyo.

"Oh, no," she said. "It was not your fault. I think it was seeing you here under this tree alone."

"I had to stop. The rain was so heavy. I was afraid for my uniform."

"Do you like school, Hideyo?"

He hesitated.

Takike laughed, not cruelly. "I think I know how you feel. My husband says you are a brilliant student, but that the other students make life miserable for you. You are brilliant, but you do not understand. If you understood, it would make school more bearable. The other students do not dislike you. They dislike themselves. They want to be intelligent, to be good students, but they are not endowed as you are. You remind them of what they are not, what they cannot be. And in your case the dislike is intense because of your hand."

Hideyo stiffened. She looked at him. There was tenderness in her glance.

"I know about your hand, Hideyo. Everyone in the village knows. You have a deformed hand, but a brilliant mind. Don't you see? That is incongruous. The two do not seem to belong together. The students who torture you with their taunts and forever hound you are sound in body. They have no physical deformities, yet their minds cannot match yours. This is bitter medicine for them. They would love you with condescension if you had a deformed mind to go with your deformed hand. But God acts in mysterious ways. Although he denied you physically he has blessed you mentally."

The rain had let up, but Takike made no move to go. Hideyo was captured in the spell of her words.

"You must try to forgive me, Hideyo," she continued. "I pray that I have not hurt your feelings."

"No," he said hoarsely. He swallowed. Her words had been sincere and thoughtful. It was the first time anyone had spoken to him thus about his hand, and he felt only gratitude.

"What will you do with your life, Hideyo?"

"I am not sure. Until now I felt that my whole life was crippled. I feel now that I want to devote myself—

my whole being—to a great task . . . Does that sound foolish?"

"Foolish? Only adults are foolish."

"I would like to be of more help at home. My mother works too hard. But with one hand . . ."

"Has a doctor ever seen your hand?"

"Yes. Nothing can be done."

"There are doctors elsewhere."

"What would be the use? The fingers are mostly gone. I can do nothing with the hand."

"There is a very good doctor in Wakamatsu. His name is Watanabe. He studied in Tokyo and in America, too."

"But he would never bother with me."

"Oh? And why not?"

Hideyo smiled. They stood under the tree, smiling at each other. The rain had ended. They looked up. The sky was clearing.

"Good-by, Hideyo," she said softly.

Hideyo bowed very low.

A Special Kind of Man

Watanabe-san held Hideyo's wrist. The early-morning sunlight lit the table on which Hideyo rested his arm. He stared at the doctor's silver instrument as it probed the stumps of his fingers. No matter how much it hurt, he would not—must not—show pain.

Watanabe-san looked at him. "Your hand is too tense," he said. "Do not look at it." Hideyo shifted his gaze to the sunlight coming through the partially curtained window.

Suddenly the sunlight turned to sparks that pierced his brain. He swallowed, then glanced at the doctor. Had he shown any sign of pain? He looked at the wall. Above the desk, on a shelf, was a row of books. He tried to make out the titles. Suddenly the books seemed to explode into fragments. He gasped.

The doctor put the instrument aside, then bandaged the hand. "That is all for now," he said. He went to a wash basin, pushed up his sleeves, and washed his hands. Then he reached for a towel. He looked at Hideyo as he dried his hands.

The doctor had dark eyes and his straight hair was streaked with gray. He tossed the towel aside.

"Did a doctor ever look at your hand?"

"When I was a baby."

"Was it that fool—the doctor in Inawashiro? Of course, it was; you do not have a doctor in your village." Watanabe-san picked up a cigar and lit it. He puffed on it rapidly and turned his eyes away. "Why did you not come to me sooner?"

"We are peasants, Watanabe-san," said Hideyo.

"What? What did you say?"

"We are peasants," Hideyo repeated softly.

"There are no more peasants. Don't you know that?" The doctor's voice was hoarse. He shoved the cigar into his mouth.

Hideyo smiled to himself. Feudalism had been abolished in 1871, eighteen years ago. Everyone knew that. But his mother still thought of herself as a peasant, for her life had not changed. She worked just as hard as she had when she was a girl.

Watanabe-san clamped down with his teeth on the cigar. "Times are better now," he said. "A man can make of himself anything he wishes—if he has the ability." He walked to the door and stepped out. Hideyo followed him.

The sun's rays seemed to pierce the hilltops. "Have you ever seen a hospital?" said Watanabe-san.

"No, sir."

"Come with me," said Watanabe-san.

Hideyo followed the doctor to a hut at the edge of the clearing behind the house. It was dark inside the hut and there was a heavy odor of sweat and vomit. The doctor stepped around a small bamboo partition.

"Good morning, Watanabe-san," said a young girl's

voice. Her head was raised from the mat where she lay. She was smiling weakly.

The doctor knelt down beside her. "How is my little princess today?"

"Better," she said.

Watanabe-san placed his hand on her forehead, then pressed back her eyelids.

"When can I go home, Watanabe-san?"

"Maybe soon," he said. The girl glanced at Hideyo. "This is Hideyo Noguchi." Hideyo smiled. Watanabe-san blew a kiss to the little girl, then walked further into the hut.

An old woman lay in the semidarkness, motionless as a mummy. Watanabe-san knelt down and drew the blanket up around her shoulders. The woman's eyes, glazed and expressionless, stared vacantly. Watanabe-san placed his hand on hers for a moment, then slowly came to his feet.

There were voices coming from the end of the hut. Hideyo followed Watanabe-san. A man with thick hair and a bony chest was sitting up, arguing with a young attendant.

"What is wrong?" said Watanabe-san.

The attendant, a boy a little older than Hideyo with a heavy lower lip, motioned to the man. "He wishes to leave, Watanabe-san."

The man leaned back on his elbows and turned his

gaze away from Watanabe-san. "I must leave," said the man. "My family needs me."

"Your family has enough to do without taking care of you," said Watanabe-san.

"I am no longer sick."

"Lie down. Be quiet."

The man lay back. Then he raised his arms toward Watanabe-san. "It is not right that I should stay here, leaving my family to struggle without me."

"Your wife is a good woman; your children are able," said Watanabe-san. "When you are ready, you will go back to them. Now rest."

Outside, Hideyo blinked in the sunlight. Watanabe-san relit his cigar. He puffed on it for a moment. Then he took it out of his mouth and stared at its burning end. There were dark rings under his eyes. He turned now, his shoulders stooped, and walked toward the house. On the steps he paused and looked back at Hideyo. "You will come again next week," he said, and started to go in.

"Wait," Hideyo almost shouted. "I forgot." He reached into his pocket and took out a knotted handkerchief. He untied the knot with his teeth and right hand, took out several coins, and held them up to Watanabe-san.

The doctor looked at Hideyo, then rubbed his cheek with his thumb. "How did you get this money?"

"My mother and sister and I worked in a neighbor's paddy at night, after our own work was done, for the past year," said Hideyo.

Watanabe-san bit on the cigar, then took the coins and put them back in the handkerchief. He tied the ends together and placed the handkerchief in Hideyo's pocket.

"Next week," he said, and turned away.

Hideyo walked along the dirt road that led to Inawashiro. When he could see the Great Stone near the peak of Bandai clearly, he would know that he was halfway home. Several miles before Inawashiro he would turn off onto a narrower road that led to Okinajima. From Wakamatsu to his village it was twenty miles. He would be home in about five hours.

That morning he had left for Wakamatsu early, when it was still dark. His mother had wanted to go with him, but he had insisted that he go alone. If the news was bad, he wanted to be the one to tell her—to lie a little, if need be, so that she would not be disappointed.

But, he knew now, the news was good. Watanabe-san had not taken payment for his services. The money could be used for winter clothing. Of course, they would have to repay Watanabe-san in some other way. A debt was a debt; it was a matter of honor.

The best news, of course, was that Watanabe-san

wanted him to come again. This could only mean there was a chance that something could be done for his hand.

He looked at the hand now. He had never been able to pick up anything with it. The stumps of his fingers were rigid and unbending. He would endure any amount of pain if Watanabe-san could bring life to his hand.

He stopped and picked up two stones. With his right hand he threw the first stone beyond the distant pines. He glanced at the stone in his left hand. He knew that even without the bandage he would not be able to throw it beyond the bend in the road. He let the stone drop to the ground.

He gazed at the road ahead. At least he was going home. He had never thought of the suffering of others until this day. The little girl, did she cry herself to sleep? The old woman would die alone, away from her loved ones. And the man with the bony chest who worried about his family . . .

If only a doctor could be a magician—could cure people quickly. But, of course, a doctor was only a man, although a special kind of man—one who could call a sick girl "princess" and place a comforting hand on a lonely old woman.

Watanabe-san was only a man—a special kind of man.

A Voice Within

Hideyo was almost used to the odor of sweat and vomit. The first day he had worked at the hospital the odor had made him ill. Azu, the other attendant, had laughed when he had rushed out to be sick after the first morning. That was at the start of the summer vacation, two weeks ago. Now the only thing that had not changed was Azu himself. He still did all he could to make Hideyo's work difficult.

Hideyo scrubbed the basin hard. He knew that in a moment Azu would come out to inspect his work. Perhaps this time Azu would be satisfied, would not find fault. It was curious. Azu had never said anything about his hand. For that Hideyo was grateful. He knew that Azu wanted to be a doctor some day. He was several years older than Hideyo and smart; Watanabe-san had only to tell Azu something once and he understood immediately. Of course, he had been at the hospital a good deal longer than Hideyo. It was too bad that the two of them could not be friends. Perhaps Azu was right; he was clumsy and careless. But today he would clean the basins, scrub the hospital floor, and burn the old bandages, and Azu would not find a single fault with his work. He would do his tasks carefully, very carefully, and everything he did would be perfect.

He held up the basin now and looked at it closely. It was spotless and shone clean and bright. He could see his face clearly in it. He smiled and his image smiled back at him.

"What are you doing?" It was Azu.

"I—I . . ."

"Are you finished with the basins, yet?"

"This is the last one, Azu."

Azu took the basin and scrutinized it. He turned it over. Then he went into the hospital, took a sheet of paper from a small table near the doorway, and ran the edge of the paper along the bottom of the basin, where the lip ended. He held the paper up and smiled. Then he shoved the paper at Hideyo.

"Look at that dirt," he said. "The basin is filthy. You can't even clean a basin properly." He threw the basin into the bucket of suds. "Do it over again." He walked back into the hut.

Hideyo knelt down beside the bucket, reached in and pulled out the basin, and picked up the brush. He gripped the brush hard. For a moment he pictured himself rushing in and throwing the contents of the bucket at Azu. How foolish Azu would look, dripping from head to foot, suds running down his face, over his heavy lower lip. But only in his imagination could Hideyo commit such an act, because of Watanabe-san.

Hideyo looked at his left hand. He had picked up the basin with that hand, something he could never have done until a few days ago. He let the basin slide back into the water, then reached in with his left hand and picked it up again. The stumps bent enough for him to grip the basin's side. Watanabe-san was bringing life to what were left of his fingers. Each time the doctor worked on the hand the rigid stumps yielded a bit. All his life Hideyo would be grateful to Watanabe-san. And he was willing to work there for the rest of his life to repay him, no matter what Azu did.

Someone inside was crying. It sounded like Aki, the "little princess." Had Azu gone to her side? The crying continued. Azu came out. From the grim line of Azu's mouth Hideyo knew he was going to get Watanabe-san. The crying grew louder, and Hideyo stepped inside.

Aki was doubled over on the bed, her face buried in her hands.

"Aki," he called softly. "Aki."

She looked at him, her eyes filled with tears.

Hideyo smiled. "What is wrong, Aki?"

"I saw lightning and heard thunder," she said.

"There is no storm," said Hideyo. "The sun is out. You must have been dreaming."

"No. No, I was not dreaming. I was awake. There was lightning and thunder that roared. The lightning struck at me and I tried to cry out but the thunder covered my voice. I was not dreaming, Hideyo."

"You are safe now, Aki. The lightning and thunder are gone."

"Why did it come, Hideyo? Why?"

Hideyo patted her hand. "Lie still, Aki." Watanabe-san and Azu came in.

"Hello, little princess," said Watanabe-san. He knelt down by her side.

"Get back to your work," Azu ordered. Hideyo left them. In a moment Azu rushed past him toward the house. He came back with a small bottle of medicine.

After several moments, Watanabe-san left the hospital. His face was pale. The rings under his eyes were very dark.

It was quiet in the hut now. Hideyo walked slowly to the doorway and stepped inside. Aki lay on her back, her eyes open, her breathing heavy. Hideyo looked at Azu. "Will she be all right?" he whispered.

Azu shrugged. "She has tuberculosis."

"Is there nothing more that can be done?"

"We could use moxa, like the older doctors do, but Watanabe-san says that is a waste of time. He knows the modern treatments. Have you finished your work outside?"

"Yes, Azu."

"Well, I will inspect it later," said Azu. "It would be best not to scrub the floor now. Instead you can get rid of the bandages. Be sure the wind is blowing in the right direction."

"Yes, Azu."

Behind the hospital was a wooden barrel with a wooden top. Beside the barrel was a flat wheelbarrow. Hideyo picked up the barrel and placed it on the wheelbarrow, then pushed the wheelbarrow down the slope behind the hospital. He had to grip the handles of the barrow hard, because the slope became steep near the bottom. He almost lost his grip with his left hand.

At the bottom of the slope was a narrow path that wound around some low bushes. Then the ground was clear. In the center of the clearing was a deep pit.

Hideyo stopped near the pit and rolled the barrel onto the ground. He untied the cover, then tipped the barrel so that its open end was just over the edge of the pit. The blood-specked bandages, soiled dressings, and stained wads of cotton emptied into the ash-strewn pit. With a small tinderbox Hideyo struck a spark which he blew into a flame. The flame leaped up. Smoke, thick and black, curled skyward.

Hideyo stared at the fire. It was good to see the flames destroy the refuse. Lighting the fire and seeing it burn through the pit was always strangely enjoyable. He watched in fascination as the fire hungrily consumed the pile.

When there were only ashes left, he sat by the edge of the pit and looked at the smoldering heap. A thin wisp of smoke drifted upward. The fire had done its work quickly.

Suddenly something darted overhead. It was a small bird. It flitted through the trees, then flew high toward the sun and slowly, in the sun's bright rays, disappeared from view.

The fields, trees, and sun fitted together, it seemed, into a single large-canvassed painting. Everything was still and perfect. But slowly Hideyo became aware of the stench from the pit. He came to his feet. As he did so he heard a voice within him say, "I will become a doctor." He stood still and listened to the voice in quiet reverie.

The Miracle of Life

The vast expanse of blue sky loomed over the terrain.
The hospital seemed dwarfed by the immensity of sky.

Aki's father's face was clean-shaven and bony, and
the corners of his eyes were wrinkled. His dark liquid
eyes were intent on Watanabe-san.

Watanabe-san's voice was soft, almost apologetic.
The woman bowed her head, showing the gray streaks
in her hair. The man spoke briefly to her. They were
silent for a moment, and then the woman turned and
went inside. The man slowly sat down on the ground
before the hut.

Watanabe-san walked away from the man, his lips
pressed together. The man stared straight ahead as
Hideyo picked up the water bucket and stepped inside. Placing it on the table, Hideyo reached for the
wooden ladle. He dipped the ladle into the bucket and
carried it out to the man.

Without a word the man took the ladle, sipped a
little water, and handed it back to Hideyo. Then he

got to his feet and Hideyo led him inside. Hideyo pointed to the screen at the far end of the hut. Taking off his large straw hat, the man stepped behind the screen.

Hideyo picked up the bucket and filled the clay pitchers on the table. Then, with the empty bucket in his hand, he went outside. The path to the well ran like a dark wound through the grass. Around the base of the well the ground was muddy.

Aki would not die, he told himself. She had looked well lately. There had even been color in her cheeks yesterday. Hideyo lowered the bucket. It hit the water with a hollow thud. Maybe Watanabe-san was wrong.

But Watanabe-san had never been wrong. Hideyo pulled on the rope. There was a slight ache high in his chest. He coughed and tears came to his eyes. He was a little tired, that was all. He reached for the bucket through a blur of tears. The ache filled his chest now.

Aki had smiled yesterday. Watanabe-san was not there. He had not seen how happy she was. He would not have sent for her parents if he had seen her yesterday. . . . But, of course, Watanabe-san *had* seen her yesterday and last night.

Hideyo looked up. Someone was calling him. He set the bucket down. No, it was someone sobbing inside the hut.

Hideyo went to the doorway. The sobbing was coming from behind the screen. It was a woman crying.

The ache inside his chest surged up. He leaned his head against the doorpost and shut his eyes tight.

It was still early, but Hideyo could not study. He would finish the chapter on circulation another night.

Lying on his side, he curled up under Watanabe-san's desk. His arms and legs felt weak, as though the muscles were made of straw. For the past two months he had studied nights when his work was done.

The medical books were difficult, and Watanabe-san was usually too busy to answer his questions. He would have to continue studying on his own. It would become even more difficult, he knew. Many of the books in Watanabe-san's library were in English. Somehow he would have to learn that language. But he would not worry about it now. He would rest . . . wonderful rest.

It seemed as though he had just dozed off. Watanabe-san was at his bench. The lantern flickered as Watanabe-san turned.

"I did not mean to awaken you." Watanabe-san held a slide up to the light and peered at it.

"Watanabe-san . . ."

"Yes?"

"Aki looked so well yesterday."

"That is the way with tuberculosis." The doctor

turned to Hideyo. "Would you like to see what killed Aki?"

He picked up a slide and placed it under the microscope, then adjusted the lens. "Look, Hideyo."

At first the boy could make out nothing. Then it seemed as if the microscope were wobbling. Slowly, under the lens, there appeared rod-shaped specks, flicking in continuous, uneven rhythm.

"Tubercle bacillus," said Watanabe-san. "The killers of Aki."

"Can they not be destroyed?"

Watanabe-san shook his head. "Several years ago the killers were still unknown. The last major step—their destruction—is yet to come."

Later, when Watanabe-san had left, Hideyo sat before the microscope. The killers of Aki were known, but they could not be destroyed. Not yet—one day. He turned and looked at the books above the desk.

There was so much to be learned. But Hideyo was not discouraged. Each night, like a caterpillar, he had inched closer to his goal. Already, in a few months, he had learned much about the miracle of life.

The medical books he had been studying had taken him beyond appearances, had taught him that life was a miracle—that man was very small and God very large.

No one could come close to matching the achievement of life itself. A man had first to learn that life was a miracle. This *had* to be learned before one dared try to correct imperfections in that miracle.

He looked up at the window. The moon, over the dark, silhouetted hills, was divided by the lines of a tree branch. In a while, the moon would be high over the hills, its light transforming the thatched roof into silver.

Hideyo went to the shelf and took down a book.

The Samurai

A rickshaw raced past him, the coolie's feet slapping against the ground. Hideyo stared at Wakamatsu's main street.

The big wheels of the rickshaws were spinning blurs. The half-naked coolies with sweating, tattoed bodies ran swiftly, their legs moving in steady rhythm, as though the rickshaws they were pulling were afterthoughts. Farmers trotted along, their sandals shuffling softly, the long poles balanced on their shoulders bending under the weight of loads slung from the ends. Tails whipping at flies, black oxen pulled their carts. Men and women, middle-aged and old, trudged beneath their piles of brushwood. Barefoot, shouting children darted through the crowd.

Hideyo crossed the street, then stood a moment, looking about. A samurai was coming toward him. Hideyo stepped to him and bowed. The samurai glanced his way, then walked on, his left hand resting on the hilt of his long sword, his head high. Hideyo watched him go. He was one of the few samurai who still carried a sword, although the government had long since forbidden it.

Two boys rolled near Hideyo's feet, laughing as they wrestled. Another boy looked down at them, grinning. Hideyo approached the boy.

"I am looking for a house. Can you direct me?"

"Can you not read numbers?"

"I can read numbers, when I can find them."

"What is your town?"

"Okinajima."

"Okinajima!" The boy laughed, then spit on the ground. "A place fit only for pigs."

"Who is he?" said one of the boys, coming to his feet.

"A peasant lost in our great city."

Hideyo walked away.

The three boys followed him. "Where are you going, peasant?" They ran in front of him. "Where do you go, peasant?" One of them pointed at Hideyo's hand. "Look. He is a cripple. How did you get that? Let us see." A second boy grabbed Hideyo's sleeve. Hideyo pushed him away. The other two jumped on Hideyo, and he fell to the ground. Squirming, he brought his right arm free and swung hard. He struck a boy in the ribs with his fist. The boy yelled. Hideyo brought up his left foot and kicked at one of the boys.

The other boy twisted Hideyo's head and pressed it against the ground. Hideyo rolled free.

"Stop him!"

He picked himself up and began to back up. The three boys spread out. Hideyo backed into a vegetable counter and they rushed him. He picked up a cabbage and flung it at them. They grabbed his arms and pushed him into the vegetable stand. The wooden counter crashed to the ground, and cabbages rolled into the street. The shopkeeper began yelling at them.

"Stand away!" roared the samurai, who had stopped to watch. "Let them fight."

One of the boys kicked Hideyo with his heel. Hideyo grabbed his foot and tripped him. Another boy fell across his chest, pressing his forearm against Hideyo's throat. Hideyo's outflung hand touched a splintered piece of wood. He whacked the side of the boy's face with it and twisted free. Coming quickly to his feet, he charged the other boy with his head, butting him in the stomach. The boy went down with a grunt.

"Look out!" the samurai yelled.

A boy was coming at Hideyo, a clublike leg of the broken counter in his hand. Hideyo grabbed the boy's wrist, brought his right foot behind the boy, and flipped him back. Lying on the ground, the boy flung the club at Hideyo; it grazed his head, stunning him.

"Get him! Get him!" shouted the boy, getting up

from the ground. He looked around. His companions were gone. He glanced at Hideyo, then took off.

A big hand slapped Hideyo on the back. The samurai laughed. Hideyo touched the side of his head. His hand was smeared with blood.

The samurai cupped Hideyo's face in his hands and looked at the wound. "Nothing. A trifle." He pulled

out a handkerchief and wiped Hideyo's head. "Is your
father a samurai?"

Hideyo shook his head.

"You are a samurai."

"I am the son of peasants."

The samurai placed his hand under Hideyo's chin.
"You are a samurai—above the others because courage

is in your heart. Now come." He tossed a few coins at the shopkeeper. "I will accompany you. Where are you going?"

"I am looking for the home of an American missionary."

"A foreigner?" The samurai shook his head. "Foreigners, dogs, goats, and barbarians. Now we welcome them all to our shores." He looked at Hideyo. "What is the name of the missionary?"

"The Reverend Taylor Wells."

"We will find him." The samurai looked about, then waited as a young man carrying a closed umbrella approached. The young man bowed. The samurai nodded. "We are looking for the home of an American, an American missionary . . ." He looked at Hideyo.

"The Reverend Taylor Wells," said Hideyo.

"He lives in the stone house on the hill." The young man pointed to a low hill on the outskirts of the city.

Ghostly white against the red tint of the setting sun, the stone house stood partially hidden by tall cedars. They set off along the narrow road that led toward it.

The samurai strode with his left hand on the hilt of his long sword. A scrawny dog scurried across the street. A little boy standing in a doorway sucking his thumb looked up wide-eyed at the samurai. A man squatting against the side of a house came to his feet and bowed from the waist.

Hideyo had to quicken his pace to keep up with the samurai. His hand brushed against the samurai's kimono. The touch of the silk was light and cool. Never had he seen such a kimono. And the samurai's *zori* —sandals—were made of silk embroidered in threads of silver. He looked at his own rice-straw sandals. At least he had these. The boys he had fought with had been barefoot.

Hideyo brought his hand up to his forehead. The bleeding had stopped, but he could not meet the American missionary looking this way.

"What is it?" The samurai turned and looked at him. "Well?"

"Nothing," said Hideyo.

"Are you in pain?"

Hideyo shook his head. "Perhaps I will make a poor impression on the missionary."

The samurai strode up to the nearest house. Standing before the door, he bellowed, "Open up!"

The door opened a crack and a face peered out.

"Bring water."

The face disappeared. The samurai waved Hideyo forward.

A man hurriedly brought out a bucket of water, then bowed and backed into the house. The samurai tossed his handkerchief to Hideyo, who caught it. Hideyo dipped the handkerchief in the water and washed his face and hands.

"What is your name?"

"Hideyo. Hideyo Noguchi."

"It is important for you to see the foreigner?"

"I wish to learn to read English."

"It is necessary for you to read English?"

Hideyo nodded.

"When I was a boy we dreamed of growing up to become samurai."

"I will become a doctor."

They started out again.

"A tutor does not instruct for nothing."

"I will repay him with work."

"The American will have servants. There can be nothing he needs."

They turned off onto a dirt road that wound up the hill. Long-leaved chestnut trees formed a green umbrella over the road. White birches, straight and slender, stood out like fine brush strokes against the dense green of the woods.

The samurai began to breathe heavily. There were deep lines in his face that Hideyo had not noticed before.

Hideyo stopped.

"What is wrong?"

Hideyo sat down. "I have pebbles in my shoes." He beat the soles of his sandals hard and examined the inside of the sandals closely. The samurai was breathing more easily now, and Hideyo slowly came to his feet.

They continued until they reached a white wall at the edge of a clearing. The wall encircled the house, which was white with gray roof tiles.

Hideyo pulled on a cord by the wall door. The bell above the door rocked back and forth, its ringing sharp and loud. A dog barked inside. The wooden door opened.

A servant peered at Hideyo; he did not see the samurai, who was standing a little to the side.

"Is your master at home?"

"What is it you want?"

"I wish to speak to him."

"He is busy." The servant started to close the door.

The samurai strode forward and grabbed the servant by the ear. "He does not hear too well, does he? Perhaps his ears are on backward." The servant winced and fell to his knees. The samurai released his hold. Wide-eyed, the servant stared up at the samurai, then suddenly bowed with his forehead touching the ground.

"Get your master."

The servant jumped to his feet and ran inside.

The samurai looked at Hideyo. "We will see what kind of man the foreigner is."

The Americans

Dr. Wells had the largest nose Hideyo had ever seen. Never had he even imagined such a nose. What he had heard about foreigners was true. There had been no exaggeration.

"You wish to speak to me," said the foreigner. His nose was pointed at the samurai. Hideyo stared, fascinated.

"The boy wishes to speak to you."

The foreigner swung his nose down. Something glinted in the sunlight. Hideyo tore his gaze away from the foreigner's nose. A golden chain, long and shiny, hung down from the foreigner's waist, the lower end disappearing into a slit in the lower garment.

What kind of clothing was this? Each leg was wrapped in dark, coarse cloth. And what did the foreigner have on his feet? They were covered—completely and tightly covered—in shiny, black material. Could he really walk in these?

"What are you staring at, young man?"

"I am sorry . . . I have never seen a for— . . . an American before."

"What do you want?"

"I would like to study with you."

"The Bible?"

"What is that?"

"A holy book."

"I wish to study English."

"With me?"

"I would repay you with my labor."

"I do not give lessons in English."

"I would study hard. The lessons could be short."

"No. I am much too busy."

"Whatever time you could spare."

"Why?"

"I must learn to read English to continue my studies. I will be a doctor."

"A commendable aspiration, but I am not a teacher. I am a missionary."

Hideyo was silent.

"You could take one pupil," said the samurai.

"Who are you?"

"I am the boy's friend."

"I do not have the time. You must excuse me." As he started to go back into the house, a woman appeared in the doorway.

"Charles, I did not know we had visitors."

"They were just leaving, Mary."

"Oh?" She had a round face and blue eyes. Hideyo had never seen blue eyes. "Hello," she said, smiling. "I am Mary Wells."

The samurai and Hideyo bowed. "I am Toson Yorozu," said the samurai. "The boy is Hideyo Noguchi."

"You both look tired. Would you care to have some tea with us?"

"I don't think they can stay, Mary."

The samurai looked up at the American, who was standing on the steps, then at the woman. "We would be honored," said the samurai. The American stared at his wife. She held her head high.

"We usually have our tea outside," she said. "Would you mind?"

"Not at all," said the samurai.

Gripping her wide skirts, the woman led them around to the back of the house. Beneath a tree bright with pink blossoms, in a corner of the yard, was a dark cedar table.

A boy and girl were playing in back of the house. The boy wore the same strange kind of lower garment as his father.

A maid came out the back door, and the missionary's wife spoke softly to her.

The boy had blue eyes, like his mother, and very light skin. He edged toward the samurai and looked at him shyly. "Are those real swords?" he asked.

"Yes, real swords." There was a hint of a smile in the samurai's deeply lined face.

"Don't stare, David." The mother smiled at the boy.

The maid set a tray on the table. Mrs. Wells poured the tea while the missionary sat quietly, looking down at his hands. There were gray streaks in his long dark hair.

The girl was laughing, throwing a round yellow object into the air. It landed on the ground, and to Hideyo's amazement, went right up again. She caught the yellow object, threw it up again, and again, when it hit the ground it bounced.

"Kathy, come here, dear."

The girl came forward, holding the round object in her hands. The woman turned to Hideyo. "I want you to try it," she said. She took the plaything from the girl and handed it to him.

It was so light that Hideyo could easily hold it with one hand. "Throw it up," said the woman, smiling.

Hideyo threw it up. When it hit the ground it bounced, and Hideyo laughed.

The woman laughed, too. She looked at her husband. The tightness in his face was gone.

Hideyo handed the plaything back to the woman. "Thank you," he said.

"Do you think we might have an extra ball, Charles?" the woman said. "One the children don't use any more?"

The man looked at his wife for a moment, then nodded. He rose and went inside.

Mrs. Wells stirred the tea in her cup. "My husband works hard," she said, "and there are times when he becomes depressed, thinking that he is accomplishing little."

"His work is very difficult," said Yorozu. "Foreign religions, especially Christianity, have long been regarded with distrust in our country."

"I am glad you understand," she said. She smiled. Her teeth were like those of a young girl. Wisps of her hair, above her temple, shone in the sun. Her blue eyes were bright. The three of them sat quietly in the sunlight.

The missionary returned, holding a ball. He handed it to Hideyo. "This is for you," he said softly.

Hideyo took it. "Thank you," he said.

"You are welcome."

They sipped their tea. The American looked at Hideyo over his cup, then winked. Up in the branches overhead a bird sang a brief tune, the notes echoing in the stillness.

To Tie a Knot

It was very hot, the sun-soaked air an invisible weight on Hideyo as he worked. His face glistened with sweat, which ran into his eyes, blurring his vision, and seeped into the corners of his mouth. His robe, soaked through, stuck to his back, and rivulets slid down his chest like drops of rain.

Hideyo wiped the sweat from his eyes and peered into the microscope. He turned the knob and adjusted the lens. The bacilli moved in nervous rhythm—animals invisible to the eye, visible now under the powerful lens. The secret killers that could destroy armies.

Hideyo raised his head. His eyes stung from the sweat. He picked up a cloth from the table, rolled it into a band with his right hand, and placed it against his forehead. Then, holding the cloth to his forehead with his left hand, he tucked the ends over his ears with his right hand. Now he removed the slide from under the microscope and placed it carefully in a wooden rack on the table. Using a small cloth, he began to wipe the lens of the microscope gently, with short, circular motions.

He thought of the samurai who had been the head-man in Okinajima when he was a little boy, and re-membered watching him as he sat on the steps of his house, his large sword laid across his lap, gently clean-ing the blade with a soft cloth. And he thought of the dueling games the boys in the village had played with bamboo sticks. Each boy carried two play swords, a long sword and a short sword, like the samurai of old. But he had been able to hold only the long piece of bamboo, and they had laughed, saying he could not be a samurai because he did not have two swords. He had fought them with his one play sword, and later, with the water from the stream that trickled down Bandai, washed the blood from his face.

He looked now at his left hand. Watanabe-san had brought life to the hand, but he could not bring back flesh and bone. There was only half a thumb and a tiny stump where his little finger had once been; the three middle fingers were completely gone. Thanks to Watanabe-san, Hideyo could move the stumps and grip some objects. But he could not tie a knot.

Hideyo took the sodden cloth from his forehead and wrapped it around his leg just above the ankle. Press-ing down with the stump of his thumb, he pushed one end of the cloth under the other with his right hand.

He held the lower end in his right hand. Then with the stumps of the thumb and little finger he tried to grip the other end. Sweat rolled into his eyes and he shook his head hard. He stretched the stump of the little finger down as far as he could. It almost touched the corner of the cloth. He stretched the stump of the thumb across the palm of his hand, biting his lower lip. The muscle on the inside of the thumb felt like a sharp sliver of wood driving down into the stump. A bead of sweat ran down the side of his nose, over his lips, and down his chin. The stumps were barely touching the cloth. He tried to stretch them further. The muscles in his shoulder and neck tightened. He was able now to place a little pressure against the end of the cloth. Again he tried to stretch the stumps. He gasped, his chest heaving. Sweat poured into the corners of his mouth. He ran his tongue over his lips. The muscles in his back and neck were as hard as wood.

Hideyo relaxed his hand and flexed the stumps. In a moment he would try again, as soon as he stopped gulping air. This day his stomach muscles had not cramped. His body was becoming accustomed to the daily effort. He took a deep breath, then gripped the end of the cloth with his right hand and again reached out for the other end with the stumps of his left hand. His face hardened into a mirthless grin as he forced the stump of the thumb down against the cloth. He closed his eyes. Sweat rolled down his face, collecting under his chin, sliding down his neck and chest. He gasped for air. He stretched the little finger toward the cloth. His face aflame, he brought the stump of the little finger against the end of the cloth and pressed the stumps tight against each other. With a quick jerk, he pulled, and the cloth tightened around his leg.

He sank back, then looked at his leg. He had not tied a knot, but he had tightened the cloth. He gazed at the left hand resting on his leg. He had been able to grip the cloth with the hand. That was the important thing.

The room seemed to tilt. Hideyo's wrist struck the table and he lowered his head. The slides in the rack glistened in the sunlight. Sweat stung the corners of his eyes. The slides looked like stacked rows of armor. He stared at them, his vision blurred by sweat.

Not a Crime

Hideyo bolted upright. The sunlight was strong. It must be late. He jumped to his feet and rushed to the door. The sun was resting on the peaks. It was not too late after all, although he was usually up when the sun was only edging over the mountains.

Outside on the porch was a bucket of water. Hideyo carried it inside and poured some water into the tin pot on the fire pit. He stirred the embers, then took the bucket back outside. He cupped his hands and splashed water onto his face. Then he pressed his dripping fingers gently against his eyelids.

The water was cold. It felt good, but his eyes burned. He had stayed up late, reading. English was not difficult. With Dr. Wells's help during the past year, he had made good progress in the medical books written in English. Americans were lucky. Their language was not as difficult to read as Japanese. He would be finished with school next year and he was still learning the different forms of picture writing.

Back inside, Hideyo took a cup from a corner shelf and went to the fire pit. He poured a little water from the pot into the cup and sipped it. It was cold. But he had no time this morning to make tea. He gulped the rest of the water down.

Outside, a breeze brought the scent of pine to him. Birds swept down through the pines in long glides. When did birds sleep? Did they ever sleep? If only he could do without sleep . . . there was so much to learn. But he was doing better than he had the first summer, sleeping now only four hours a night.

Yosa, the attendant, looked up and smiled as he stepped into the hospital hut.

"How are they?" Hideyo asked.

"Ihara was a little restless during the night," said the boy. "The others slept well."

"All right, Yosa."

Still smiling, Yosa stretched, then stepped out. Hideyo checked the shelf above the table. There were enough bandages for now. Next week he and Yosa would get more. He checked the basin that held the forceps and scissors. The solution in the basin was low. He took a bottle of carbolic-acid solution from an upper shelf and poured some of it into the basin. Then he poured some into a smaller basin.

Watanabe-san came in and Hideyo bowed.

"Azu is not here yet?"

"I have not seen him, Watanabe-san. I can assist you until he comes."

Swiftly Hideyo took a large flat tray with handles from the table and placed the basin with the scissors and forceps on it, then the smaller basin. Carefully he carried the tray to the end of the hut, where Watanabe-san was looking at a boy with an infected foot. The boy was asleep.

Watanabe-san knelt and placed his hand on the boy's forehead. Then he looked at the bandaged foot.

"The scissors."

Hideyo reached into the larger basin and handed the scissors to Watanabe-san. The boy opened his eyes.

"Good morning, Ihara."

The boy grinned at Watanabe-san.

"I am going to change your bandage. It may hurt— but only a bit. Another bandage, the same size."

Hideyo went to the shelf. He took down a roll of bandage and brought it to Watanabe-san.

"And your mother and father—dip the bandage in the solution."

Hideyo dipped the bandage in the smaller basin with the carbolic acid solution.

"And your mother and father say that your friends—" Watanabe-san took the bandage from Hideyo. "Lift his foot. They say your friends keep coming to them, asking when you will be back." The boy groaned. Gently Watanabe-san placed the first layer of bandage around the boy's foot. " 'Yes, Ihara is very lucky,' your friends are all saying. 'We must work in the fields while Ihara is resting.' " The boy grinned.

"You can go." Hideyo looked up. It was Azu.

"May I stay, Watanabe-san?" The doctor nodded.

Hideyo watched as Watanabe-san placed the bandage on the boy's foot. Azu glared at Hideyo.

Ihara squirmed and bit his lip hard.

"I am almost finished, Ihara. You are looking at a boy who will be treated like a prince—lift his foot higher—when he gets home . . . like a prince while he hobbles around . . ." Watanabe-san leaned back. "That was not bad, was it?" The boy shook his head. Watanabe-san rose. "You are a brave boy." Ihara smiled.

The sun, directly overhead, beat down on the roof, but in the shade under the eaves it was cool. Hideyo placed the end of the bandage around his foot. Then he took it off. Watanabe-san had placed it on the skin gently. He began again, then stopped. He had the end under his foot; Watanabe-san had placed the end on top of the foot. He started once more.

This time it was right. Carefully he brought the roll under his foot, making certain the second band overlapped a bit. Then he brought the roll up. It felt tight. Was that the way it was supposed to feel?

He brought the roll down and under again. Then

he brought it up and around his ankle, above the anklebone, as Watanabe-san had done. Then across the foot and under. Now, the two ends—bringing them together was the difficult part. He gripped one end with his right hand, then slowly gripped the other end with his left. Crossing the ends, he lost his grip with his left hand. He tried again, this time getting a firmer grip. He brought the two ends across each other, brought one end under, pulled gently, then crossed the ends again, brought one end under again, and pulled. The knot tightened. He looked at his work. It looked right.

Someone was standing by him. He looked up. It was Azu. "You took that bandage without permission." His voice was hoarse.

"Watanabe-san would not mind, Azu."

"Take it off."

"But Azu—"

Azu shook his fist at Hideyo. "You'll be sorry!" His lower lip was trembling.

"I was just practicing, Azu."

"Who told you you could take that bandage? You are not supposed to take anything without permission!"

"But Azu—"

"You will take off that bandage, clean it in the solution, and return it. And from now on you will ask before you take anything! Remember that!"

"What is this shouting?"

Watanabe-san glanced at Azu, then at Hideyo, who got to his feet.

"He took a roll of bandage without permission."

Watanabe-san looked at Hideyo's bandaged foot.

"He took the bandage and sneaked around back here—"

Watanabe-san held up his hand. "I want to talk to Hideyo." Azu, breathing heavily, glared at Hideyo, then turned and left them. Watanabe-san watched him go.

"Azu is angry. Do you know why, Hideyo?"

"I did wrong. I took the bandage without permission."

"Sit down, Hideyo." Watanabe-san knelt down beside him. "Yes, you did wrong."

"I am sorry, Watanabe-san."

"But you did not commit a crime. Azu is angry with you because he fears you. He wants to become a doctor, too. But you are learning well and he is afraid you will find more favor with me than he does. Do you understand?"

"Yes, Watanabe-san."

"So, from now on—so as not to aggravate him unnecessarily—you will get permission before you borrow anything."

"Yes, Watanabe-san."

"You did not finish your lunch. Pick up your bowl."

Hideyo reached for the bowl by his side. "You did well, assisting me this morning." The doctor looked at the bandaged foot, then smiled. "I see you observe well, too." He placed his hand on Hideyo's shoulder. "Finish eating."

"Yes, Watanabe-san."

Friends

Hideyo and Yosa walked together to the Wells house, Yosa carrying the basket. The servant answered the door, then went inside.

"Do you think the foreigners have old clothes?" Yosa asked as they waited.

Hideyo nodded.

Yosa sighed. "I hope so. I am tired of walking."

Mrs. Wells came to the door. "Hideyo." She smiled. Hideyo and Yosa bowed.

"This is my friend, Yosa. He works with me in the hospital."

"Hello, Yosa."

"We have been collecting old clothes for bandages," said Hideyo. "We thought you might have some old clothes that you could spare."

"Let me think. Yes, I think I do—if you don't mind some very old ones."

"All the clothes we bring in are sterilized before they are used," said Hideyo.

"Please come in." They followed her into the house. "Sit down. I'll only be a moment."

Hideyo and Yosa stood just inside the doorway. Yosa gazed about the room. "Oh, the poor foreigners."

Hideyo smiled. "They are not poor."

"But look . . . look at all those things. Those monster chairs, all those tables, that desk, those big—boxes."

"They are called cabinets."

"But how can they walk around in here? How can they avoid bumping into things? At night it must be dangerous."

Hideyo smiled. He knew how Yosa felt. He had felt the same way the first time he had stepped inside the Wells house.

The front door opened. Hideyo turned. "Hello, Hideyo." It was David. He looked at Yosa. Hideyo stepped forward.

"David, Yosa." David put out his hand. Yosa looked at it, and then at Hideyo, who clasped his own hands together. Yosa nodded, took David's hand and clasped it, then bowed, still holding David's hand.

David smiled, looking at Hideyo. "Are you waiting for my mother?"

"Yes."

"Would you and Yosa like to see what I caught?"

Hideyo looked at Yosa, who stared open-mouthed at David.

The boy reached into his shirt. "He's down here.

There, I have him now." He brought his hand out, and Hideyo and Yosa bent closer.

"A big frog," said Hideyo. "Where did you get him?"

"Down at the creek, by the willows."

Mrs. Wells came in carrying some clothes. "This is all I could find, Hideyo. Maybe next time I'll have more for you."

Hideyo took the clothes. "Thank you, Mrs. Wells."

"If you're looking for old clothes, there is Toshiaki," said David. "He is one of the richest merchants in Wakamatsu. His house is just past the temple."

"Toshiaki?" said Yosa. "We have been to him before. He would send us away. Perhaps turn his dogs on us."

"We have not tried him in a long time," said Hideyo.

"Come," said David. "I will show you the way. I know a short cut."

"Good-by, Mrs. Wells," said Hideyo. "We thank you." Hideyo and Yosa bowed, then followed David out.

They cut through the woods, along a path that wound up a hill. Ahead, at the top of the hill, was the temple, silhouetted against the sky. The boys turned off the path, went past clumps of underbrush, then through a grove of tall pines, their footsteps cushioned on thick, browned pine needles. A low stone wall stretched before them. They climbed the wall. A rock loosened and tumbled down the hill, crashing through thick underbrush. David pointed. "The house is just beyond those birches," he said.

"I will go," said Hideyo.

"No," said Yosa. "He is a difficult one. This requires a special skill." He took the clothes out of the basket. "Wait for me here." He picked up the empty basket.

David and Hideyo sat down by the stone wall.

They waited. A dog barked. Hideyo leaned forward. More dogs barked and Hideyo got to his feet. "He will be all right, Hideyo," said David. "The dogs are mean-looking but cowardly."

Hideyo picked up a small rock and tossed it down the hill. "All morning Yosa and I walked through the streets of Wakamatsu asking for old clothes. A woman threw a bucket of water at us. And an old man spit on the ground near our feet. They say bad things about Watanabe-san because he practices modern medicine and does not believe in the old ways. They still believe in acupuncture and moxibustion. Especially the older ones."

"What is acupuncture?"

"Needle pricking. A doctor takes small, fine needles made of gold or silver and with a hammer drives them into the skin."

"Into the skin?"

Hideyo nodded. "Then he twists each needle down

for about half an inch, sometimes more, to where the pain is located. The needles are taken out after a minute or two."

David stared. "What is moxi—?"

"Moxibustion. The doctor takes a tuft of wool-like material and twists it in the shape of a cone and puts it on the bare skin. Then he takes a burning splinter and sets the tuft afire. If one is very sick, more than one tuft is set afire."

David shook his head. "Do doctors still do these things?"

"Some do; not Watanabe-san. He despises those methods. Watanabe-san is an educated man. He has studied at universities."

"Why does he stay in Wakamatsu? He could go to a large city—to Tokyo."

"This is the place where he was born."

"My father has asked to be transferred to Tokyo."

"Why does he want to leave here?"

"He thinks he has failed. The people here are not interested in Christianity."

"Would it be any different in Tokyo?"

David shrugged. "I don't know."

"Do you want to leave?"

David shook his head. "I like it here."

"Do you miss America?"

"I was a small boy when we left there."

"Tell me about America—what you remember."

"It was so long ago. We had milk on the table—"

"Milk?"

"Yes, milk from cows. I think it was good. Anyway, we had it every day."

"Did you have school?"

David nodded. "We had a teacher whose face looked like old leather. He had a very soft voice, but if you were late or cut up during lessons, his voice made the timbers shake."

Hideyo smiled.

"And in the winter we slid down the hill on sleds— our fathers made them from pieces of lumber. Sometimes four or five of us would get on one sled and we'd all end up in a pile of snow. Then at Christmas we'd bring in a fir tree from the woods, and there was candy and presents. We still do that, but now it's not the same. My father has changed."

"Would you like to go back to America one day, David?"

"I would like to see my father smile."

They were silent. David picked up a small rock and tossed it. Hideyo turned. "Here comes Yosa." He was carrying a basketful of clothes. Hideyo and David ran to him. Yosa set the basket down.

Hideyo stared at the basket. "How did you manage to get so much?"

"It is all a matter of acting," said Yosa.

"How did you do it?" David asked.

Yosa smiled. "I approach the honorable one's door, empty basket in hand. When he appears, majestic and not a little irritated to see only a boy, I bow—very low. Like this." Yosa knelt and brought his head down until it touched the ground.

" 'Go away!' shouts the noble one. 'You were here before. I have no more old clothes. Besides,' he says proudly, 'in my house there are nothing but fine clothes.' But once again I bow low."

Yosa brought his head down again, acting out the scene. "Then I look up and there is the honorable one standing with his fists on his hips, a scowl on his face." Yosa smiled. "Now my acting skill is challenged. I take the empty basket and lift it up. 'Look, noble one. Look. I must return to Watanabe-san with an empty basket. That good doctor—who one day may be your own doctor—will look at me with reproachful eyes, as though it were my fault that the sick people he cares for will be without fresh bandages. Oh, it breaks my heart to think of those poor creatures lying there in the hospital . . . the bandages they have on now old, worn, falling apart . . . their cries of joy as they hear my voice. But what will I be bringing them? An empty basket.' "

Yosa bowed low once more. He giggled. Hideyo laughed, picked up the basket, and dumped its contents on Yosa's head. They wrestled for a moment, laughing so hard that the dogs began to bark.

The Gift of Joy

Hideyo curled up under the desk. His nose itched. That night he would return to Okinajima for the start of school in the morning. He would go directly to school, and after school he would go home. If he left at three in the morning he would be in school when Kobayashi-san began the class.

He rubbed his nose. His belongings were gathered together in his *furoshihi*—bandana. He had already said good-by to Watanabe-san and all the others except Yosa, whom he would see that night. When he returned next summer he would be finished with school. He had learned much this summer, more than the first summer, when he had done only the menial tasks around the hospital. This summer he had been responsible for the bandages and for the care of the forceps and scissors in the hospital. He had learned a great deal watching Watanabe-san. He had even assisted the doctor once. And from his study of the books in Watanabe-san's library he had learned anatomy.

Best of all he had learned to tie a bandage. He could hardly wait to show his mother. She would be happy that he could now use his left hand almost as well as his right. No longer would she have to worry about him or cry in her sleep. It was almost as though his childhood accident had never happened. People would no longer laugh at him when they saw what he could do with the hand. Still, he knew he would continue to hide it.

The itching had stopped and now he sneezed. The temperature had gone down a little, that was all. The nights were cooler. Soon the days would be cool, and it would be time to harvest. This year, using both hands, he would have less difficulty cutting and threshing the grain. And there would be a larger vegetable crop.

Last year, for the first time, he had wielded the mattock to loosen the soil in the hilly ground near the end of the rice field. It had been very difficult keeping a grip on the handle with his left hand, but he and his mother together had turned over nearly half the patch. This spring it had been easier for him to wield the mattock, and he alone had broken the soil in the vegetable patch. He had been able to do as much as a man—as much as his father could have done had he been at home.

His father had left a crippled boy, but now the crippled boy could do a man's work, could cut and thrash the grain and wield a mattock. It did not matter any more that he was gone. They would be able to manage now without him. His father would have stared in surprise to see how well they could manage on their own. The one time his father had come, long ago, Hideyo had been only a baby. He had been sitting on the ground in front of the house, scooping up dust with his right hand and letting it stream down through his clenched fist.

"Where is your mother?" his father had asked, looking down at him a little angrily. Hurrying toward the rice paddy, he had turned to stare at Hideyo. Then he had disappeared.

Later, Hideyo's sister had told him that the thin-faced man with the tattered sandals was their father.

Hideyo turned over, and opened his furoshihi. Carefully he took out a small mirror and the *suzu*. The mirror was for his mother; the suzu—small bells—were for Inu. Then he took out a pair of sandals tied together with a piece of string. They were for his father. Someday, perhaps, he would return. How proud he would be of his son, earning money working for Watanabe-san, studying to be a doctor. "Only fifteen years old," his father would boast, smiling at the other farmers. "My son is a boy who honors the family name."

And together, with his father's hand on his shoulder, they would go through the village. "There is Hideyo with his father," the villagers would whisper, and they would bow in greeting . . . and there would be no laughter.

Hideyo sat up. Laughter was coming from outside. It was probably Yosa coming on duty. He replaced the articles in the furoshihi and tied it.

He would miss Yosa and David. He smiled, remembering the day Yosa had gone to Toshiaki's house and returned with a basketful of old clothes. It had been fun. Before he knew Yosa he had almost forgotten how good it was to laugh. But with Yosa it was different. Yosa laughed often. When he didn't laugh, he smiled— a big, happy smile. Yes, Yosa had the gift of joy. He was lucky.

He had not said good-by to Yosa. Hideyo went to the door, slipped on his sandals, and walked down the steps. Fireflies pricked the blackness with tiny sparks. A hazy, pink moon tried to hide behind the tallest trees. Hideyo's feet crunched on the gravel path. The hospital smell reached his nostrils. The night air was still. He stepped inside. A dim lantern hung over the entrance. Yosa, sitting near the door, looked up at Hideyo.

"I thought you had left."

"Soon."

"You have a long walk ahead of you. You should be resting."

Someone coughed. The boys were silent. The coughing stopped.

"How has it been?" Hideyo asked.

"Not bad. I think it will be a quiet night."

"How is it, working at night?"

"All right."

"Does it get lonely?"

Yosa shook his head.

Hideyo sat down next to him. "Will you be starting school tomorrow?"

"School?" Yosa smiled. "I went to lower primary school, and then I had to work. There are seven children in my family."

"How is it for you, working here?"

"It is easy. But sometimes it is not easy to stay awake." He grinned.

"What do you do to stay awake?"

"I think about things . . . about the things that happen in a day. Did you know that when it is still dark, even before the sun comes up, the rooster crows? I heard it this morning—I like to sleep late on my days off, but this morning my small brother woke me with his crying. I could not go back to sleep again, and I lay awake in the dark. Then I heard a faraway cry—like a human voice. It was almost musical. Alone in the dark, the rooster sang. Then it was still, and slowly, so slowly, the night crept away and light stretched across the sky. I felt as though I had been reincarnated, as though I had left one life and were beginning another." Yosa smiled.

Hideyo looked at his hands. "What will you do with your life, Yosa?"

"I had thought of becoming a priest, but I don't know. I do not see things in the right way—in the way a priest should. I have too many eyes. I see things that are gray—and black—but I also see things in brighter hues." He smiled. "Too often, I sit at the bright end of the rainbow."

"Even here?"

Yosa looked about at the darkened forms. No one stirred. "One night Miki could not sleep. It was the pain. Watanabe-san had already given her a large dose of morphine. I sat by her, holding her hand. She is not old, but her hands are withered, like an old woman's. I talked to her, to get her mind away from the pain. I told her she had the same eyes and hair as my sister—she doesn't, but I said it anyway. I told her that my sister was very beautiful and sought after by the sons of wealthy merchants, but that she was even more lovely. And slowly her face relaxed and she turned to me and smiled. She knew—I'm sure she knew—that I was lying—although my sister is ugly and almost any woman is a better sight than she is. Anyway, Miki looked up at me, and do you know, Hideyo, I don't think I'll ever forget that smile . . .

"And later, when the pain had eased and she had fallen asleep . . . she looked like a little girl."

The boys were silent. The only sound was the heavy

breathing of the sleeping forms. Slowly, Hideyo got to his feet. He looked at Yosa.

"I will write to you."

"I will write to you, Hideyo."

Hideyo smiled. "Good-by, Yosa."

"Good-by."

Stars sprinkled the heavens. The hazy moon had gone and now the night silhouettes were sharp and clear. Carrying the furoshihi, Hideyo stepped quietly into the night. Far ahead, above Okinajima, a bright star shone. Hideyo winked at it.

Man of the House

Hideyo was shivering. He pushed aside the straw covering and jumped to his feet. He slid into his clothes and rushed to the door. Snow was falling. The paddies were freezing beneath the snow. He ran down the steps, slipping on the last one. Snowflakes touched his head and shoulders. The soft snow cushioned his steps. The cold brushed against his neck and chest as he ran. Shivering, he looked out over the snow-covered fields to the vegetable patch on the slope of the hill. Like charred bodies, the blackened leaves of the sweet potatoes jutted up from the snow.

Hideyo fell to his knees and dug into the snow with both hands. The snow was powdery. He scratched into the dry, flaky soil, gripped a potato, and gently eased it up out of the ground. It was frozen. A sliver of fear sliced through his stomach. He ran back to the house.

His mother opened her eyes as he burst in. "Quick, Mother, the potatoes!"

She reached out for Inu and shook her. "Wait, Hideyo," she called. "Cover your feet."

Hideyo glanced toward the corner of the room. He knew there were only four burlap bags there. "You and Inu use them," he said.

Outside, snow drifted down and made it difficult to see. Through the netting of snow he heard shouts nearby. Other farmers were running to their fields. A dog howled somewhere in the village, its cry almost smothered by the heavy snowfall.

Hideyo knelt and burrowed into the snow. His mother dropped a basket near him. Inu came toward them. "Inu," he shouted. "The carrots and radishes." She turned and ran to the other end of the patch. His mother was on her knees, struggling with the soil.

With the forefinger of his right hand Hideyo dug around a potato. This one was not frozen. Carefully he placed it in the basket. Perhaps the sudden cold wave had not killed too many. They would harvest the crop this day, but they would have to hurry. The temperature could plunge below freezing again. Another hard frost would kill the whole crop.

He dug his blackened hands into the snow. The fingertips of his right hand were beginning to tingle. The snow made his hands slippery. The potatoes came up from the funnels in the snow black with mud.

Hideyo was nearing the end of the first row. He looked in the basket. There were three potatoes inside.

Three potatoes. A deep, hollow fear spread through him. Most of the crop was frozen. He clenched his muddied hands and struck them against the ground.

"Hideyo."

He turned. His mother was kneeling in the snow, her dark eyes fixed on him.

"Are you all right?"

"I'm all right, Mother." Suddenly he brought his hand up, cupped it around his mouth, and shouted, "Inu!" There was no answer. He stood up, but he could not see her.

"Inu!" his mother shouted. Her voice disappeared in the falling snow.

"I will go, Mother." He ran stiffly, his feet nearly numb. He could not see her. Then he heard a sob.

Inu was kneeling on the ground, her head hanging down. Frozen radishes were scattered around her like drops of blood on the snow.

"Inu."

Hideyo knelt beside her and put his arm around her. Inu raised her head. Snowflakes hung in her hair like diamond crystals.

"All of them?"

She nodded.

"It is all right, Inu. We will manage."

"The potatoes?"

"The cold has not killed them all. "

"You are sure?"

"Yes. Why, already Mother and I have nearly filled the basket."

"Will there be enough?"

"Don't worry, Inu. We will be all right. But don't tell Mother yet about the carrots and radishes."

Hideyo helped her to her feet and looked at her. Her face was pinched and tired. He brushed the snow-

flakes from her shoulders. Then, hand in hand, they walked through the snow.

Later, Inu brought out some o-mugi, and they ate hurriedly, surrounded by the falling snow.

Hideyo's hands were so numb with cold he could not grip the sticks to bring the barley to his mouth. He laid the sticks aside, tipped the bowl up to his mouth, and gulped the porridge. It brought warmth to his insides, but his hands and feet were nearly frozen.

Hideyo stuck his hands inside his robe and pressed them against his chest. Then he brought them up under his armpits. He glanced around at the remaining rows. There was still a few hours' work ahead of them. He raised his right foot and brought the heel down against the ankle of the other foot. It would have been better to stand and stamp his feet to get the circulation going again, but his mother would see him. He brought his hands out and blew into them.

"Hideyo."

He looked up at Inu.

"Come inside and warm your hands by the *hibachi* for a while."

"No, Inu."

"Just for a little while. . . ."

He tried to grin. "I don't think I can walk."

She knelt beside him. "Your feet . . . oh, Hideyo."

She took off one of his straw sandals and wrapped

her hands around his bare foot. "Do you feel anything?" He shook his head. "Take my sacks."

He shook his head again. "We will be finished soon."

Pressing her hands around his foot, Inu watched the
falling snow. Her dark eyes were deep-set. Snow crystals clung to her hair. "Where Father is, in Hokkaido,
it often snows like this."

"Do you think about him much?"

She shook her head. "No longer." She looked at Hideyo. "You are the man of the house now."

"Has Mother been in to warm herself?"

"Yes. We both have. Now you should go in."

"There is only a little daylight left. We must get this
work done before night comes."

"Let me help you here, Hideyo."

"No. I'm all right. Go to Mother, Inu."

She got to her feet. "Yes, Hideyo."

It was getting dark. How long had it been since Inu
had brought out the o-mugi? He had lost track of time.

With his clenched fist Hideyo reached out to his foot
and beat on it. Each blow sent sparks of pain up his
leg. He had to stop. His foot would crack, like a piece
of ice. He took hold of the basket and dragged it along
to the next row.

The ground seemed to be swaying.

He stuck his right hand under his armpit, pressing
against it with his arm. With his left hand he stabbed
into the snow and scratched around a root. Then using

his right hand, he pulled out the potato. It was frozen. Now he placed the left hand under his right armpit and with his right hand dug into the snow. Pain shot up through his fingers. He stopped and beat his fingers against the edge of the basket, but the pain made him gasp. He stared at his hands, pressed them against his chest, and closed his eyes.

The face of Watanabe-san appeared before him. The face smiled at him. Hideyo opened his eyes. He would swallow the pain. He bit his lips and dug into the snow with both hands. The pain jumped into his chest. He swallowed. For a moment, the ground seemed to heave up at him. The snow came closer, then receded.

Far off a voice called him. He tried to turn his head. His mother was calling.

"In a moment, Mother," he whispered. "I'm almost finished." He felt the soft snow against his face. And it was quiet and warm.

The Hidden Spring

The boat swayed. Another pitch of the boat and he would fall into the water. He awoke.

It was day. From the corner of his eye he could see tiny puffs of clouds above the nearby trees. He was not in a boat. It had been a dream. He was safe.

The swaying again. He opened his eyes. He had dozed off. It was still day. Above the trees the sky was now clear, without a cloud. He started to raise his head but became aware of the pain, like a knife point digging into his arm. He groaned.

Someone called his name. "We do not have far to go. You must be brave." His mother's voice sounded very close. Then he felt the ground swaying once more. He raised his head. Inches away was the back of his mother's neck. He was on her back. She was carrying him.

"Mother!" She turned. "Put me down, Mother."

"It is all right, Hideyo."

"But you can't. I won't let you."

"You cannot walk, Hideyo."

He looked down at his feet. They were dangling above the ground, tied in rags.

"I will try. Please let me try, Mother."

"Be still, Hideyo."

"Please, Mother. Please. You can't . . . I won't let you. Mother!" He buried his face in her back.

Watanabe-san looked down at him. He was smiling. He raised a bowl to Hideyo's lips. The broth was hot.

Hideyo looked at his bandaged hands. His bandaged feet stuck out from under the end of the blanket.

"When can I go, Watanabe-san?"

"You are lucky to be going back with no permanent harm. Frostbite can be serious. Your mother got you here in time. In a few days you will be able to return home."

The doctor put the bowl down.

"Thank you, Watanabe-san."

He nodded. "Now rest."

"Is my mother all right?"

"Yes."

They were silent.

"I insisted that your mother stay overnight and rest. She left this morning."

Hideyo bit his lip. He turned his face away from Watanabe-san.

"Do not think solely of your mother's suffering. Think of her joy, too. When I told her that you would soon be all right, her face was radiant, like a young girl's."

"But to come so far, Watanabe-san . . . so far."

"Yes, Hideyo, a long distance. But what was she carrying on her back—a load of sticks? Her endurance came not only from her arms. It came also from a hidden spring." He grinned. "I am talking, and you should rest."

"I'm all right, Watanabe-san."

The doctor gazed down the row of patients. "You will be coming back in the summer?"

"Yes, Watanabe-san. I will be finished with my schooling."

Watanabe-san rubbed his chin. "I am glad you will be here, Hideyo. I have received a letter from the central government. I am to report for military duty."

"For military duty?"

"Yes. The army is in need of doctors."

"But they cannot call you." Hideyo sat up. "You are needed here."

The doctor placed a hand on Hideyo's shoulder and eased him down. "It is my duty. I must go."

"But your patients, Watanabe-san. . . ."

"They will be looked after. There will be Azu, Yosa, and yourself. What you and the others have learned will be put to good use. The surgical cases you will send to Shoin-san. And you will send Azu or Yosa to him when you are in doubt about the diagnosis or treatment of a case. But there is time enough for all the instructions when you return in the summer."

"When will you be leaving, Watanabe-san?"

"I am to report to Sendai next month. But I have written to the commanding general there requesting a delay until the summer, when you will be here. I believe he will grant the request; we are not at war yet."

Hideyo remembered now the rumors he had heard of a war with China. "Do you think there will be war?"

"I don't know. If there is, I may be away a long time. Will you remain here as long as I am gone?"

"I will be here when you return, Watanabe-san, no matter how long you are away."

Watanabe-san stroked his chin. He grinned. "I overheard Yosa tell Azu that now they would have to address you as Noguchi-san. Azu did not laugh. Yosa told him you might grow a mustache to look older. Azu told him to shut up. I took Azu aside and explained why I had selected you."

"Azu has been here longer than I."

"I know that. That is why Azu expected that I would choose him. But a true doctor must have compassion as well as knowledge and skill. In Azu there is no hidden spring. Perhaps, working with you, he will discover it."

A voice called at the other end of the hut. Watanabe-san rose. "I think it is the woman I admitted today. Try to rest."

Hideyo could not sleep. Images tumbled over each other. His mother walking in the snow, bent under the weight of his body. The blue sky. Watanabe-san looking down at him.

Someone coughed in the dark, and then it was still.

He stared into the darkness. In a few days he would be leaving. He would be well. But those here with him, what did tomorrow offer them? What hope?

He shut his eyes. He saw his mother standing in the fields, in sunlight, the green rice shoots around her feet. Her face was pale, the skin weatherworn as old leather and the creases deep from her nose to the corners of her mouth; but the eyes were clear, dark, and gazing happily, not seeing the fields.

She would be thinking of him, Dr. Noguchi, her son. A peasant's son who had become a man of learning, healing the sick and bringing hope to their tomorrows. Her son. And her joy would make the world seem young again. To her, he would be like a flower growing up out of the hard soil, the loveliest flower because it had blossomed in a patch of thorns.

Someone coughed again. Then it was silent. Hideyo could hear his heart thumping. He opened his eyes. He would work as he had never worked before. Not for himself, but for her . . . for Watanabe-san . . . for all who knew pain.

Good Medicine

Hideyo stumbled and almost fell headlong. Yosa laughed. Then, his elbows resting on the tops of his stilts, he smiled at Hideyo.

"Try it again, Hideyo. I'll wait."

Hideyo shook his head. He picked up the bamboo stilts and climbed onto them once more.

"Keep them straight, Hideyo. Straight! Look out!" Hideyo tumbled backward into the dust. He lay on his elbows, grinning up at Yosa, who almost lost his balance he was laughing so hard.

Hideyo picked himself up. "I can't do it, Yosa."

"You can. It's not hard, once you get on them. Put your right foot up first and steady yourself with the other stilt. Lean on the left one more. Now, get your weight down on your right foot. Easy . . . good. Now, your left foot. Watch it. Keep them apart—you can bring them closer later. Get the feel of them. Don't look down at your feet. There . . . that's it. Good. Now try to turn, easy. Very easy. . . . How is it?"

"Look out, I'm going to fall."

"No. You're doing fine. Move one foot, slowly . . .
slowly . . . the other. Lift it gently . . . that's it.
Shift your weight before each step. Don't look down.
You have it now. Just relax a bit."

Hideyo looked at Yosa and grinned. "It feels good."

"Sure, it's fun. We used to play with these all the
time when we were young. Didn't the boys in your
village every play stilt-riding?"

"They did. Many times I watched them."

Yosa glanced at Hideyo's hand. He grinned. "Now
you can do it as well as they. Right, Hideyo?"

Hideyo smiled.

Yosa waved his arm. "Come on, Hideyo." Yosa set off along the path in front of Watanabe-san's house. Hideyo followed.

"Not too fast, Yosa."

Yosa turned. "I'll wait for you on the road. From there we'll go together." Gripping the top of the stilts tightly, he moved along the path in long steps. A light breeze rumpled his hair. He smiled to himself, then turned and shouted, "How is it, Hideyo?"

"I'm ten feet tall."

Yosa laughed. At the road he stopped and looked back at Hideyo, squinting in the sunlight. In the distance, Hideyo's figure looked tiny on the high stilts, as if he were floating above the ground. As Hideyo approached, Yosa saw that his left stilt was dragging a little.

"You all right?" he asked as Hideyo came abreast of him.

Hideyo nodded, then looked around. "You can see over the cedars to the pond." He looked toward the mountain. "Bandai looks bigger—and its peak whiter. And the sky . . . I can reach up and touch it." He smiled, and they set off together.

Dust billowed up from the dirt road. Pines stretched beyond the road into the distance. Behind them squatted the mountain, which rose high above the valley. An echo rippled across the valley. The temple bell. Its echo died away slowly. Then all was still, but for the thumping of the boys' stilts on the road.

They turned off onto a path bordered with high grass. The cedars overhead hid Bandai. Circling the file of cedars, the path curved to the pond. The water shimmered in the sunlight.

The boys stepped down from the stilts and sat by the edge of the pond. A giant willow caressed the ground on the other side. An air bubble floated on the water. Hideyo flipped a pebble into the pond and the ripples widened. At the edge of the cedars, a squirrel sat up.

Yosa tied a string around one of the bamboo stilts. At the end of the string was a pin bent into a hook. While Hideyo stared at the water, Yosa stepped to the edge of the pond, then brought the rod back over his shoulder. He swung the rod over his head in a wide arc. The line leaped out across the pond, the hook sinking into the water.

"You will not fish?"

Hideyo shook his head.

Sitting holding his pole, Yosa looked out at the water. "I hope they will not be stubborn. At least one of them—a big fat one—should cooperate."

"I would like to see Azu's face if we brought back a good one."

"You must accept that he will not change."

"He doesn't do his work properly."

Yosa looked at him. "I know." He grinned. "But that's the only way he has of defying your authority."

"I have been easy with him."

Yosa nodded. "But that doesn't change things, does it?"

"If Watanabe-san had given me a choice, I would have said no. Then he would have had to pick Azu."

"Azu in charge? I would have quit. You are bad enough—working us like coolies."

Hideyo grinned. He reached out, broke off a blade of grass, and put it in his mouth. Yosa got slowly to his feet and leaned forward. The line tightened. He yanked up the rod. The line whipped over the water and he pulled it in. "The whole bait, eh?" He grinned. "All right, hungry one. I will try again."

Hideyo took the blade of grass from his mouth. "Do you think Watanabe-san will be changed?"

"He will be older."

"I mean, will the war have changed him?"

"I have not seen war. I do not know."

Hideyo gazed at the water. "He should be coming home soon."

"Even if the war ended tomorrow, there would still be the wounded to care for."

"But he has served long enough."

Yosa looked at him. "It has only been a little more than a year."

"That is long enough."

"War is slow. It takes a very long time to kill enough men."

"You have not seen war."

"I know that wars end only after thousands of men have died."

Hideyo shaded his eyes with his hand.

"He has not written this month."

"We will get a letter soon."

Yosa set his rod down carefully by the edge of the pond. He picked up one of Hideyo's stilts. "Give me your line." He took the line from Hideyo and tied it around the top of the stilt.

"I am sorry, Yosa." Hideyo fell back on the grass. "I feel as old as Bandai."

"That is all right, lazy one. I will fish for both of us."

"It was fun on the stilts."

"Didn't I tell you it would be? But no, you are stubborn like these fishes. All you care about is staying around the hospital."

"I am responsible, Yosa."

"Yes, but what has happened to you? You have become ill-tempered like a money-hungry merchant. I am not a wise doctor like you, but I know that a little fun and a change of scene is good medicine."

Hideyo grinned.

Yosa held both rods, one in each hand. "I have never tried this before, but I should have a double chance for a meal now." He gazed at the water where the weeping willow was reflected. The surface of the pond shone like steel.

The rod Yosa held in his right hand jerked forward. Quickly he set the other rod on the ground. "Come, once more. Bite. Bite well, and up through the air you will fly. Go ahead . . . a big bite."

Yosa waited. The line tightened. He yanked up the rod, and the fish slid through the water. He reached out and pulled in the line, hand over hand, then stepped into the water and grabbed the fish. Lashing back and forth, it leaped out of his hand. He cupped his hand over it as it squirmed in the dust.

"Hideyo. . . ."

Hideyo lay on his side, his head nestled on his arm, his eyes closed. Yosa pulled out the hook and placed the fish in the hollow stump of a tree. He glanced at Hideyo. There was a fly on his shoulder. Yosa reached down and swept it away.

The Face of Evil

Azu watched Hideyo as he raised the woman's chin and peered at her eyes. They were red and swollen. Hideyo rested his hand on her shoulder for an instant, then stepped to the medicine cabinet.

"You will use the silver nitrate?"

Hideyo looked at Azu. "No, the boric lotion. Bring the cotton."

Hideyo set the boric-acid solution down on Watanabe-san's desk, and Azu placed the cotton beside it. The woman stared at the bottle and pressed her hands together. Then she looked up at Azu and started to smile. But Azu went past her to the doorway and stood gazing out at the porch.

There was an old man there, and a woman with a child. The old man came slowly to his feet, but Azu shook his head. The old man sat down again. The child whimpered, and his mother put her arms around him.

Azu turned and looked at Hideyo. He was applying

drops of the boric-acid solution to the woman's eyes. Her fingers gripped the edge of the stool. Hideyo reached for a wad of cotton and gently wiped her eyelids. She suppressed a cough and her eyelids flickered. When Hideyo straightened up and put the wad of cotton aside, her grip on the edge of the stool eased.

"That is all," he said. "You will come again in a week's time."

The woman nodded her head. As Hideyo picked up the bottle of boric lotion and started for the cabinet, she slid from the stool onto her knees and bowed her head to the floor by his feet.

Hideyo put the bottle back in the cabinet, closed the door, and glanced at Azu. Their gazes met for a moment, and then Azu turned his eyes away.

"There are two more out there," Azu said. His voice was hoarse.

"Is the boy we looked at yesterday here?"

Azu nodded and went to the doorway. The old man was standing there, waiting.

"Not yet, old man."

"I have come far."

"Sit down!"

"What is the trouble?" Hideyo asked.

Azu turned to him. "This old one wants to come in now."

The old man looked at Hideyo, then took off his

large straw hat and nodded his head. Wisps of hair hung over his pink bald head. "I have come a long way . . . as on a pilgrimage." The old man smiled. His toothless gums shone with saliva.

"You will wait your turn, old one," Azu ordered.

The old man did not look at Azu. "Your assistant is a fine example of our progressive nation," he said to Hideyo.

"I have respect for those who deserve it. And I am not his assistant," Azu snapped.

The old man looked at him. "I do not believe you respect anyone, young man."

Hideyo moved aside. "Come in." He turned to the woman. "You may bring in the child."

The old man stepped in, and Hideyo pointed to the stool. "Please sit there," he said. He glanced at Azu. "I will need a blood sample from the boy."

"He will not let me go near him—you remember yesterday."

"Then I will see to the boy. You will take care of the old man?"

Azu nodded. Hideyo went to the washbasin. "I will be with the boy in a minute," he said to the woman. She smiled.

Azu looked at the old man. "What is wrong?"

The old man eyed him for a moment. "An evil spirit has entered my body."

Azu snorted.

"Of course, you do not believe in evil spirits, my young one. What do you believe in?"

Azu placed his hands on his hips. "I have no time to waste."

"All right, my impatient young one." The old man pulled up his kimono. On his thigh, just above the knee, was a large dark sore.

Azu knelt. "You should have come sooner."

"I have never been ill. I thought it would go away."

"Well, it will not go away, old one."

"I thought you might apply something. The older doctors tried herbs."

"And failed." Azu grinned. "Didn't they?"

The old man looked at him. "You do not accept the old ways. Do you, young one?"

"The past is ignorance."

"And we are old fools?"

Azu nodded. "Old fools."

The man came to his feet.

"What is wrong?" Hideyo stood behind the old man, towel in hand.

"An ulcer."

"Did you get the chlorine solution?"

"I will."

"Wash it first with hydrogen peroxide."

"I know."

"I do not want him to treat me," the old man said softly.

"Go to the child. Put on a tourniquet and find a good vein," Hideyo said to Azu.

"I told you, he will not let me go near him."

"Smile at him."

As Hideyo knelt down by the old man, Azu went to the child. The boy looked at Azu and clung to his mother.

"Put out your arm," said Azu.

He pushed the boy's sleeve up and tied the tourniquet around his arm. The boy stared down at the tourniquet.

"He will not hurt you, Toku." The woman brushed her lips against the boy's cheek. His eyes were very dark in his pale face.

Azu took hold of the boy's arm and wiped it with iodine. He picked up the syringe. The boy stiffened. "Hold him," Azu said.

The boy twisted. "No! No!"

"Hold him still!"

The mother looked at Azu, wide-eyed. "We will come back—perhaps another day."

Hideyo went to them and placed his hand on the boy's shoulder. Then he turned to the mother. "We must have a blood sample. Yesterday's examination did not indicate anything definite. We will wait a moment, then try again." He looked at Azu. "Give the old man some chlorine solution. I have washed the sore. Tell him to keep off his feet. And ask him to come again in a few days."

The old man watched as Azu took a small bottle from the laboratory table and filled it with solution.

"You are to take this home with you," said Azu, not looking at the old man.

"I am to drink it?"

"Place it on the dressing. Keep it wet."

"Is that all?"

Azu looked at him. "That is all."

The old man took the bottle. "Thank you." He clutched the bottle against his chest, bowed, and shuffled out of the room.

Azu watched him go, then turned toward Hideyo, who was leaning over the washbasin.

Hideyo straightened up. A face he did not recognize was staring at him from out of the mirror. After an instant he realized that it was Azu's.

"The old man has left?"

"Yes."

Hideyo put the towel aside and turned to the boy. "We will try again," he said to the mother.

He looked at the boy. "What is your name?"

"Toku."

"Put out your arm, Toku." The boy looked at his mother. She nodded to him. The boy put out his arm.

Hideyo picked up the syringe. The boy stiffened. "No," said Hideyo. "You will not show fear."

"It is shameful to show fear, Toku," said his mother softly. The boy clung to her.

"You will not shame your mother," said Hideyo. "Put out your arm."

The boy glanced at Hideyo, then turned and looked at his mother. She returned his gaze without speaking. The boy bit his lower lip, then slowly extended his arm. Holding the boy's wrist, Hideyo pressed the needle into the skin. The boy stared at the syringe. Hideyo released the plunger.

"Good, Toku." He smiled. The boy put his arms around his mother's neck. "Bring him again tomorrow," Hideyo said.

She nodded. "Thank you." She bowed, then put her hand behind the boy's neck and bent his head down before Hideyo.

The woman stepped out, the boy peering silently over her shoulder at Azu.

Hideyo turned to Azu. "You go ahead. Bring the sterile saline for the woman with the burns. I will be there in a moment."

"Should we not use the picric acid?"

Hideyo shook his head.

"But the picric-acid solu—"

"I said the saline solution!"

Azu stared at him, then swung around and went out.

Hideyo turned to the basin and grasped the pitcher. He filled the basin with water, spilling some of it over the edge. Gripping the bar of soap, he plunged his hands into the water.

Anger churned within him. Always Azu spoiled it, the joy he took in his work. Yosa had been right, that day in the fall when they had gone fishing. Nothing would change Azu. Hideyo had tried to give him more responsibility, letting him take care of patients on his own. Still Azu continued to defy him.

He glanced into the mirror. For an instant he did not recognize himself. Then he recalled Azu's face in the mirror. He had not immediately recognized him, either. Why? The frustration that was gnawing at his insides at this moment had subtly distorted his own features. What had distorted Azu's face, he realized now, had been frustration, too.

But about what? Had he done something—said something? This day had been really no different from all the others since Watanabe-san had left. It had been but another day with Azu, as difficult as always. Hideyo picked up the towel and dried his hands.

Was it because he was too much like Watanabe-san— brisk, positive, authoritative? But he had to be that way. He was responsible. He had to see that things were done, and done right.

Was it simply that Azu still resented his being in charge?

He tossed the towel aside. Whatever the reason, Azu could feel frustration, too. He stepped to the doorway and looked out.

The air smelled clean and carried a hint of warmth. Soon it would be spring. Cherry blossoms would transform the hills with pink snow, and wild roses would spot the fields with red. Soon the hospital would be an island surrounded by a sea of color.

Hideyo stepped out. Azu was waiting for him. He would let Azu take care of the woman with the bad burns. He would say, "You take care of her, Azu. I'll assist you." Then, later, he would praise his work.

Homecoming

The man was still too far away to be sure. The tiny figure silhouetted against the pinkish sky could be a farmer. Hideyo felt a tightness edging through his chest. But it could be him. His last letter had been from Yokohama. From that port he had written that it would not be long, maybe a few weeks. That had been more than a month ago.

The figure was not a farmer. Yet, it was not like him either—it seemed shorter, the steps heavier. But there was no doubt now, the man was in military uniform— an officer, with a sword trailing by his side.

Slowly Hideyo came down the steps. The figure waved. It was Watanabe-san. The name pounded up through Hideyo's chest. He started forward but checked himself. He pressed his knuckles hard against his chin. His heart seemed to be throbbing in his stomach.

You must not run, he told himself. Walk slowly. He raised his hand and waved. Watanabe-san smiled. His face was dark, much darker than Hideyo remembered, and there were deep lines in his cheeks. The face was thinner, too. Was this man Watanabe-san?

"Hideyo." The man hurried forward, his sword clicking against the scabbard.

Should he bow now? Should he, too, hurry forward? He stood still. Smiling, Watanabe-san ran forward, awkwardly, his elbows jutting out, the sword like a third leg. He stopped a few yards away, his breathing hard. The buttons on his faded uniform shone like jewels.

Hideyo bowed very low, then looked up at the doctor through a haze of tears. Suddenly his feet were carrying him over the road, and his face was pressed against the rough army cloth.

"I did not recognize you," said Watanabe-san, his arm on Hideyo's shoulder.

"I did not recognize you," said Hideyo, looking up at him. They both began to laugh.

The two of them walked together. The house and the hospital beyond it stood like stone blocks in the fading sunlight. On the slope of the first hill, the cherry blossoms gleamed red in the dimming light. On the crest, a low, twisted pine seemed carved out of the hill.

Watanabe-san slowed his steps. "It has been a long time," he said softly. "So much has happened, but here—things have not changed."

They turned onto the gravel path. Hideyo looked at Watanabe-san. Beneath the army cap, his hair was completely white.

"Tell me of the war, Watanabe-san."

"What do you wish to know about it?"

"Was it exciting?"

Watanabe-san stopped. "War—exciting? War is stupid, senseless destruction."

They went up the steps of the porch. Hideyo hurried ahead and opened the door. Watanabe-san stepped in and looked around the room. He moved to the laboratory table and ran his hand along its surface. He touched the microscope and glanced at the box of slides, the flasks, and the instruments on the tray. He turned and looked at the desk. Then he smiled, loosened his tunic, and unbuckled his sword.

Hideyo took them and put them down on a chair. Watanabe-san stepped to the washbasin. He washed his hands and lathered his face. Cupping his hands, he splashed water on his face. He smiled. "It is cold," he said. Hideyo handed him a towel. He rubbed his face hard, then wiped his arms and hands.

He looked into the mirror and rubbed the skin beneath his nose with his thumb. "I will shave later." He grinned. "You can introduce me to the patients as a visiting doctor." He put his arms into the white jacket Hideyo held for him. The sleeves reached only to his forearms.

"Is this mine?"

"Yes, Watanabe-san."

The doctor looked at his wrists jutting out from the sleeves. He glanced at Hideyo, then stretched his arms out in front of him. The sleeves slid up to his elbows. He burst out laughing.

"Mine? But what happened? I have lost—I have lost, not gained weight." He leaned against the desk, laughing.

He looked at the sleeves and shook his head, his laughter slowly subsiding. "What—what happened to the jacket, Hideyo?"

"I have been using it, Watanabe-san."

"Did you cut it down?"

"Oh, no, Watanabe-san. But I did keep it clean."

"How often did you wash it?"

"Every day, Watanabe-san."

"I see."

The doctor took off the jacket and picked up the army tunic. He left the sword on the chair. Buttoning the tunic, he said, "You can introduce me as Dr. Watanabe, home from military service." He smiled and placed his arm on Hideyo's shoulder.

The Gift

Everyone was waiting outside the train. It was better than waiting inside. Some were sitting on the embankment, their backs to the train. A few had wandered down the high bank and stood now in small groups by the tall marsh weeds. A stream, narrow and swift, sparkled as it rushed through the weeds. Hideyo cupped his hand in the stream and sipped the water. It chilled his mouth.

He leaned back. The train, black and sooty, framed the top of the embankment like the ramparts of an ancient castle. The sun's rays glared off the tops of the cars.

Inside the cars it had been like an oven. Perhaps the train would be delayed until the sun set. It would be better to wait than to go back into the train while the sun was still up, baking the steel plates. Hideyo looked toward the front of the train. He could not see the conductor. Whatever was delaying the train was farther ahead on the track.

He sat down and removed his sandals. Sitting at the edge of the stream, he thrust his feet into the water. Deeper down the water was cold. The current tugged gently against his feet. The bed of the stream was paved with white pebbles.

He was hungry. In the furoshihi by his side were some pickled plums his mother had given him. If he ate them now, then what would he eat when he reached Tokyo? He would have to spend some of his money, but he could not do that. He had exactly eighty-two yen after paying the train fare. Most of that would have to go for tuition; the little remaining would have to last until he got work.

Perhaps he could have one plum, saving the rest for later. Yes, one plum. He began to untie the furoshihi but stopped. He could wait. Had he not eaten well that morning? His mother had kept filling his cup with rice, insisting that he eat more. . . . His last meal at home. And then at the train station, Yosa had given him two apples, which he had eaten at noon on the train. But one plum would ease the gnawing in his stomach. Just one. His hand was still on the furoshihi. He took his hand away. This would be part of it, Hideyo knew. He had learned to combat fatigue, to ignore it. He would learn to live with hunger.

He would have to live with it for a long time. The first part of the government examinations for the medical license would be given in October, the second part the next October. Somehow the eighty-two yen would have to see him through until then, permitting him to take at least some of the courses of study. Whatever job he found would only help keep him alive. He had already decided to eat barley instead of rice, since barley was cheaper. But the tuition and books he could not do much about, unless he was able to buy second-hand books. He had heard that Tokyo was a very big city, many times larger than Wakamatsu. Perhaps he could find bookstores with cheap secondhand medical books.

He would manage somehow. He had to. He could not expect any more help. He had already received much. It would not be right for his friends and his mother to give more. Besides, what more could his mother give? During the last four years she had saved fourteen yen, which she had managed to put aside from the money he had earned working for Watanabe-san. He had not expected money from her and had protested when she first offered it to him. "All the money I earned was for you," he told her. But she had insisted that he take the money and he could not refuse.

Now he remembered something else in his furo-shihi. He pulled his feet out of the water, and kneeling by the stream, untied the bundle. He took out a small packet wrapped in paper and unfolded it gently. In-side was a note written in graceful letters. It read: *May you live long as the pine, Hideyo.* At the bottom were the signatures—two in English and three in Japanese: The Reverend Taylor Wells, Mrs. Taylor Wells, Dr. Kanae Watanabe, Sakae Kobayashi, and Toson Yorozu. He smiled, remembering how Yorozu-san had befriended him that day long ago when he had fought with the boys in Wakamatsu. "You are a samurai," he had said, "because you have courage in your heart."

Courage. But the ache in his stomach was sharp. How many plums were there? He reached into the furoshihi. There were eight. If he had two now, he could have six this night when the train arrived in Tokyo. Then tomorrow—well, tomorrow he would buy some barley, enough to last a week. But no, he could not spend money for food on his first day in Tokyo. He would make the plums last, eating half of them tonight and the rest tomorrow.

Tomorrow he would go to the college and register. Perhaps someone there could recommend a room for him. He had heard of students living with families, paying for a room. How much would that be? Perhaps he could share a room with another student. Or perhaps he could do as he had with Dr. Wells—pay his way by doing odd jobs around the house, gathering firewood, caring for the hibachi, keeping the garden clean. That would be payment for a room. Somehow he would manage. He would make the money last.

He closed the furoshihi, putting aside four of the plums. These he put inside his shirt. He would eat them tonight. He looked up at the train. The conductor was still not in sight. People were lined along the side of the embankment, squatting on their thighs, their feet digging into the gray stones. The men wore white knotted handkerchiefs around their heads; several of them smoked long clay pipes. Near the bottom of the embankment a boy lay on his side, asleep; his little brother, strapped to his back, was also asleep.

Inu had carried Hideyo on her back when he was an infant. When would he see her—or his mother—again? Or Watanabe-san? What was he doing at this moment? Late in the afternoon he was usually at the clinic, working at his desk—that same desk under which Hideyo had slept. He remembered Watanabe-san behind that desk for the first time after he had returned from military service last year. Sitting back in the chair, Watanabe-san had smiled up at him. "You have done well in my absence," he had said. And then they had talked of the future, of Hideyo's hope of going to medical school in Tokyo and preparing for the medical license examinations.

"Somehow I will find a way to help you," Watanabe-san had promised.

Now the conductor was calling, waving his arm, waving the passengers back on board. Hideyo picked up his furoshihi and headed up the embankment. He passed the boy who was asleep and touched his shoulder. One by one they climbed back into the car. The engine ahead belched up black smoke. Hideyo gripped the iron railing and pulled himself up into the car.

The boy carrying his little brother sat down across from him. Unloosening the straps, the boy swung the child around to his lap. Hideyo glanced out the window. In the distance dark-blue mountains walled the horizon, and stretches of wheat yellowed in the sunlight. It would be time to harvest soon, and it would be a good harvest, because the rains that spring had been heavy but not severe. The day Watanabe-san had given him the money, it had been raining. Holding a small package under his straw raincoat, the doctor had stepped into the office, drenched.

"This is for you," he had said, holding out the package. There was a note inside and seventy yen. "A gift from us," Watanabe-san had said. Hideyo's stomach tightened now, remembering.

The car kicked forward and lurched. Then, steel banging against steel, the train edged ahead. The child whimpered, his large dark eyes peering up at his brother. The train whistle, shrill and piercing, cut through the countryside. Tears filled the little boy's eyes. Again the whistle pierced the air. The child screamed. The boy held the child in his arms and rocked him. The little boy sobbed, clinging tightly to his brother, his tiny knuckles like pebbles. Sobbing shook his whole body.

Reaching inside his shirt, Hideyo took out a plum. Gently loosening the little boy's grip, he placed the plum in the child's hand.

The Animals

Hideyo stood with his back to the entrance of an old monastery. The smell of incense was strong; behind him, in the dimly-lit interior, yellow-robed monks moved as noiselessly as shadows over the dark, polished floors. The wide stone steps in front of Hideyo led to a gravel path that curved slightly to the tall iron gate. The boys were standing at the gate, waiting for him.

The three of them together reminded Hideyo of the *ronins* of old, who wandered the countryside, living by threat of their long swords. Binshi was the clown of the three, with long stringy hair and an unwashed face. Matsuo, the leader, was short and pudgy; Arakawa was thin, with sad, intelligent eyes. They were not students; they had no jobs—and no homes, probably.

Hideyo had met them a few days ago near the college. They had asked if he wanted a job. "We're in the book business," Binshi had said, laughing. All Hideyo had to do was take out a few books from the college library. They were friends of a merchant who paid good prices for scientific books. Hideyo had refused.

Matsuo had stared pointedly at his hand. "No one will give a cripple work."

"We know where you live. We followed you yesterday," Arakawa had said. "If you work with us, you could live like a human being."

"In a palace," Binshi had said, laughing.

Hideyo had not seen them again until this day. They had told him they would come. All he had to do now was walk down the steps and join them. But he could not move. His legs were like the stone pillar against which he leaned.

The sunlight spread its spring warmth over the gravel path and the carefully trimmed grounds. A slight breeze pushed through the entrance, a reminder of the winter that was fleeing. Hideyo looked out over the white stone wall at the rooftops and the dark line of mountains, aloof from the city.

Maybe it would be different with winter leaving. Spring brought joy to people's hearts. If he tried to get a job now, his chances might be better. Someone might let him prove his worth.

Maybe this day he would go to the Kanda and Shimbashi districts again. Perhaps one of the merchants he had talked to before would smile and nod his head. Perhaps . . .

But he would be careful in the Shimbashi district.

The last time the rich odors from the food stalls had made him nauseous.

This morning there had been a bowl of warm broth in the corridor near his cell door. Was it the thin monk with the pale face, or the younger one with the sad eyes? One of the monks—he still did not know which one—from time to time left food, sometimes a bowl of barley, near his door. There was compassion even in this cruel city within the walls of the monastery.

During the past six months, the city had smothered his hope. It was a sprawling city, ugly in vast stretches and fascinating in spots: handsome parks, clusters of beautiful homes, and a moat-fringed palace, all surrounded by barren fields, shanty villages, torn roads, and hurrying hordes of people.

For days, in the beginning, he had walked the city streets, responding eagerly to the sights and sounds like a child at his first festival. He was fascinated by the crowds—it was as though all the people in Japan were pressed together in one city, filling the walks, spilling over into the streets—the streets that were ruptured everywhere by immense holes.

But it was a city, he soon learned, that had no need for a youth with a crippled hand. There were too many looking for work, all of them with two good hands.

Hideyo had hidden his hand, of course. But the hand in the kimono always brought suspicious glances, and refusals, often polite. Each refusal devoured his hope, bit by bit.

A deep sadness filled his heart. Spring would change nothing. He walked toward the three at the gate slowly, as though his legs were weighted. Near the end of the gravel path a small fountain splashed water into a stone pool. He stopped and threw a handful of water into his face. His reflection looked up at him from the pool. His eyes were like pieces of charcoal against the pallor of his face.

Hideyo pushed open the gate and stepped between Arakawa and Binshi.

"You kept us waiting," said Matsuo. "Let's go."

Hideyo did not look at Matsuo. "I thought you would get someone else."

"It would be best if we did not get anyone at all," said Binshi. "Four is unlucky."

"Quiet, *baka*," said Matsuo. "And do not walk so close to me. You stink like an earth-grubber."

"Farmers are cleaner than the bunch of you," Hideyo said softly.

"I think this fool is right," said Matsuo, nodding his head toward Binshi. "Four is unlucky."

"No, wait," said Arakawa. "We need this one." Arakawa glanced at Hideyo.

A rickshaw came hurtling from a side street, narrowly missing Matsuo. "Baka! Idiot!" yelled Matsuo, shaking his fist at the coolie.

The coolie stopped and put down the shafts of the
rickshaw. Matsuo darted across the street and down an
alleyway, his short legs flying over the cobblestones.
The coolie, with quick strides, reached the alleyway,
but Matsuo had disappeared. He turned and stared at
the three of them, then strode back to his rickshaw.

Binshi laughed, placing his hand over his mouth.
"Did you see that? Matsuo ran like a frightened pig."
He doubled over and slapped his thighs.

The alley was black with shadows, the cobblestones

smooth and slippery. A girl in a dirty kimono stood against a wall, sucking her thumb, a thin cat rubbing against her leg. A thick layer of garbage stretched along the sides of the alley. Hideyo held his breath. Binshi and Arakawa strode together, their gaze fixed on the end of the alley.

A bamboo fence, part of it down, separated the alley from a steep hill that plunged down to a canal.

"Where did that fool go?" said Binshi, leaning over the fence.

Arakawa pointed to a small bridge in the distance. "He's probably down there. Come on."

Slowly they made their way down the slope. The soft, gray clay was slippery under their feet. The canal, its water a muddy green, cut through the first stretch of level ground. On the other side of the canal, rows of low shanties spread to a dark line of hills. The boys walked along the canal to the low concrete bridge. In the shadows beneath the span crouched a figure. It was Matsuo.

He came out, his eyes avoiding theirs.

Binshi grinned, his chin jutting out. "Well, look who's here."

"Shut up!"

"You've taken us out of our way," said Arakawa.

"So?"

Arakawa gazed at Matsuo. "Next time be careful who you call a fool."

"I can outrun any of them."

Binshi lifted his knees, running in place. "Like a frightened pig—little legs flying, tail wagging behind."

Matsuo stepped forward and swung at Binshi. Jumping back, Binshi kept running in place. "Come catch me. If you can."

Matsuo clenched his fists.

"Wait!" Arakawa stepped between them.

"Come, ugly pig. Catch—"

"Enough!" shouted Arakawa.

Binshi grinned. His hair hung loosely down the sides of his face. Matsuo reached out to push Arakawa aside.

"Stop it!" Arakawa glared at Matsuo. They stood face to face.

"I am in charge," said Matsuo thickly.

"You're in charge," said Arakawa, "but let us get on with our business."

"First, I must teach this one not to call me an ugly pig."

Binshi laughed, then stepped back. Arakawa waved his arms at them. "Go ahead, bash your heads in, for all I care." He went to Hideyo and sat down beside him. Hideyo, his heels against the wooden wall of the canal, gazed at the muddy-green water drifting past.

"I was only joking, Matsuo," Binshi said.

"I am only joking, too—" Matsuo lunged and grabbed Binshi by his *obi*. Binshi fell forward, Matsuo yanking him down by his sash. Pressing his knee against Binshi's neck, Matsuo thrust his hand into Binshi's hair and seized a handful near the scalp. He pulled and Binshi screamed.

"I am only joking, Binshi."

Hideyo started to get to his feet. Arakawa gripped Hideyo's shoulder. "Stay out of it. You are not one of us." He looked at Hideyo, then leaned back against the soft clay, his hands by his side. He looked up at the sky.

Binshi yelled again.

"I am only joking." Matsuo spoke through clenched teeth, his face down close to Binshi's head.

"When will he stop?"

Arakawa did not look at Hideyo. "He must take it out on someone. Today it is Binshi; tomorrow it will be someone else."

An animal scurried over the bridge. It was a rat, its tail long and pointed. It disappeared in the shadows under the bridge.

Binshi screamed.

"I am still joking, Binshi."

Hideyo bolted up. "Stop it!"

Matsuo turned to Hideyo. Beads of sweat gleamed on his forehead. His eyes, dark and glazed, were fixed on Hideyo.

"What is wrong, honorable doctor?" he asked hoarsely. "Don't you like the way we play?"

Binshi was sobbing, his face pressed into the clay. Hideyo looked at Matsuo. "I am going," he said.

"Then go," said Matsuo. "Starve alone."

Arakawa stood up. "It will be difficult to get another student."

"The three of us can manage," said Matsuo.

"They will not let us in the library."

"But if I washed. . . ."

Arakawa shook his head. "With those clothes?"

"Maybe this one."

"Binshi! They would throw him out on sight. Look,

we have gone over this before. Not one of us has a
chance of getting inside the college library—or any library in this city. And even if we managed to get inside, how could we get a book out?"

"You could hide it under your kimono."

"You forget easily, Matsuo. Don't you remember
when Binshi tried that at the private library near
Ueno Park? Binshi remembers it. I do not care to be
beaten with bamboo rods—like a common criminal."

Binshi raised himself to his knees, still sobbing.

"You disgust me," said Matsuo. "Stand up! You look
like an animal."

"Animals," Binshi sobbed.

"Come on, get up," said Matsuo. "We will find another student. Hurry up!"

Arakawa helped Binshi to his feet. "Come, miserable one. Time for us to be on our way."

They scurried up the hill, pulling Binshi with
them.

To Stay Alive

As the sound of Binshi's sobs died away Hideyo picked
up a lump of clay and tossed it into the muddy water
of the canal. He had no strength to climb the hill. He
would spend the day here and sleep in this place under
the stars. He leaned back. The ground was soft. He
closed his eyes.

He saw his home: Bandai, its white cone jutting up
into the sky; the blue expanse of Lake Inawashiro
sparkling in the sunlight. He opened his eyes. It would
be better not to think of home.

He sat up. It was beginning to rain, drops dotting
the water in the canal. In a moment it would be pour-
ing. He started up the hill, but halfway up it, his knees
sank to the ground. Raindrops fell on his bent neck.
Slowly he raised his head; then, clawing at the ground,
he climbed the hill.

At the top, he leaned wearily against the wall in the
alley. The alleyway was deserted, except for a cat
pushing its nose in the garbage.

He heard a door slam nearby. A rickshaw raced past
the entrance to the alley, and a woman ran across the
street. A man, out of sight, shouted something. Hideyo
looked down. The cat was pressing against his leg.
Yellow stains streaked its side. The cat miaowed, looking up at him with large, liquid eyes. Hideyo bent
down and stroked the cat's back. Its fur was sticky from
the rain. The cat placed a paw on his knee, rubbing an
ear against its scrawny leg. Hideyo picked the cat up.

The rain was cold. A man with a large straw hat,
head bent, fought his way through the wind-swept
rain. Hideyo pulled his collar together and crossed the
street. He stopped beneath a small tree near the curb.
The cat lay quietly in his arms, its head pressed against
his chest. He could not go back to the monastery with
the cat. There was a shrine in the park. It was not far
away.

He hurried through the rain, the wind cutting
through his kimono, rivulets of water sliding down his

back. He gripped his collar tighter. It would be better to run, but he could not trust his legs. And it did not matter—his kimono was soaked through. His sandals, too.

The stone wall of the park stretched in a long line, its iron railing like soldiers' pikes. Two women beneath umbrellas ran past him, their wooden *getas* ringing on the wet pavement. A gust of wind struck him as he turned into the park entrance.

He could see the top of the *torii*—the gateway to the shrine—now; its high, curved crossbeam resembled a huge, dark bird in flight. Rain pattered on the leaves overhead, and cherry blossoms lay helplessly on the wet stones.

Hurrying along the flagstone path, Hideyo passed beneath the high arch of the torii. On both sides of the path tall granite lanterns stood like sentinels. Ahead, nearer the shrine, bronze lanterns shone darkly in the rain, their curved tops like ancient helmets. At the end of the path the shrine stood deserted.

Hideyo went to the foot of the stone steps. Rain spilled over the steps in tiny waterfalls. Hideyo put the cat gently on the ground. Then he clapped his hands together twice sharply, and with his hands pressed together, bowed his head.

The cat rubbed against his legs, but he kept his eyes shut tight. The cat miaowed. He opened his eyes. The

cat, stretching its mouth wide, miaowed again, and he knelt and picked it up.

Hideyo sat on the wooden base of the shrine, watching the rain pour down in tapered streams from the edge of the curved roof. At least they were out of the rain. He wiped his forehead with the back of his hand, then slipped his feet out of his sandals. He turned his body and lifted his feet up onto the wooden ledge. The wood was smooth and dry. Near his feet was a wooden box. There were copper coins inside, he knew, thrown there by worshipers.

Hideyo closed his eyes. His mother was proud and happy. He had passed the first part of the examination. He had told her nothing of the nightmare of living. Watanabe-san and Kobayashi-san had guessed. They had sent a few yen each month.

He lowered his head onto his forearms. The sharp, dank smell of the cat, which lay on his lap, made him nauseous. He raised his head.

Leaning against the side of the shrine, Hideyo stared at the rain-enshrouded trees. A long time ago, he remembered, he had talked with Kobayashi-san's wife under a tree in the rain. To dedicate himself to a great task, he had said. To stay alive was a great task, too.

He closed his eyes. His head felt light. The rain cascaded down. It was like sitting near a waterfall.

Slowly he was floating away, the waterfall receding, the water plummeting down softly . . . very softly.

A Job

It was dark and still. Hideyo sat up. The rain had stopped. He swung his feet down. How long had he slept? In a corner of the shrine, the cat uncurled itself and stretched.

Th stone lanterns along the path seemed alive. In the darkness their flickering lights were like giant fireflies. The cat pressed against his leg. Suddenly Hideyo remembered something.

Several days ago, he had tried for a custodial position at the Takayama Dental College. He had learned of the job from Dr. Chiwaki, a lecturer at that college. It was not much of a job, only cleaning lamps, and the pay was just two yen a month, but it was a job. The custodian had seemed interested at first. What had gone wrong? Not the hand—the custodian had not seen it.

Had he said something wrong? The custodian had asked only a few questions: Did he have another job? What did he do during the day? The man had listened politely, but then he had mumbled something and left Hideyo abruptly.

What had annoyed the man? Perhaps if he returned there now and spoke to him again. . . . There would be no harm in that. Hideyo went down the steps. Soon it would be daylight. Already dawn was turning the sky pink.

The streets were deserted. Shallow puddles of water lined the curbs. The houses had been washed clean by the rain. The roof tiles cut sharp silhouettes against the pink sky.

He crossed the bridge, the cat treading behind him. The river Sumida swirled softly by. On the far bank, a lone willow sagged, its branches tugged by the current.

Hideyo turned onto a path that led to a large iron gate. Beyond the gate, at the far end of the grounds, stood a white, two-story building. The grounds seemed larger now. A few days ago the area in front of the building had been jammed with students, their voices a confusing, suppressed roar. Now it was still, except for the crunch of his steps on the gravel. The building's high, curved windows seemed to be eyeing him. A tiny bird landed on the peak of the roof, then fluttered away.

Suddenly he stopped because of the pain. Daggers seemed to be stabbing into his stomach. He had not eaten since yesterday morning.

He turned his gaze to the door of the building. He would not knock. He would not stand on the doorstep like a beggar. He almost tripped on the stairs, but he pushed the door open and stepped in.

A man was standing by a window. He looked at Hideyo.

"What is it?"

"I came here several days ago."

"I remember."

"I am willing to work here."

"You are a student, are you not?"

"Yes."

"I do not wish to hire a student. I'm sorry."

"My classes will not conflict with the work."

"I have had students work for me before. They were afraid of work. Is that your cat?"

Hideyo turned. "I forgot he was with me. I will put him out."

The man looked at the cat. He had a wide, straight mouth and alert, deep-set eyes. He stepped closer.

"Is this the way you treat an animal? He's filthy." He stooped down before the cat.

"I picked him up in an alley. He was alone with no one to look after him."

"I see . . ." He gently stroked the cat. "So, you are a student." The man glanced at Hideyo.

"I am not afraid of work."

"Do you know how to mop floors?"

"Yes."

The man was silent a moment. He stood. "I do not promise anything. . . ." He went to a closet beneath the stairs, opened the door, and pointed. "The supplies are here. The soap is on the shelf. I've got to go upstairs. Keep the cat inside—there are dogs that wander around the grounds." He grinned. "They are good dogs but bad with cats." He started up the stairs.

Hideyo stepped into the closet. There was a deep sink opposite the doorway. He turned on the tap, placed his mouth against the running water, and drank. Then, cupping his hands, he filled them and knelt before the cat. The cat pushed its nose into the water and drank.

Hideyo leaned over the sink and splashed water onto his face. He wiped his face with the back of his sleeve.

He placed the pail under the tap and the water roared into it. He pulled the pail up out of the sink, lowered it to the floor, and dunked the mop in the water, soaking the bundle of yarn. He squeezed the water out of the mop, then took the bar of soap and rubbed it over the yarn.

Gripping the pail in his right hand and balancing the mop in his left, he crossed the front hall. Sunlight filtered through the heavily curtained windows. He set the pail down and pushed the mop into the water, soap foaming up to the surface. Resting the yarn on his left hand and twisting it with his right, he wrung it out. Spreading his legs wide, he plopped the yarn down in the corner. He thought of nothing now but cleaning the floor and doing the job well.

From what seemed to him a long distance away, Hideyo heard a voice.

"I said, what is your name?"

Hideyo straightened up. There was a clamp of pain in the small of his back. The man was standing on the first step of the stairs.

"I'm sorry. I did not hear you come down."

The man gazed at the floors. They shone like glass in the sunlight.

"Where is the cat?"

"In the closet. I had to put him there while I worked."

The man glanced at Hideyo, then stepped carefully along the side of the stairway.

"Do you want me to work on the lamps?"

"There is time. What is your name?"

"Hideyo Noguchi."

"I am called Matsumoto. Where did you learn to mop floors?"

"In Wakamatsu. I worked in a hospital."

"You are studying to be a doctor?"

"Yes, at the Saiseigakusha."

"Have you been in Tokyo long?"

"Since October last. I will take the final examination this October."

"You have worked before—in Tokyo?"

"No."

"I can only pay two yen a month. And maybe an occasional meal—when my wife gives me extra. When is your first class?"

"At nine. I am finished with my classes at two. The college is just across the Sumida."

"I know. If you get here by three, it will be all right. You should be finished by eight or nine. On Saturdays you will help me with the grounds." The man glanced at the window. "The sun is up. You have had breakfast?"

"No."

"Breakfast is important." Matsumoto glanced at Hideyo. "One must start the day with the necessary strength." He turned abruptly and went into the closet. The cat stuck its head out from behind the doorpost. Matsumoto came out with a bento box, which he handed to Hideyo.

Hideyo looked at him questioningly. Matsumoto reached for the pail. "Don't just stand there," he said. "Go on out. I'll finish this."

On the steps, Hideyo opened the box. Inside was rice and a pair of chopsticks. He shook a little rice onto

the cover of the box for the cat, who was pushing against his arm. Then he raised the box to his mouth. It was difficult to hold the sticks. His hand was trembling.

To Help Extend the Light

The breeze, not chilling, more like spring than fall, caressed Hideyo's body, cooling his near-feverish excitement. The water rhythmically rose and fell beneath the bow of a boat, which creaked softly. A leaf glided down, swaying a bit as the sunlight struck it, then touching the bridge and falling to rest on the water. Hideyo's reflection looked up at him. It was like looking at someone else. The face showed no trace of excitement. It appeared calm—an underwater Buddha. He grinned.

He was not himself today. And the world was not itself. Not this day. He was no longer a student. Now, he was Dr. Noguchi. He smiled. Gripping the wooden rail of the bridge, he looked out at the river that rippled to the sea, at the sunlight dancing on the surface. He tried to envision the world beyond the horizon, hidden and mysterious. He gripped the wood hard.

He would write this night to his mother and Watanabe-san. He could imagine her happiness when Kobayashi-san read the letter to her. She would cry a little, of course, embrace Inu, and perhaps rush with the letter to the villagers. At night there would be a group of friends with her in the house, drinking tea, the insects singing outside in the dark, and they would talk of him, the honor he had brought to his mother and to the villagers.

And Watanabe-san.. . . . He would sit at his desk, relaxed, one leg crossed over the other, the way he usually sat, peering down at the letter. What would he feel? Pride? Happiness? The boy with the crippled hand who had come to him years ago—Tembo—sitting with teeth clenched while he separated the scar tissues of the hand. The boy, now a young man, writing to him: "I have succeeded, and the pain and suffering of others will never let me rest in peace."

Hideyo relaxed his grip on the railing. He had seen lotus flowers in a pool one day in Ueno Park. Large, beautiful lotuses—the flowers he would have liked to bring to his mother, to Watanabe-san and Kobayashi-san this day.

Someone was crossing the bridge, and Hideyo glanced over his shoulder. It was a woman in a peach-colored kimono. Her getas sounded on the wooden deck of the bridge. He had never before really heard the melody of getas: *kara-koro, kara-koro, kara-koro.* The melody dropped to a minor key as the woman stepped from the bridge onto the paved road. He listened to the song receding.

Silence. He had never really listened to it either. Life continued softly, quietly. The sea rising and falling; the breeze caressing the trees; a leaf drifting down; a near-motionless sea gull, a speck against the sky. The world pulsated quietly, as though through a giant stethoscope. Perhaps, this was the way God heard it.

Hideyo felt the insistent beating of his own heart, the rhythmical beating in his throat. He had not told his news to anyone yet. Would Matsumoto be at the college now?

No, it was still early. He would not be there until eight-thirty. Too long to wait. He would shout it to the sky.

He smiled, remembering the German professor with the white beard who had looked so solemn, and how his own heart had become like a stone from fear as he stood before the desk waiting for the answer.

He remembered the professor's gentle, cold query. "Yes?"

"I am Hideyo Noguchi."

The professor had not recognized him, of course, he realized now. To him Hideyo was just another face among the hundred that had peered at him in the lecture hall each day. And what had it meant to him as he thumbed through the list of those who had passed the examinations? "Noguchi . . . Hideyo?"

"Yes."

To him, only a name.

Hideyo's breathing had ceased as the small eyes looked up at him. Then the head bowed slowly.

Hideyo smiled now, remembering. All he could think of at the moment was the professor's beard touching the page, like a flaxen cloud.

Outside, the sun was bursting through the sky. Half-blinded by the light, Hideyo began to run with the abandon of a child. Out of breath at last, he had stopped at the bridge. He had come there frequently to escape the city; now he came to savor his joy.

He had run all the way from the college. He smiled, shaking his head. If only Yosa could have seen him. He had leaped over a cart standing by the curb, the shouts of the man trailing briefly after him. And where the paved walk cut down steeply, near the government buildings, he had fallen. Fallen hard on his knees and elbows. But he had picked himself up, not feeling the pain, still running.

Now he bent over and pulled up his kimono. His knees were bruised and bloodied. He looked at his elbows. They were red, the skin roughened, and his right forearm was scraped. He almost needed a doctor. Hideyo smiled to himself.

My body is bruised, he thought, but I feel wonderful.

Standing on his toes, Hideyo stretched his arms

wide. This night he would not fight his fatigue. He would sleep all night, gorge himself on sleep—a feast for his body. And tomorrow he would take Matsumoto's sons to the park. It was the least he could do for the family.

Since the spring he had shared their home and their meals. They had asked nothing of him in return. Not that he had been merely a burden to them. He had made life a little easier for Matsumoto by doing the job well.

Still, Hideyo owed them much, for a place to sleep and for food. He had offered to pay Matsumoto for room and board, but Matsumoto had refused.

He had slept in a corner near the two boys, behind the partition that separated them from their parents. Sometimes Matsumoto and his wife kept him company while he ate his supper, but usually the whole family was asleep by the time he came home. During the night he used the kerosene lamp, turning it down low, just enough to study by, not enough to disturb them.

It was a good family. They should be the first to share his joy. Matsumoto would arrive at the college soon. Dr. Chiwaki, too. Hideyo would stop by his classroom and tell him the good news. The teacher had been kind to him and had expressed interest in his career.

Hideyo had already applied for a position at all the city hospitals. At the Juntendo hospital there would be a vacancy soon. Perhaps next week he would hear from them. The pay was little more than he was making working with Matsumoto, but it was a beginning.

Hideyo leaned his arms on the bridge and looked out at the sea.

There would be a time, maybe in the new century that was near, when people would live in a world free of disease. Perhaps even in his lifetime—or the lifetime of his children. But there was so much to be done, so much to be learned. Knowledge was like a deep pit. The deeper one probed, the deeper the darkness became. But he would not be probing the darkness alone. Perhaps by the time he left this world, the darkness would not be so immense. To help extend the light, leaving the world a little less dark than he had found it—that would be a worthy accomplishment.

A Brilliant Discovery

The man's sweat-covered chest gleamed in the sunlight. He twisted his head and his chest heaved, the ribs outlined against his skin. His head fell to the side, toward the sunlight squeezing through the porthole. His eyes, dark and glazed, stared vacantly. His lips widened in a gentle smile and he spoke in a low voice.

Hideyo knelt by the man, holding his wrist. The pulse was rapid. He turned to the captain. "Are there other Chinese on board?"

The captain, standing in the doorway of the cabin, shook his head, his round face impassive. "He is the only one."

"Will he die?"

Hideyo looked at the cook, kneeling across from him. "Do you know anything about him? What part of China he's from?"

The man shrugged his shoulders. "He came on board in Shanghai as my assistant in the galley."

"When was that?"

"A few days ago."

Hideyo turned to the captain. "When exactly?"

"Four days ago," said the captain.

"How did he appear then?"

"I would not have taken him on if he had looked sick."

Hideyo stood. "When did he become ill?"

"Yesterday. He collapsed in the galley. What is wrong with him?"

Hideyo did not answer. Taking the captain by the elbow, he led him outside. He closed the door and motioned him toward the end of the corridor. There, Hideyo turned to him. "The man is dying."

"What is it, Doctor?"

"I'm not sure. I'm going ashore. I will be back. In the meantime, no one else is to go inside that cabin. And no one is to leave the ship. It is under quarantine."

The captain's head was silhouetted above the dark hull of the ship as the small boat moved toward the shore. Hideyo stared at the oars dipping into the waves.

Had the captain suspected? Had he revealed his fear to the captain? In the northern provinces of China, the epidemic was killing hundreds each day. And in India, where it had begun, the dead and dying were being left in the streets, the fear and stench depopulating

cities and villages. But Japan had remained uncontaminated. So far.

Of course, he could be wrong. He would find out soon. He glanced impatiently at the ramshackle houses cluttering the shore.

Above him a sea gull cried. It would be good if he were wrong this time. The small boat rose up gently. It was likely he was wrong. There were none of the usual symptoms he had read about—no dark areas of

hemorrhages on the skin or swellings in the groin or under the armpits. Nothing, except a high fever, a rapid pulse—and the fact that the man was Chinese. Hardly enough to diagnose an illness or to justify his suspicion.

But the man was dying. There was no doubt of that. If it was what Hideyo feared, there would be little he could do except ease the pain. There was no way of loosening the death grip of the disease. Nor was there any way of stopping it from spreading once it came into a country. The Black Death, it was called in ancient times. The Black Death—bubonic plague—in Japan. He straightened up.

"Hurry with those oars!"

Hideyo peered through the microscope at the specimen of blood. Ever so slowly, with his right hand, he turned the knob, adjusting the lens. He pressed his eye against the end of the microscope. For a moment, he felt a sense of relief. He had been wrong. There were no bubonic-plague bacteria. But he continued adjusting the lens. His hand trembled. Yes, he had been wrong. How foolish of him to jump to that conclusion on so little evidence. He was inexperienced. He had a great deal to lea— His hand stopped and froze on the knob.

Slowly, oval-shaped organisms came into view, bunched together, still. *Pasteurella pestis,* bacteria causing bubonic plague.

He raised his head. His throat felt parched. He ran his tongue over his lips. He peered into the microscope again. He had seen correctly. There were the invisible killers.

He leaned back. There was a tightness in his stomach. The man would die. But maybe it was not too late. Hideyo slid off the stool.

He ran along the wharf. The men were waiting in

the small boat. Getting a firm grip on the handle of his bag, Hideyo turned off onto the pier, his feet thundering on the boards as he ran. The small boat bobbed up and down. He climbed down the pier ladder and leaped into the boat.

"Hurry."

The men strained on their oars. Ahead of them, the ship rested on the glassy surface of the harbor, the yellow flag of quarantine high on its mast.

Late that night Hideyo swung his feet off the bed. The excitement of the day would not allow him to rest. He went past the laboratory bench to the door. On the porch, fast-winged moths flew around the orange lantern.

He stood on the edge of the porch, near the steps. Overhead, the moon cut a white hole in the sky. Suddenly, from the darkened wharf, came the sound of wooden blocks being struck together. The night watchman was making his rounds.

Clack-clack-clack. The night watchman appeared. His hands, holding the wooden blocks, seemed to be clasped in prayer. Hideyo waved to him. The night watchman raised his arm.

"Good evening, Doctor."

Hideyo watched him disappear into the darkness. The people could sleep secure tonight, unaware that death had been kept at sea.

Hideyo sat on the porch steps. A ship's bell rang in the night, its sound clear, vibrating. He glanced at the moonlit surface of the water. The ships in the harbor were like dark mountains.

He had done all he could. The man was still alive and there was a chance he would survive. The man alone was fighting the Black Death. If the ship had docked, the plague, at this moment, would be creeping through the land, the diseased rats from the ship carrying fleas to infect others with the plague.

Tonight, when he had submitted his report, the port superintendent had commended him for preventing what might have become a national catastrophe. "A brilliant discovery, Dr. Noguchi," the superintendent had said, the words of praise singing inside of him then and again now.

A ship's bell rang once more, echoing in the night. He gazed past the dark ships to where the water met the sky, the stars distant fireflies. For the past two years, since becoming a doctor, he had often thought of that far-off land that David had spoken of when they were boys. Sometimes he felt as if he were living with one foot here and the other foot there.

He lowered his gaze. *The streets are paved with gold in America.* The peasants believed this. Nonsense, of course. But in a way they were right. America was paved with gold . . . the gold of opportunity. There, he might be able to devote his life to research.

An Interesting Place

Jordan stepped to the row of cages at the end of the room. He pointed to the last cage on the top. "We got that one in yesterday. A timber rattler."

Dobie peered through the glass window. "He looks asleep—or dead."

Jordan tapped the side of the cage. The rattler raised its head, its tongue darting out. The round yellow catlike eyes stared at Dobie.

"He looks even meaner than my old chemistry professor."

Jordan laughed.

Hideyo raised his head from the microscope and looked up at the window above the laboratory bench. The dying rays of the autumn sun shone through the panes.

"It takes them a few days to get used to being in captivity," Jordan said.

Hideyo grinned. Jordan was enjoying himself, lecturing Dobie, showing off his knowledge, although Jordan had been assisting him only a few weeks. For almost a year after arriving in America Hideyo had worked alone. The year before that, as a quarantine officer in Yokohama, he had worked alone too. It was good having an assistant now.

"Why does it keep flicking out its tongue?" Dobie asked.

"That helps the snake to smell," said Jordan. "Each time the tongue flicks out it picks up odors from the air."

Hideyo stood up and reached for a tube on the rack.

"Doesn't this one rattle?" said Dobie.

"I'm sure he does. They usually do when they're nervous," Jordan said. "Sometimes one will start and then they all join in."

"I've heard it from my lab. Quite a racket." Dobie turned to Hideyo. "Nice collection of pets, Doctor."

Hideyo smiled. He poured the top fluid in the tube into the sink. "It is kind of you to look after our animals while we're gone."

"Not at all, Doctor. We can't have anything happen to these animals. Are you all set for the big day?"

"I think so. Jordan, the salt solution, please."

"How do you feel?" Dobie asked Hideyo.

"Scared."

Dobie smiled, his handsome face marred by bad teeth.

"Guess who will be there?" The sunlight glinted off Jordan's eyeglasses.

"Theodore Roosevelt." Dobie grinned.

"Dr. Osler," Jordan said. "Think of it, Dobie—Dr. William Osler."

"Dr. Weir Mitchell and Dr. Hideyo Noguchi of the University of Pennsylvania will be there, too," said Dobie.

Hideyo shook his head. "The National Academy of Sciences never heard of me. I was only invited because of Dr. Mitchell."

"But when they hear of the research you have done—" Jordan said.

"Research?" Hideyo shrugged. "Dr. Mitchell has devoted many years to snake-venom research. I am only a beginner."

"No one knows as much as you about snake venoms and how they act on the blood," said Jordan.

Dobie glanced up at the wall clock. "I have a supper appointment. Want to cue me in on my baby-sitting chores, Jordan?"

Jordan stepped away from the laboratory bench. "You won't have to feed them. I've already taken care of that."

"How often do they eat?"

"Once a week. The water moccasins have appetites like horses. The copperheads and rattlers are content with a medium-sized rat once a week."

Dobie looked at Jordan. "It takes them that long to eat a rat?"

"Oh, they don't chew it. They eat it whole—swallow
it, in fact. Head first. Come here, I'll show you something."

Jordan pointed to a cage, just above the floor. "Look
at the bulge inside that rattler. Fed him a rat yesterday. He's still digesting it. It takes them a couple of
days to digest an animal completely, bones and all."

Dobie stared at the rattler. "Are the rats alive when
you put them in there?"

"Yes, why not? The snakes kill them as fast as we
could. Those fangs are like hypodermic needles. One
bite and the rat kicks once or twice, then keels over
dead."

Dobie turned from the cage. "Do they get anything
else besides rats?"

"Sometimes a rabbit."

"A rabbit?"

Jordan nodded. "Swallowing a rabbit is no problem
for a rattler. Their jaws have four sections—two upper,
two lower—and each section moves independently.
When they swallow a rabbit they seem to be crawling
over it."

"Delightful. What do you want me to do?"

"Well, if it's a hot day, open the windows. Close the
blinds, too; they can't take too much heat. The main
thing is to check the water in their cages. Don't open
the top. Just pull out the drawer in front of the cage
and take out the pan. Be sure you fasten the hook after

you replace the pan. They can push open the drawer if it's left unlocked." Jordan reached into his pocket. "Just remembered—here's the key to the lab door. Be careful when you close it or you'll startle them. They're deaf, but they do react to vibrations."

"Deaf?"

"You could hit a gong near their heads and it wouldn't bother them. They can't hear sounds carried through air. But if you were to walk heavily past their cages, they'd rear right up, because the vibrations pass through the cages to their bodies."

"Jordan."

"Yes, Doctor."

"We'll put this one on the bench."

"What are you going to do?" Dobie asked nervously.

Jordan glanced at him. "The rattler—the one that arrived yesterday—we're going to milk it."

Hideyo and Jordan carried the cage to the laboratory bench.

"Push the vial stand a little closer, Jordan."

Hideyo unlocked the cover of the cage and set it on the bench. A soft buzz came from inside, and the snake's head rose up through the opening. The head swung to and fro gracefully, as though manipulated by invisible strings.

The snake leaned over the side of the cage; its body was sulphur-yellow, banded in black.

Hideyo's right hand darted out, grabbing the snake

behind the head. Its jaws sprang open, the fangs gleaming daggers. Its rattlers shrilled.

Hideyo pulled the snake out of the cage. "Grab the tail."

Jordan reached for the tail as it whipped the air.

Hideyo pressed the head toward the glass vial. Like a sprung rattrap, the fangs clamped into the parchment-topped glass.

"Do you have him, Doctor?"

"I have him." Slowly Hideyo massaged the snake's head with his index finger. Venom dribbled into the glass. The snake's body squirmed. Jordan's breathing was the only sound in the room. Dobie edged away from the bench.

Hideyo glanced over his shoulder. "All right, Jordan?"

"Okay."

Hideyo lifted the head and with one sweep of his arm pushed the snake back into the cage, head first. He threw the cover on and locked it.

Dobie stared at the venom in the glass. "It almost looks like orange juice." His voice was hoarse.

"Don't drink it," Jordan said, grinning.

Dobie looked at the cage. "I'm glad I only wrestle with chemical formulas. How can you touch these slimy beasts?"

"They're not slimy, Dobie. Their skin is as dry as the bark of a tree. Would you like to feel one?"

Dobie shook his head. "No, thanks."

"You're looking a little pale, Dobie," said Jordan.

"Interesting place you have here, Doctor. I have to be going now." Dobie stepped to the door.

Jordan looked at Hideyo, and they smiled at each other.

A Bend in the River

The stillness was interrupted by a click as the door downstairs closed. Hideyo turned back to the papers scattered on the laboratory bench. Footsteps echoed up the stairs. It sounded like Jordan. He tossed his pen onto the bench and slid off the stool. For the first time he noticed that it was daylight. The white porcelain of the lab sink reflected the sunlight coming through the window above it.

Now he became aware of his body. His muscles felt sore and his eyes seemed connected to taut wires. Standing on his toes, Hideyo stretched his arms upward and yawned.

"Doctor." Jordan stood in the doorway. "What are you doing here?"

"What do you mean?"

"You're supposed to be at the station."

"Station? What day is it?"

"Monday."

"But what happened to Sunday?"

Jordan leaned against the doorway and shook his head. "Doctor, you're going to give me an ulcer." He grinned. "Are you packed?"

"Packed? Why, no. I was going to do it on Monday—this morning."

"The train will be at the station in ten minutes. You won't have time to go to your room."

"But my clothes—"

"I've got an extra shirt. It'll be a little big for you but you'll manage. Let's go, Doctor. We've got to catch this train."

"The next one . . . ?"

Jordan shook his head. "The next one leaves tonight. Doctor, we've got to hurry."

"Yes, Jordan." Hideyo unloosened the buttons on his white laboratory coat. "I stopped in here Saturday morning—wanted to finish the article on Japanese medicine for the encyclopedia, outline the plans for Wednesday's experiments, and compile the notes for tonight. Are you sure it's Monday?"

"Doctor, we'll miss the train."

Outside, the sunlight made Hideyo blink. He paused on the steps of the building for a moment. Jordan took his arm.

"We'll walk, Doctor. At this hour it will be difficult to find a cab."

They passed the iron gates of the medical school.

Ahead of them, in the direction of the Schuylkill River, smoke hung over a factory chimney.

Hideyo was tired. Perhaps he could sleep on the train. His eyes felt as if they were two stones. He had not finished the plans for Wednesday's experiments. But there would be time this night.

"Where are we staying tonight, Jordan?"

"I've made reservations in a hotel in Washington, Doctor."

"What time will we be getting back tomorrow?"

"In the afternoon, at three."

"Is your luggage at the station?"

"Yes, Doctor."

"I can carry my briefcase, Jordan."

"I have it, Doctor. Watch your step." They stepped off the curb and crossed the street.

Jordan pulled out his vest watch. "We'll never make it."

"How much time do we have?"

"Four minutes."

"Well," Hideyo said with a smile, "there's no problem. We'll run."

They ran side by side along the street, past the red-brick buildings, beneath the row of shop awnings. A white horse pulling a wagon came toward them, the horse's hoofs clip-clopping on the paved street. The driver stared. Hideyo waved at him.

They could see the river now—flat, glistening in the

sun. Many times in the past year, before returning to his room, Hideyo had walked along the bank of the wide Schuylkill, the jumble of buildings on the other side looking like firefly-dotted hills in the night.

Jordan was breathing heavily. Hideyo reached for the briefcase. "No, Doctor."

Hideyo smiled. "It's all right, Jordan."

They came in sight of the bridge, its span high over the water. The station, a massive pile of brick, loomed up at the other end of the bridge.

Jordan grinned, his long, straight hair falling over one eye. "The train hasn't come in yet. You go ahead, Doctor. I'll meet you at the station."

Jordan sprinted ahead, toward a row of shops across from the station.

Hideyo continued over the bridge, past the iron railing. The station, with its broad dormers, reminded him of a Buddhist temple. Near the entrance, a heavy bald-headed man sat before his shoeshine stand. Hideyo walked under the high canopy and through the open door into the station.

It took his eyes a moment to adjust to the semidarkness of the interior. He went to the right, into the main area of the station. It was like being inside a huge cave. He glanced up at the high, arched ceiling. He grinned to himself. Everything in America was big.

Footsteps rang out behind him. Jordan almost ran into a porter. He stopped in front of Hideyo, smiling, his face flushed, holding a paper bag in his hand. "Okay, Doctor. This way."

"Your suitcase, Jordan?"

"It's on the platform, Doctor. I left it there with the porter."

They went down the steps. The smell of steam and coal dust rose up from the platform area. The tracks sparkled like sword blades. In one corner of the platform the porter was leaning against a handcart next to the stacked luggage.

The train bell rang slowly, lazily. Hideyo peered over the edge of the platform and down the tracks. The steel snout of the engine inched forward, steam hissing up from under its wheels. With a sudden belch of steam the train moved to the platform. The steam floated up, revealing the coal-black steel plates of the cars. The engineer, with a long mustache and coal-bearded face, gazed out the engine window.

The train hissed softly as the passengers climbed aboard. Hideyo followed Jordan down the center aisle of the car.

"Here, Doctor." Jordan slid between two seats facing each other. He lifted the suitcase and placed it on the rack above the window. He motioned to Hideyo to sit on the side facing the front of the train.

Hideyo sat, resting his elbow on the ledge of the window. He realized now how tired he was. His bones seemed to be embedded in the seat. The sound of a paper bag being opened made him look up. Jordan reached into the bag on his lap. Smiling, he pulled out an orange. "Know you like oranges. Figured you were hungry . . ." He reached into his pocket and took out his penknife.

"Don't peel it." Hideyo reached for the orange. "Thank you, Jordan." He held the orange in the palm of his hand. "You know, Jordan, I never had an orange when I was a boy. They were too expensive." He bit into the orange.

"I've never seen anyone eat the skin."

Hideyo smiled.

"The bakery wasn't open yet. I would have gotten you—"

"This is fine, Jordan. Thank you."

The car door clanked shut. Slowly, the train slid out of the station, past a maze of tracks and a string of cars. Then they had a clear view of the river, silver-hued in the early sunlight.

Hideyo placed the orange on his lap. He was hungry but he felt too tired to eat. He rested his head against the windowpane.

Across the river he recognized the wide expanse of Franklin Field, and beyond it, the cluster of buildings that was the University of Pennsylvania.

He remembered the first time he had walked through the complex of old, handsome buildings. Professor Flexner had been surprised to see him. He

grinned now, remembering. Professor Flexner had never expected to see him again. They had met only once, and briefly, in Tokyo. He had told Dr. Flexner that he would like to come to America. That was all. And one fall day a year ago he had arrived at Professor Flexner's office at the university. He knew no one else in America.

Professor Flexner had offered Hideyo the only field of research open at the university when he arrived—snake venom. Hideyo knew nothing about it, but he had eagerly accepted because he was penniless—he had used his last coins for a meal that morning.

Hideyo's cheek pressed against the windowpane. This night he would be one of the speakers at the National Academy of Sciences in Washington, D.C. Dr. Osler, the most famous doctor in America, would

be there, as well as other distinguished doctors. If only his mother and Dr. Watanabe could be there too. He would write to them tonight. They would share his joy.

The train curved around a bend in the river. In an open stretch of field, between the river and the train, a boy ran, waving at the train. Hideyo waved back at him. The boy stood in the field waving. Hideyo watched him disappear into the distance.

Epilogue

In any story based on the life of a real person, the reader is entitled to know which important incidents and characters are fictional and which are not.

All the main points in this book about Hideyo Noguchi's boyhood and youth are true. Hideyo's hand was severely burned when he was an infant, and because of his deformed hand, his school days were a torment. The classroom scene and the stone fight in the graveyard, both imaginary, illustrate this. Hideyo's school days were brightened only by the friendly interest of a teacher, Kobayashi, and his wife, and this interest in the crippled student continued even when Hideyo had grown into manhood.

At the time when Hideyo was growing up, Japan, though still a tradition-bound nation, was undergoing revolutionary changes. After centuries of isolation, the mountainous string of islands was rapidly becoming part of the modern world. In the fictitious encounter between Hideyo and the samurai on Wakamatsu's main street, the aging samurai represents the old order in a Japan that was eagerly adopting the new.

A peasant's life is hard enough, but with his father gone, life for Hideyo, his mother, and his sister was particularly harsh. Hideyo became "the man of the house," and he took his responsibilities with a deep seriousness that is difficult, perhaps, to imagine today. Its depth is illustrated by the invented frostbite incident. (Frostbite was a common occurrence in that snow-plagued area of Japan.)

Hideyo did, in fact, become a devoted apprentice to Dr. Kanae Watanabe after the doctor operated on his hand. It is also true that his brilliance as Dr. Watanabe's assistant aroused jealousy among some of the other apprentices, an attitude personified by the imaginary Azu. Hideyo also had friends among his co-workers, however, and the character of Yosa suggests the lasting friendships Hideyo actually formed during his apprentice days.

It is true that Hideyo studied medicine virtually on his own, and that in order to read the medical books in Dr. Watanabe's library, he learned English from missionaries. The Wells family is fictitious but typical of missionary families of the time.

Dr. Watanabe did leave Hideyo in charge of his practice when he was called for military service. Upon his return he was so impressed by the work Hideyo had done in his absence that he gave the boy the assistance he needed to continue his studies in Tokyo.

Hideyo's student days in Tokyo were among the unhappiest of his life. Although the incident with the street gang is fictitious, it is true that, due to financial distress, he associated briefly with a group of Tokyo toughs. He finally managed to find work as a janitor at the Takayama Dental College in Tokyo.

As a quarantine officer in Yokohama, Dr. Noguchi did discover bubonic-plague bacteria in a Chinese crewman, thus preventing what might have been a catastrophe—a national epidemic of the dread disease.

A short time later, in 1900, Dr. Noguchi came to America and began research work on snake venoms at the University of Pennsylvania. His intense dedication to his work there earned him the respect and admiration of his associates, who are represented in the book by the character of Jordan.

As a result of his brilliant snake-venom research, Dr. Noguchi was awarded a Carnegie Fellowship for study abroad, and under the fellowship, he continued his research in Denmark. Back in America, Dr. Noguchi wrote a book on snake venoms which was the first major work in the field (it is still a valuable reference today).

In 1904, Dr. Noguchi joined the staff of the Rockefeller Institute for Medical Research (now the Rockefeller University) in New York City. Here he labored for many years, making important contributions to the study of snake venoms; of microorganisms, particularly spirochetes; of diseases such as general paralysis, syphilis, and the South American diseases Oroya fever and verruga peruana. His dedication to his work became legendary among his fellow workers at the Rockefeller Institute.

He did not spend all his time in the laboratory, however; he traveled a great deal, going wherever he felt he was needed.

While investigating yellow fever in Africa, Dr. Noguchi contracted that disease and died.

The news of his death was announced throughout the world. The *New York Times* carried a front-page story headlined: DR. NOGUCHI IS DEAD, MARTYR OF SCIENCE. Dr. Noguchi is buried in Woodlawn Cemetery in New York City. The inscription on his tomb reads:

HIDEYO NOGUCHI
BORN IN INAWASHIRO, JAPAN,
NOVEMBER 24, 1876
DIED ON THE GOLD COAST, AFRICA,
MAY 21, 1928
MEMBER OF THE
ROCKEFELLER INSTITUTE
FOR MEDICAL RESEARCH
THROUGH DEVOTION TO SCIENCE
HE LIVED AND DIED FOR HUMANITY

DAN D'AMELIO lives with his wife and four children in Smithtown, Long Island, not too far from the New York suburb where he grew up. During his high school and college years he was devoted to music and led his own dance band. Mr. D'Amelio graduated from New York University in 1953 with a major in English and a minor in music.

As a writer, his first working experience was on the editorial staff of CBS. Subsequently, he worked for the Associated Press in New York City, and within a short period of time was teaching journalism and English, as well as writing on weekends and evenings. At the end of his first year of teaching, he received a citation as the "outstanding beginning high school teacher in the East Islip, Long Island, School District."

It was during this period that Mr. D'Amelio was asked to take over a class of mentally retarded children for two weeks until a regular teacher could be found. "Those two weeks became four years," he writes, "—my most gratifying and rewarding years in teaching."

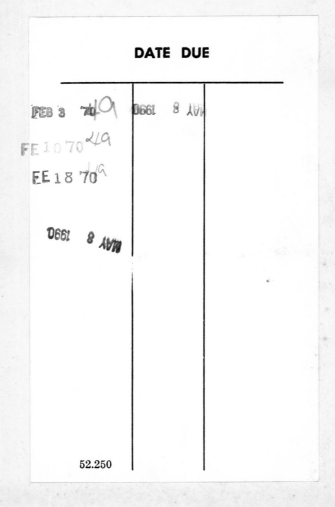

THE BEST
HOME
BUSINESSES
FOR THE 90s

THE INSIDE INFORMATION
YOU NEED TO KNOW TO SELECT A
HOME-BASED BUSINESS THAT'S
RIGHT FOR YOU

PAUL and SARAH EDWARDS

A Jeremy P. Tarcher/Putnam Book
published by
G. P. Putnam's Sons
New York

Acknowledgments

We're told that it's unusual for authors to have three books published at the same time by the same publisher. Yet this book is proof that it can happen and it is due to the extraordinary team of people at our publisher, Jeremy P. Tarcher, Inc. To Jeremy Tarcher we owe a continuing debt for his vision that resulted in his publishing *Working From Home* when it was regarded as something short of a fad in 1985, because he recognized that people are seeking alternatives to the 9-to-5 routine and that it's both possible and profitable to make it on your own working from home.

We thank Rick Benzel, our editor for our three new books, *Best Home Businesses for the 90s, Getting Business to Come to You,* and *Making It on Your Own.* Rick's support, creativity, good sense, and problem-solving ability has come through many times in the course of developing these books.

We are especially grateful to Robert Welsch for his special vision and role in bringing these books about. We don't know how many hours of sleep Paul Murphy and Susan Harris will have lost to get these books out on time, and we are grateful. To Mike Dougherty, Lisa Ives, Michael Graziano, Lisa Chadwick we say "thank you" for helping us to get our message out that there are positive alternatives for people in a rapidly changing world.

We appreciate the hundreds of people we interviewed for these books, many of whom came to us by way of the Working From Home Forum on CompuServe and our radio shows.

A Jeremy P. Tarcher/Putnam Book
Published by G. P. Putnam's Sons
Publishers Since 1838
200 Madison Avenue
New York, NY 10016

Library of Congress Cataloging-in-Publication Data

Edwards, Paul.
   The best home businesses for the 90's : the inside information you need to know to select a home-based business that's right for you / Paul and Sarah Edwards.
      p.   cm.
   ISBN 0-87477-633-3

   1. Home-based business.   I. Edwards, Sarah (Sarah A.)
II. Title.
HD2333.E34   1991
658'.041—dc20   91-25210
                                                                          CIP

Manufactured in the United States of America
20 19 18 17 16 15 14 13 12 11

CONTENTS

■■■■■■■■■■■■■■■■■■■■■■■

Part 2: The Rest of the Best238

Appendix: Lists of Top-10 Best Businesses264
Index266

INTRODUCTION

■ ■

Finding the Best Business for You

Our purpose in writing this book is to point you toward the most viable options for joining the over 20 million Americans making money from their homes so you can enjoy the freedom of being your own boss. Whether you're looking for new ideas or already have some idea of what you'd like to do, this book is designed to help you narrow down the many possibilities and find a business that's right both for you and for the economic climate of the 1990s.

There are literally hundreds of possible home-based businesses. And you'll find many books filled with interesting, ingenious ideas about businesses you could start. But haven't you ever wondered if many people are really making money in those businesses? We certainly have. The fact that something is a clever idea that could be done at home doesn't mean people can make money doing it.

In fact, the people we talk with want to know which businesses are truly viable. They've heard about work-at-home scams; they've heard stories about businesses that fail. So they want to know:

- which businesses are actually succeeding
- who can succeed in these businesses
- how much it costs to start them
- how much money you can actually make from them

We wanted to be able to answer these questions with confidence, so we set out to identify what we consider to be the best home-based businesses to start, given the realities of this decade. Before we introduce you to the businesses we've identified and outline what's involved in operating them, we'd like you to know how we went about picking them.

1

When we began research on this book, we felt somewhat humbled by the task of selecting what we think will be the best home businesses for the 1990s, especially in providing specific information about their viability. We decided, however, to set specific criteria and make sure the businesses we chose would live up to their reputations.

First, we drew on our own experience. We've been working from home ourselves since 1974, and ever since we began writing our book *Working from Home* in 1980, we've been tracking which businesses people have been running successfully from home. Through the *Working from Home Forum* we operate on CompuServe Information Service, the many seminars we've taught on operating a home-based business, and the call-ins we've had from *The Home/Office Show*, which we host on the Business Radio Network, as well as our Los Angeles radio program, we've developed a sense about which businesses are doing well.

To project what people *will* be doing successfully is a somewhat different task, however, from describing what people have been and are doing now. Fortunately, we've always been future oriented. We began reading the World Future Society's *Futurist* magazine in 1970, and forecasts from pundits like John Naisbitt, Alvin Toffler, and Faith Popcorn have stimulated us to think about what their projections mean for home businesses.

In addition, we were engaged by At Home Professions to research which home-based businesses would be the best ones for which to develop training programs. From this research, we identified specific businesses that are more in demand and easier to access than others.

To screen our selections, we also went to the Bureau of Labor Statistics in Washington, D.C., where we examined the job projections this government office develops and interviewed the experts who synthesize the information that forms the basis for the bureau's projections. Although these projections focus on outside jobs, we find that their work is relevant to home businesses as well. For example, growth in certain job categories may signal other business opportunities, and sometimes the shrinkage of jobs in a category is compensated for by the emergence of small businesses that can be operated from home.

Once we identified businesses that seemed to have a good future, we had to address the issue of what qualifies a business as the *best*. Income possibility was certainly one criterion. We also considered other issues like lifestyle considerations, since today people want more than money from their work. In sum, to be one of our best, a business had to meet a variety of criteria, including the following:

Real Businesses with a Successful At-Home Track Record

Too many people fall prey to an endless stream of scams disguised as business-opportunities promising that you can make thousands of dollars a week starting immediately working from home with no background or experience.

Unfortunately, such offers look too good to be true because they are too good to be true.

If such schemes were valid businesses, wouldn't everyone be doing them? Wouldn't you meet lots of people who have become wealthy in such businesses? In fact, if these so-called opportunities were real, wouldn't most people on your block be self-employed and doing one of them, and wouldn't you all be driving Mercedes? But when you think about it, have you ever met anyone who is making good money from one of these schemes? We haven't. After all the years we've been in this field, we haven't met a single person who is making a lot of money from a get-rich-quick scheme.

We have, however, met tens of thousands of people who are working from home successfully year after year, and every one of them is earning a living by using his or her own talents, skills, and experience. The businesses we've selected for this book are the types of businesses these successful people are running. They are *businesses*; not *business opportunities*. In fact, we hesitate to put the words *business* and *opportunities* together anymore because too often the combined term has come to refer to mythical businesses anyone can start tomorrow and make a fortune from.

The home businesses in this book do not pretend to be such opportunities. Not just anybody can start many of the businesses we've identified immediately. Truly profitable businesses are not like unskilled jobs on an assembly line. They require a combination of interests, skills, aptitudes, background, knowledge, and contacts that meet real needs people have. But everyone has some interests, talents, skills, aptitudes, and background. Therefore, in describing each business, we have attempted to honestly portray what's required and what you can expect, so you can objectively and realistically match your own strengths to a truly doable home business.

Good Income Potential

We have selected only businesses that can and are producing a sufficient income for people to support themselves in a reasonable lifestyle. Living at the poverty line is not our idea of a good life. So missing from our list of the best are businesses like astrology, handicrafts, and pet breeding, from which it's difficult for most people to make more than a part-time income. While such pursuits are popular and many people are doing them at home, we have included a business only if it has the potential to produce a good, steady, full-time income.

We recognize that what constitutes a good income is highly subjective. What for some would be ample would for others be insufficient, so we've been as specific as we can be about potential earnings.

To make sure that people are in fact making money in the businesses we've selected, we conducted interviews with professional and trade-association executives from each field whenever possible. We also did in-depth interviews with owners of the businesses that were likely candidates for our list. In addition to determining whether people are making an adequate living from these businesses, we also wanted to know what they are able to charge and how they go about getting business.

In fact, we were surprised to learn that four businesses that were on our original list and that seemed to have great potential are not profitable. Many people who are trying to succeed at them from home are struggling instead of thriving, and consequently we yanked them from our final list.

We found, for example, that according to the National Institute on Adult Daycare, the costs of meeting state and federal regulations make adult day care unprofitable for 51 percent of eldercare providers. We also determined that there's not a broad enough market to make advertising brokering viable for very many people in a given area, and not at all in major parts of the country. And although we think used-equipment broking will emerge as a viable business, we found very few people who were making sufficient money as used-computer brokers at this time. For the business of checking employment applications, not only did we not find people making a livelihood at it, but we discovered that computer databases that will give employment histories are now readily available to employers for under $100 a search.

In short, while all the businesses we describe can provide what many people find to be adequate full-time incomes, we suggest that, in selecting the best business for you, you carefully consider how much income you need and want.

Reasonable Ease of Entry

While we have found that many professionals like accountants, software engineers, and psychotherapists are doing well working on their own from home, we have excluded any business that requires a specific college degree. We consider this important because as corporations continue to reduce the number of people they employ and as jobs go out of existence, many people need to do something other than what they were originally trained to do or have had previous experience in. Few people have the time and resources to go back to school full-time to prepare for a new profession, although in today's world education is not a one-time event.

Some of the businesses we've chosen can be operated with any general background. Your existing skills, aptitudes, and experience may ideally qualify you for many of them. Some businesses, however, require certain skills and experience that you may need to pick up by taking some course work or working for a period of time in a particular field. Should you not have the required background for the businesses that interest you the most, you will find specific steps outlined for how you can gain whatever background you need.

So while some of the businesses you'll find most appealing may require that you take time to gain certain skills or experience, keep in mind that the best investment you can make is an investment in yourself. An investment in building experience, education, and training is never wasted. Even if preparing yourself for your chosen home business would take a year or more, that period of time will most certainly pass whether you pursue the needed preparation or not. So if you start now, you'll be ready to succeed that much sooner.

In fact, a Canadian study of entrepreneurs showed that those who succeed are the ones who have prepared themselves prior to starting their business so that they have the necessary skills and expertise to make it. The successful ones begin with realistic expectations for how much they can earn and then do their homework for at least six to nine months—taking courses and calling on experts, for example.

What we can assure you is that the businesses described in this book do not require that you be without a job while you prepare yourself for them. In fact, for some of the best businesses, like being a private detective, the ideal way to learn is to first take a job working for someone else in that business. While you may have to take a pay cut at first in order to do this, you can think of it as a way to get paid for on-the-job training.

Also keep in mind that even if a business requires no prior experience, if it is in a field you know well, getting started will be much easier. You will be able to use contacts you already have, and your reputation in the field could be valuable in qualifying you. The greater your experience in a field, the shorter and less challenging your learning curve will be once you get out on your own.

Low or Modest Start-Up Costs

We have also selected businesses that do not require tens of thousands of dollars to get under way. Some businesses, like cleaning services, can be started for as little as a few hundred dollars, while others, like a desktop video business, require sophisticated computer technology and an initial investment of over $10,000.

In calculating start-up costs, we're assuming that you will be starting your business in a home office space other than on the kitchen table. People have started successful businesses from kitchen tables, but by setting up a specific desk and office area devoted to your business, not only will you avoid unnecessary backaches and eyestrain, but you'll be able to work more productively, and you and your customers, family, and friends will also be more likely to take your new business seriously.

The fact that you will be working from your home without the overhead of office or storefront rent means you will be able to start most of the businesses we've selected for this book on a part-time basis while you still have a job. We think starting out while you have the security and cash flow of a job is the safest way to finance a home-business start-up and to carry you through the months it takes to launch a business.

In addition, as soon as you start your own business, whether full- or part-time, you can convert some of your costs of living into tax-deductible business expenses (which as a salaried employee you're not eligible for) thereby reducing your annual federal and state income taxes. By starting your business while you still have a job, you can actually use the federal tax system to help fund your start-up costs. Doing this involves changing the number of allowances you claim on your W-4 so that you have several hundred additional dollars each month in take-home pay. Before doing that, however, we recommend seeing a tax consultant to make sure that you set up your home office so that such expenses are deductible.

Ability to Operate from Home

Not all businesses can be run from home profitably. In fact, we found that upon close scrutiny several businesses that you might think would be good home-based candidates are really not best suited to be operated from home. Auto brokering, with its state licensing requirements, was one such business. Catering services was another. Although we learned that most successful caterers started their businesses from home, invariably they left their home as soon as possible because of important legal and zoning problems and space limitations; so we removed this business from our list of the best.

All the businesses in this book can be operated successfully from home without employees. Most of them, however, can also be expanded by hiring employees or using subcontractors who may either work on your premises or from their own homes. Such expansion is not necessary, however, in order to earn a decent living.

In fact, we've talked with many people who expanded their home business only to find that while adding employees increased their gross revenues, once they paid for salaries, fringe benefits, and insurance, they decreased their net income. What's more, some people who expanded by adding personnel also found that they had to work longer hours and contend with more aggravation. By cutting back to what they could handle themselves, they ended up netting more income with greater satisfaction.

So for each of these businesses, growth is an option, not a prerequisite to success.

Variety: Something for Everyone

The businesses we selected are varied enough that virtually everyone can find something to do from home. Whether you prefer to be outdoors or at a desk, work with people or manipulate information, use your hands or your head, be alone or with others, get involved with computers or stay away from technology altogether—whatever your interests, hobbies, talents, experience, and preferences, you should be able to find a business in this book that's suited to you.

Sometimes when we talk about these businesses, someone will say, "Who would ever want to do that?" But we've learned that there is someone who can find satisfaction in doing virtually any task imaginable. There are people whose brain endorphins start to flow when they're busy cleaning things, and they're perfectly happy running a cleaning service or auto-detailing business. For others who are turned on by doing highly detailed work, a business like bookkeeping or medical transcription is enjoyable.

Still others enjoy the thrill and challenge of standing in front of an audience, even though most people list public speaking as their greatest or second-greatest fear. For them, corporate or computer training is a perfect match. Someone who loves helping people solve problems might relish running a collection business. Should nurturing others be your passion, becoming a facialist could meet your needs. Ultimately, enjoyable work is in the *brain* of the beholder!

What the Business Profiles Will Tell You (And What They Won't)

In describing the businesses we've selected, our objective is to give you the best possible information we could obtain so that you can make a true comparison and a well-informed choice among the businesses we believe offer the best potential in these nervous '90s. The first 50 business are what we consider to be the *Best of the Best*. These businesses have an established track record of success and a strong continuing demand.

The *Rest of the Best*, which follow, are businesses that are sometimes less well known and at this time less common. They are being done successfully though, and are well suited to grow and flourish in this decade. Some of the Rest of the Best are so new that it was hard to discover much about them, in which case we have included as much information as we could find.

Each Best of the Best profile begins with a general description of the business, the types of customers and clients it serves, and what makes it a good business for the '90s. We then go on to address the following issues.

☑ Knowledge and Skills You Need to Have

This section lists what you need to know and be able to do in order to operate this business, as well as any special training or licenses you may need. Here we also highlight the aptitudes, preferences, talents, and tolerances each business demands, as identified by people we've interviewed who have enjoyed and succeeded at doing it, as well as people who have not done well or enjoyed the business.

In short, this section of the profile gives you the opportunity to determine whether you already have or would be willing to acquire the needed capabilities and competencies the business requires. Sometimes the businesses of most interest to you will be a perfect match. You'll say, "Hey, I could do that right now!" At other times, however, you'll find that you have *some* of what it takes but need to develop additional skills and talents. For example, you might be able to start a business doing professional-practice management for chiropractors by taking on a relative as your first client, but you may need to develop your knowledge of billing procedures. Or you may have the expertise but not the interest or the contacts.

Not only can reviewing these profiles help you make sure you are qualified to start a given business; it can also help you avoid the mistake of focusing only on the potential opportunities a business provides. One person who came to one of our seminars learned this lesson the hard way. He decided to start a medical-transcription business because he knew there was a high demand for it and it paid well. And indeed, when we met him he was making $60,000 a year. But, not being someone who enjoys sitting still, he said the work was driving him crazy. So he was attending our seminar to find a business he would enjoy more.

The special training some of the businesses require may be acquired through community colleges, trade schools, and professional associations, or by working for/apprenticing with an existing business in the field. Some industries provide on-the-job apprentice programs through trade and professional associations. And reputable trade schools will readily provide information on attrition and graduation rates and provide references.

Where there are specific training programs available that are particularly well suited to people wanting to learn at home, we've listed these resources in the section titled "Where to Turn for Information and Help."

⬛ Start-Up Costs

This section indicates what someone starting each business can expect to spend in order to get the business under way. Each item will usually have a low and high figure. The low figure is for what we consider to be a minimally equipped office; the high figure is for the optimally equipped office. Prices are as of early 1991.

To be competitive today, most businesses require an adequate investment in office furniture; business cards, letterhead, and envelopes; and a computer of some kind. While these start-up expenses add up to a minimum of around $2,000, do not let this amount deter you. You may have some of the needed items already. You may be able to delay some purchases until your business produces the income to buy them. You can buy used equipment and furniture. You may be able to lease items, although leasing is more expensive than buying, even if you finance your purchases.

You may notice that some of our start-up costs appear somewhat higher than those you might read about in other publications. The reason for this is that while we heartily recommend that people bootstrap their business, we don't recommend trying to limp by with less than a minimally professional setup. So although you might be able to forego some of the items we recommend initially, these are the expenditures you should anticipate and plan for.

Office Furniture.   Unless the business requires something special, we have calculated standard office furniture to run around $600 at the low end and $800 at the high. This range is based on the following: a standard four-drawer filing cabinet at $150, a desk at $200 (with $200 you can buy a new economical steel desk, a used wooden desk, or a hollow-framed door placed upon two two-drawer filing cabinets), a basic ergonomically designed chair at between

The Five Basic Skills Required for All Businesses

There are five basic skills we believe anyone must have to run any kind of business. Altogether they are required for *all* the businesses in this book, we don't repeat them in each business profile. And while we don't discuss these skills in the book, the other books in our series of Working from Home Guides do. So if you are lacking in any of these vital areas of expertise, we have indicated throughout this chapter when you can turn to the other books in our series for help.

1. Basic money-management skills. While you don't need to have a lot of money to start a business successfully, you do need the ability to make the most of the money you have. Being able to focus on the bottom line and pay attention to the numbers is as essential as the ability to price your products and services, manage your cash flow, and make sure you collect payment for the work you do. If you are lacking in these skills you can get training in business courses, books, and so forth.

2. A marketing mindset. You aren't truly in business until you have business. No matter how much your product or service is in demand or how great a job you do, if people don't know about you, you won't have much business. You must be able to make your business visible to the people who need it, and this means understanding marketing.

3. Self-management skills. To make it on your own, you must become a goal-directed and self-motivated individual. You must be able to get yourself started each day, stick to business, and close the door on work at the day's end.

4. Time-management skills. In your home business, you will need to wear many hats, from chief executive officer to janitor. You'll have to do the business, get the business, and run the business. This means you'll need to manage your time effectively to make sure the most important and urgent things get done in a timely fashion.

5. Basic office organization. Since one of the roles you will probably play is that of your own office administrator, you will need to be able to organize, equip, and manage your office space so that you can work effectively in it, having a place for everything and keeping everything in its place so that you can find it easily when you need it.

For more information on mastering these five basic skills, refer to the other guides in our series: *Working from Home, Getting Business to Come to You* (with Laura Clampitt Douglas), and *Making It on Your Own.*

$200-$400 (to keep your costs at the low end of that range, name-brand chairs can be purchased used or from companies like BIF, which sells such chairs on sale for $200), a printer table or stand for $100, and $50 for office supplies and accessories.

Computer hardware and software. Unless the business requires a higher-performance computer, our estimates for computer costs are based on your buying an IBM compatible 286 computer, costing around $1,000, including monitor. In the first five months of 1991 computer prices decreased almost 40 percent, which means it's entirely possible that you'll even be able to get a more powerful 386 SX or a low-priced Macintosh within this budget. Software prices are based on discounts widely available by mail or in stores that heavily discount software. Under printer prices, where we think a dot matrix printer is adequate, we have indicated a price of $300, which will allow you to buy a 24-pin dot matrix printer producing near letter quality. Where we think a printer producing a higher quality image is important, we have specified an inkjet printer, such as Hewlett-Packard's Deskjet or Canon Bubblejet at $500, or a laser printer available now at three price levels—a low priced laser at $650, such as an Okidata or a Panasonic, a Hewlett-Packard Laserjet III at $1600 or a Postscript printer at $2500. A low-budget solution for obtaining word-processing software is to use an integrated program, such as *Microsoft Works, Lotus Works,* or *Toolworks Office Manager,* that includes basic spreadsheet, database, and communications functions as well.

Business cards, logo, stationery. We've generally indicated $200 at the low end to cover business cards, stationery, and so forth. However, we've found that by using a home-based desktop-publishing service that has an arrangement with a print shop, you can get a high-quality designed logo, 1,000 business cards, letterhead, and envelopes for around $600, and the extra expenditure can greatly enhance your image.

Brochures. Altogether we have heard of people spending $4,000 to produce 250 brochures, this is not necessary or advisable today. For example, rather than spending $1,200 for design work alone, by using free-lance professionals or college students to design your materials, you can keep the costs in the range we have quoted in the profile. And you can cut your costs down even more dramatically if you use a personal computer and laser printer to create the brochure yourself. Colored foils and high-quality textured paper can be used with a laser printer to produce a very striking brochure at a minimal cost. For example, by using a laser printer and buying paper from Paper Direct, a mail-order source of quality paper, you can create 500 brochures for $100.

In fact, business consultant Alan Gregerman, president of Venture Works, in Silver Spring, Maryland, recommends that many businesses use what he calls a customized brochure. Using your computer with word-processing or desktop-publishing software and a laser printer, you can create a basic format for your brochure and then tailor the content for each person or company to whom you send it. In such cases your brochure becomes a custom-made proposal at a fraction of the cost of a standard printed brochure. Gregerman finds that such a brochure has great impact. This does require purchasing sophisticated word-processing software such as *Word Perfect, Microsoft Word, Ami Professional,* or *Wordstar,* or desktop publishing software, and investing the time to learn to use it effectively.

Organizational dues. Because making business contacts through formal or informal networking is one of the most effective methods for home businesses to get business and because feeling a sense of isolation from one's peers is one concern people have about leaving the traditional office setting, we have included $250 in start-up expenses for joining one or more professional, trade, or business organizations.

Special expenses. Beyond the basic costs listed above, we have also included any expenses that are particular to a business. Some businesses, for example, demand specialized equipment, more sophisticated computer technology, or specific software. An export agent or publicist, for example, must have a fax machine. An errand service needs a radio pager or cellular phone. Some businesses, like association management, require that you join organizations in order to market or establish yourself.

In some cases, you'll be able to postpone buying more costly equipment by leasing it or by contracting out for services. Few desktop publishers, for example, have equipment capable of producing printouts at 1200 dots per inch, so they use service bureaus when they need to provide that level of clarity. Buying used equipment will also cut down your initial costs.

Costs not included. Our start-up estimates do not include the costs of an answering machine, telephone equipment, or telephone services because there is a wide range of options available for meeting these needs, including converting your existing equipment, using an outside service, and so forth. At the minimum, however, you will need one separate business telephone line and either an answering machine, an answering service, or voicemail for taking calls when you are not in your office. These costs should be added to the start-up estimates you'll find in this book.

Other than the cost of initial organizational dues or brochures, our estimates of start-up expenses do not include the costs of marketing your business. Such costs are reflected instead as part of overhead estimates, which we've put in the section titled "Potential Earnings." Nor do our estimates include what you will need to cover initial operating expenses or your living expenses. If you have a job or your spouse has a job, you may be able to cover your ongoing expenses in that way until your business begins to generate income sufficient to support your lifestyle. Otherwise you should have some other plan to cover your living expenses and overhead for at least three, and preferably six to nine, months while you get your business under way.

Later in this chapter you will find a list of the five most common plans used to finance home-business start-ups.

🔼 🔽 Advantages and Disadvantages of Each Business

Selecting a business is always a matter of balancing the best aspects with those that are least desirable. Every business has its pros and cons. These two entries will help you identify businesses that may be especially appealing to you as well as those with characteristics that you would find disagreeable. They are intended to help you avoid businesses that won't be of interest to you and businesses you would only abandon later.

If you hate to work under the pressure of deadlines, for example, you won't want to consider technical writing or book indexing. But if you want to be in a business that holds the potential for establishing a steady stream of repeat business, being a facialist or running a mailing-list service could fill the bill.

💲 Pricing

This section in the profiles answers one of the most common questions people starting a home-based business ask. In most cases, we give a range of fees or prices. These ranges are based on several variables.

First, unless otherwise indicated, the prices stated are typical for urban areas. Also local prices can vary substantially from one part of the country to another and competition in a given community may push prices downward or drive the rate higher. For example, we found desktop publishing to be a particularly competitive business in large cities. The hourly desktop-publishing prices ranged from $25 to $35 in Dallas to as high as $125 in Los Angeles. We believe, however, that the more typical range is between $40 and $65.

The prices you can charge are also affected by your particular background, skills, and contacts and by the type of clients you decide to serve. For example, nonprofit organizations typically operate on tighter budgets than marketing departments for large corporations. They therefore are likely to hire people who will charge less for the same service a corporation might be paying more for. Student and educational markets also pay a lower range of fees.

In setting your own prices, you should make calls to comparable businesses in your area to find out what the going rate is for the business you are considering. If you charge too much, you're apt to wait a long time for that first customer; but if you charge too little, colleagues and prospective customers may very well question your capability. So do check local prices before setting yours, and remember that what other people charge should be only one factor in determining your prices. In the 1990 edition of *Working from Home*, we added a new chapter (chapter 21) on various pricing strategies and the procedures for setting your prices.

📇 Potential Earnings

The figures stated in this section are based on estimates of what you can earn from operating the business full-time without employees. By working full-time, we mean spending 40 hours a week or more doing work for which you are paid, as well as marketing and administering your business. For many of the businesses, the income estimates are based on being able to bill 20 hours per week (1,000 billable hours per year). Some occupations such as bookkeeping and word-processing, however, can bill out closer to the standard 40 hours per week. In still other businesses, like corporate training and wedding planning, we presume you are billing a certain number of days or events each week.

Typical annual gross revenue for a programmer, for example, is $40,000. This figure is based on billing 20 hours per week, 50 weeks a year (1,000 hours a year) at $40 an hour. Many programmers, however, are able to bill in excess of 40 hours a week and earn up to $100,000 per year.

We have attempted to be conservative in our income estimates, as research has shown that having realistic expectations of what you can earn is an important criterion for business success. Our figures do presume, however, that the business owner is successful in effectively marketing the business and therefore has ample business coming in.

For most of these businesses, you can exceed these projections by hiring an employee or using subcontractors. This is especially true when the business involves selling your time as the only or the principal source of revenue, as is the case with word-processing or transcribing court reporters' notes. There are only 174 hours in each week, and producing revenue in more than 25–30 of these hours is difficult when you must not only *do the business* but also *get the business* and *run the business*.

Overhead. In calculating overhead, which covers the basic costs of being in business (like marketing, telephone, business taxes, insurance, postage, printing, supplies, subscriptions, and so forth), we indicate whether the overhead for this business is high, moderate, or low. These estimates are based on information gathered directly from successful business owners and, whenever possible, from reports by national trade associations such as the Professional Association of Innkeepers International and the American Society for Training and Development.

We consider low operating expenses to be 20 percent or less of your gross income, moderate to be 25 to 40 percent, and high to be greater than 40 percent. We have used these estimated ranges for several reasons. First, we find that most home-based business owners do not know exactly what it costs them to operate, beyond the calculations they do for income-tax purposes. But the tax system is designed to collect taxes, not to serve as an information system for financial planning. While how much you can deduct from your taxes does reflect your business expenses, the amount you deduct depends on how disciplined you are in keeping records of things like automobile usage for business purposes and how well you engineer social engagements to make them tax deductible. Therefore, actual expenses and deducted expenses can often vary. In our estimate of overhead, no allowance is made for using your home or automobile unless this is a significant part of operating your business (for example, a bed-and-breakfast inn or an errand service).

Second, many home businesses have wide latitude in what they must spend for overhead. Furniture used in the home office may be a $500 Steelcase chair, or it may be an "early relative" dining-room captain's chair that costs nothing.

Best Ways to Get Business

When we ask operators of successful home businesses to tell us the best way to get business, over and over again they tell us the same thing:

The best source of business is referrals from satisfied customers. In fact, they tell us that once a home business is established, most business comes from word-of-mouth. For example, Steve Burt, a resume writer in Gainesville, Florida, put it this way: "If you do a good job for someone, take a little extra time to talk with them, or give a client something extra, I guarantee you'll get referral business."

But, of course, you can't get referral business until you have business. So to avoid the proverbial chicken-or-the-egg dilemma we have limited our list of best ways to get business to those that can help you get your initial clients and customers. In this category, you'll find the most likely and cost-effective ways to market each business based on our interviews with people who have successfully established these businesses.

We've included this information for two reasons. First you're not *in business* until you *have business,* so it's crucial in selecting a business to know that there are identifiable methods others have used and found reliable for bringing in business. Second, in your own business you may spend up to 40 percent of your time marketing, so it's important to select a business for which the most reliable marketing methods are ones that you feel comfortable doing. Therefore, in reviewing the businesses, we suggest considering this section as another important way to judge which businesses are best suited to your talents, interests, and personality.

In general, we have usually not listed advertising because, for a home business being started with limited capital, it can be costly. In the process of writing our book *Getting Business to Come to You* with marketing expert Laura Clampitt Douglas, we interviewed over 100 successful home-based businesses earning over $60,000 a year and discovered that the most successful marketing methods for home-based business are often the least expensive ones. The most successful home-business owners use their time and energy, not their money, to market themselves.

Finding the best marketing method is always an experiment, so you can use our list as a starting point to test various methods until you find the ones that will actually be the most effective in your community with your prospective clients and customers. The fact that a method does not appear on our list does not mean it will not work for you. What's most important is whether you're comfortable with using a method and whether it is effective in reaching the people you need to reach.

For step-by-step information about how to use these methods, refer to our book *Getting Business to Come to You*. It also includes recommendations for how to name your business to achieve maximum marketing effectiveness, proven start-up strategies, instant business-getting techniques, and methods for getting repeat business.

Ann McIndoo, successful computer tutor whose business, Computer Training Systems, is located in Diamond Bar, California, offers this marketing suggestion for whatever business you are in: build a client and prospect database of everyone whom you could work with, and then whenever you aren't busy, make unbillable moments productive by giving them a call. She finds it always generates work.

⊞ Related Businesses

This section provides the names of other businesses that are related in terms of the type of work done, skills required, or markets served.

⊡ Franchises

Where appropriate, we have included a section with the names and addresses of franchises that are available for starting the business being profiled. We have discovered a growing number of franchises that can be operated from home. Buying a franchise instead of starting a business from scratch has advantages in that a proven franchise provides a tested formula for starting a business that has worked for others. It can save you from making costly errors, shorten your learning curve, and help you make a profit more quickly. There are trade-offs in buying franchises, however: start-up costs are often higher, and franchising organizations require that you follow their procedures instead of doing it your own way.

⬚ First Steps

If you decide you would like to pursue a given business, this section provides suggestions on how to obtain the knowledge and skills you will need, as well as ideas for getting your business under way. To gather this information we asked people who are in the field what advice they would give to someone wanting to start this business.

▯ Where to Turn for Information and Help

Here we list books, trade associations and professional organizations, special training programs, and magazines and newsletters recommended by people in the field that can be of value to someone starting out in each business. For products over $50, we have indicated the current price.

How to Choose a Business That's Right for You

Selecting a business from among the many that are viable requires finding a match between two things: (1) your particular interests and capabilities, and (2) what people will pay for in your community. Finding this match is vital to your success, and this book is designed to help you find the best possible match. As you read through the businesses we've profiled, you can begin by making a list of those that hold the greatest appeal to you and in which you believe you could do well.

Finding Something You Want to Do That You Do Well

Being able to do a good job is a must in any business. A poor or even mediocre job usually guarantees that you won't have return customers, but that's not all. Sometimes clients and customers will refuse to pay for inferior work, and worse yet, an unhappy client usually tells at least seven other people what poor service he or she received. So first and foremost, you must be confident that you will be able to do a high-quality—if not superior—job in whatever business you select.

Obviously, having a background in the business and a track record of success would therefore be ideal. For example, if you have worked as an employee for a florist doing gift baskets and have received rave reviews on your work, you're in a position to feel confident about your ability to do a good job in your own gift-basket business. Or if you've been doing bookkeeping on a salary for several years and your clients respect you and refer others to you, you're certainly well positioned to start a bookkeeping service.

But what if you don't like what you've been doing? What if you're looking for a change or if what you've been doing can't be done from home? You still have many options. You can look for a business in another field that utilizes skills similar to those you've acquired. For example, if you're good at bookkeeping but want to do something different, you could look for businesses that involve financial management, attention to detail, or record keeping.

If you are seeking a complete change, you can turn to hobbies or other interests and talents you have. When work repairing televisions dried up for Ted Laux, for example, his wife pointed out that he had years of experience cataloguing and indexing his extensive record collection and therefore might enjoy starting a book-indexing business. She was right. That's exactly what he did.

In fact, while being good at your business is essential, our research shows it's not sufficient. You also need to enjoy it. We think it's profoundly sad that so many people feel they're squandering the precious moments of their lives doing work they dislike. We also believe that a hefty percentage of business failures, physical illnesses, and addictions of mankind can be traced to choosing the wrong job or business.

And most important, succeeding as your own boss is almost always a matter of taking the initiative and going the extra mile despite the stresses that accompany any business. Picking a business you like and that likes you is essential to staying motivated through the ups and downs of being on your own. It could even mean your business or personal survival.

Besides, it feels good to wake up in the morning eager to get to work because you like your work so much. We believe one's work should be stimulating, exciting, enjoyable, interesting, and fulfilling. And since your work is likely to be one of the primary ways you express what you have to contribute to life, your work should also be a platform through which you can give the best you have.

Therefore, in selecting a business, use your interests, talents, and likes and dislikes as a filter through which to examine the businesses we've profiled. If you are not fully confident about your ability to do a particularly appealing business, you can take the time to build your skills through practice, attending courses, or even apprenticing for a while before going out on your own.

What follows is a series of worksheets designed to help you identify what you are most interested in doing. If you already have a good idea of what type of business you want to do, you may wish to skip these next few pages. Before you do so, however, consider that it could be useful to compare your intended choice with other possibilities before you fully commit to it.

Determining If There's a Need

Once you've identified two or three businesses you think you would enjoy and do well at, we suggest that you invest a few weeks, even a few months, to test out whether you are likely to find ample customers for these businesses in your local community.

That fact that a business appears in this book means that many people are succeeding at running this business from home. Clients and customers in many parts of the country are willing to pay for what these businesses offer. The market looks good for others to succeed in this business. But as we said before, the demand for a business varies from community to community. A community can become oversaturated with a particular business.

In fact, we found that while many people were succeeding in these businesses, in all cases there were others who were not. Therefore, before you invest time and money in starting a particular business, it is crucial that you determine if you will be able to find enough people who are willing to pay you if you open such a business in your community. Here are several ways you can go about checking out the actual need for a business in your community.

1. Look in the yellow pages and/or other directories where such a business might be listed and see if there are other such businesses. How many listings are there? If there are a number of similar businesses, this is a good sign that there's a strong market for the business, but you will need to determine whether they are doing well and whether the market can support yet another one. Should the market be oversaturated, only the best are going to survive.

Questionnaire 1
Questions to Ask Yourself in Choosing a Business

1. Based on your education, your current or past jobs, and any special interests and hobbies, what three things do you know the most about? This expertise could be the basis for a business.

2. What other experiences in your background could you draw upon for a business?

3. What do people tell you that you do well? Think about the times you've heard someone say, "You know, you really ought to start a such-and-such, you're so good at that." Maybe they're right. And maybe they would be your first customer.

4. What things do you like doing most? Think, for example, about these questions.

   What do you like to do on your day off?

   What kinds of things do you leap out of bed for?

   What magazines, newsletters, and books do you enjoy reading?

   What headlines catch your eye?

   What things did you love doing most when you were a child?

   What is it you've always said you were going to do someday?

   If this were the last day of your life, as you looked back on your life what would you say you wished you had done?

5. How much do you want to be involved with people? All the time? Sometimes? From a distance? Not at all? The answers can help you rule in or out businesses that have a lot of or very little people contact.

6. How many hours a week are you willing to invest in your business? Do you want a full-time or a part-time business? Be realistic about this. The amount of time you're willing to invest is what separates full time from part time and profits from losses.

7. How much money do you need to make? How much money do you want to make? Each week? Each month? Each year? You'll notice that some of the businesses can charge considerably more than others, so choose a business that will produce the income you want and need.

8. What resources do you have available to you in terms of property, equipment, and know how? These resources could become the basis of a business. If you look around your home, you may have many untapped resources right under your nose such as a personal computer, a van, a spare room, an automobile, a camcorder, your kitchen stove, vacuum sweeper, backyard, or mailbox.

9. Do you want to start a business from scratch, or would you prefer a franchise or direct-selling organization such as Amway or Avon that will train you in what to do?

Questionnaire 2
What Do You Like and Do Best?

Circle the work activities on this list that you like to do, and use the list to help stimulate your thinking as you complete Questionnaire 3.

Information-Oriented Work

Working with words
Working with numbers
Analyzing
Compiling
Creating
Evaluating
Finding
Keyboarding
Organizing
Synthesizing

People-Oriented Work

Advising
Caring
Communicating
Helping
Informing
Organizing
Negotiating
Performing
Persuading
Planning events
Teaching

Thing-Oriented Work

Cleaning
Making
Organizing
Repairing
Working with animals
Working with food
Working with plants
Working with tools

If you discover there are no such businesses in your area, this could mean that there's an unmet need and the community is ripe for such a business—or it could mean that there is not enough need to support such a business. You'll need to investigate further.

2. Call your competition. Find out what services they actually offer and whom they serve. You might be able to specialize in some aspect of the work that they do not provide, or you might offer your services to a market they are not serving. Let them know you are thinking of starting a similar business and ask if they ever need to refer out overload or if there is a type of clientele they cannot or don't wish to serve and therefore are turning away. Also, find out how long they've been in business. This will give you an idea of how persistent a need there is for this business.

In a good market, while there may always be one or two people who fear competition, the majority of competitors will tend to be forthcoming with information and even glad that others are joining the field. Some will even offer to help you. But if you find that all or most of the people you talk to are consistently closed-mouthed or are complaining about business, this could mean there's not enough business to go around.

Questionnaire 3
Business Selection Worksheet

Your Long List

List your six best or strongest skills, talents, abilities, capabilities, or aptitudes.

1. _____

2. _____

3. _____

4. _____

5. _____

6. _____

List the six subjects or fields you know the most about, are the most competent in, or have the most experience and expertise in.

1. _____

2. _____

3. _____

4. _____

5. _____

6. _____

3. *Read business, trade, and professional journals* related to your field. These periodicals, especially local ones, can provide a wealth of information about the demand for a business. Sometimes they list new businesses and bankruptcies, track sales volumes, cover booms and busts by region or area, and feature success and comeback stories. Also read the trade journals your potential clients read to see what their concerns are and to follow emerging trends.

4. *Attend local business, trade, and professional meetings.* Follow the topics addressed at these meetings and listen to the table talk. Are people singing the blues or whistling "Dixie"?

5. *Talk directly to potential customers.* Locate and contact potential clients to find out how they are currently being served and if they are happy. Listen to what they complain about. See if you can identify how you could provide faster, cheaper, or better service.

Your Short List

Now narrow the long list down to the three skills and subjects that you like most, in rank order.

Skills   Subjects

1. _____   1. _____

2. _____   2. _____

3. _____   3. _____

With this short list in mind, you can look through the profiles for the businesses that best correspond to what you know about, what you're good at, and what you enjoy.

Some people also find it useful to make a list of the things they dislike doing, because a negative filter can prevent you from entering into a business that has a fatal flaw for you. If a business is otherwise appealing to you, however, consider the possibilities of working with someone else who would do those aspects that for you are disagreeable. That person might be a partner, a subcontractor, or an employee. For example, a desktop publisher who isn't an especially fast typist can subcontract with a word-processing service to do text entry. Many partnerships form because one person is good at being the *inside* person, handling production and administration, while the other is the *outside* person, handling sales and customer contact.

---

6. Talk with the chamber of commerce and local government planning agencies about the size of your market and community developments that will affect your business potential.

7. Analyze the marketing literature of your competitors to see how they are addressing the market and what they are and are not offering.

Check Your Zoning

Zoning regulations vary from community to community, so another important step in determining which business is best suited to you is to determine what restrictions, if any, have been placed on the type of work you can do from home.

Zoning regulations typically divide communities into residential, commercial, industrial, and agricultural zones, with subdivisions within these categories. Even in residential areas, many zoning regulations allow so-called home occupations. But some communities prohibit working from home altogether in residential zones, or allow certain activities but not others. In some locales, for example, you can't have clients coming to your home. In others, you can't have employees, use your address in advertising, or sell retail.

Questionnaire 4
Other Criteria for Selecting the Right Business

Circle the answer that best describes the business you want.

Income Potential

How much money you think you need to:
- survive? How much do you need to get by?

  Under $25,000 $25,000 to $50,000   Over $50,000
- thrive? What do you need to meet or exceed the standard of living afforded by your job?

  Under $25,000 $25,000 to $50,000   Over $50,000
- get rich? How much money would you really like to make?

  Under $25,000 $25,000 to $50,000   Over $50,000

Where You Want to Work

Work at home   Work from home

Amount of People Contact

Mostly working with people   Some work with people   Not a people business

What's Required

A business I'm already prepared to enter.
Something that will require me to learn new talents and skills.

Start-Up Money Needed

Low—under $2,500   Moderate—$2,500—$7,500   High—over $7,500

Therefore, it's important to find out specifically how your home is zoned and what business activities can and cannot be legally carried out on your premises. To determine if your home can be used for business purposes, you will need to check the zoning ordinances at either your city hall or your county courthouse. To know whether you need to check with the city or the county, a general rule of thumb is that if you would call the police for an emergency, you are governed by city zoning; if you would phone the sheriff's office, you deal with the county.

For more information about zoning and specifically what you can do if you are not zoned to do the types of businesses you wish to do from home, refer to chapter 9 of *Working from Home*.

Choosing One and Only One

Once you've gathered the needed information and weighed what you've discovered, we urge you to settle upon one *single* business to pursue. We think it's an error to diffuse your efforts by trying to start up several businesses at once. Instead, we urge you to focus your energy on one undertaking. This will greatly maximize your chances for success.

Focusing on only one business will enable you to be sure that the message you deliver to other people about what you do in your business is clear. We know too well the glazed look that comes across people's faces when they hear someone go into describing three or more things he or she can do for them.

In the '90s people want to trust their business to experts; they want to do business with people who are specialists. And few people will believe that you can be an expert in multiple fields. There is rarely enough time to do all that needs to be done in one business, let alone in multiple businesses. So select the *one* business you want to pursue and develop a plan for how you will proceed.

Tailoring a Business to Get the Right Fit

If you don't immediately find a business that suits your needs and those of your community, don't despair. Having read about the types of businesses that are doing well and the kind of skills and background you need to do them, you can use this information to create a unique business tailored to you and your community. Many of the most successful home businesses we discovered came about in just that way. Of course we could not include those businesses in this book, because very few people would be able to build such unique enterprises, but here are a few examples.

PHIL ABLIN of Rockport, Texas, had been a securities broker for 16 years and was looking for a change. His hobby was fixing things around the house, but instead of simply becoming a general repairman he created a unique repair business based on his personal experience of living in a resort area. He returned to the community where he was raised and became the House Doctor, doing maintenance and repair for absentee home owners on Key Allagro Island, a resort area on the Gulf Coast of Texas. Although his first job was weeding a flower bed for $3.75 an hour, he now grosses $150,000 a year.

DON CRESCIMANNO of Honolulu, Hawaii, has put a unique twist on event planning. He has an event clearinghouse. Crescimanno was a physicist working for major corporations like Hewlett-Packard and Rolm before he began to feel tied down by administrative duties and decided to make a change. Recognizing that Honolulu has an average of 550 events going on every week, he created CAT-NET, a voicemail system telling business subscribers about upcoming events. He also helps stage 200 events himself every year, including art openings, theater parties, cruises, and private parties.

DAVID ELIASON had been a radio news director in Dubuque, Iowa for three years when his job was eliminated. He decided that rather than leaving town to find a similar position, he'd stay in Dubuque and do something he really enjoyed. He turned his hobby of dabbling with electronics into a home-based business called Professional Audio. He designs and installs sound systems for churches, auditoriums, racetracks, office buildings, and theaters and grosses $200,000 a year.

RITA TATEEL of Los Angeles may be the ultimate proof of how with ingenuity you can turn even the most unlikely interests into a business. Instead of matching specialists with businesses who needs them, she matches celebrities with events that need them. Burned out from her social-welfare career, she created Celebrity Source, which provides celebrities for fund-raising events. She says of her business, "Ninety percent of what I enjoy outside of work is an element of my work, even watching TV and going to parties."

We know hundreds of stories such as these, so use the businesses in this book as a springboard to create a business that is perfect for you.

Preparing A Business Plan

The profiles in this book should not be confused with a business plan. This book is intended to stimulate your thinking and provide information to help you choose the best business. If you've done the things we suggested above, however, you will be well along the way to gathering the information you'll need to prepare a solid plan.

A business plan is simply a road map. It sets out your goals. It outlines where you're going with your business and how you plan to get there. As a home-based business you will probably not be seeking investors or getting a loan to start your business, so preparing a business plan is not for someone else's benefit. It's for you—so you'll know *what* you're doing and *how* you're doing at each step along the way. Having such an operating plan to guide your daily activities can prevent you from making costly mistakes.

There are three key parts to such a business plan:

1. Three descriptions of your business. Three brief statements, one of 25 words, one of 65 words, and one of 125 words, that describe what your business is, whom you serve, and what benefits you provide will help you know precisely what you intend to do and will enable you to talk successfully about it with business contacts, potential customers, and clients.

You can use the 25-word description as part of your standard introduction of yourself and who you are. The 65-word description is the answer you can give to the question, "What do you do?" or your reply to the statement "Tell me more about your business." The 125-work description can be used as the basis for writing advertising and brochure copy describing your business.

2. A plan for how you intend to market your business. Identifying as thoroughly as possible the people who need what your business has to offer and how you will let them know about your business can help you select the best marketing methods to make sure you have enough business. In this portion of your plan you should:

- define exactly who your customers or clients are
- identify who your competition is
- clarify what advantages you have over your competition in terms of price, service, quality, variety, ease of use, and so forth
- determine how big your market is and if there are enough buyers for you to reach the level of income you desire or need
- identify how you will let the people who need your product or service know about what you have to offer

3. Financial projections. Identifying how much you need to earn in order to survive and thrive, and then checking out the going prices in your community, can help you know what you will need to charge and how many clients or customers you will need to have each month to reach your income goals. You should also identify which start-up expenses you will have and identify how long you will need to supplement your income before your business can support you. Keep in mind that a business can take anywhere from three months to over a year to turn a profit. So you should have a plan for how you will cover your living and operating expenses during that period. Some people advise that to be on the safe side you should double the time you think it will take you to break even. With careful planning, however, most home businesses are basically able to finance their start-ups themselves. (In chapter 3 of *Working from Home*, we have listed many ideas and variables to consider in starting up your business, including five ways to finance your venture.)

Opening Your Business

Once you know what you want to do and have a solid business plan, there are a number of important details you must take care of to actually set yourself up in business, such as selecting which form of business you wish to operate, getting the necessary licenses and permits, setting up and equipping your office, opening your business bank account, setting up an easy-to-follow record-keeping system, and having your letterhead and stationery printed. In this country, however, taking care of these details is the easiest part of starting a business. Let's go through them one by one.

Dealing with Legalities

In operating on your own, you must choose one of three forms of business. Your business can become a sole proprietorship, a partnership, or a corporation. We recommend beginning as a sole proprietorship unless your business faces the danger of being sued for damages or you will be working with a partner. You should consult an attorney and an accountant, however, in selecting the form for your business.

The name you select for your business is one of the most important decisions you will make, so once you've selected your name, you will need to register and protect it.

If you are a sole proprietorship you will need to file a fictitious business name with the secretary of state or with your local county clerk, depending on state law. If your business is a corporation, you will need to reserve the name with the secretary of state.

You may wish to trademark your name to protect it from use by others. You do this through your state; if you meet the qualifications, you may also register it with the U. S. Patent Office in Washington, D.C. Federal registration takes about one year to 18 months and currently costs several hundred dollars.

Because state, county, and local regulations vary from place to place, you will need to determine whether your business requires any of several licenses and permits. These could include a city or county license, a state sales permit if you need to charge sales tax, a federal employer's identification number and any other special licenses.

Even if you are not required to have one, we recommend that you get an employer's ID number. It will cost nothing, but will convey the image of a substantial business. You can get a federal ID number from the nearest Internal Revenue Service office.

Setting Up Your Financial System

When you open your business you should set up a separate business checking account. We recommend selecting a small or local neighborhood bank where your business will be noticed and valued.

If you're happy with your existing bank, you may want to open your business account there because they already know you. Find out what the bank's

---

Five Home-Business Start-Up Steps

1. Deal with the legalities. Determine the form of your business. Select and register your business name. Obtain and file needed licenses, permits, and registrations.

2. Create a financial system. Establish a bank account and your credit. Set up your bookkeeping and accounting system. Get needed insurance.

3. Set up your office space. Select an adequate location for your home office. Get needed equipment, furniture, and supplies. Establish your telephone service. Set up your mail service.

4. Develop your business identity on your logo, cards, and stationery.

5. Establish your work schedule and start getting business.

---

policy is on holding checks deposited for collection, however. Some banks won't credit your account for checks over a certain amount until the checks have cleared. This could cause cash flow problems for you, so accept only immediate access to your funds.

Cash flow is the lifeblood of being self-employed. Making sure you collect what you are owed is like making sure you get your paycheck. The best strategy for having ample cash on hand, of course, is to make sure you have plenty of business. But you also have to make sure you get the money you're owed in a timely fashion. To keep your cash flowing, get money up front, take deposits, get retainers, and require partial or progress payments. Request payment in cash at the time of sale or delivery of your service. Take bank cards instead of extending credit. Experts claim that offering MasterCard or Visa can increase your business 10 to 50 percent. Unfortunately, most banks will not offer MasterCard or Visa merchant accounts to home-based businesses. In chapter 14 of *Working from Home,* however, you will find a list of sources through which you can obtain merchant status.

If you must bill your clients or customers, always bill promptly instead of waiting until the end of the month. Also offer discounts of 2 to 5 percent if payment is made within 10 days from the date of the invoice. And be sure to act promptly on any overdue account.

One of the best ways to make the most of your money is to keep careful track of it, so set up a reliable bookkeeping and accounting system right from the beginning. The purpose of keeping good records is to enable you to know how your business is doing. With good records, you'll know where you're making a profit and where you aren't. You'll know what your costs have been, where you can cut expenses, and in which ways you'll need to modify your plans and projections. Good records also will enable you to take the greatest advantage of allowable tax deductions and will protect you should you be audited.

Today the easiest way to keep simple, accurate records is to use a computer with software like *Quicken* or *One Write Plus.* Such programs keep your bank balance for you and can quickly print out income and expense reports.

To help make sure you get the basic insurance you need to protect your home office and your business, refer to chapter 11 in *Working from Home* in which we discuss which types of insurance you might need and under what circumstances you need it.

Setting Up Your Home Office

Where you locate your home office and how you set it up are two of the most important factors in determining whether you'll be able to run a business successfully at home. Many people are concerned about interruptions from family or distractions from household activity; others worry that they'll feel compelled to work morning, noon, and night, because their work is always there.

Where you put your office and how you set it up can protect you from these potential problems. For a full treatment of this topic (including claiming your tax benefits) see chapters 5–8, 10, and 17–19 in *Working from Home*.

Developing Your Business Identity

Selecting the right name for your business may be one of the most important business decisions you make. If your name is memorable, distinctive, pronounceable and understandable, it can be a valuable sales tool. On the other hand, if your name is hard to pronounce, confusing, and difficult to spell, it can actually cost you business.

In chapter 4 of our book *Getting Business to Come to You,* you'll find a list of rules for naming your business and the pros and cons of the five most common strategies for choosing a business name. We suggest that you follow these guidelines to select several possible names for your business. Then list your top choices on a sheet of paper and ask several potential customers which company they would be most inclined to contact and why.

Once you've selected your name, you need to create a graphic image for your business cards and stationery. Now that you're in business, your cards and stationery are more than paper you use for correspondence. You should think of them as miniature billboards for your business. They create a first impression for people with whom you don't have face-to-face contact. Some of the people you do business with may know you only through your stationery.

So think about your graphic image as part of your promotion and sales effort. Design your logo, cards, and stationery to make a statement about your business. Make sure they convey the image you want to create. For example, if you are a computer consultant, you might want to project a modern, high-tech look, so you could use a paper, type style, and design that convey a clean, sleek, and forward-looking image. On the other hand, if you are an errand service, you might want to convey a warmth and friendliness in which case you may choose a paper, type style, and design that are rounded, warm, soft and reminiscent of the familiar past.

Don't leave these important decisions up to a typesetter or to the standard format at your print shop. In chapter 4 of *Getting Business to Come to You* we outline how to create a business image that sells itself.

Establishing Your Work Schedule

Even though as your own boss you are free to work when and if you want, we urge you to set up a work schedule. A schedule not only will help you organize your work, but will also help your family and friends know when they can and cannot interrupt you. Business contacts will know when they can best reach you. A schedule will even help you to avoid having your work take over your life, because it will tell you not only when it's time to start working, but also when it's time to stop.

If you are operating a part-time business, we suggest that you make a commitment to work at least eight hours a week in your business. And don't plan to squeeze all eight hours in on Saturday. Spread the eight hours throughout the week, so that you'll be sure to get some work done even when things you want to do come up on the weekends. In Part II of *Making It on Your Own,* we provide guidelines for managing your time so you can balance the three principal aspects of being your own boss; getting the business, doing the business, and running the business.

Having completed these five basic start-up steps, not only will you be in business, but you will be in position to make sure that you have business.

PART I

■ ■

The Best of the Best

■ ■ ■ ■

ABSTRACTING AND INDEXING SERVICE

If you like to read a variety of books, magazines, or other printed material, an abstracting and indexing business may be of interest to you. Abstracting and indexing services embrace three possible businesses: back-of-the-book indexing, indexing and abstracting for computer databases, and abstracting for in-house corporate use.

Back-of-the-book indexing. Many authors do not have the time or desire to index their own books. Also, they're often so immersed in their own specialty that they are unable to construct an index of key words and subjects that would be useful to a layperson. Therefore they or their publishers hire independent indexers to create an index as the last step prior to printing a book.

Computer-database indexing. A whole new field of indexing and abstracting services for computer databases is now open to people working from home. Such abstracting consists of reading journal articles and condensing the information into a format—typically 10 to 15 sentences each—for inclusion in databases. Some databases consist only of key words, in which case they are only indexed, but many require a full abstract.

Currently there are 4,000 to 6,000 databases that are accessible directly or through information utilities such as Dialog, BRS, Dow Jones, and CompuServe. Other databases are available only on CD-ROM. This is a field that will grow for the next five to eight years, until most databases offer full-text services. Even then, there will be a need to create the key-word indices to which people can turn to search for specific information before accessing full-text services.

Corporate abstracting. The third market for indexers/abstracters is corporations that want to have important market or trade information abstracted for in-house use or to offer as a service to clients. In order to save their staff or customers valuable time, such companies will often employ outside services to read articles and books pertaining to their business and abstract the information into concise summaries.

Nancy Mulvany, whose business is called Bayside Indexing Services, says, "There is a huge market beyond regular book indexing. There is so much material going on-line today, and people are waking up to the fact that it has to be indexed."

☑ Knowledge and Skills You Need to Have

- You need sufficient knowledge in the subject areas you are abstracting—or a broad enough general knowledge and interest—to be able to ferret out central ideas and relevant information from printed materials on a wide range of subjects.
- You have to read a book differently than you normally would. You need to be able to skim through and pick out key points, condense the points into the required number of lines, and pick out the key words that someone would use to search for that information.
- You need confidence in your ability to communicate the material you're abstracting clearly and concisely.
- For some databases, word-processing skills are needed, altogether a lot is done on paper forms provided by database owners. Little abstracting work is transmitted by modem.
- If you do database abstracting, you must be familiar with on-line computer databases and the abstracts that appear on them.

✴ Start-Up Costs

	Low	High
Computer with modem and hard disk	$1,000	$2,500
Fax machine	——	$ 400
Printer	$ 300	$1,600
Word-processing software	$ 250	$ 250
Office furniture, especially an ergonomic chair	$ 600	$ 800
Business cards, envelopes	$ 200	$ 400
Reference books and dictionaries	$ 75	$ 250
Total	$2,425	$6,200

Advantages

- The work can be interesting and stimulating intellectually.
- You can learn a great deal about a variety of subjects.
- The ability to focus on key points and to summarize concepts in a clear and concise matter is helpful for doing other kinds of writing.

Disadvantages

- Indexing is a high-pressure job because it must be done on time and deadlines are often tight. In abstracting and indexing, databases, for example, turnaround times can be one to two weeks. In book publishing deadlines may be very tight.
- The work is highly detailed and requires concentration, precision, and careful organization.
- In book publishing, work is often particularly intense during certain seasons.

Pricing

Back-of-the-book indexing: $1.50 to $6 per printed book page you read to index, or $8 to $40 per hour. Indexers who use computer indexing software receive the higher fees.

Abstracting: $4 to $12 for doing a full abstract with index.

Potential Earnings

TYPICAL ANNUAL GROSS REVENUES: $30,000, based on billing 1,500 hours per year at $20 an hour. A back-of-the-book indexer, however, taking 3 weeks to do a 300-page book, will index 17 books a year, at $3.00 a page, he or she will earn $15,300. The best earnings are being made by those who are abstracting and indexing for computer databases.

OVERHEAD: Low (20 percent or less).

Best Ways to Get Business

- Directly soliciting publishers and database companies by sending samples of your work to the appropriate personnel. If your background is relevant to a company's specialty, emphasize your background. The quality of your work must be at least equivalent to in-house work.
  - To locate book publishers, you can refer to *Writer's Market,* by Writer's Digest, or *Literary Market Place,* published by Bowker. New editions come out each year. Send a sample index to the production manager along with your query letter.
  - Since many database publishers hire only local free-lancers, in order to find database publishers in your area, decide which type of data-

base you want to work with and search a directory like the *Epsco Index and Abstract Dictionary* or *Cuadra Directory of Online Databases* to identify publishers in that field by address.

- To get corporate work, contact corporate librarians and the department responsible for technical writing.
- Responding to the occasional newspaper classified want ads.
- Volunteering to index a book without charge to establish yourself with a publisher for the first time.
- Responding to classified ads for indexers in the *Library Journal* (Bowker Magazine Group, 249 West 17th Street, New York, NY 10011; 800/669-1002) and in the publications of the Association for Information Management (703/490-4246).

First Steps

If you have no experience in indexing, first steps would include learning indexing software and reviewing indexes in a variety of books. Try looking up subjects of interest to you in indexes. Begin indexing materials that are not indexed, and use these as samples of your work. Once you know you can create a good index, begin using the marketing methods listed above.

Where to Turn for Information and Help

BOOKS

Abstracting and Indexing Career Guide, by M. Lynn Neufeld and Martha Cornog, National Federation of Abstracting and Information Services, 112 South 16th Street, Philadelphia, PA 19102; (215) 563-2406.

Freelancers on Indexing, American Society of Indexers, Box 386, Port Arkansas, TX 78373; (512) 749-6634. Transcript of a panel discussion.

Indexes and Indexing, by Robert L. Collison. Tuckahoe, NY: John de Graff, 1972.

Starting and Maintaining an Indexing Business, American Society of Indexers, Box 386, Port Arkansas, TX 78373; (512) 749-6634. A compilation of answers to questions asked of San Francisco-area indexers.

ORGANIZATIONS

American Society of Indexers, 1700 18th Street, N.W., Washington, DC 20009; (202) 328-7110.

MAGAZINES AND NEWSLETTERS

Index and Abstract Directory, Ebsco Publishing, Box 1943, Birmingham, AL 35201.

Indexing: How It Works. A two-day course offered by National Federation of Abstracting and Information Services, 112 South 16th Street, Philadelphia, PA 19102; (215) 563-2406.

United States Department of Agriculture Graduate School offers reasonably priced courses in indexing. Write for a catalogue: Graduate School, USDA, South Agriculture Building, 14th Street and Independence Avenue, S.W., Washington, DC 20250. Or call to speak with a counselor at (202) 447-5885.

■ ■ ■ ■

ASSOCIATION-MANAGEMENT SERVICE

Organizations of all types, especially professional and trade groups, often need someone to manage and administer their operations. Since many organizations have grown beyond the size that volunteer officers can effectively manage, but are not large enough to justify hiring full-time staff and renting office space, they turn instead to people who make a living administering professional and trade associations.

The association manager provides a cost-effective solution to staff an organization. He or she also enables the organization's volunteer leadership to concentrate on program and policy issues rather than administrative tasks and provides continuity of the organization during leadership changes.

Actually, association management services, also called *executive director services,* have existed for over 100 years. What association managers specifically do depends on which functions their clients want them to handle. However, to serve clients well, they need to be prepared do just about everything an organization needs to have done. They may collect dues, keep membership lists, prepare association newsletters, answer phone calls, handle incoming mail, mail out information about the organization, and keep the financial records, pay bills, make arrangements and take reservations for membership meetings, and events, help raise funds, and book speakers for meetings as well as national conventions. They may also get involved in membership development, professional education, lobbying, and marketing. With today's office technology, all the tasks involved, however, can be done from someone's home.

Your clients might include small national organizations like the Association of Flying Dentists, state and local trade or professional associations like the American Society of Training and Development, or hobbyist organizations like the Lake Amphibian Flyers Club, a group of 400 individuals worldwide who pilot Amphibian aircraft on lakes. One association manager, Bill Goddard, also finds churches to be in the market for executive director services, because they, too, have many administrative needs but often do not have the budget to hire full-time staff.

An alternate route to becoming an association manager is to start your own association. For example, Goddard points out that "no one has ever started a national association of waterfront homeowners. Yet environmental regulations give them reason to band together around issues like public access to water. Selling ads in the association magazine alone could net a good income. Think of all the companies who would like to reach people who own waterfront property." Any new field, like desktop video services or environmental testing services, also could become the basis for a thriving association. Goddard believes there are plenty of organizations that need professional management.

☑ Knowledge and Skills You Need to Have

- You need to know an industry or be able to tap into knowledge about an industry through someone you know who will show you the ropes.
- You need to be able to manage an office at the secretarial level or higher.
- You need to be good at organizing paper, information, and people. You'll be handling lots of details and administrative snafus and making sure everything runs smoothly and that everyone is taken care of.
- You must have a personal computer and be able to type and do mailing lists and simple bookkeeping.
- You will be working with volunteers, most of whom are involved with the association as a labor of love or for professional development. You'll need to have a sensitivity to these people and refrain from barking directions and orders to motivate them.
- You'll need to have political savvy to handle personality and ego conflicts that arise within the association.

✿ Start-Up Costs

	Low	High
Computer with hard disk	$ 1,000	$ 2,500
Inkjet or laser printer	$ 550	$ 1,600
Office furniture, especially an ergonomic chair	$ 600	$ 800
Business cards, letterhead, envelopes	$ 200	$ 600
Brochure	$ 100	$ 2,000
Organizational dues	$ 250	$ 250
Total	$ 2,700	$ 7,750

👍 Advantages

- You get to attend and possibly travel to many interesting meetings and conventions.
- This business provides a lot of visibility. The people you're involved with are often leaders in their industry.
- The work offers ample variety to keep anyone from being bored.
- When you do your job well, your efforts will be greatly appreciated.

⚏ Disadvantages

- Navigating organizational politics can be tricky.
- You're on call. You need to be available when your clients need you. So sometimes you will be very busy.
- Organizational meetings are often held in the evenings or on weekends.
- Except for associations organized around hobbies and avocations, which typically don't operate on rigid time lines, you're apt to find that there will always be some big event or project in the works, so your vacations and time off will be pretty much confined to December and August.

⑤ Pricing

Like attorneys, professional association managers operate on a monthly retainer. The amount of the retainer depends on what functions you will be doing and the amount of time they will involve. Clients are uncomfortable knowing the meter is running while you're working. So you may need to estimate how much of your time the tasks will take each month and, based on a hourly rate, negotiate a fixed monthly fee. Hourly rates generally range from $25 to $75.

⚏ Potential Earnings

TYPICAL ANNUAL GROSS REVENUES:

- For managing other associations: $52,500, based on 1,500 billable hours a year (30 hours a week for 50 weeks) at $35 an hour.
- For running your own association: $20,000 to $30,000, based on an organization with 400 members, each of whom pays $35 to $50 a year for dues.

OVERHEAD: Low (20 percent or less).

⚏ Best Ways to Get Business

For starting your own organization:

- Mailing to a list of potential new members.
- Publicity and advertising in the publications they read.

For engaging existing associations as your clients:

- Contacting the presidents of professional and trade associations directly. Refer to *Encyclopedia of Associations,* from Gale Research which is available in most libraries.
- Networking with professional, trade, or industry groups.
- Volunteering to do seminars on administration and management for association leadership teams.
- Responding to classified ads for churches seeking employees.

▌ First Steps

If you don't have any administrative experience, you might volunteer to administer a small group to which you belong. Or you could get elected to office in an organization to gain the experience of running an organization.

If you already have administrative experience of some kind, begin by finding a niche you could serve, such as medical associations or business organizations. Survey the officers of such organizations regarding their likes and dislikes in administering their organizations.

▢ Where to Turn for Information and Help

ORGANIZATIONS

American Society of Association Executives, 1575 I Street, N.W., Washington, DC 20005; (202) 626-2723. Although the ASAE is geared to salaried professional staff and large association management companies, it has useful publications and local chapters.

Institute of Association Management Companies, 104 Wilmot Road, Suite 201, Deerfield, IL 60015; (708) 940-8800. This organization serves association management companies. However, no current members are home-based. Minimum dues are $750 a year.

■ ■ ■ ■

AUTO DETAILING

If you have a van and are willing to roll up your sleeves and work, you can earn good money in an auto-detailing business. Auto detailing goes beyond what a car wash can do to make an automobile look and feel like new.

Believe it or not, auto detailing is a growing business. Americans now own 120 million cars, and that number may double during the 1990s! Our love affair with the automobile continues despite the fact that auto prices have come to resemble housing prices. In 1990, the average new car cost $16,000—50 percent of the median U.S. family income, up from only 36 percent in 1980. As a result of this steep rise in new-car prices, Americans are holding on to their cars longer. But for many people, you are what you drive, so they want their cars to look like new even though they have to keep them a little longer.

But keeping an older car looking decent means making sure it gets more than the occasional wash, and that's where auto detailing comes in. Home-based auto detailers work on their clients' premises, where they polish and clean the cars inside and out, right down to the finest detail. It takes about three hours to thoroughly detail a car. So if you work quickly you can do two to three cars a day. In addition to working for individuals, you can also work with used-car dealers or companies with fleets of cars that routinely need to be detailed.

This is an ideal business for someone who likes to work out of doors, derives satisfaction from paying attention to detail, and enjoys making sure things are immaculately clean.

☑ Knowledge and Skills You Need to Have

- The primary prerequisite is a willingness to roll up your sleeves and get your hands dirty doing physical work.
- Although no special skill or experience is needed, you do need to know or be willing to learn techniques for thoroughly cleaning an automobile.
- You have to have the ability to communicate with customers and the desire to please them.

🐖 Start-Up Costs

	Low	High
Polisher	$ 300	$ 400
Air washer	$ 55	$ 75
Wet-dry vacuum	$ 100	$ 650
Towels, brushes	$ 100	$ 100
Supplies	$ 500	$ 500
Business cards, letterhead, envelopes	$ 400	$ 600
Flyers, brochure	$ 200	$ 500
Portable water-supply equipment	$ 100	$ 100
Generator	$ 800	$ 1,200
Minivan	$4,000	$12,000
Total	$6,555	$16,125

👍 Advantages

- You can work outdoors.
- Virtually anyone can learn to do auto detailing.
- This business can easily be started as a part-time or sideline business.

👎 Disadvantages

- It's hard physical work.
- Your business is subject to weather conditions.

💲 Pricing

Retail to the public:	$100 to $300 per vehicle.
Wholesale to car dealers and fleet owners	$55 to $60 per vehicle.
Per hour pricing:	$25 and up.

🔲 Potential Earnings

TYPICAL ANNUAL GROSS REVENUES: $39,600 to $57,600. The low end figure is based on detailing 15 cars a week wholesale at $55 per vehicle for 48 weeks a year; the high end is based on 12 cars a week retail at $100 a car for 48 weeks a year.

OVERHEAD: Moderate (20 to 40 percent) due to van maintenance, marketing, and supplies, which run about $5 to $10 per car

🔲 Best Ways to Get Business

- Directly soliciting corporations, rental-car agencies, funeral homes, limousine companies, government agencies that maintain fleets of cars, used-car dealers, car dealers who send trade-ins to auctions, banks that resell repossessed cars, and insurance agencies and body shops that deal with damaged cars. Leave a brochure, flyer, or well-done business card and follow-up periodically by phone.
- Approach upscale car owners as they park their cars in parking lots and handing out your card, flyer, or brochure.
- Networking and making personal contacts in organizations, such as trade and business associations.
- Listing in the yellow pages and placing advertising in publications your potential clients are likely to read.
- Prominently featuring your business and phone number on the body of your van.

🔲 Related Business

AUTO PAINT TOUCH-UP. A complementary business to auto detailing; for more information contact Color Tech Systems, 579 Interstate Boulevard, Sarasota, FL 34240; (813) 378-1193.

🔲 First Steps

The people we've talked with who are doing this business successfully learned how to do it in one of two ways. Some simply watched people wash cars, tried out different cleaning products and methods, and talked with automobile body-shop equipment and supply dealers, asking for advice about which products and equipment to buy. Automobile body-shop equipment and supply dealers can be found in the yellow pages.

Another way to learn this business is with the assistance of a training company like The Curtis System Advanced Automotive Care which sells a system (for $1,895 to $4,450) to start and run an auto detailing business. This program is not a franchise; you pay only for the one-time fee and for additional supplies as you need them. For additional information including a videotape describing this business write or call them.

▢ Where to Turn for Information and Help

CLEANING PRODUCTS

Cyclo, 1438 South Cherokee Street, Denver, CO 80223; (800) 525-0701. Also provides information about pricing and other facts about starting an auto-detailing business.

Glo-Shield Glass, 3060 Whitestone Expressway, Flushing, NY 11354; (718) 463-1035.

Production Car Care Products, 1000 East Channel Street, Stockton, CA 95205; (209) 943-7337.

Super Gloss Manufacturing Company, 3431 West Clarendon, Phoenix, AZ 85017; (800) 221-1842.

ORGANIZATIONS

The Curtis System Advanced Automotive Care, Box 250, Mountain Road, Stowe, VT 05672; (800) 334-3395.

International Car Wash Association, 1 Imperial Place, 1 East 22nd Street, Suite 400, Lombard, IL 60148; (708) 495-0100. Serves both car washes and auto detailers. It provides a wealth of membership services including a monthly newsletter, library and training aides, customer surveys, cassette education programs, advertising slicks that can be adapted for local advertising and a telephone hot line.

VIDEO

Auto Detailing, Entrepreneur Magazine, 2392 Morse Avenue, Box 19787, Irvine, CA 92713; (800) 421-2300; in California, (800) 352-7449. Shows how to clean, degrease, glaze, and paint a car and make the inside look like new.

■ ■ ■ ■

BED AND BREAKFAST INN

A bed and breakfast inn is truly a *home* business, because your home becomes the business. Once upon a time, when homeowners had more space than they needed, they took in boarders. Today's version of this long-lost practice is a bed and breakfast inn, which offers travelers the comfort of a home environment at a cost less than what a hotel would charge for a comparable room.

The idea of bed and breakfast inns developed in the 1980s. Though at this writing they represent less than one percent of the hotel industry, they are a well-established option for today's travelers. Whereas there were only 400 bed and breakfast inns in the United States in 1975, today there are over 15,000. And Pat Hardy, codirector of the Professional Association of Innkeepers International, foresees a doubling of B&B inns during the '90s.

Pat points out that with their emphasis on service, bed and breakfast inns have influenced the traditional hotel industry to offer new services to their guests such as concierges and complimentary breakfasts. Pat, who is also a coauthor of the book *So You Want to Be an Innkeeper*, predicts that urban inns and small executive retreats will do particularly well in the '90s.

This is an ideal business for someone who loves to have houseguests, decorate, and keep a beautiful home. The location of a bed and breakfast inn is of particular importance, however. You need to live in a desirable area that will draw travelers who are interested in staying at a bed and breakfast inn. Inns are commonly located in areas that draw tourists or business travelers who want a small, more private and personal overnight experience.

The more rooms you have available to convert into guest rooms the better. Profitability with four or fewer guest rooms is difficult, according to a national study by the Professional Association of Innkeepers International. Smaller inns with a higher occupancy rate than is typical for urban inns can make money, as can those located in the West, where the weather is more suitable for year-round travel.

☑ Knowledge and Skills You Need to Have

- Although no specific experience is required for this business, being an innkeeper requires that you like all kinds of people and are willing to serve them; they will be coming into your home and expecting you to take cater to their needs.

- You need to be a good housekeeper and cook who's willing to roll up your sleeves and get your hands dirty keeping things clean, attractive, and in good running order.

- You need to be able and willing to listen, observe what people want, and respond to their needs so you can provide the extra touches that will make your inn memorable—such as having umbrellas available for your guests if it's raining.

- Innkeepers must be able to respond calmly and quickly to crises and sudden changes in plans.

⚙ Start-Up Costs

Acquisition cost. If you are converting your existing home, you will not have any acquisition costs; however, if you're buying a home in order to go into this business you can expect to pay $35,000 to $70,000 per guest room in California; less elsewhere.

Renovation cost. If you are converting portions of your existing home into guest quarters you can expect to spend $20,000 to $40,000 per guest room in California; less elsewhere.

Working capital. To open an inn in your home you should allow for $6,000 per room up-front to cover the costs of utilities, towels, insurance, marketing, maintenance, and so forth.

👍 Advantages

- You can live in any desirable location in the country.
- Almost any life experience, from housework to marketing, can be effectively applied to operating an inn.
- Operating an inn provides an increased opportunity to enjoy a family life. This business can be an opportunity for couples to work together and for parents to be with their children. Also, this is a business in which children can easily be involved.
- For people who like being domestic, being an innkeeper is a way to earn an income while their property appreciates in value.
- This business provides many perks. You save on child-care costs. Expenses such as the interest on your home, the cost of operating your car, your insurance, eating out, magazines, cleaning supplies, and even travel become tax deductible.

👎 Disadvantages

- As an innkeeper, you need to be at home most of the time, and you're tied to the telephone.
- You are on the job seven days a week—no weekends off.
- Many states deem inns with more than six rooms to be subject to the state's hotel laws. Meeting such regulations involves a greater degree of red tape and higher costs for making sure your home adheres to the more demanding standards these laws require.

💲 Pricing

Average fee per room in 1990:	Standard Rate	Corporate Rate
Northeast	$116	$91
Midwest	$ 92	$72
South	$ 92	$63
West	$100	$86

📠 Potential Earnings

1990	Net Profits	Occupancy Rate	Gross Income
1 to 4 rooms	$ 8,000 net loss	44%	$ 42,000
5 to 8 rooms	$12,000	46%	$111,000
9 to 12 rooms	$63,000	51%	$245,000

OVERHEAD (INCLUDING INTEREST EXPENSE ON REAL ESTATE)

1 to 4 rooms   108%
5 to 8 rooms   77%
9 to 12 rooms   63%

AVERAGE OCCUPANCY RATES

National   38%
Northeast   51%
South   45%
West   66%
Rural   45%
Village   60%
Urban   65%

*All data provided by the Professional Association of Innkeepers International.

Best Ways to Get Business

- The most effective source of business is getting your inn listed in travel and guide books.
- Happy guests will generate referrals, so one of the best business-getting strategies is to provide a quality room, spectacular breakfasts, and some other distinguishing service.
- Reservation services in your community or region can refer business to you for a percentage of the fee you receive, usually between 10 and 35 percent. You can find reservation agents in your local yellow pages or through the national association for such agencies, listed below.
- Travel sections of newspapers and magazines, even TV news and talk shows, sometimes do feature stories on unique, charming, and colorful inns, so sending out news releases can lead to valuable visibility.
- To get repeat business, do regular mailings to your former guests announcing special services, offering special discounts, and informing them of upcoming events or activities in your community.

First Steps

1. Be a guest at a bed and breakfast inn yourself, particularly ones listed in books for tourists. Read critiques to see what's recommended and what's not.
2. Attend workshops of the associations listed in the resources below.
3. To gain experience, consider taking work as an inn sitter for vacationing inn owners.

Where to Turn for Information and Help

BOOKS

The Bed and Breakfast Cookbook, by Pamela Lanier. Philadelphia: Running Press, 1985.

Bed and Breakfast USA, edited by Betty Rundback. New York: E. P. Dutton. Published annually.

So You Want to Be an Innkeeper, by Mary F. Davies, Pat Hardy, Joanne M. Bell, and Susan Brown. San Francisco: Chronicle Books, 1990.

ORGANIZATIONS

American Bed & Breakfast Association, 1407 Huguenot Road, Midlothian, VA 23113; (804) 379-2222. Offers an inn rating program.

Bed and Breakfast National Network, Box 4616, Springfield, MA 01101. An organization of bed and breakfast reservation services. It will send you a list of reservation agencies with which you might want your inn to be listed.

Professional Association of Innkeepers International, Box 90710, Santa Barbara, CA 93190; (805) 965-0707; fax (805) 682-1016. Offers a free kit, called the Aspirers Intro Kit.

NEWSLETTERS

Innkeeping, Box 90710, Santa Barbara, CA 93190; (805) 965-0707; fax (805) 682-1016. Monthly; $56.

SOFTWARE

The Front Desk, Eugene McAllister, Box 1706, Guerneville, CA 95446; (707) 869-3121. Handles reservations, mailing lists and billing. $215.

■ ■ ■ ■

BILL AUDITING SERVICE

This is a win-win business for the '90s. Companies spend a lot of money on gas, electricity, water, insurance, telephones, and a wide variety of goods and services they purchase from other merchants. The bills they receive are often difficult to understand, especially utility bills, which are among the most complicated. Nevertheless, many of these bills are simply paid, without their accuracy being verified. But sometimes meters are misread, miscalibrated, or broken, or data is entered or calculated incorrectly; decimal points can be misplaced, or discounts overlooked. Often lots of money can be recouped by carefully checking these bills. And that's what a bill auditing service does.

Also called an *overcharge collection service,* an auditing service verifies bills against purchase orders, checks to see that goods have been delivered, compares charges against what the laws, tariffs, or contracts allow, and checks the math, the tax rate, and other rate classifications to make sure their clients have not been overcharged. When overcharging is found, the auditor negotiates a refund and splits both the savings of past overcharges and future savings.

Auditors usually limit their services to commercial and industrial clients who have utility or other bills amounting to at least $2,000 to $3,000 each month. But with over 5 million business establishments in the United States, there is an abundant number of prospective clients. And with telecommunications experts estimating that 70 to 80 percent of all bills have errors in them, there should be ample interest.

Utility-bill auditing is growing especially fast because after deregulation utility bills have become increasingly complex and most companies simply assume they are correct. Clients may include schools, government agencies, churches, hospitals, retail stores, hotels and motels, grocery stores that stay open all night, nursing homes, auto dealers . . . any company that uses a lot of electricity, water, or phone service. For example, a company that has multiple water meters that are being separately billed might save hundreds or thousands of dollars by something as simple as combining these meters so that the readings are reflected in one bill. A savings of $300 a month over 12 months for 3 years is an $10,800 savings and represents a $5,400 fee for the auditor.

Other areas offering opportunities for auditing are sales taxes, freight bills, insurance payments, credit-card charges, and property taxes. However, county tax officials are more adversarial in granting property-tax reductions.

☑ Knowledge and Skills You Need to Have

- You need to know the applicable laws, tariffs, and regulations well enough to spot errors.
- You need to be able to do basic math and use a calculator accurately.
- Essentially, auditors find errors, so you need some analytical ability. You need to have an eye for money in the way that an editor has an eye for words.
- You need to have the instincts of a detective and the creativity of a budget-stretching parent of 10 children in finding ways to save your clients' money.
- This is a detail business. You must have a penchant for detail and correctness.
- You need to know and understand how utility-company tariffs apply.

▣ Start-Up Costs

	Low	High
Calculator	$ 50	$ 150
Computer	$1,000	$2,500
Inkjet or laser printer	$ 500	$1,600
Spreadsheet and word-processing software	$ 100	$ 700
Office furniture, especially an ergonomic chair	$ 600	$ 800
Business cards, letterhead, envelopes, contracts, agreements	$ 200	$ 600
Fact sheet or brochure	$ 100	$1,000
Totals	$2,550	$7,350

▣ Advantages

- This business helps sell itself because the benefit is obvious and customers pay you from the refunds you obtain for them.
- It is a year-round and recession-proof business. Companies always welcome an infusion of cash and future lowered overhead.
- The business can offer more than a one-shot service. Clients can be sold on paying for savings over a three-year period.
- The income potential is excellent, with the potential of large sums of passive income from future savings for which you do no additional work.
- Competition is relatively low.

▣ Disadvantages

- There is a 60-to-90-day lag between when the claim is made and when you get paid.
- You are paid only if you find savings.
- The utility tariffs in some states, such as New York, do not provide many opportunities for savings.

▣ Pricing

Auditors charge 50 percent of past and future savings. Average fees run from $1,000 to $3,000 on refunds. Because you may negotiate a contract in which a business agrees to pay you for savings it will realize over three years, your income from that client may continue for three years without additional effort by you.

▣ Potential Earnings

Once seasoned, an auditor can do 1 to 2 claims a day. A slow rate is 2 to 3 claims a week.

A claim that takes you 8 to 12 hours to do manually in the beginning can be done in 20 minutes once you develop an eye for what you're looking for.

TYPICAL ANNUAL GROSS REVENUES: $100,000 to $300,000 a year, based on 2 claims a week producing $1,000 each for 50 weeks or 2 claims a week producing $3,000 each for 50 weeks.

OVERHEAD: Low (20 percent or less).

Best Ways to Get Business

- Direct solicitation of businesses that are likely users of large amounts of energy, such as stores that stay open all night or coin laundries.
- Using direct mail followed up with telephone calls; start by making at least 50 calls.
- Networking and personal contacts in business organizations.
- Serving on fund-raising committees of causes and organizations.
- Contacting influential individuals such as accountants, business consultants, lawyers, bankers, and bankruptcy trustees who can refer clients to you.
- Giving speeches on how much money can be saved by auditing.
- Getting publicity for your work in newspapers and trade papers.

First Steps

The easiest way to acquire the knowledge you need for this business is by working for a corporation whose bills you will eventually audit, such as a utility, an insurance company, a government regulatory agency, and so forth. If you don't have such experience, however, you need to learn the laws, regulations, tariffs, and billing procedures of the type of audits you plan to do. (A training program that provides this information is listed below). You can expect a three-to-six-month learning curve; however, you can start this business part-time.

Where to Turn for Information and Help

TRAINING

Auditel Marketing Systems, 12033 Gailcrest Lane, St. Louis, MO 63131. (314) 567-1980. (800) 551-9282.

Utility & Tax Reduction Consultants, 1280 Iroquois Avenue, Naperville, IL 60563. (708) 369-3072. (800) 321-7872.

■ ■ ■ ■

BOOKKEEPING SERVICE

The mushrooming number of small businesses is good for bookkeeping services because entrepreneurs often need assistance in understanding the ins and outs of financial record keeping. As Chellie Campbell, of Cameron Diversified Services, points out, "While doing business is getting more complex, people are not getting better at handling their money. Today virtually everybody needs some professional guidance."

Also, as the complexity of doing business and the intricacy of tax laws increase, fewer small-business owners have the time or the ability to do the necessary financial record keeping themselves, yet many can't hire full-time personnel to carry out these functions. As a result, bookkeeping is a good business year-in and year-out. Bookkeeping services do well even during difficult economic times because at such times businesses are specially careful about their money.

Every business performs some aspects of its bookkeeping, so what you do for your clients depends upon which services they need and which services you wish to provide. Bookkeeping services range from making deposits, reconciling bank statements, recording transactions, and keeping the books to doing payroll, billing, and accounts receivable and payable, and preparing financial reports for tax or accounting purposes. Accounting, which is not in the purview of the bookkeeper, involves interpreting the financial statements and determining how to best use that information in business and tax planning. Sometimes people confuse bookkeeping with accounting, especially since software manufacturers refer to their products as accounting software when in fact this software simply helps keep track of information and does not interpret it. Bookkeepers keep the records; accountants analyze them.

Bookkeeping is a business you can start with a personal computer. And although no computer experience is needed, by using a personal computer a bookkeeping service can operate at a high degree of efficiency. In fact, bookkeeping services that stick to manual methods find the computer to be their greatest source of competition.

Bookkeeping services can be conducted from your home office by going into your clients' offices periodically. Mobile bookkeeping services have also become popular. A mobile bookkeeper can travel to an office with a laptop computer and software or use a van equipped with computer, printer, and electrical generator as a traveling office. Bookkeeping services may choose to specialize in the type of businesses they handle or serve a variety of clients.

☑ Knowledge and Skills You Need to Have

- You must know how to do bookkeeping accurately and reliably. This includes knowing basic principles of bookkeeping and what types of information must be kept in what form for legal and tax purposes.

- You need a clear, logical mind and enough real-world experience that you recognize whether the numbers make sense when they're tallied.
- You need to be thorough, dependable, and accurate.
- You need to enjoy paying attention to details.
- You need sufficient communications skills to handle people who become emotional about money matters and to give advice effectively.
- You need honesty and integrity. If you would go along with a client who asks you not to report or to hide income, it's in your interest to find a business that is less apt to tempt your integrity and get you in trouble. Also, a client who will ask you to use questionable practices may also have no compunction about not paying your bill.

■ Start-Up Costs

	Low	High
Personal computer with hard disk	$1,000	$2,500
Printer	$ 300	$1,600
Calculator	$ 50	$ 150
Accounting software *(One Write Plus* is a good program for services that don't provide payroll preparation)	$ 200	$2,500
Office furniture, especially an ergonomic chair	$ 600	$ 800
Business cards, letterhead, envelopes	$ 200	$ 600
Organizational dues	$ 250	$ 250
Totals	$2,600	$8,400

Add $4,000 to $12,000 for a van-based mobile service.

■ Advantages

- Bookkeeping is an essential, not discretionary, business activity, therefore it is generally recession resistant.
- Bookkeeping is not hard to sell because businesses know they need it.
- The business allows you to learn about both business in general and specific kinds of businesses.
- If you like numbers, the work is involving and challenging.

■ Disadvantages

- Bookkeeping is very technical and demands careful attention to detail. Mistakes can result in your clients' facing substantial interest assessments and other penalties from the government.
- People get emotional if they're not satisfied with their results and tend to blame the bookkeeper when the message is bad news.

- Collections can be a problem unless you use retainers and refuse to work when clients get behind.
- You need to keep current about tax-law changes relative to payroll and record keeping.

💲 Pricing

Charges range from $15 to $50 an hour; higher-end fees are paid for preparing financial statements, analyzing balance sheets, and tax preparation, particularly corporate tax returns; manual entry commands lower fees. Some bookkeepers also charge for travel time to clients' offices.

🏦 Potential Earnings

TYPICAL ANNUAL GROSS REVENUES: $18,000 to $60,000, based on working 1,200 hours a year (or 24 billable hours a week) at $15 to $50 a hour. Some people are able to bill more hours per week.

OVERHEAD: Low: (20 percent or less).

📈 Best Ways to Get Business

- Focused advertising and promotional efforts within a 20-to-30-minute drive of your home.
- Personal contacts with small businesses.
- Networking in business and trade organizations such as the chamber of commerce.
- Yellow-pages advertising.
- Overload or referral business from CPA firms, other bookkeeping firms, and financial planners.
- Making speeches and offering workshops on financial topics.

➕ Related Businesses

Tax-preparation service. From bookkeeping, you can also branch into this business. Although you can learn to do simple tax preparation by attending one of H&R Block's tax-preparation courses offered around the country each fall, to be able to handle significant tax preparation you should become an enrolled agent. This is a special status first created by Congress in 1884. As an enrolled agent, in addition to being able to prepare tax returns, you are also eligible to represent your clients before the IRS and the tax court. You can become an enrolled agent by passing a two-day examination given by the Treasury Department. The National Association of Tax Practitioners (720 Association Drive, Appleton, WI 54914, 1-800-558-3402) offers a training seminar to prepare for the examination and Thomas Tax Seminars, 4833 Skycrest Way, Santa Rosa, CA 95405, 1-800-257-3825, offers a home study course for the exam. The National Association of Enrolled Agents (6000 Executive Boulevard, Suite 205, Rockville, MD 20852, 301-984-6232) is the professional association of enrolled agents. Some states license tax preparers.

Bill-paying service. Many people need or want help taking care of their finances. That's what a billing-paying service provides. You create a budget for each client and then pay the monthly bills.

▓ Franchises

AFTE Business Analysts, 13831 Northwest Freeway, #335, Houston, TX 77040; (713) 462-7855. Provides a week-long training program and computer software to enable someone with no bookkeeping background or experience to begin this business. The franchises fee is $2,500.

Advantage Payroll Services, 800 Center Street, Auburn, Maine 04210; (800) 323-9648. This franchise is based on entering payroll information on a personal computer; the information is then transferred by modem to a central corporate mainframe computer in Maine. The franchise fee is $14,500.

BINEX-Automated Business Systems, 4441 Auborn Boulevard., #E, Sacramento, CA 95841; (916) 483-8080. Puts you in business doing consulting, computerized accounting, financial planning, and tax preparation. There is no specific franchising fee, but start-up and training costs are under $12,000.

General Business Services, 20271 Goldenrod Lane, Germantown, MD 20874; (800) 638-7940. Requires a business and management background. You provide financial management and tax-planning services to small businesses. The minimum franchise fee is $15,000.

▐ First Steps

If you have no prior background in bookkeeping, you can learn this skill from community-college courses, books, or on-the-job experience. If you have a background already, your first steps might be talking with other bookkeeping services, selecting and learning to use the software, and identifying clients.

▢ Where to Turn for Information and Help

BOOKS

Simplified Accounting for Non-Accountants, by Rick Stephan Hayes and C. Richard Baker. New York: John Wiley and Sons, 1986.

Small Business Accounting Handbook, Small Business Association Publications, Box 15434, Fort Worth, TX 76119. The SBA also has many other free or low-cost publications, such as *Keeping Records for Small Business* and *A Handbook of Small Business Finance.* Write for a list of publications.

MANUALS

Mobile Bookkeeping Service Business Guide, Entrepreneur Magazine, 2392 Morse Avenue, Box 19787, Irvine, CA 92713; (800) 421-2300; in California, (800) 352-7449. Entrepreneur also offers audiotapes.

GOVERNMENT RESOURCES

The Internal Revenue Service offers seminars on federal taxes. State and municipal tax offices are a source for information about rules for sales tax and local income taxes.

MAGAZINES AND NEWSLETTERS

Practical Accounting, Warren Gorham and Lamont, One Penn Plaza, 42nd Floor, New York, NY 10119; (212) 971-5000.

COURSES

McGraw-Hill's NRI Schools offers a course in bookkeeping and accounting. McGraw-Hill Continuing Education Center, 4401 Connecticut Avenue, N.W., Washington DC 20008.

United States Department of Agriculture Graduate School offers reasonably priced correspondence courses in accounting. Write for a catalogue: Graduate School, USDA, South Agriculture Building, 14th Street and Independence Avenue, S.W., Washington DC 20250. Or call to speak with a counselor at (202) 447-5885.

■ ■ ■ ■

BUSINESS BROKER

Business brokers bring together a client who wants to sell a business with someone who wants to buy a business. They focus on selling businesses with assets under $300,000 exclusive of any real estate the business owns. They function much like a real-estate broker. In fact, in sixteen states, business brokers are required to have a real-estate broker's license.

Business brokering is a growing home-based business. The U. S. Department of Commerce estimates that there are 16 to 18 million businesses in this country and that 20 percent change hands every year. Ninety percent of these businesses have under $300,000 in assets. So there are plenty of opportunities for business brokers. In fact *Inc.* magazine predicts that buying, not starting a business will be the rage for the '90s because failure rates for businesses that are bought are lower than those for businesses started from scratch or even franchises.

Under real-estate laws, brokers must represent one side or the other. Ninety-nine percent of brokers choose to represent those who are selling a business. They must locate such clients and obtain a listing agreement. The most successful home-based brokers specialize in selling a particular size or type of business, such as gymnasiums, dairies, or funeral homes, or businesses in a particular geographic area. A new area of activity for business brokers is assisting businesses in selling a portion of their businesses, usually 25 to 40 percent, as a method for creative financing.

Finding people who want to buy a business is not difficult. Brokers tell us that advertising in the business-opportunities sections of newspapers draws 6 to 12 inquiries per ad. Nine out of ten people who buy businesses are first-time buyers. Tom West, owner of the Business Brokerage Press, says business brokers spend about 40 percent of their business time out of the office calling on sellers to get listings, 40 percent dealing with buyers, 10 percent working with attorneys and 10 percent doing analysis.

☑ Knowledge and Skills You Need to Have

- This business requires considerable perseverance and patience to get listings and to find the right match between buyers and sellers. While some sales happen quickly, the time between getting a listing and closing a sale may be several months to over a year.

- Brokers need to have the ability to read and evaluate financial reports such as profit-and-loss statements to be able to represent their clients honestly and effectively.

- You need to be familiar with the legal aspects of selling a business.

- Brokers must have good sales skills. First you must convince an owner to sell and have you represent him or her. Then you must sell buyers on the merits of the businesses you represent.

- A broker needs to have good communication and interpersonal skills to build a strong relationship with both buyers and sellers. You must be able to listen and empathize in order to structure deals that will be satisfactory to both parties. And you must be able to negotiate successfully with buyers, attorneys, accountants, and sellers.

- You should have a conference area or separate office space in your home for meeting with people who are interested in the businesses you represent.

- A real-estate broker's license is required in the following states at this time: Alaska, Arizona, California, Colorado, Florida, Georgia, Hawaii, Idaho, Michigan, Minnesota, Nevada, Oregon, Tennessee, Utah, Washington, and Wisconsin.

⚙ Start-Up Costs

	Low	High
Computer with hard disk	$1,000	$2,500
Printer	$ 300	$1,600
Word-processing, spreadsheet, and bookkeeping software, and special software for evaluating businesses	$ 650	$1,000
Office furniture, especially an ergonomic chair	$ 600	$ 800
Business cards, letterhead, envelopes, and listing forms	$ 200	$ 600
Totals	$2,750	$6,500

👍 Advantages

- Being able to serve your clients well is easy because buyers will come to you. Brokers fail only if they don't get listings.
- The costs of starting this business are minimal and expenses are low.
- You are like a matchmaker. When you do your job well everyone is happy.
- Fees are high; overhead is low.
- There's little to lose if this business isn't right for you; you should know this within six months.

👎 Disadvantages

- Getting businesses for sales is just plain hard work. You will probably need to specialize to succeed.
- You don't make any money until the sale is complete.
- You may not have the patience, persistence, and interpersonal skills necessary to enjoy this business, but you won't know until you try.

💲 Pricing

Ten to 12 percent of a business's selling price, with a $10,000 minimum, is the standard fee.

🖬 Potential Earnings

TYPICAL ANNUAL GROSS REVENUES: $100,000, based on 1 sale a month for 10 months of the year at a minimum fee of $10,000 each. Some brokers earn much, much more. As Tom West says, "With a $10,000 minimum, it's all up to you."

OVERHEAD: Low (20 percent or less). Note: a good answering service is necessary. You need to have a live person answering your phone. To get premium service, voluntarily pay the answering service $50 more a month.

▣ Best Ways to Get Business

- Contacting business owners directly by phone, mail, or in person.
- Soliciting listings by going up and down the street talking to business owners.
- Networking in associations if you're specializing in some industry, or in other organizations of business owners.
- Getting referrals from lawyers, accountants, and bankers.
- Purchasing lists of names of franchises and private companies for sale all over the country.

✚ Related Businesses

Two businesses using similar skills are:

Commercial-mortgage broker. Brokers who have contacts with many real-estate lenders can help clients secure real-estate loans with the best possible terms. Some work in the residential market; some with commercial properties. They charge a commission for these services. You need to be a licensed real-estate agent to do this or work with someone who is.

Venture-capital broker. Brokers who match owners of undercapitalized businesses with sources of money receive a percentage of the money raised and sometimes an equity position in the venture. Four hundred thousand of the 600,000 new businesses starting up every year need additional funds. But according to venture-capital broker André Brady, only one in 1,000 will get funded using only venture capital. But by using creative financing, like various forms of leasing, bridge loans, second mortgages, accounts-receivable financing, and real-estate loans, the broker can close a deal for about one in 20.

Tronsoft, Inc., can help you enter venture-capital brokering. For more information write to Tronsoft, 133 West de la Guerra, Santa Barbara, CA 93101; (805) 564-3048. An excellent resource to learn about creative financing is *Guerilla Financing,* by Bruce Blechman and Jay Conrad Levinson, (Boston: Houghton Mifflin, 1991).

▣ First Steps

- If a real-estate broker license is required in your state, contact the state agency responsible for licensing realtors for the procedures necessary to become licensed.
- To gain experience in this business, you might begin by working for an established broker.
- If you have no experience with analyzing financial statements, take a community-college class or other adult-education course in basic business finance.
- Talk with other business brokers.

▣ Where to Turn for Information and Help

BOOKS

The Business Brokers Reference Guide, Business Brokerage Press, Box 247, Concord, MA 01742; (617) 369-5254. Cost: $54.

Guide to Buying and Selling a Business, by James Hansen, Business Brokerage Press, Box 247, Concord, MA 01742; (617) 369-5254.

ORGANIZATIONS

International Business Brokers Association, Box 704, Concord, MA 01742; (508) 369-2490. A professional organization for business brokers, with over 800 members. It offers a certification program and regular conferences.

Institute of Certified Business Counselors, 3485 West First Avenue, Eugene, OR 97402; (503) 345-8064.

MAGAZINES AND NEWSLETTERS

The Business Broker, Business Brokerage Press, Box 247, Concord, MA 01742; (617) 369-5254.

MANUALS

30 Days to a Successful Brokerage, Business Brokerage Press, Box 247, Concord, MA 01742; (617) 369-5254. Cost: $90.

TRAINING COURSES

Business Brokerage Consultants, 1998 County Road 427 N, Suite 6, Longwood, FL 32750; (407) 331-8133. A home-study course on becoming a business broker that includes a manual, audiocassette tapes, and telephone consultation. $165.

SOFTWARE

ValuSource, 1939 Grand Avenue, San Diego, CA 92109; (800) 825-8763. Offers two choices: *Value Express* for businesses under $300,000, and *ValuSource* for larger businesses.

REFERRAL SERVICES

Two services to help you find buyers and sellers are:

Franchise Broker Network, 3617A Silverside Road, Wilmington, DE 19810; (302) 478-0200.

Nation-List Headquarters, 1660 South Albion Street, No. 407, Denver, CO 80222; (303) 759-5267.

■ ■ ■ ■
BUSINESS NETWORK ORGANIZER

A business network organizer solves two of the most common problems small-business owners face: marketing their business, and not having time to spend with colleagues and associates. A networking organizer sets up groups of small-business owners to meet regularly, usually weekly, in order to give each other business referrals and to help one another get business. Each group or club has only one person from any particular type of business or profession, so there's no competition among the members of the group.

Such networking organizations provide a structured way for professionals and business associates to refer clients and customers to each other. Also called *word-of-mouth marketing,* getting business through referrals from other people has been a common practice for a long time. Increasingly, however, instead of making contacts in traditional service and fraternal organizations like the Rotary, Eagles, Elks, Lions, and Moose, small businesses are making valuable business contacts through what's called networking organizations. These organizations are sometimes referred to as *leads clubs* or *networking groups.* The Network, founded by Ivan Misner in 1985, is an example of such a group.

Initially, business networking groups were informal in nature. However, Misner observes that "despite good intentions, it's easy for informal networking meetings to turn into coffee klatches and social gatherings as people seek to keep meetings friendly and to please everyone." That's where networking as a business comes in. The business network organizer sets up and runs networking groups, which follow a system of procedures to help the members stick to the business of getting business for each other. In fact, Misner's fast-growing Network has a 160-page manual that outlines a proven framework for enabling members to network effectively.

The Network has become a full-time business for Misner, who is beginning new types of networks and franchising the original one. Even when someone chooses to manage a network as a sideline venture, the operator of a network can also market his or her principal business in the process of meeting the hundreds of people who pass through the typical networking meetings over several months.

While some critics believe that networking is a fad, Misner says, "Networking has proven to be as much of a fad as having a sale." In fact, Tom Peters, coauthor of *In Search of Excellence* and *Thriving on Chaos,* advises small businesses to devote 75 percent of their marketing time and money to developing a structured word-of-mouth network. Networking is as it always has been—the most reliable and cost-effective way for a small business to make sure that it has business.

☑ Knowledge and Skills You Need to Have

- You need to have an outgoing personality.
- You need to be comfortable speaking in front of groups and able to speak well extemporaneously.
- You must be able to motivate, lead, and educate people in the skill of networking.
- You have to be able to set up and run an organization.

👍 Advantages

- The market for networking organizations is expanding.
- Running a networking group provides an excellent opportunity to market another business or profession.
- You make many valuable contacts throughout the business community.

👎 Disadvantages

- Unless you run multiple chapters, a networking organization will not provide a full-time income. But it can be a route to expand another business.
- Networking means constantly attending early-morning meetings.
- Members who don't use what the organization teaches about effective networking techniques may blame the networking organization for not providing them with enough business leads.

🐷 Start-Up Costs

	Low	High
Computer with hard disk	$1,000	$ 2,500
Laser printer	$ 650	$ 1,600
Copy machine	$ 900	$ 1,500
Accounting, database-management, word-processing, and desktop-publishing softwares	$ 750	$ 1,000
Office furniture, especially an ergonomic chair	$ 600	$ 800
Business cards, letterhead, envelopes, brochures, and manuals	$5,000	$ 7,500
Total	$8,900	$14,900

The above figures are for starting up on your own. If you are starting as a franchise, your costs will range from $4,000 to $25,000.

💲 Pricing

Members pay $200 to $1,000 a year.

▣ Potential Earnings

TYPICAL ANNUAL GROSS REVENUES:

- If you set up and run the organization yourself: $120,000, based on $6,000 per chapter and 20 chapters.
- If you run a chapter as part of a franchise: $18,000.

OVERHEAD: High (over 40 percent; includes room rentals, promotional materials, and mailings).

▣ The Best Ways to Get Business

- Personal contacts.
- Attending and exhibiting at trade shows.
- Using direct-mail advertising to small businesses and professionals.

▣ Franchises

American Business Associates, 475 Park Avenue South, 16th Floor, New York, NY 10016; (212) 689-2834. In business since 1983 and with four franchisees at the time of this writing, provides seven days training. The franchise fee is $25,000, and financing is available.

The Network, 1341 Ancona Drive, La Verne, CA 91750; (800) 825-8286 outside Southern California, or (714) 624-2227. In business since 1985, the Network has 140 chapters in 15 states. Newly franchised in 1991, the franchises are actually part-time businesses. To become a franchisee, you must begin as a regional director for the Network. There is no fee involved to become a regional director, and the Network pays all costs of launching your first chapter. It provides several days of on-site training and a 160-page operating manual. If the chapter does well and the relationship is mutually satisfactory, there is an opportunity to franchise. The fee is $4,800 to $5,000.

▣ First Steps

If you've had experience networking and getting business through word-of-mouth marketing, develop procedures for running your network. Then begin recruiting a membership. Don't start a networking group until you have at least 20 paid members. To recruit members invite people to free networking meetings at which you describe the organization and demonstrate the process; then follow up by phone with those who are seriously interested. Don't begin a second chapter until your first one is thriving.

If you have had no experience with networking, your first step should be to join a network or two and become familiar with what works and what doesn't.

🔲 Where to Turn for Information and Help

BOOKS

The First Five Minutes, by Norman King. Englewood Cliffs, NJ: Prentice-Hall, 1987.

How to Work a Room, by Susan Rowane. New York: Warner Books, 1988.

Is Your "Net" Working? by Ann Boe and Betty Young. New York: Wiley, 1989.

Networking for Success, by Ivan Misner, AIM Consulting, 1341 Ancona Drive, La Verne, 91750; (800) 825-8286 (outside Southern California) and (714) 624-2227 (in Southern California).

NATIONAL NETWORKING ORGANIZATIONS

American Business Associates. See the "Franchises" section above.

LEADS, 279 Carlsbad, Carlsbad, CA 92018; (619) 434-3761.

LeTip, 4907 Morena Boulevard, Suite 13, San Diego, CA 92117; (800) 255-3847.

The National Association of Women Business Owners, 600 South Federal Street, #400, Chicago, IL 60605; (312) 922-0465.

The Network. See the "Franchises" section above.

■ ■ ■ ■

BUSINESS PLAN WRITER

Today a new business begins every 24 seconds. Most of these new businesses are small businesses. In fact, small businesses employ half the nation's workers and provide two out of every three first jobs. While most small businesses start up without a formal written business plan, research shows that those with a good business plan increase their likelihood of success. A business plan is like a road map. It shows entrepreneurs where they're headed, gives insights into whether their concept is feasible, and lays out estimates and projections of expenses and revenues. As a business grows, a formal business plan is also needed in order to seek loans, attract outside investors, get acquired, or franchise an operation.

The market for this business is best in regions where businesses are starting up or expanding. Linda Elkins, who makes a full-time living writing business plans in Annapolis, Maryland, finds she gets most of her business from companies that are just beginning, followed by those seeking second-round financing. Linda points out that, in this business, "you are basically a translator. You listen to your client's ideas, review their financial data and the other information they have gathered, and then put this information into the clearest, most direct format possible." Sometimes your job is also to point out additional information the client needs to gather in order to formulate a good plan.

Software programs are available to make writing business plans easier, quicker, and more professional. These programs also make it easy to examine and present alternative scenarios for a business, using spreadsheets and what-if scenarios.

✔ Knowledge and Skills You Need to Have

- You need to have the ability to see a business situation from the viewpoint both of the owners and of potential funding sources.
- Good business writing and grammar skills and a high level of organizational skills are required.
- You need to have enough of a background in business to understand the financial and marketing aspects of running a business.
- You need the ability to present yourself credibly as an expert who can be relied upon.
- You need the ability to motivate and inspire cooperation from your clients.

🐷 Start-Up Costs

	Low	High
Computer with hard disk	$1,000	$ 2,500
Laser printer	$1,600	$ 2,500
Word-processing, spreadsheet, chart-making, and business-planning software	$1,200	$ 1,800
Desk furniture, especially an ergonomic chair	$ 600	$ 800
Business cards, letterhead, envelopes	$ 400	$ 600
Brochure and promotional material (Customized brochures are suitable)	$ 100	$ 2,000
Organizational dues for networking	$ 250	$ 250
Total	$5,150	$10,450

👍 Advantages

- There is little competition. Few people specialize in business plan writing.
- The work is challenging and varied.
- You have the opportunity to learn about new people and new business ideas.
- It can be very rewarding to assist others in achieving success.
- If you take an equity interest in a client's business as part of your fee, you have the potential to strike it rich.

⬛ Disadvantages

- Because business start-ups and expansions are sensitive to economic cycles, this business may be subject to feast-or-famine cycles.
- Because you're often working with new or changing businesses, you may encounter clients who have collection or legal problems.

💲 Pricing

Fees range from $2,000 to $5,000 for each business plan. Proven consultants can charge as much as $25,000 per plan. You can take part of your fee in cash and the remainder in stock, equity, or a percentage of capital raised with the plan.

Some people charge $5,000 and work with the client until the client is satisfied with a final plan. Others charge less but provide a maximum of two drafts, with each additional version costing more.

For a few hundred dollars, you can also offer to write a detailed outline or to edit a plan your client has written. Small jobs such as these can create a referral base.

🏦 Potential Earnings

TYPICAL ANNUAL GROSS REVENUES: $24,000 to $100,000 based on 12 plans a year at $2,000 a plan or 20 plans a year at $5,000 each.

OVERHEAD: Low (20 percent or less).

🗾 Best Ways to Get Business

- Networking through personal contacts at organizations such as trade and business associations for those industries or fields in which you have experience; it's recommended that you join two organizations and become active in both.
- Teaching courses on starting a business, entrepreneurship, and small-business management.
- Making contacts with bankers, venture capitalists, and people at universities or organizations that run new-business *incubator* workshops, offer mentor programs, or have an entrepreneurship center.
- Showing a sample of your own business plan; an example can be more important than a brochure.

👤 First Steps

- Begin by reading about and studying business planning and learning to use business-planning software.
- Do a plan or two without fee to gain experience.

📘 **Where to Turn for Information and Help**

BOOKS

Many books on starting a business contain outlines for developing a business plan. Here are several:

The Business Plan: A State of the Art Guide, by Michael O'Donnell, Lord Publishing, One Apple Hill, Natick MA 01760; (508) 651-9955, 1988.

The Complete Handbook for the Entrepreneur, by Gary Brenner, Joel Ewan, and Henry Custer. Englewood Cliffs, NJ: Prentice-Hall, 1990.

How to Prepare and Present a Business Plan, by Joe Mancuso. Englewood Cliffs, NJ: Prentice-Hall, 1983.

SOFTWARE

Software such as the following packages can take you and your clients step-by-step through developing a business plan.

BizPlan Builder, Jian, 127 Second Street, Top Floor, Los Altos, CA 94022; (800) 442-7373.

Ronstadts Financials, Lord Publishing, One Apple Hill, Natick MA 01760; (508) 651-9955.

Success Inc., Melbourne House, 18801 Cowan, Irvine, CA 92714; (714) 833-8710.

Venture, Star Software, 363 Van Ness Way, Torrance, CA 90501; (213) 533-1190.

■ ■ ■ ■

CLEANING SERVICE

Modern life leaves most of us with very little time for cleaning up. According to studies reported in *American Demographics* magazine, most people today feel like they're having to squeeze more and more into less and less free time. And it's no wonder. Over half of all households consist of two-career couples. More than 40 percent of all households consist of a single person. Almost a quarter of all families today have only one parent. Almost every sixth person in the work force works more than one job.

So who has time to clean? And who wants to anyway? Housecleaning ranks as American's most disliked daily task, even less popular than grocery shopping, cooking, and going to work. According to a survey by Spiffits (manufacturers of premoistened towels), 13 percent of us hate cleaning and 66 percent merely tolerate it. A survey by *Family Circle* magazine of 35,000 working women and homemakers shows that 42 percent end up ignoring household chores. And a *Good Housekeeping* survey shows that two-thirds of women are unhappy with the way they keep house because they can't keep up with the standards by which they were raised.

It's just this type of dilemma that has made residential and commercial cleaning services one of the fastest-growing segments of the economy, with the number of such companies more than doubling in the last five years. Home cleaning alone is a $92-million-a-year industry. The Bureau of Labor Statistics says there will be more than half a million people cleaning things for others by the year 2000.

The cleaning industry provides many opportunities, and cleaning businesses are among the easiest businesses to start profitably from home. The standard cleaning or janitorial service is the most common. You can serve either residential or commercial clients. Specializing in cleaning tasks that the general services don't provide is also a profitable way to start a cleaning service. Examples of specialties are apartment preparation, carpet cleaning, floor cleaning, ceiling cleaning, drapery and upholstery cleaning, window cleaning, venetian-blind cleaning, air-duct cleaning, pool cleaning, drain cleaning, chimney cleaning, and yard and lawn services, which are a form of cleaning, too.

All these businesses can be run from home, although, of course, the cleaning is done on the customer's premises. You can do this business alone or as a family, or, if you choose, you can hire employees to do the actual cleaning. In some communities you can earn a good living specializing in offering only one type of cleaning service. In other communities you will need to offer a combination of services in order to make a good living throughout the year. Just how good an opportunity cleaning services can be is evidenced by the large number of franchises and training and licensing programs available to help you set them up. Further information follows about each of the various types of cleaning services.

☑ Knowledge and Skills

One of the greatest advantages of starting a cleaning service is that there is very little formal knowledge or experience needed. You simply need:

- the appropriate equipment and supplies
- knowledge of how to use them
- the willingness to work hard and produce superior results

🔧 Advantages

- Generally start-up costs and overhead for all types of cleaning services are low.
- You can get free technical expertise from janitorial supply houses and product manufacturers.
- Usually there are ample customers who need these services.
- By adding crews of workers, your business can grow very large and still be home-based.
- You can build a base of regular clients who will use your services repeatedly.

🔧 Disadvantages

- In general, most types of cleaning businesses have a low status image, which must be overcome by creating a very clean, neat, and professional identity.
- Cleaning is hard, dirty work. You'll have to be willing to roll up your sleeves and get your hands and clothes dirty.
- Some cleaning is seasonal or periodic in nature.
- Unless you hire employees, your income is limited by the number of hours you can work in a day. And when you hire crews, you will need to bill, which can lead to collection problems.

💲 📇 Pricing and Potential Earnings

See the individual cleaning businesses described below.

📋 Best Ways to Get Business

- Taking out classified ads in weekly community newspapers. This is one home business for which advertising works very well. Find the local paper that produces the best results and advertise there indefinitely.
- Listing in the yellow pages.
- Distributing flyers in neighborhoods or business districts.
- Calling directly on businesses that could use your services.
- Sending direct mail offering some type of introductory discount, and then turning each customer you get into a regular weekly or monthly account.
- For more periodic types of services, keeping names of past clients in a computer database and calling them periodically.

🚶 First Steps

- Take advantage of free training and expertise from janitorial supply houses.
- Wait until you see what character your service takes before you invest in significant amounts of supplies and equipment.
- If you do commercial cleaning, you can start as a sideline business because you are usually working evenings and weekends. In contrast, residential customers expect cleaning to be done during weekday hours.
- Residential cleaning costs less to start because commercial services are often required to have a bond and the equipment needed is larger and more expensive.
- For equipment you use infrequently, rent rather than buy.
- Offer to help out other services on days you don't have business. You can learn from them and they can help you in return when you get busy.
- Carry a pager or use an answering service to make sure you don't miss calls while you are working.

Air-Duct Cleaning

Cleaning heating and air-conditioning ducts involves using vacuums and other equipment to remove dust and debris from the ducts in commercial or residential buildings. This is actually an environmentally oriented business, because inefficient heating systems can waste 50 percent of the energy they generate, and clogged air-conditioning systems waste electricity. And it's a year-round business: air-conditioning in the summer; heating in the winter.

Duct cleaning has traditionally been done using a truck-mounted super-powered vacuum. Such equipment, however, runs from $25,000 to $50,000 and may leave much of the finer debris. Air-Care, however, has developed a system that is totally portable and removes not only the heavy build-up and debris, but also the finer dust that increases growth of bacteria, mold, and mildew. Air-Care's program is not a franchise; it's a dealer program in which for a $15,000 fee they provide all the equipment, training, and promotional materials for you to use their methods in your business.

Using this system, people can charge an average of $500 per job and do 2 jobs a day. Therefore, if you specialize in air-duct cleaning and work 4 days a week, 50 weeks a year, you can gross $200,000 per year. Air-duct cleaning can also be an adjunct to general cleaning, chimney cleaning, or carpet cleaning. For more information contact Air-Care, Air Duct Decontamination Division, DPL Enterprises, 5115 South Industrial Road, Suite 506, Las Vegas, NV 89118; (800) 322-9919.

NRI Schools, McGraw-Hill Continuing Education Center (4401 Connecticut Avenue, Washington, DC 20008), offers a home-study course in air-conditioning, heating and refrigeration. And International Correspondence Schools (925 Oak Street, Scranton, PA 18540), offers a career diploma program in air-conditioning and refrigeration.

Carpet Cleaning

Carpet-cleaning services can serve both residential and commercial clients and can be easily started on a part-time basis. Wall-to-wall carpeting is commonplace in both homes and offices, but since cleaning carpets requires special equipment, most people hire someone instead of trying to do it themselves. Carpet-cleaning methods today include steam, dry extraction, and carbonation. Some carpet cleaners also clean draperies and upholstery.

Costs for start-up run around $3,000 to $4,000 depending on the type of equipment you buy. You should also have a station wagon or van, because equipment does not fit well into a regular car. When you're first starting you can rent machines by the day. You can charge a flat fee such as $150 per job, or you can charge by the square foot (preferred) or by the room. Prices range from 10 to 25 cents a square foot depending on how much carpet there is, how dirty the carpet is, and whether it can be done by machine or must be done by hand. You can also charge for such extras as preconditioning, stain removal, and stain guarding. Usually this works out to be somewhere between $25 to $60 an hour, for an annual gross income of $30,000 to $60,000.

No real background is required, but you do have to have good equipment and know how to use it. Edward Svadlenka, who owns Mighty Clean Enterprises, finds that there's plenty of business. If you want to learn more, here are additional resources:

BOOKS

Carpet Cleaning Service Business Guide, Entrepreneur Magazine, 2392 Morse Avenue, Box 19787, Irvine, CA 92713; (800) 421-2300. Cost: $69.95.

The How-To Handbook of Carpets, Carpet and Rug Cleaning Institute, 208 West Cuyler Street, Dalton, GA 30720; (404) 278-3176.

ORGANIZATIONS

The Carpet and Rug Cleaning Institute, 208 West Cuyler Street, Dalton, GA 30720; (404) 278-3176. A trade organization for rug manufacturers that has information about types of carpets and carpet care.

NEWSLETTERS

Cleantalk, Cleaning Consultant Services, Box 1273, Seattle, WA 98111; (206) 682-9748. Covers how to start a home cleaning/window-washing service and offers referrals.

TRAINING PROGRAMS AND FRANCHISES

If you're interested in this business but don't want to go it alone, here are four companies you can affiliate with that will teach you the ropes.

Chem-Dry Carpet Cleaning, 3330 Cameron Park Drive, #700, Cameron Park, CA 95682; (800) 841-6583. Offers its franchisees a patented carpet-cleaning method that uses carbonation. This method has two major benefits: lack of environmentally toxic chemicals, and quicker drying time. The franchise fee is $9,950 plus a flat $175 monthly royalty. In business since 1967.

Host, 16th Street, Box 1648, Racine, WI 53401; (800) 558-9439. Offers a free or very low cost three-hour training program in its dry-extraction carpet-cleaning system, available through local janitorial-supply distributors. Host equipment and products can be purchased for around $2,000; once you have purchased the system you can attend the three-day Host School in Racine, Wisconsin, for free.

Rug Doctor Pro, 2788 North Larkin Avenue, Suite 5A, Fresno, CA; (800) 678-7844. Offers a franchise as a carpet, upholstery, drapery, ceiling, and wall cleaning service for residential and commercial customers. In business for 18 years. The minimum franchise fee is $5,000, and start-up costs run from $10,000 to $20,000, depending on the equipment needed. Financing is available.

Von Schrader Company, 1600 Junction Avenue, Racine, WI 53403; (800) 626-6916. Will provide training, equipment, and uniforms for room, carpet, upholstery, and wall cleaning. The fee is $2,895. This is not a franchise.

Ceiling Cleaning

Although most commercial facilities need to have acoustical ceilings cleaned, most cleaning services don't provide this, so there is a need. You can buy one of the many chemical cleaning packages available from ceiling-cleaning distributors, who will instruct you in how to use them. Or you can tie in with a company like Ceiltech, which offers a start-up ceiling-cleaning program for $3,500. Ceiltech estimates that you can earn $150 an hour using its system to clean ceilings. Or ceiling cleaning can be an add-on service to a general or carpet cleaning service. For more information you can contact Ceiltech at 825 Gatepark Drive, #3, Daytona Beach, FL 31224; (800) 756-9299 or (904) 239-9426.

Air-Care also has a ceiling-cleaning system. When you become an Air-Care dealer, the company provides all the equipment, training, and promotional materials for $12,500. Contact Air-Care, Air Duct Decontamination Division, DPL Enterprises, 5115 South Industrial Road, Suite 506, Las Vegas, NV 89118; (800) 322-9919.

(See also Rug Doctor Pro and Steamatic above for ceiling-cleaning franchise opportunities.)

Chimney Cleaning

Did you know there are 25 million fireplaces in the United States and sooner or later they all need cleaning? In fact, failing to clean a chimney that's being used regularly can cause a serious fire hazard. So if you live in a climate and community where people burn wood in their fireplaces regularly, you can earn up to $400 a day as a chimney sweep. This is a low-overhead business. All the equipment you need fits easily into a car. In addition to a specialized vacuum and a set of tools, you need a ladder and the knowledge of how to do the work.

Garry Trotter was working in a grocery store when he started a part-time business as a chimney sweep. Within five months he had made more money than he earned in a year at his grocery job. He knew it was time to become his own boss, full-time. His business, Thee Chimney Sweep, is now available as a franchise. It offers a comprehensive three-week training program and all needed equipment. The franchise fee is $7,500, and there is no royalty. Contact Thee Chimney Sweep, Route #8 Box 36 Northeast, Rome, Georgia 30161; (404) 232-5261.

Floor Cleaning

In his book *Cleaning Up for a Living,* Don Aslett says there are few good floor-care professionals, and yet stripping, waxing, sanding, and refinishing hardwood floors is certainly a service needed by homeowners and business establishments like restaurants. The necessary equipment can be purchased from a wholesale janitorial service for less than $2,000. And you can charge considerably more per hour than a general housecleaning service.

A company called Hardwood Floor Restoration offers a start-up package for this business that costs from $8,000 to $10,000 and includes equipment, supplies, training manuals, videos, and phone consultation. The company can be reached at 2270 Pope Road, Douglasville, GA 30135; (404) 739-6946.

Mobile Power Washing

Using a truck equipped with a tank that holds hundreds of gallons of hot water that is propelled through high-pressure hoses, mobile power washers go where large things need cleaning. They clean construction sites; aluminum siding; old brick, cement, and marble on buildings being restored; farm, industrial, and construction equipment; garbage trucks, airplanes, and boats; parking lots; restaurant freezers and vent hoods; awnings and signs; air-conditioning units, phone booths, shopping carts, and hotel dumpsters. They also travel to residences to clean driveways, patios, kitchen floors, siding, basements, pool decks, and mobile homes.

When Greg Souser bought power cleaning equipment he thought he would use it to bring in some extra income each month. Little did he know his home-based company, Tri-State Mobile Power Wash, would become a $100,000-a-year business. Souser borrowed $10,000 from the bank to launch the business. He works with a partner and spends 50 percent of his time cleaning, 30 percent selling, and 20 percent administering. He likes the regularity of working with his monthly accounts. His company motto is We Wash Anything, Anywhere, Anytime.

The equipment runs from $800 to $10,000, depending on how much water pressure it has, how many gallons per minute it produces, and whether it has hot and cold water. It is available through industrial steam-cleaning equipment suppliers, which can be found in the yellow pages.

Two guides provide information about this business: *Mobile Exterior Surface Cleaning,* and *Construction Cleanup.* They are available from Entrepreneur Magazine, 2392 Morse Avenue, Box 19787, Irvine, CA 92713; (800) 421-2300.

If you'd prefer not to go it alone, here are several companies with programs to get you started.

Sparkle International, 26851 Richmond Road, Cleveland, OH 44146; (216) 464-4212. Offers a franchise that includes a customized van with the mobile cleaning unit installed. All training, chemicals, and equipment are included, along with marketing and sales information. Franchise fees run from $7,500 to $45,000, and you can get a protected territory. In business for 26 years.

Wash America, 943 Taft Vineland Road, Orlando, FL 32824; (407) 855-2215 or (800) 331-7765. Provides you with seven hot-and-cold water systems in a trailer complete with pumps, heater, storage tank, chemicals, hoses, sandblasting equipment, and the ladders and clothing you need to use it. Not a franchise. Total cost is $5,000 to $24,000. Some financing is available.

Express Wash, 908 Niagara Falls Boulevard, North Tonawanda, NY 14120; (416) 466-4164. Provides a start-up package for a mobile car/boat/plane wash. The package, which costs from $1,695 to $1,995, includes supplies, training, and a cleaning system.

Wash on Wheels Marine Clean, 5401 South Bryant Avenue, Sanford, FL 32773; (407) 321-4010. Although Wash on Wheels also offers franchise opportunities for outdoor and indoor pressure-cleaning services, their Marine Clean franchise is a boat-and-yacht cleaning service. The down payment is $7,900 and includes the franchise fee, training, and equipment.

Pool Cleaning

If you live in a community where many homes have year-round swimming pools, pool cleaning can be a way to earn a steady, regular income working out of doors. As anyone who has a swimming pool knows, pools have to be cleaned properly and on schedule or you've got trouble. Therefore, most pool owners turn this task over to someone they can rely on to make sure it gets done right.

You do need to learn how to do this business, because it involves using various hazardous chemicals, which must be used in the proper ways. If you don't have any experience, chemical manufacturers provide some training, as do stores that sell spas and swimming-pool equipment. The best route, however, would be to work for a time as an assistant to someone in the business.

Start-up costs, including equipment and supplies run from $500 to $1,000. You can earn $50,000 or more a year. A guide called *Pool Cleaning and Repair* is available for $69.95 from Entrepreneur Magazine, 2392 Morse Avenue, Box 19787, Irvine, CA 92713; (800) 421-2300.

Residential and Commercial Cleaning

You can start a residential cleaning service by investing $1,000 in basic professional cleaning supplies and equipment. For start-up on a shoestring, you can use the supplies and equipment on the premises of your clients or you can use your household equipment until you can have enough income from the business to purchase additional equipment. Fees for general housecleaning run from $50 to $75 a day or $10 to $20 per hour for the average home, depending on the going rates in the community. Income from working full-time by yourself can be $20,000 to $30,000 a year. You can earn more if you work as a husband-and-wife team or hire teams of individuals to work for you.

Commercial cleaning services are also in demand. Although large office buildings contract with janitorial services that provide crews to clean all the offices each night, smaller buildings and small retailers also need cleaning services. These contracts can become a steady, reliable source of business. Commercial janitorial services can charge more than residential services, and a one-person service can earn about $50,000 a year.

One way to learn how to run a cleaning service is to work briefly for an established service. In addition, here are several resources you can use to learn about starting a cleaning or janitorial service.

BOOKS AND MANUALS

Cleaning Up for a Living: Everything You Need to Know to Become a Successful Building Service Contractor, by Don Aslett and Mark Browning. Crozet, VA: Betterway Publications, 1991.

Comprehensive Custodial Training Program: Instructor's Guide, by William Friggin, Cleaning Consultant Services, Box 1273, Seattle, WA 98111; (206) 682-9748. A comprehensive guide to training employees.

Everything You Need to Know to Start a Housecleaning Service, by Mary Pat Johnson. Cleaning Consultant Services, Box 1273, Seattle, WA 98111; (206) 682-9748.

Is There Life after Housework?, by Don Aslett. Cincinnati: Writer's Digest Books, 1980. Step-by-step instructions for cleaning every area of the home in 75 percent less time. Includes sample contracts.

AUDIOTAPES

How to Start a Cleaning or Janitorial Service, by Lynne Frances, Here's How, Box 5172, Santa Monica, CA 90409. For the self-employed professional cleaner.

VIDEOS

Home Care Series, 2 vols., by Don Aslett, Article One Publishing, Box 1682, Pocatello, ID 83204. These videos demonstrate professional housecleaning methods. Although they are designed for people to use in cleaning their own home, you can also use them to learn cleaning methods for starting a business.

NEWSLETTERS

Cleantalk, Cleaning Consultant Services, Box 1273, Seattle, WA 98111; (206) 682-9748. Covers material on how to start a home cleaning or window washing service and offers referrals.

ORGANIZATIONS

Building Service Contractors Association International, 8315 Lee Highway, Suite 301, Fairfax, VA; (800) 368-3414. Trade association for commercial cleaning companies. Offers educational programs, printed materials, and networking for members.

FRANCHISES

There are many franchises that will help you get started in this business. The following ones encourage you or allow you to operate from home.

Classy Maids, Box 160879, Altamonte Springs, FL 32716-0879, 800/445-5238. In business since 1980; franchise fee is from $5,900 to $9,500, which includes the cost of supplies, uniforms, and so on. Financing is available for half the fee over four years.

Jani-King, 4950 Keller Springs Road, Suite 190, Dallas, TX 75248; (800) 552-5264; in Texas, (800) 533-9406. Specializes in commercial cleaning. In business since 1969. Variable franchise fee.

ServiceMaster, 855 Ridge Lake Boulevard, Memphis, TN 38119; (800) 338-6833. In business since 1947, one of the oldest home-based franchises and the biggest such business in the world, with 4,029 franchises. The franchise fee ranges from $6,000 to $17,500; financing is available for up to 65 percent of the total cost.

Steamatic, Inc., 1601 109th Street, Grand Prairie, TX 75050; 800/527-1295. Specializes in commercial and residential cleaning services, working primarily with insurance companies on settling claims for fire and water damage from accidents or natural disasters. In business since 1946. In addition to general cleaning, Steamatic franchisees learn how to clean carpets, upholstery, draperies, electronics, and air ducts, as well as how to do wood restorations and fire and flood repair. Steamatic is also heavily involved in environmental cleaning. Franchise fee ranges from $10,000 to $17,000, and financing is available.

Window Cleaning

You've undoubtedly heard the saying *We don't do windows.* But virtually every residence and business establishment in the country has windows, and someone has to clean them periodically. This demand has led to specialized window-cleaning services.

Clean windows are particularly important to retail shops which count on a clear view of their merchandise. And retailers make good clients because they need their windows cleaned frequently and regularly. Although you actually charge per pane, per side, or per story, you can earn what amounts to $15 to $25 an hour for residential clients and $20 to $35 an hour for commercial clients. And since there's plenty of work, you can work a full 40 hours a week and earn about $50,000 a year.

One advantage of this business is that you are working outdoors. Dan Rastorfer, of Silverstreak Services, tells us the work doesn't need to be boring because you can work while listening to a radio or tape headset and you meet a lot of interesting people. Start-up costs can be as low as $200 for a pail, a bucket, squeegees, and ladders. You need average motor abilities, and it helps to be somewhat ambidextrous and have no fear of heights.

You do need to have health insurance, however, because there is a risk of injury. You should also have liability insurance, which runs about $2,500 a year (more if you have employees). A related service is removing window paint from store windows after holidays and sales.

How to Start a Window Cleaning Business: A Guide to Sales, Procedures and Operations, by Judy Suval, Cleaning Consultant Services, Box 1273, Seattle, WA 98111; (206) 682-9748.

Window Washing Service Business Guide, Entrepreneur Magazine, 2392 Morse Avenue, Box 19787, Irvine, CA 92713; (800) 421-2300. Cost: $69.95.

American Window Cleaner, 27 Oak Creek Road, El Sobrante, CA 94803; (415) 222-7080. "The voice of the professional window cleaner."

Window Blind Cleaning

Miniblinds, vertical blinds, and venetian blinds adorn the windows in millions of households and office buildings across America. But if you've ever tried to clean these blinds, you know why most cleaning services not only don't do windows, but don't do blinds, either. A blind-cleaning service, however, can make up to several hundred dollars per job. Start-up costs and overhead can be very low. And little specialized skill is required.

You can buy specialized equipment to clean the blinds faster and more efficiently. This equipment runs from $500 to $20,000, and you can find out about it through cleaning and janitorial supply houses. *Mini-Blind Cleaning/ Installation,* a guide that describes the equipment and supplies you need, along with other guidance on starting this business is available for $69.95 from Entrepreneur Magazine, 2392 Morse Avenue, Box 19787, Irvine, CA 92713; (800) 421-2300.

S. Morantz, Inc. has created a specialized blind-cleaning machine. The Morantz family has been in the blind-cleaning business for 60 years. They provide you with the special equipment they've developed, teach you how to use it, and support you in developing your business for a fee that ranges from $10,000 to $20,000. Contact S. Morantz, Inc., 9984 Gantry Road, Philadelphia, PA 19115; (215) 969-0266.

■ ■ ■ ■

COLLECTION AGENCY

There's nothing new about the idea that businesses often need help in collecting money owed to them. For many years, businesses have hired agencies to collect on delinquent accounts. But what is new is that the collection business is changing in ways that give a home-based collection service a distinct advantage in serving small businesses, particularly health-care providers.

In large collection agencies, the people hired to make collections work on commission and often are financially hard up themselves. Motivated by their own desperation, they tend to harangue the accounts they're assigned to and often are encouraged to do so. According to Michael Kelly, who operates a home-based collection service in Columbus, Ohio, this is not the most effective approach. People who own their own collection business and have chosen it as a career adopt a more professional, problem-solving approach with debtors and are able to collect on a higher percentage of accounts than the traditional, high-pressure, hard-nosed collection agent.

Another advantage for home-based collection services is that big agencies do not collect on most accounts. Statistics show that 20 percent of people who are delinquent on their accounts will pay after receiving only one dun notice in the mail. The big agencies make no attempt to collect on smaller bills after that initial mailing, putting their people to work on collecting only the larger bills that will produce a sizable commission when paid. With lower overhead, however, a home-based collection service can afford to collect on accounts of all sizes, thereby increasing the money collected for its clients, and still make sufficient money to prosper.

Using a personal computer and special collections software, a home-based collection service can become very efficient by reducing the time and labor required for handling mailings and accounting. Using on-line database services can also reduce the cost of tracking debtors.

There are two specialty areas you might want to focus on:

Health-care providers. Today three out of every four dollars sent out for collections are for hospital and medical bills not covered by insurance. For the most part, the people who owe money for their health care will pay on these debts if dealt with appropriately.

Day-care businesses. Collecting on unpaid bills for day care is another growing area for collections. With more women working and having to place their children in day care that may cost as much as $125 per child a week, parents can get behind on day care payments as much as any other kind of debt.

Other typical collections customers are grocery stores (bad checks), cable-television operators, and department stores.

Collecting money from people is regulated by both the Federal Fair Debt Collection Practices Act and state laws. State laws typically require people who do collections to be bonded and licensed; however, obtaining a license is usually not difficult.

✔ Knowledge and Skills You Need to Have

- To do well in this business you need to have good communication skills. You need to be able to persuade businesses to hire you while their outstanding accounts are still young, and to convince the people you contact to pay the bill you're collecting on.
- Patience is essential. You must be both firm and fair with the people who owe money. Rather than haranguing them, you need to see them not just as debtors but as people with money problems whom you can assist.

- A collector needs to have high self-esteem. You need to be able to keep your self-esteem intact in the face of rejection when people refuse to pay their bills or lie to you.
- Basic budgeting skills are needed so that you will have sufficient knowledge to advise debtors on how to begin solving their financial problems.
- You need to know the Federal Fair Debt Collection Practices Act and the laws in your state regarding collections.
- If you will be collecting on medical bills, you need to have an understanding of health-insurance policies and billing practices.

Start-Up Costs

	Low	High
Computer with hard disk	$1,000	$ 2,500
Printer	$ 300	$ 1,600
Specialized collections software or a combination of word-processing, database, spreadsheet, and bookkeeping software	$ 80	$ 2,495
Telephone headset	$ 40	$ 70
Office furniture, especially an ergonomic chair	$ 600	$ 800
Business cards, letterhead, envelopes	$ 200	$ 600
Brochure	$1,000	$ 2,000
Organizational dues	$ 250	$ 250
Totals	$3,470	$10,315

Advantages

- This work is both challenging and rewarding. When you help make it possible for someone to pay a bill, everyone wins.
- Sometimes you're able to help people solve their financial problems and avoid having to go into bankruptcy.

Disadvantages

- People may return your phone calls at all hours of the day and night.
- The standard working hours—from 10 A.M. to 8 P.M.—may be inconvenient.
- Hearing about people's financial problems all day long and having people become angry with you or lie to you can be emotionally draining.

Pricing

Commissions range from 25 percent on young accounts to 50 percent on those that must go to court.

▣ Potential Earnings

TYPICAL ANNUAL GROSS REVENUES: $30,000 to $60,000, based on a 25 percent commission for collections of $10,000 to $20,000 per month.

OVERHEAD: Moderate (20 percent to 40 percent; includes leasing a postage meter).

▣ Best Ways to Get Business

- Directly soliciting potential clients by phone or in person. (To see doctors, find out which day of the week they see pharmaceutical reps and ask to be placed on the schedule.)
- Networking in organizations of professionals and small business owners.
- Writing articles for publications that are read by your target clientele.
- Speaking and offering seminars at meetings and trade shows attended by professionals and small-business owners.

▣ First Steps

If you have no background in doing collections work, a good way to gain the experience you need is to take a job for several months with a collection agency. If you have experience, subscribe to *Collector* magazine and review back issues to prepare yourself to get under way.

▣ Where to Turn for Information and Help

KEY REFERENCE

The Fair Debt Collection Practices Act, U.S. Code Annotated. St. Paul, MN: West Publishing Company. Updated annually. Available in libraries.

ORGANIZATIONS

American Collectors Association, Box 35106, 4040 West 70th Street, Minneapolis, MN 55435; (612) 926-6547.

MAGAZINES

Collector, American Collectors Association, Box 35106, 4040 West 70th Street, Minneapolis, MN 55435.

SOFTWARE

Cash Collector, Jian Tools for Sales, 127 Second Street, Top Floor, Los Altos, CA 94022; (800) 442-7373; in Canada, (800) 346-5426. Cost: $179.

Debtmaster, Comtronic Systems, 33305 First Way South, Suite 210, Federal Way, WA 98003; (206) 874-4034; fax (206) 874-9534. Single-user version, $2,495.

■ ■ ■ ■

COMPUTER CONSULTANT

A computer consultant combines the varied roles of hardware and software expert, programmer, technical writer, and business adviser. Although freelance programmers often call themselves consultants, there is a distinction between what the consultant does and what the programmer does. Whereas programmers are valued for their specialized knowhow and are paid to write code, computer consultants take a broader view of an organization and its computer needs.

The consultant asks people what they want to achieve and explores possibilities for how a computer can help them accomplish it. Thus, while programmers work on fixed, objective targets, consultants deal more with broader, moving targets. According to consultant Nigel Dyson-Hudson, "The programmer is like the chief scientist sitting atop a triangle of ever more highly specialized knowledge. Consultants, on the other hand, work on an inverted triangle; the more skilled they get, the broader their knowledge must become."

Another distinction between a computer consultant and a programmer is that whereas programmers accomplish their principal tasks working alone, consultants usually interact with people as an integral part of their work. Martin Schiff, who has a consulting firm, Custom Data Solutions, in Florida, finds that he spends about 50 percent of his time interacting with clients and running his business, and only about 30 percent of his time writing code. (Some consultants don't write any code.) Martin's other activities include installing equipment, providing network upkeep, and helping clients use other products. Some consultants also purchase equipment for the client. Others also design for mainframe computers.

Although Schiff now gets nearly all his business from referrals, he originally got his work from people he met in person and by participating on CompuServe and local bulletin-board systems. By sharing information, swapping or evaluating code, and answering questions, people recognized that Martin knew what he was talking about and decided to hire him. He now has clients from as far away as Alaska, and he has never even seen half of them. He works directly on their computers via telephone using the software program *PC Anywhere,* a remote-access software package.

Schiff believes computer consultants have the best of both worlds; you're on your own, but you're working with established businesses. He says, "The outlook for computer consultants is good. As computers grow more and more powerful and become even cheaper to buy, more and more businesses will need help making the most of them."

☑ Knowledge and Skills You Need to Have

- Technical knowledge of hardware and software is a must.
- You need to know how a business works and where to find the answers you don't have.
- You need to be able to inspire trust. You need to have the ability to communicate on the client's level and know how much information he or she really wants to know. You need to be able to convey with confidence that you understand a client's situation and can take care of it.
- In order to market yourself as a consultant, you need to have a specialty, but you must also have an overview of everything in the field so you can provide the entire solution. Once you have a client, you don't want to have to refer him or her to someone else. But you do need to know when to bring in a subcontractor and whom to choose.

🐷 Start-Up Costs

	Low	High
IBM-compatible 386 or 486 or Macintosh SE computer*	$2,500	$ 6,000
Inkjet or laser printer	$ 500	$ 1,600
Software appropriate to your specialty and other popular software programs	$1,000	$ 3,000
Office furniture, especially an ergonomic chair	$ 600	$ 800
Business cards, letterhead, envelopes	$ 200	$ 600
Brochure	$ 100	$ 2,000
Organizational dues	$ 250	$ 250
Totals	$5,150	$14,250

*You need to have access to computers that are as advanced as the computer systems of your clients.

👍 Advantages

- In this business, problems are opportunities. Essentially, as a consultant, you're in the business of solving problems.
- People are grateful when you help them.
- You can often work any time of the day or night you wish as long as the job is done on time.
- If you're good at getting business, you can do this work from anywhere in America.
- You perform varied activities, and there is seldom boredom or repetition.
- The demand is high. If you're good, you don't have to be concerned about competition.

⚡ Disadvantages

- At least part of the time, you may have to work under time pressures due to client deadlines.
- You must devote considerable time to keeping current in the fast-changing computer field. To stay current, computer consultants typically read 10 to 20 hours a week.
- If you must work on fixed bids you have to be skillful at estimating, as project costs can easily exceed estimates.

💲 Pricing

Computer-consulting rates typically range from $25 to $135 per hour. Factors that influence rates include:

- Community size. Rates are higher in metropolitan markets.
- Client size. Rates are higher for large corporations.
- Specialization. Rates vary depending on which industries you serve, what types of problems you solve, and which hardware and software you work with.
- Length of project. Some consultants discount for long projects.
- Whether you work through a broker. Brokers who refer you to or place you with clients typically pay lower rates because they are lining up clients for you.

Bidding by the job is risky for the inexperienced consultant. A high bid that protects the consultant may scare off a potential client; a low bid can cause heavy losses for a consultant if the project costs exceed estimates.

📟 Potential Earnings

TYPICAL ANNUAL GROSS REVENUES: $45,000, based on billing 20 hours per week, 50 weeks a year (1,000 hours per year) at $45 an hour. Many consultants, however, earn up to a $100,000 a year and some as much as $300,000 a year.
OVERHEAD: Moderate (20 to 40 percent).

📇 Best Ways to Get Business

- Networking and making contacts in any of the following ways:
  - Helping people at computer and software user-group meetings and special-interest groups, without expectation of compensation.
  - Answering questions on on-line computer services and local bulletin-board systems.
  - Joining and participating in organizations such as trade and business associations, particularly in industries or fields in which you have experience, and letting people know what you do.
  - Joining or forming a business referral group.

- Speaking to civic, trade, and professional organizations.
- Teaching courses in adult-education programs and colleges; offering seminars at conferences and trade shows.
- Writing articles and books targeted to your clientele.
- Sending a newsletter to past and prospective clients.
- Working for your former employer.
- Acting as a distributor for a quality hardware or software product while it is catching on but prior to its becoming a standard.

First Steps

1. Work as an internal consultant for a large company for a period of time.
2. Start with either a cash reserve to cover you for a year or a contract in hand that is large enough to cover your overhead and living expenses to the extent that you do not have reserves or a spouse's income.
3. Identify a niche or specialty.
4. Join the Independent Computer Consultant's Association, especially a local chapter. Through contacts there you may be able to get sub-contracts or referrals if you have a specialty.

Where to Turn for Information and Help

In addition to the resources below, see also those listed under *Computer Programmer* and *Management Consultant*.

BOOKS

Exploring Requirements: Quality before Design, by Donald Gause and Gerald M. Weinberg. New York: Dorset House, 1989.

Handbook of Walkthroughs, Inspections, and Technical Reviews, by Daniel P. Freedman and Gerald M. Weinberg. New York: Dorset House, 1990.

How to Be a Successful Computer Consultant, by Alan R. Simon, New York: McGraw-Hill, 1990.

Peopleware: Productive Projects and Teams, by Tom DeMarco and Tim Lister. New York: Dorset House, 1987.

The Secrets of Consulting: A Guide to Giving and Getting Advice Successfully, Gerald M. Weinberg. New York: Dorset House, 1985.

ORGANIZATIONS

Independent Computer Consultants Association, 933 Gardenview Office Parkway, St. Louis, MO 63141; 1-800-GET-ICCA. The ICCA sponsors the Consult Forum on CompuServe Information Service.

■ ■ ■ ■

COMPUTER PROGRAMMER

Programmers are the people who prepare the step-by-step instructions—called *programs* or *software*—that a computer follows in order to perform tasks. There are two types of programmers: *applications programmers,* who write programs that solve problems and carry out tasks like payroll and inventory management; and *systems programmers,* who write programs that tell the computer how to carry out its own internal operations. *Systems analysts* go a step beyond programmers; they help clients find ways to computerize their operations.

The Bureau of Labor Statistics has identified programming as one of the fastest-growing occupations. The number of programmers is expected to grow by 45 percent between now and the year 2000. That's 250,000 new programmers, just about equivalent to the 1990 population of Las Vegas, Nevada. And much of this work is going to free-lancers. Increasingly programming is being done on personal computers or at work stations that do not need to be near a centralized data-processing department. As a result, companies are reducing their number of core employees, and more programming work is being *outsourced* to outside contractors.

Free-lance computer programmers may create one-of-a-kind programs to help clients run their businesses, or they may customize off-the-shelf software programs so the client can avoid the cost of creating a program from scratch. As Chris Nelson of New York, who operates his own company under the name S/Wizardry, Ltd., says, "The opportunities are enormous. Companies are more inclined to work with outside programmers because they don't have to make as much of a commitment as when they hire a permanent employee. They can try out a consultant, and if he or she doesn't work out they don't have the complications of terminating an employee. They can more easily find someone who will do the job."

A programmer will begin by developing an understanding of the tasks the client wants the computer to perform, how much material will be processed, and in what form it will be needed. Once the programmer has a full understanding of what needs to be done, he or she may have to design, write, or modify the program that will do the job. Then the programmer must test and implement the program. In fact, David Lake of Boulder, Colorado, who has been an independent programmer for the past ten years, says, "I spend two hours of my time testing for every hour of programming. I hire people to try to break my programs. If they do, I fix it."

Dave Bennett, a San Diego programmer, has written around 40 applications over the past three years. He says of the field, "This work is growing more challenging and complex. Windows, Unix, Macintosh, and OS/2 programming are taking us a geometric step beyond DOS programming."

✔ Knowledge and Skills You Need to Have

- First, you need to be able to do computer programming. How much knowledge you need depends on whether you will work with clients who have problems for which you must design solutions or clients who already have solutions in mind and want you to program their solutions. Some routine applications programming can be performed by workers with a high-school education. However, most companies would expect applications programmers, particularly free-lancers, to have some post-high-school training at a college or technical school. Systems programmers usually have a college degree and a strong knowledge of the computers they work with.

- Working as an independent programmer requires more expertise than you will be able to learn by simply taking a community-college course on programming. You need to be able to do more than write code. Most programmers find they must be familiar with the operations of a wide range of hardware and software.

- Ideally you should have two to five years of programming experience, so that you know how long it will take you to complete various projects and thus can tell a client with confidence what you will charge for a finished project.

- Working as a free-lance programmer requires that you have better communications skills than you would need if you were employed as a programmer. You need to have some business savvy and be able to listen, ask questions, and draw out the needs of your clients. You also need to be able to build a good rapport with your clients, negotiate amicably, and avoid office politics.

- You must be willing to sell your services and market yourself—skills that are sometimes unfamiliar to programmers.

◼ Start-Up Costs

	Low	High
IBM-compatible 386 or 386 SX computer or Macintosh equivalent for development work	$2,500	$ 6,000
Network system file server set for at least two computers	——	$ 3,500
Printer	$ 300	$ 1,600
Communications, compiler, and miscellaneous software*	$1,700	$ 2,500
Office furniture, especially an adjustable chair	$ 600	$ 800
Business cards, letterhead, envelopes	$ 200	$ 600
Organizational dues	$ 250	$ 250
Totals	$5,550	$15,250

*You often can get free software by doing beta testing.

📖 Advantages

- Programming is one of the fastest-growing occupations. Programmers are in demand and are respected as experts.
- You can work on a wide variety of projects.

📖 Disadvantages

- As software becomes easier to use, the inherent difficulty of directing computers shifts to programmers.
- While it's necessary to specialize in a particular *platform* (the hardware or operating system that computers run on), uncertainty as to which platforms will be in future demand heightens the risk of your skills becoming obsolete.
- Sometimes the more interesting projects are not the most profitable ones.
- Some clients will change their minds about what they want you to do at various points during a project, causing you frustration and costly time.
- Many clients want you to do the work on their premises.
- Often you are dealing with people who don't know how their business works, and you must tactfully help them articulate what they need.

💲 Pricing

Programming rates range from $15 for students doing coding to more than $100 an hour. You will need to bill $30 to $40 an hour to make a living.

(Note: the pricing information given for *Computer Consultant* applies to programmers as well.)

💻 Potential Earnings

TYPICAL ANNUAL GROSS REVENUES: $40,000, based on billing 20 hours per week, 50 weeks a year (1,000 hours a year) at $40 an hour. Many programmers, however, are able to bill in excess of 40 hours a week and can earn up to $100,000 per year.

OVERHEAD: Moderate (20 to 40 percent). As a home-based programmer, you need to constantly upgrade your own computers and software.

📑 Best Ways to Get Business

- Turning your former employer into a client.
- Assisting people at computer and software user-group meetings and

special-interest group sessions, and answering questions on on-line computer services and local bulletin-board systems.

- Making personal contacts in trade and business associations and other organizations, particularly in industries in which you have experience.
- Joining or forming a business referral group.
- Getting referrals from other professional contacts such as business consultants and accountants.
- Teaching classes on programming for businesspeople.
- Getting listed as a consultant for referrals with companies with whose software you work.
- Writing articles or columns about how a computer can make a business more productive.
- Contacting computer stores about what you do. Retail computer stores can be a great source of business. A customer who has taken the initiative to go to a computer retailer is already sold on using a computer but may need custom software (or software customization like spreadsheet models, database applications, and so forth).
- Checking bulletin boards at colleges and universities for companies seeking help.

⬛ First Steps

Computer courses are available at most universities and community colleges. There are also many commercial trade schools that teach computer programming. To develop your skills you might consider doing temporary work through technical job shops until you feel you can take on clients on your own. To develop the social skills you need and to market yourself, Dave Bennett suggests you "learn to play golf and then get out on the course with business men and women."

⬛ Where to Turn for Information and Help

BOOKS

Read the design and technical books about the platform for which you write.

The Programmer's Survival Guide, by Janet Ruhl. Englewood Cliffs, NJ: Prentice Hall, 1989.

The Psychology of Computer Programming, by Gerald Weinberg. New York: Van Nostrand Reinhold, 1971.

ORGANIZATIONS

CompuServe Information Service, 5000 Arlington Centre Boulevard, Columbus, OH 43220; (800) 848-8199. Many forums are named and focused on specific hardware and software.

Society for Technical Communication, 901 North Stuart Street, Suite 304, Arlington, VA 22203; (703) 522-4114. The society has local chapters, some of which have employment referral services.

Software Publishers Association, 1101 Connecticut Avenue, N.W., #901, Washington, DC 20036; (202) 452-1600. If you write software you may be eligible for membership. Members have access to form contracts that can be adapted for use with clients.

MAGAZINES AND NEWSLETTERS

Computer Language, Miller Freeman Publications, 500 Howard Street, San Francisco, CA 94105; (415) 957-9353.

Databased Advisor, Databased Solutions, 4010 Morene Boulevard, #200, San Diego, CA 92117, (619) 483-6400.

Dr. Dobb's Journal, M&T Publishing, 501 Galveston Drive, Redwood City, CA 94063; (415) 366-3600.

PC Techniques, Coriolis Group, 3202 East Greenway #1307-302, Phoenix, AZ 85032; (602) 483-0192.

■ ■ ■ ■

COMPUTER TUTOR AND TRAINER

Just as driver education has become the standard way to prepare new drivers to operate motor vehicles, computer tutoring has become established as the way for people to learn how to use computers and the software programs written for them. Although there are many computer training programs available in community colleges and commercial facilities, independent computer tutors have an advantage because they can take the training to their clients and customize it to their needs.

Computer tutors generally work on the client's premises, teaching in classroom style or doing one-to-one coaching, or they may go into a company to help an office automate: they assist in setting up the computer systems to do what the business needs to have done and then teach the employees to use both the hardware and software.

Most successful tutors specialize in working with particular industries or particular software applications. Ann McIndoo, for example, has a company, Computer Training Systems, that specializes in working with law firms ranging in size from the solo practitioner to firms with 300 lawyers. She especially likes to work with medium-sized firms, those with 10 to 25 lawyers, because they can make decisions relatively quickly. McIndoo says, "Because you have to go through their committee structures, larger firms take a longer time to approve a training project. And the larger the company, the more the red tape. Also, managing a large project becomes a challenge in and of itself." Midsized firms, however, are large enough to keep McIndoo busy and provide enough variety to make them interesting and profitable.

About 60 percent of McIndoo's work involves one-to-one tutoring with individuals. The rest of her time is spent training small groups or running two-to-three-day classes for four to six people. She also offers public workshops for 10 to 12 people, for which she rents a training room equipped with computers. She also helps clients install and customize their software.

Other good markets for computer tutors include the medical field and the construction industry.

☑ Knowledge and Skills You Need to Have

- To be a computer tutor, you must be able to operate a personal computer and have a thorough knowledge of at least one software program that an ample number of people need to learn. Although you can learn to use appropriate software on your own, some software manufacturers will train and certify you to teach their software. Some of these courses are free; others are for a fee. Once you are certified, the manufacturer can also become a source of referrals, so becoming certified is to your advantage.

- You need to be familiar with whatever field you decide to work in so that when clients ask questions about how to use the software to do their work, you will understand what they're talking about and be able to answer in a way that makes sense to them.

- Computer tutors need good communications skills in order to listen to and interpret students' needs.

- Good presentation skills and the ability to communicate directions and technical information in simple, clear, and concise language are important.

- You need to have patience with novice computer users as they learn. They may make repeated mistakes, ask obvious questions, and often need ample encouragement and reassurance.

- You should have sufficient writing skills to prepare correspondence, proposals, documentation, training materials, and curriculums.

▣ Start-Up Costs

	Low	High
Computer with hard disk (as good a computer as clients have)	$1,500	$ 2,500
Laser printer	$ 650	$ 1,600
Software necessary to serve your customers' needs (some software companies will give you free software or a special discounted consultant/trainer price	——	$ 2,000
Training cost to become certified for the software programs you teach	$ 500	$ 4,000
Modem	$ 100	$ 600
Fax	$ 400	$ 1,000
Office furniture including a table for assembling training materials	$ 500	$ 800
Comb binding machine	——	$ 550
Business cards, letterhead, envelopes	$ 200	$ 600
Customized brochure and/or presentation folder	$ 100	$ 2,000
Organizational dues	$ 250	$ 250
Totals	$4,200	$15,900

▣ Advantages

- Responding to the varied requests of clients provides a challenge and keeps the work interesting.
- Helping people to become more productive and develop confidence in using technology is satisfying.
- You're learning all the time because you need to keep pace with the growing edge of technology and new updates of the hardware or software you teach.

▣ Disadvantages

- You must deal with people's resistance to technology and to change.
- People's egos become involved when learning something new, so sometimes you must work with people who don't want to be in a student role and who don't like someone else telling them what to do or knowing more than they do.
- This has become a competitive business, so you must stand out and specialize.

▣ Pricing

Hourly tutoring fees range from $85 to $125. Don't be surprised, however, to find hobbyists offering to tutor individuals for as low as $10 an hour. To command professional prices you must target your market and take your work and yourself seriously.

Price workshops so that clients perceive a savings in what it would cost their employees to learn on their own. A fee can be calculated at somewhat less that the employees' rate of pay multiplied by the time it takes to train them. For example, if employees earn $15 an hour and your program is 4 hours long, you might charge $50 per student.

🖳 Potential Earnings

TYPICAL ANNUAL GROSS REVENUES: $50,000 to $125,000, based on training 3 days a week, 42 weeks a year, at $50 to $125 dollars per hour.

OVERHEAD: Low (less than 20 percent). Primary expenses are telephone and office supplies.

🖻 Best Ways to Get Business

- Giving speeches about the benefits of computerizing. This is the fastest, cheapest, and easiest method.
- Networking and making personal contacts through the professional, trade, or business associations of the field in which you are specializing.
- Sometimes, as in the legal field, you cannot join the professional association and therefore must network through other civic or business organizations. You can also network in computer and software user groups; manufacturers can direct you to user groups in your area.
- Getting certified or licensed by, and listed to get referrals from, the software company whose packages you teach.
- Asking satisfied clients for referrals to others who need training.
- Soliciting referrals from manufacturers, resellers, and suppliers who serve the same types of companies you work with.
- Sending direct-mail advertising to companies that have purchased particular software packages. These names are available, listed by zip code, from software vendors. Without such a highly qualified list, direct mail is too expensive.
- Providing a quarterly newsletter highlighting information about software upgrades, user tips, and new equipment to past, present, and potential customers and everyone else you meet who could refer business to you.
- Advertising in computer publications or specialized trade publications for your target market, such as a legal journal or magazine.

🔗 Franchises

COMPUTOTS, Box 408, Great Falls, VA 22066; (703) 759-2556. Franchisees teach computer classes to preschool children at private schools and daycare centers. In business since 1983; franchise fee is $15,000.

🔋 First Steps

Doing computer tutoring is like speaking a foreign language—you can't fake it. Therefore you must have a solid knowledge of the software packages and equipment you will be training others to use. If you are a computer user now, begin by teaching the programs you know well, or spend some time polishing up and deepening your knowledge of the programs you will be teaching. Often training and licensing to teach a package are available from the software manufacturer.

Select a market that you will specialize in (for example, law firms, construction firms, dental offices). Your niche should be in a field in which you are knowledgeable and comfortable, and which you enjoy. If possible, specialize in marketing your services to a field in which you have been working. Survey that field to identify what people like and dislike about using computers.

If you must enter a field in which you are not familiar, volunteer to do a project for a company in the field of your choice in exchange for your learning the ins and outs and special needs of that field. Take ample time on that first project to learn as much as you can by observing and asking questions. If possible, join and become active in the professional or trade associations in the field and subscribe to publications in the field.

If you currently do not have experience using a computer and software or have only limited knowledge, your first step will be to become computer literate yourself. There is a rich array of computer training programs available in most communities. Contact local college and university adult-education programs to find those in your area.

📖 Where to Turn for Information and Help

BOOKS

The Computer Training Handbook: How to Teach People to Use Computers, by Elliott Masie and Rebekka Wolman, National Training and Computers Project, Sagamore Road, Raquett Lake, NY 13436; (800) 34-TRAIN. Cost: $44.

Also see books listed under *Corporate Trainer.*

ORGANIZATIONS

Computer Training Forum on CompuServe Information Service. The Computer Training Forum is a special interest group of computer trainers who communicate through their computers. GO DPTRAIN is the on-line address of this forum on CompuServe. CompuServe Information Service, 5000 Arlington Center Boulevard, Box 20212, Columbus, OH 43220; (800) 848-8199 or (614) 457-0802.

The Micro Computer Trainer, 606 Ninth Street, Box 2487, Secaucus, NJ 07096-2487; (201) 330-8923. A monthly newsletter offering practical solutions and strategies for the microcomputer training professional.

■ ■ ■ ■

COPYWRITER

Businesses and organizations often have a need to describe their products and services in written materials that represent them to the world. The copy in advertising, direct mail, brochures, and newsletters not only needs to be written clearly and concisely, but also must capture attention, impress, inspire trust, and motivate the reader to buy or to call for further information. Rarely do small-business owners have the time, talent, or knowhow to prepare these materials themselves, however. And often they can't afford to employ a full-time copywriter to do it for them. So instead they turn to free-lance professional copywriters.

Copywriters prepare copy for a wide variety of materials: ads, brochures, instruction manuals, grant proposals, media kits, feature stories, ghostwritten magazine articles, catalogues, company names and slogans, consumer-information booklets, captions for photographs, product literature, annual reports, product names and packaging labels, marketing communication plans, speeches, telemarketing scripts, video scripts, and storyboards. Their clients include major corporations, doctors and lawyers, small manufacturers, automotive dealers, banks, health clubs, consumer electronics firms, and direct-mail catalogues.

Don Hauptman is a New York-based free-lance copywriter whose specialty is writing copy for subscription newsletters selling for hundreds of dollars a year. These newsletters accept no advertising and are not sold on newsstands; therefore, they must be sold by mail, and they rely on strong copy to sell. Don has built his business by speaking, writing articles, networking with professionals, and keeping in touch with clients and prospects by sending newspaper clippings of things of interest to them.

☑ Knowledge and Skills You Need to Have

No specific background is required to be a copywriter. However, you need:

- the ability to write clear, interesting, arresting, and compelling copy.
- curiosity about how something works and a sense of what makes something appealing, unique, better, interesting, beneficial, and so on.
- the imagination to say something in a way that hasn't been said before.

- the self-discipline to see a project through even when ideas don't flow readily.
- a logical, organized mind that can assimilate information, synthesize it, and integrate it into a theme or message.

🐄 Start-Up Costs

	Low	High
Computer with hard disk	$1,000	$2,500
Printer	$ 300	$1,600
Word-processing software with spell-checking, grammar-checking, and thesaurus software	$ 350	$ 350
Office furniture, especially an ergonomic chair	$ 600	$ 800
Business cards, letterhead, envelopes	$ 200	$ 600
Dictionaries and reference books	$ 100	$ 300
Totals	$2,550	$6,150

👍 Advantages

- There is no fixed schedule for this work. You can do it anytime you want.
- This is creative work—taking plain, even dull information and creating something original.
- You have the opportunity to try out your creative ideas and discover how your work influences people.
- This work is concrete and finite. When you finish a project, you have something in your hands that didn't exist before.

👎 Disadvantages

- Sometimes you will need to work under the pressure of tight deadlines.
- Nonwriters don't appreciate how long it takes to write.
- The actual copywriting is something you must do alone.
- You may come up against a wall because the subject is difficult to write about.

💲 Pricing

Prices for copywriting are very regional. You can charge by the hour, by the day, or by the job.

By the hour. Fees can range from $10 an hour for a student to over $150 an hour for professional speech writers, with average fees running from $60 to $75 an hour.

By the day. Fees for consulting on a direct-mail project range from $1,500 to $2,000 a day.

By the job. Fees range from $2,000 to $7,000 for a direct-mail package. You will be working on an estimate so to price a job you need to have records of your hours spent on projects over the years so you will know how much time a job will take you and price it accordingly.

🖳 Potential Earnings

Robert W. Bly, the author of *The Copywriter's Handbook,* has surveyed attendees at his workshops in cities across the country. He has found that people who approach copywriting as a business typically earn:

- $20,000 to $40,000 a year during their first two years, which he calls Phase I
- $40,000 to $80,000 a year during what he calls Phase II
- $80,000 to $175,000 a year when they become real pros during Phase III, which often occurs in three to five years.

OVERHEAD: Low (20 percent or less).

📷 Best Ways to Get Business

- Talking to everyone you know and meet and showing them samples of your work. Send samples to your friends and colleagues. Let them know what you really do at a level they understand.
- Networking in organizations, such as trade and business associations, particularly in industries or fields in which you have experience.
- Developing affiliations with related professionals like graphic designers, photographers, and printers who can refer business to you.
- At the conclusion of a successful project, asking for a reference letter you can use in talking with prospective clients.
- Dropping off samples of your work at the offices of other businesses in your clients' buildings, offices, or business centers, indicating that you work for their neighbor and would like them to see a sample of what you do.

✋ First Steps

1. Take courses offered by local writers' groups, extension programs, colleges, and universities.
2. Join special-interest sections of writers' groups that meet to read their material to one another and compare notes.
3. Develop a look for a business card and letterhead that is an advertisement for what you do.
4. Join an organization of people who can refer you to clients—for example, printers, graphic designers, and photographers.
5. Create a portfolio of at least five samples to show to clients.
6. Read books and go to writers' workshops. Never assume you're done learning.

Where to Turn for Information and Help

BOOKS

Breakthrough Advertising: How to Write Ads That Shatter Traditions and Sales Records, by Eugene Schwartz. New York: Boardroom Books, 1984. Cost: $50.00

The Copywriter's Handbook, by Robert W. Bly. New York: Henry Holt and Company, 1985.

Create the Perfect Salespiece, by Robert W. Bly. New York: John Wiley, 1985.

How to Make Your Advertising Make Money, by John Caples. Englewood Cliffs, NJ: Prentice Hall, 1986.

Looking Good in Print: A Guide to Basic Design for Desktop Publishing, by Roger C. Parker. Chapel Hill, NC: Ventana Press, 1988.

Scientific Advertising and My Life in Advertising, by Claude Hopkins. Chicago: Crane Books, 1966.

Secrets of a Freelance Writer: How to Make Eighty-Five Thousand Dollars a Year, by Robert W. Bly, New York: Henry Holt and Company, 1988.

Selling Your Services, by Robert W. Bly, New York: Henry Holt and Company, 1991.

Tested Advertising Methods, by John Caples. Englewood Cliffs, NJ: Prentice Hall, 1986.

Words That Sell, by Richard Bayan. Chicago: Contemporary Books, 1984.

ORGANIZATIONS

International Association of Business Communicators, 1 Hallidie Plaza, Suite 600, San Francisco, CA 94102; (415) 433-3400.

MAGAZINES AND NEWSLETTERS

The Direct Response Specialist, Stilson and Stilson, Box 1075, Tarpon Springs, FL 34688; (813) 786-1411. Monthly newsletter on selling by direct mail and direct response advertising. Useful source of knowledge for writing copy that will sell.

Writer's Digest Magazine, 1507 Dana Avenue, Cincinnati, OH 45207; (513) 531-2222.

Writer's Digest Book Clubs Bulletin, (800) 876-0963. Books about writing that are not in the bookstores.

SOFTWARE

The increasing availability of CD-ROM with reference material for writing will be a boon to writers. Writers will be able to instantly find quotes, look up rules of usage, and so forth. Such software that you can run on your hard disk is already available such as:

Writer's Dreamtools, Slippery Disks, Box 1126, Los Angeles, CA 90069. Events Day by Day lists, by day and date, thousands of birthdays and historical events, the feast days of every saint, and holidays around the world; there's also space for users to add their own information. Cliches and Catch Phrases lists more than 12,500 cliches and catch phrases. A Slang Thesaurus provides words that meet all your criteria, neatly organized by part of speech. Mail order only. Cost: $35 each or $79 for all three.

■ ■ ■ ■

CORPORATE TRAINER

As jobs demand more, workers need additional training. The American Society for Training and Development (ASTD) claims that in order to do their jobs more effectively, 50 million people—42 percent of the workforce—need additional training in various areas including technical skills, management, customer service, and basic skills. Meeting this need will require investing $15 billion each year on training above the current $30 billion dollars now being spent annually.

In the past, employee training in large organizations was usually provided by an in-house staff. Today many companies no longer keep such a staff on the payroll, however, and are turning instead to independent trainers who come in as needed to teach their particular area of expertise. Even companies with large training staffs use outside trainers to teach specialized skills. As long ago as 1987, employers were spending $112 million a year on private consultants, most of which are one-or-two-person firms.

While corporate training is an expense that is customarily cut during economic downturns, training programs that hold special promise during the '90s include teaching the basic literacy skills (reading, writing, and math), computing skills, sales training, management skills, and customer-service training. The need for basic literacy training alone is expected to grow at a rate of 17 percent a year and perhaps even more. Trainers are also called upon even in the worst of times to help a company handle particular crises and challenges.

Most corporate trainers specialize in one or two areas. Usually trainers conduct their programs on the premises of their clients; however, some trainers rent hotel or conference facilities to conduct programs to which multiple employers can send their personnel. Trainers are usually expected to provide visual aides and accompanying written course materials. Some also develop and sell their own manuals, books, and tapes.

Kathryn Dager, whose firm, Profitivity, focuses on customer-service training, says of this field, "Nothing is more satisfying than working with a company and seeing the entire company become more successful as a result of the new skills its employees have mastered."

☑ Knowledge and Skills You Need to Have

- To be effective you must have a skill or area of expertise you know well and that others need to learn.
- Trainers need excellent stand-up presentation and teaching skills. You must be able to break down the skills or information in a way that others can easily understand and quickly learn.
- Trainers should have good interpersonal communication skills and be able to help a group go through the process of learning.
- It's important for trainers to have resolved any personality issues they may have. Such issues surface easily when teaching before a group and not only hinder the learning process but prevent trainers from getting good evaluations from students, even if they have otherwise done a good job.
- Trainers must have the ability to sell themselves and an intangible product like training.
- You need good writing skills to write proposals and prepare workbooks and correspondence. You also need to design slides and other visual aides.
- Being reasonably physically attractive and fit is helpful, because as a trainer people will be looking at you for hours at a time.

🐄 Start-Up Costs

	Low	High
Computer with hard disk	$1,000	$2,500
Laser printer	$ 650	$1,600
Word-processing software with desktop-publishing capabilities, or separate desktop-publishing software	$ 250	$ 750
Comb binding machine to bind workbooks	$ 275	$ 550
Fax	$ 500	$1,000
Office furniture	$ 600	$ 800
Business cards, letterhead, envelopes	$ 200	$ 600
Brochure	$ 100	$2,000
Totals	$3,575	$9,800

📖 Advantages

- Training can be intellectually stimulating. You earn your living using your brain. Also, watching people master new skills and become more effective is very rewarding.
- By working with many companies in an industry, you can have an impact on the entire field.
- If you like to perform, this is an opportunity to be onstage frequently.

- Top trainers make excellent money.
- Training provides the opportunity to create books, tapes, manuals, and other products that can add to your fees and provide ongoing passive income.

■ Disadvantages

- Training is a difficult product to market. You are often selling intangible or indirect benefits that can be hard to measure. You must continually address the questions *What's the guarantee that it will work?* and *What makes you a better trainer than someone else?*
- You may be spending 80 percent of your time selling your services.
- In order to get work, you must penetrate the many barriers between you and the executive who will make the ultimate decision.
- Unless you live in a large community with many organizations that need your expertise, you may need to travel frequently.

■ Pricing

Most trainers charge a daily rate ranging from $600 to $2,000 a day. As you would expect, fees are higher in large metropolitan areas than in smaller communities. You can charge higher fees to train trainers to teach what you know. When trainers work with service brokers, they may work for a little as $175 a day or give the broker a percentage of their fee.

Some consultants charge by the trainee, in which case they relate the per-person fee to the salary level of the trainees. So training fees for a group of 12 people earning $100 a day ($26,000 per year) are apt to be around $1,200.

■ Potential Earnings

TYPICAL ANNUAL GROSS REVENUES: $31,00 to $230,000, based on 42 nonholiday weeks a year, someone training on the 3 days a week that organizations favor for training (Tuesday, Wednesday, and Thursday) could work 126 days a year. At $600 a day, he or she would gross $75,600 a year.

OVERHEAD: Low (20 percent or less).

■ Best Ways to Get Business

- Demonstrating what you do by speaking before professional and trade associations like the ASTD, or trade shows. To reach smaller clients, try organizations like the Rotary and Kiwanis, and the chamber of commerce.
- Directly soliciting potential clients using a combination of phone contacts, mailing customized materials, and personal appointments.
- Writing articles for trade and professional journals.
- Publicity.

🏃 First Steps

Training is industry related, so you will be best served by starting to sell training to an industry in which you already have experience. For example, if you've been in banking for 14 years, work in banking. If you wish to train in an industry in which you have no experience, we recommend taking a job in that industry for a period of time so you can become familiar with its needs and make initial contacts.

Much of what you need to know can be learned from using the resources listed below. One resource is a directory of academic degree and certificate programs that you can enroll in to better prepare yourself to enter the training field. Although such formal training is not necessary to become a trainer, it will certainly shorten your learning curve if you have not already had training in your desired area of expertise. Knowing a subject well or doing something well is not the same as being able to teach someone else to master it.

In conjunction with these resources, you can gain experience in teaching and presenting by taking courses from image consultants in your area who specialize in presentation skills. These consultants can be located through the Association of Image Consultants International (509 Madison Avenue, Suite 1400, New York, NY 10022). There may also be some courses available through local community colleges, the local chapter of the ASTD, or one of the many companies that teach presentation skills, like Dale Carnegie or Walters' Speakers Academy.

Develop a step-by-step course outline for what you intend to teach. Identify the specific skills and knowledge employees will gain. Develop the accompanying written material you plan to hand out during your course. Test out your training program by volunteering to do training for nonprofit organizations or by offering it by invitation only to select contacts.

If you already have experience doing training, you can begin by finding a niche within your industry that you feel comfortable with and enjoy. Take a video training workshop to build your presentation skills, learn as much as you can about human behavior, and observe other people's workshops. Then get out and start selling your program. If selling is new to you, take sales training courses. Don't be undercapitalized. Unless you have already lined up clients before you start, you'll need a cushion to live on for three to six months while you get your initial clients.

📖 Where to Turn for Information and Help

BOOKS

How to Be a Successful Trainer without Being Tarred and Feathered, by Bud Allen and Diana Bosta. Sacramento, CA: Rae John, 1981.

An Introduction to Human Resource Development Careers, American Society for Training and Development, Box 1443, Alexandria, VA 22313. A 17-page basic introduction to the field of human resource development.

The Trainer's Professional Development Handbook, by R. Bard, C. Bell, L. Stephan, and L. Webster. San Francisco: Jossey-Bass, 1987.

Training and Development Handbook: A Guide to Human Resource Development, by R. l. Craig. Oklahoma City: McGraw-Hill, 1987. Considered to be the basic nuts-and-bolts how-to book for new trainers and a valued reference for experienced trainers.

Your Career in Human Resource Development: A Guide to Information and Decision, by R. Stump, American Society for Training and Development, Box 1443, Alexandria, VA 22313. Booklet to help readers determine whether they are suited for the human-resources field.

ORGANIZATIONS

American Society for Training and Development, 1630 Duke Street, Alexandria, VA 22313; (703) 683-8100. Offers a professional journal, a catalogue of resources, local chapters, and a train-the-trainer certificate program.

University Associates, 8517 Production Avenue, San Diego, CA 92121-2280; (619) 578-5900. This company publishes and distributes many books, tapes, and videos on training. It also offers seminars on training throughout the country.

MAGAZINES AND NEWSLETTERS

Training: The Magazine of Human Resource Development, Lakewood Publications, 50 South 9th Street, Minneapolis, MN 55402; (612) 333-0471.

Training and Development Journal, American Society for Training and Development, 1640 King Street, Box 1443, Alexandria, VA 22313; (703) 683-8129. ASTD also publishes *Technical and Skills Training* magazine.

■ ■ ■ ■

DAY-CARE PROVIDER

The era of Ozzie and Harriet is just a memory. Women no longer work only until they have babies. Today 57 percent of married women with children under six work outside the home and 70 percent of divorced women with preschool-age children work. So who takes care of the infants, toddlers, and preschoolers while mommy is at work? Day care is the solution for nearly a third of full-time working mothers.

The Bureau of Labor Statistics reports that parents spend $11 billion on child care each year, and that figure continues to grow. Not only do two-career households and single parents need day care, but according to a study by Dr. Kathleen Christenson of the New School for Social Research, 50 percent of women who work at home use some form of child care help, too, at least part-time.

What many people don't realize is that most commercial day-care is done in people's homes in what is called family day care. According to the Children's

Foundation, 1.5 million to 2 million family day-care providers are caring for 5.5 million children. These 5.5 million children represent more than four out of five children in all child-care programs. In fact, according to Warren Schmidt of Monday Morning Mom, a family day-care management service, "Many child-development psychologists contend that family day-care is the best form of child care because it provides more personal, less regimented care and a more age-appropriate curriculum."

Good day care is hard to come by. A Louis Harris survey found that fewer than 25 percent of people surveyed believe children get good child care while their parents are at work. So family day-care providers who do a good job have a loyal following of parents who are uncomfortable with the typical 50-child day-care facility. Martha Post, for example, who is licensed to care for six children in her California home, never has a vacancy.

Virtually all states require some form of licensing or registration for day care providers, although how strictly licensing laws are enforced varies from state to state. While only about one in four home-based operators are licensed, there are strong incentives for becoming licensed. First, the unlicensed day-care operator risks being ordered to close down. Second, licensed day-care providers become eligible for food subsidies, which for Martha Post means up to an extra $120 a week in funds provided by the U.S. Department of Agriculture to help pay for breakfasts, lunches, and snacks. Licensing is also needed to get liability insurance, which anyone involved in providing care to people needs to have.

The licensing process is usually simple, requiring an inspection of your home. Although specific requirements vary by state, to be suitable for family day care, the home and yard must be roomy enough for children to play in. And of course a child-care home needs to have ample toys for children to play with both indoors and out, and precautions must be taken to be sure cleaning fluids, dangerous chemicals, and other things that could hurt children are locked away. In addition, day-care centers need to stimulate children's mental, physical, and social development by providing them with learning experiences. For this reason, many teachers who no longer want to be in a classroom are able to do well in home-based day-care.

City and county zoning may also affect family-care homes. Your home may be located in an area that is zoned to permit no family day-care or that limits the number of children to three or six. The zoning ordinance may also allow you to apply for a conditional-use permit, which will require the nonopposition of your neighbors. Because the comings and goings of parents and children are obvious to neighbors and will involve additional traffic, neighbors may well complain to zoning officials if your home is not properly zoned.

To enjoy this business, you must like children and be willing to become, in effect, a professional parent—dealing with temper tantrums, tears, and fighting, and all the other problems of supervising preschool children.

While day care has less income potential than most of the businesses described in this book, it provides a wealth of psychic rewards for someone who wants to stay at home and loves working with children.

☑ Knowledge and Skills You Need to Have

- You must like taking care of and parenting other people's children.
- You need to have an upbeat personality and not be quick to get angry, because children will test you regularly.
- A knowledge of child development and how to appropriately handle various behaviors at different ages is especially useful.
- Getting along with parents requires tact and tolerance.
- You need to be able to schedule, organize, and manage four or five things at the same time.
- Making time for the various types of developmental tasks the children need to do each day requires organizational skills.
- You need to be able to give first aid.
- You need to enjoy children's games and stories or at least be able to enjoy the children's enjoyment.

☁ Start-Up Costs

	Low	High
For Six Children		
Liability insurance*	$ 375	$ 500
Toys and equipment	$1,000	$2,000
Bed and cribs or playpen for children under two	$ 350	$ 500
Fire extinguisher	$ 25	$ 50
Smoke detectors	$ 50	$ 50
Children's tables and chairs	$ 125	$ 150
Cordless telephone (so you can continue to watch children despite inevitable phone calls)	$ 75	$ 125
Business cards	$ 100	$ 100
Brochure	$ 100	$ 200
Totals	$2,200	$3,675

*You may be able to get umbrella coverage with your homeowner's policy. Without insurance, parents need to sign a notice in which you state that you do not have insurance.

ᗔ Advantages

- If you love taking care of children, this business means you can make money doing what you love.
- You can earn a living and stay home with your own children, who become part of your career.
- Operating a home-based day-care center makes you eligible for important tax deductions. You can take deductions for the rooms you use for day care even if those rooms are used at other times for nonbusiness purposes.

⬆ Disadvantages

- You are essentially confined to your home and yard every weekday. You can't run out somewhere for lunch or for errands.
- Unless you have an assistant, you can't take a day off unexpectedly to go to the doctor or dentist or just to relax.
- You can't go to your own children's school events during daytime hours unless you make special arrangements for someone to relieve you.
- For ten hours a day your conversation is limited to talking with small children.
- Normal auto insurance doesn't cover transporting children, so unless you get special insurance coverage you may have to call an ambulance if a parent can't come to get a child in the event of illness or injury.

💲 Pricing

How much you can charge depends on your local area and the level of services you provide. According to Runzheimer International, which surveys for-profit day-care rates quarterly, in March 1991 the least expensive weekly rates were $38 in Ogden, Utah, and $42 in Mobile, Alabama. The most expensive rates were $118 in Boston and $109 in New York. Runzheimer reported that the median cost of day-care in suburbs was $75 per week; however, remember that this means half of the rates were below $75 and half were above.

Day-care rates can vary widely even within a metropolitan area. For example, we found home-based day-care centers in West Los Angeles that were routinely charging $125 to $150 per week, whereas in East Los Angeles the rate was $40 a week; in Culver City the weekly rate was $95, and in the San Fernando Valley it ranged from $75 to $100.

📇 Potential Earnings

Although home-based day-care centers work best both financially and psychologically when two adults are present, the calculation below is based on a one-person operation.

TYPICAL ANNUAL GROSS REVENUES: $23,400 plus $6,240 of Child Care Food Program funds for a total of $29,640. This figure is based on 6 children at $75 per child per week. In areas where the daily day-care fees are $150 per week, the gross is a more comfortable $46,800 plus the $6,240 food-program funds for a total of $53,040.

Some states will license home facilities for up to 12 children; however, then a helper is required, which means paying someone else to assist you, which may cause a zoning problem.

OVERHEAD: High (more than 40 percent).

▣ Best Ways to Get Business

- Listing with a referral agency. Child Care Resource and Referral Agencies provide free services; they are funded with government grants. They may also provide loans for toys and other equipment.
- Networking with other family day-care providers, by belonging to a support group and receiving their overflow.
- Putting notices on bulletin boards in coin laundries.
- Advertising through classified ads in local newspapers.

▦ Franchises

Monday Morning America, 276 White Oak Ridge Road, Bridgewater, NJ 08807; (908) 685-0060. Founded by Suzanne Schmidt, who worked for 12 years as a family day-care provider herself, they offer two opportunities that could be of interest to day-care providers. The first is a family day-care management service. They train existing and new family day-care providers, who become part of their network. You set your own rates, but they screen and match you with families in need of child care and handle your collections. They also provide backup for vacations and sick leave; advertising; insurance; ongoing training classes; an equipment, toy, and book loan rotation program; and paid holidays. This service is free to the provider because the firm adds its fee to those set by the day-care provider. They also offer franchises to individuals who would like to become a family day-care management service; the franchise fee is $9,000.

▤ First Steps

1. Check your zoning to see if you can offer day care in your home. It's a good idea to talk over your plans with neighbors to avoid their opposition, even if you don't have zoning problems.
2. Contact a child-care information agency in your area (these agencies are listed in the yellow pages under Child Care) or the local family day-care association to learn about the demand for day care in your area, licensing requirements, and sources for training, such as the Red Cross and community colleges. Elementary schools are another source of information about the need for day care in your area.
3. Apply for a license or registration, according to the requirements of your state.
4. Take classes in first aid, emergency preparation (for example, earthquakes, hurricanes, tornadoes), and operating a day-care business in your home, if available.
5. Establish your rates and written policies, including hours of operation, deposits required, late fees if children are picked up late, medical issues,

holidays, notice of termination, and payment. To avoid collection problems, have parents pay on Friday prior to the next week. Never let unpaid bills go for more than one week.

6. Obtain equipment, and childproof your home. You may be able to buy used equipment and toys (wood is more durable than plastic) at garage sales and second-hand stores. You can even borrow books and sound recordings from your library.

▢ Where to Turn for Information and Help

BOOKS

Negotiated Care: The Experience of Family Day Care Providers, by Margaret E. Nelson. Philadelphia: Temple University Press, 1990.

Setting Up for Infant Care: Guidelines for Centers and Family Day Care Homes, edited by A. Godwin. Washington, DC: National Association for the Education of Young Children, 1988.

Start Your Own At-Home Child Care Business, by Patricia Gallagher. New York: Doubleday, 1989.

The Business of Family Day Care, by Helen and Dolores McCorey. Malibu, CA: Round Table Publishing, 1988.

Toddler Day Care: A Guide to Responsive Caregiving, by R. L. Leavitt and B. K. Eheart. Lexington, MA: Lexington Books, 1985.

ORGANIZATIONS

National Association for the Education of Young Children, 1834 Connecticut Avenue, N.W., Washington, DC 20009; (202) 232-8777.

National Association for Family Daycare, 725 15th Street, N.W., Suite 505, Washington, DC 20005; (800) 359-3817 or (202) 347-3356. The association offers accreditation to day-care providers who meet their state's requirements and have been providing care in their own home for 18 months. It annually publishes the *National Directory of Family Day Care Providers,* listing over 1,000 local support groups of day-care providers.

■ ■ ■ ■

DESKTOP PUBLISHING SERVICE

"If you have a background in the design field or are willing to work hard and learn how to design using desktop publishing software on a personal computer, you can start a home-based desktop publishing business," says Heidi Waldman, a home-based desktop publisher in St. Paul, Minnesota.

Today desktop publishing eliminates many steps in the process of preparing printed materials; pages no longer need to be pasted up and typeset, for example. The desktop publisher uses a personal computer and desktop publishing software to provide the services of a layout artist, typesetting service, and even a printer.

The market for desktop publishing is extensive, including businesses, non-profit organizations, and government agencies. Organizations of all kinds need printed material for both their internal and their external communications. Since the arrival of desktop publishing in 1985, a crudely typed and photocopied price list, contract, newsletter, or bulletin is no longer acceptable. Now proposals, flyers, forms, newsletters, reports, and presentation materials of all types are expected to look good and be produced quickly.

Desktop publishing has significant advantages over traditional publishing: production time is shortened, changes are not difficult or expensive to make, and, of course, overall cost is lower. Desktop publishing has advantages over word-processing, too. Even word-processing programs that have desktop publishing capabilities are limited in their ability to develop complex designs, and they don't have a full range of typographic controls.

The Aldus Corporation, producers of *Pagemaker,* one of the leading desktop publishing programs, has identified 350 different types of documents that are being created by using desktop publishing. Many desktop publishers today specialize by serving different sizes or types of clients or by offering specialized desktop publishing applications such as newsletter and directory publishing. The work is done at home, although someone skilled in desktop publishing can also get temporary work on-site for companies.

☑ Knowledge and Skills You Need to Have

- You need to have good computer skills and a knowledge of desktop publishing software.
- You should have a feel for design and an ability to write. Lawrence Miller, a designer who operates Daddy Desktop, points out that "too many desktop publishers can't write. They mistake typing for writing. They also can't design. They mistake the tools for the ability. It is possible, and desirable, to learn to design and write well, but you won't learn it in a software manual. It's a process of being aware of what you want to do, studying, and doing, taking courses and doing some more."
- Good communications skills are a must both to get business and to draw out of clients what their objectives are. Often visual concepts are difficult to articulate clearly. You must help them do that.
- You should know or be willing to learn about printing practices and procedures.

▣ Start-Up Costs

	Low	High
Macintosh or IBM-compatible computer with large hard disk and full-page monitor	$2,500	$ 6,000
Laser printer	$1,600	$ 6,000
Desktop-publishing, word-processing, and drawing software and fonts	$1,950	$ 3,450
Office furniture, especially an ergonomic chair	$ 600	$ 800
Business cards, letterhead, envelopes	$ 200	$ 600
Direct-mail advertising followed up with telephone calls	$ 500	$ 2,500
Organizational dues	$ 250	$ 250
Total	$7,600	$19,600

▣ Advantages

- The work is interesting and creative. People who dreamed of doing design work can now do it with desktop publishing.
- Desktop publishing is a rapidly growing field.
- The income potential is very good.
- There is ample opportunity to develop new skills.

▣ Disadvantages

- The field is growing increasingly competitive.
- You are often working under the pressure of deadlines, and you'll sometimes have to work nights and weekends.
- There is a constant demand to keep current with the latest advances in software.
- Unless you take necessary precautions, you risk developing repetitive-motion injuries as a result of constant keyboarding.

▣ Pricing

Desktop publishers may charge by the hour, by the page, or by the job.

By the hour. Typical hourly prices range between $25 and $65. Heidi Waldman points out that "in a metropolitan area, a desktop publishing business is not going to survive charging under $40 a hour."

By the page. Typical page prices range between $25 and $50.

By the job. Pricing by the job involves estimating how many hours the job will take and allowing a fudge factor for corrections and changes. This method of pricing is popular, because many clients prefer to pay a fixed price.

In addition, some desktop publishers charge an extra fee for higher-quality output. For example, a typical charge for a 1,270-dots-per-inch Linotronic is $12 per page; for film, $15 per page.

▣ Potential Earnings

TYPICAL ANNUAL GROSS REVENUES: $40,000 based on 4 billable hours a day at $40 per hour. Earnings may be increased by offering additional services, such as pickup and delivery, extra-fast turnaround time, high-quality printing, and a wider variety of font types.

OVERHEAD: Moderate (20 to 40 percent).

▣ Best Ways to Get Business

- Directly soliciting print shops, small service and retail businesses, professional practices, and nonprofit organizations with a portfolio of your work.
- Networking in organizations, such as leads clubs and chambers of commerce.
- Using direct mail in the form of a letter, a sales flyers, or an introductory brochure sent to a specific market in larger cities or, in smaller communities, to businesses that advertise in the yellow pages and in newspapers.
- Follow up these mailings with a personal phone call in which you ask for an appointment, to which you bring samples, perhaps customized to the prospective customer's business.
- Phoning and then writing companies that have placed help-wanted ads seeking graphic-arts personnel to do their backup or overflow work.
- Advertising in the yellow pages.
- Placing three-to-five-line ads in local publications, particularly computer publications, in which you provide specific information about your operation such as the software you use, the output you can offer, and so forth.
- Offering a discount with the first job—for instance, one hour free with a minimum two-hour job.

▣ First Steps

1. If you have no experience in the graphic-design field, you need to take several courses in design such as those available from continuing-education programs, community colleges, colleges and universities, and art schools.
2. Learn about working with service bureaus and printers.
3. Learn to use desktop publishing software and related drawing programs. Courses are available from computer schools, continuing-education programs, and desktop publishing divisions of art schools.

4. If you have experience, do market research to find a specialty market not being served before you acquire the expensive software and equipment needed for desktop publishing.

◘ Where to Turn for Information and Help

BOOKS

Desktop Publishing as a Business, by Heidi Waldman, White Bird Press, Box 11881, St. Paul, MN 55111.

Desktop Publishing by Design, by Ronnie Shusan, and Don Wright. Redmond, WA: Microsoft Press, 1989. Available in both Pagemaker and Ventura editions.

Desktop Publishing Success, by Felix Kramer and Maggie Lovaas, self-published. Box 844, Cathedral Station, New York, NY 10025.

Pocket Pal, by Michael H. Bruno. New York: International Paper Company, 1986.

Roger Black's Desktop Design Power, by Roger Black. New York: Bantam Books, 1991.

ORGANIZATIONS

Desktop Publishing Forum, CompuServe Information Service, 5000 Arlington Centre Boulevard, Columbus, OH 43220; (800) 848-8199. Once on-line, enter GO DTPFORUM.

National Association of Desktop Publishers, Box 1410, Boston, MA 02215; (617) 426-2885.

Special-interest groups of local computer and software user groups in your area can be of value also.

MAGAZINES

Adobe Font and Function. Call (800) 83FONTS for a subscription. Free.

How Magazine, F&W Publications, 1507 Dana Avenue, Cincinnati, OH 45207; (513) 531-4744. Emphasizes business aspects of graphic design.

Personal Publishing, the Renegade Company, Box 390, Itasca, IL 60143.

Publish!, PC World Communications, 555 DeHaro Street, San Francisco, CA 94107.

Step by Step, Dynamic Graphics, 6000 North Forest Park Drive, Peoria, IL 61614.

NEWSLETTERS

Before and After, Pagelab, 331 J Street, Suite 150, Sacramento, CA 95814. Tips on designing newsletters.

Cut and Paste, Data Search Publications, 6 Reina Court, Valley Cottage, NY 10989; (800) 745-4037. Focuses on marketing tips, product trends, and how-to information.

COURSES

Desktop Publishing and Design, NRI School of Home-Based Businesses, McGraw-Hill Continuing Education, 4401 Connecticut Avenue, N.W., Washington, DC 20008. This at-home study course includes a computer, software, mouse, printer, and lessons in both design and operating a desktop publishing business.

■ ■ ■ ■

DESKTOP VIDEO

Some people say desktop video is simply a term coined by marketeers to sell computers and software. But that's what they said about desktop publishing—which, of course, has now transformed the world of print media and become a burgeoning new field. We believe desktop video will impact the world of video production as dramatically as desktop publishing has affected the world of print. And in the process it's opening doors for many exciting businesses.

Essentially, *desktop video* refers to using new technologies to create full-motion video at your desk. The term is generally used to describe the wedding of television technology with computer technology. This includes sending video signals into a computer either as still images or in full motion, or sending computer-generated graphics or animation out of a computer into a video monitor or projector, thereby mixing computer-generated graphics or text with video images from a camera or videotape and using a computer for editing. The technologies that make this marriage possible include optical laser discs for video that are similar to music CDs, advanced computer-graphics software, and low-cost video-production equipment like the camcorder.

Desktop video is not a single business, however. The following are the types of services made possible in this emerging field, which is also referred to as *multimedia production.*

Desktop presentations. One of the first forms of desktop video, this involves creating animated videos for use in presentations that would previously have relied on still slides and overheads. Kevin McFarland, whose home-based company is called Desktop Video and Graphics, points out that "there are 10 million presentations made every week in the United States and most of them are using slides and flip charts. I feel like I'm on the crest of a wave."

Corporations, consultants, and professionals use presentations for sales tools, animated brochures, and instruction or training. Nancy Schuler, who with her partner, Mary Holzer, has a business called Show and Tell Systems, has been producing full-motion animation used in marketing and training presentations for five years. She says, "People are putting their message on disks and videotape so that it communicates the excitement that comes with movement and sound. Full motion is coming to be a standard for presentations."

With the ability for complete animation, otherwise-mundane statistical data can be superimposed over an endless variety of subject matter and made visually interesting. The limits are subject only to the creator's imagination. Such presentations, produced on IBM-compatible and Macintosh computers and using desktop presentation software like *Macromind, Storyboard,* and *Authorware,* can be distributed on floppy disks or transferred from disk to videotape and CD-ROM for presentations.

Free-lance media producers and independent filmmakers can also use this application of desktop video as a planning tool to produce simple storyboards and to sketch out effects—which helps them sell clients and backers on concepts.

Computer graphics. Computer-generated graphics are being integrated into many kinds of video productions. Kevin McFarland is able to save his clients two-thirds of what it would cost them to produce the same overlays and animation at a studio. Special effects created in people's homes are being sold for use in films as well.

Video production services. Turning raw videotapes shot with a camcorder into professional-looking productions good enough for broadcast television is being done with new products like NewTek's *Video Toaster.* Either by using stand-alone equipment or by adding a card to an Amiga computer, desktop video services can add titles and special effects like flips, tumbles, zooms, mosaics, trajectories, and trails to videotapes.

Many professional videographers like to shoot weddings, graduations, sporting events, conventions, reunions, retirement parties, and bar mitzvahs, but don't like the detailed work of editing these tapes. Not only can a desktop video service do the editing; it can also help the videographers produce a better finished video for their clients, making sure they have something that looks much better than what Uncle Harry could have done with his camcorder. And since videographers who use a desktop video service are adding value, they can also charge a higher price and gain a competitive advantage over videographers who do not offer these services. To gain the same advantage without a service, a videographer would have to buy expensive special-effects generators.

Of course, Uncle Harry could hire a desktop video service to turn his camcorder recordings into better-quality productions, too. With desktop video, homemade wedding videos can be made to look like *Dynasty,* and tapes of Little League games can look like Monday-night baseball.

Desktop video is being given a giant push forward by *Video Toaster.* This unlikely name, it seems, was a nickname the project directors gave this product during its development. The *Toaster* is a combination of hardware and software and is available as a stand-alone system for $4,000. If you already own an *Amiga* computer, though, you can get most of the same capabilities for $1,600 by adding a card that fits in your Amiga's video slot.

The *Toaster* generates a full network-broadcast-level video signal that is of duplicatable quality. It also can produce real-time digital video effects, which means transitions need not be limited to a dissolve or a cut, and can be an image peeling off or tumbling away to reveal another image—just like on network TV.

While the *Video Toaster* can be combined with images created on a computer, the *Toaster* creates its own images and can create a videotape with broadcast quality that includes digital video effects, 3-D animation, character generation, original artwork, and color processing. In fact, NewTek, the *Toaster's* makers, report that the *Toaster* is being used by all the major networks.

Other products are being developed with similar capabilities from companies like Avid and Digital, but the *Toaster* provides 90 percent of the capabilities equivalent to $60,000 to $100,000 worth of studio equipment, thereby making possible other businesses:

Creating television commercials for local cable companies. Local cable companies have the right to insert commercials into cable programming they carry from networks like CNN and MTV. If the station sells commercials to local sponsors, like car dealers and florists, they keep all of this revenue. However, the cost of producing television-broadcast-quality commercials has kept most local sponsors from buying commercial time from local cable companies. By using desktop-video equipment such as the *Video Toaster,* however, desktop video services can produce great-looking commercials for such local sponsors at a fraction of their former cost.

Producing special-interest videotapes. Just as books, newsletters, and some magazines are being published in people's homes, how-to and local-interest videotapes can now also be produced from home using products like *Video Toaster.*

Producing corporate videos. Videos with full motion—just like what you see on television, not animation—can be produced and used for corporate sales, training tapes, and annual reports.

Creating visualization aids. With desktop video technology you can produce video prototypes and walk-throughs of proposed buildings for architects, accident reconstructions for attorneys, and a variety of choices for landscape artists and other designers to show their clients. By using a video camera to shoot the image on the screen, you can provide still photographs of video images as well.

✔ Knowledge and Skills You Need to Have

- You need to understand images and how they fit together. This can be acquired by studying film or video in or out of college. However, learning video production involves more than doing an apprenticeship, or working for an established professional or a cable television station that has local programs. Virtually every local cable system offers such training. A background in animation, graphic design, or cartooning is helpful.

- You need to be technically and mechanically inclined. Robert Goodman, a Philadelphia film and video producer, says that to be good at desktop video someone needs to be "an artist with a technical side or a technician with a good visual sense."
- Because this is an art form, you need to be sufficiently *right-brained* that you can work without using logic for every decision, according to Jim Mack who run a video- and film-editing service in Michigan.

⬛ Start-Up Costs

	Low	High
Using a Personal Computer		
Computer with 80-megabyte hard disk	$2,500	$ 6,000
Printer	$ 300	$ 2,500
Desktop presentation/*Authorware* software	$ 400	$ 8,050
Word-processing software	$ 250	$ 250
Digitizing tablet	$ 400	$ 800
Optical scanner	$1,000	$ 2,500
Office furniture, especially an ergonomic chair	$ 600	$ 800
Business cards, letterhead, envelopes	$ 400	$ 600
Totals	$5,850	$21,500

Using the Video Toaster

	Low	High
Video Toaster (stand-alone model)	$4,000	$ 4,000
Two high-quality or professional videotape recorders (they need to be controlled by an edit controller)	$1,200	$ 4,500
Edit controller unit	$ 900	$ 900
Two color monitors	$ 600	$ 1,200
Time-based correctors	$ 750	$ 1,500
Video printer to make hard-copy prints of a screen	——	$ 1,000
Camcorder for creating your own videotapes	——	$ 2,000
Computer with hard disk	$1,000	$ 2,500
Printer	$ 300	$ 1,600
Word-processing software	$ 100	$ 250
Office furniture, especially an ergonomic chair	$ 600	$ 800
Business cards, letterhead, envelopes	$ 200	$ 600
Brochure	$ 100	$ 2,000
Totals	$9,750	$22,850

With the high-end configuration you should be able to duplicate 90 percent of what television stations can produce.

■ Advantages

- This is creative and challenging work that exercises every part of your brain.
- The people you will deal with are creative, and work is done in an informal atmosphere.
- The variety of projects provides interesting problems. Your work is not routine.
- You have the opportunity to get in on the ground floor and be a pioneer in a major new field.

■ Disadvantages

- Your work is perceived as a technical function instead of an artistic one.
- Your job is to make what you do invisible. So if your ego needs recognition, desktop video may not be your thing.
- You will often be working under tight deadlines.
- Video production is a highly competitive field, and the industry is undergoing significant transformations.
- The cost of entry is high relative to other home-based businesses.

■ Pricing

While most professionals charge on a per-project basis, hourly rates range from $40 to $100.

■ Potential Earnings

TYPICAL ANNUAL GROSS REVENUES: $40,000 to $100,000, based on billing 1,000 hours a year.

OVERHEAD: Moderate (between 20 and 40 percent).

■ Best Ways to Get Business

- Networking and making personal contacts in user groups and other organizations, such as trade and business associations.
- Directly soliciting videographers who do not wish or are not equipped to do their own editing; check under Video Production Services in the yellow pages.
- Getting on a software company's referral list.
- Sending direct mail to ad agencies, video services, video studios, and product designers.
- Teaching classes on aspects of video production.
- Placing announcements on bulletin boards in computer stores.

✚ Related Businesses

Video Data Service, 24 Grove Street, Pittsford, New York 14534; (716) 385-4773. A videography franchise. The fee is $15,950, which includes equipment and training. The primary activities for Video Data Service franchisees are taping weddings, making film-to-tape transfers, taping legal depositions, and duplicating and editing videotapes.

✊ First Steps

1. If you are artistic, take classes or apprentice at a cable station to learn the technical aspects of video production. If you are technically oriented, take courses in design at community colleges or art schools.
2. Learn to use the equipment and software.
3. Work on a volunteer basis to develop a reputation, or apprentice through a service bureau.
4. Build your reputation by doing good work.

☐ Where to Turn for Information and Help

BOOKS

Desktop Video Workbook, by David Land, Multimedia Computing Corporation, 3501 Ryder Street, Santa Clara, CA 95051; (800) 229-4750 or (408) 737-7575. This company also publishes a newsletter (*Mind Over Media*) and a directory.

Everything You Wanted to Know About Home Video Editing (But Nobody Had the Answers), by John Johnson, Video One Publications, 3474 Dromedary Way, Suite 1304, Las Vegas, NV 89116; (702) 643-2880.

ORGANIZATIONS

Professional Videographers Association of America, 2030 M Street, N.W., Suite 400, Washington, DC 20036; (202) 775-0894.

MAGAZINES

AV Video, Montage Publishing, 25550 Hawthorne Boulevard, Torrance, CA 90505; (213) 373-9993.

Camcorder, Miller Magazines, 2660 East Main Street, Ventura, CA 93003.

Computer Graphics World, Pennwell Publishing Company, Box 987, 1 Technology Park Drive, Westford, MA 01886.

Computer Pictures, Electronic Pictures Corporation, 2 Village Square, West Clifton, NJ 07011; (201) 546-4600.

Presentation Products Magazine, 513 Wilshire Boulevard, Suite 344, Santa Monica, CA 90401.

Videography, PSN Publications, 2 Park Avenue, New York, NY 10016; (212) 213-3444.

Video PROfiles, IDG Communications, 80 Elm Street, Peterborough, NH 03458.

INSTRUCTIONAL VIDEOTAPES

Introduction and Switcher Operation, TeleGraphics International, 605 Dock Street, Wilmington, NC 28401; (919) 762-8028.

■ ■ ■ ■

ERRAND SERVICE

People now are trying to squeeze more into the 24-hour day than at any other time in history. The reasons are many. Two-career couples now outnumber single-income families; jobs are demanding more than 40 hours a week; many people spend more than an hour a day just to get to and from work. In addition, exercise and fitness, once perceived as leisure, have become must-dos. The result is that many people are willing to pay others to run their errands and handle life's time-consuming minutiae.

Personal errand services do the grocery shopping, pick up cleaning and laundry, take shoes in to be repaired, take care of pets, run to the post office—whatever a client needs. Sometimes called a personal shopping service, an errand service may also pick out a last-minute gift or even find a dress for that special occasion.

Kathleen Carlson, who runs an errand service in Los Angeles, says, "As long as it's legal, we do it. However, we don't transport people and we don't pick up children. But we do take items back to stores to be returned or exchanged. We buy gifts. We take gifts to be wrapped. We make pick-ups and deliveries and do grocery shopping for small or new companies. For example, we deliver wedding cakes for a bakery. Hiring us is cheaper than hiring a driver and leasing a truck."

In this business, the best customers are regular ones who use the services several times a week. In addition to small companies that don't have their own delivery person on staff, your clients might include senior citizens, two-income families, single working women with children, and high-income individuals who can afford, for example, to hire someone to drive to every button shop in town to find a certain kind of button. So customers range from the extravagant to the frugal, and the work varies from the frivolous to the basic—from picking up theater tickets to getting in groceries.

Four years ago, Kathleen was working three days a week and had one client; now she has three full-time employees. She has doubled her gross every year and says she's making more money than she's ever made.

✔ Knowledge and Skills You Need to Have

- You need to like doing things for other people.
- You need patience to stand in lines, drive in traffic, and wait for people.
- Activities like running in and out of stores, hopping in and out of the car, climbing stairs, and lugging groceries are tiring, so you need to have stamina.
- You must be able to plan a route for your errands. By organizing an effective route you can save two hours a day.
- You have to be assertive to get help quickly. You have to be able to ask questions like where to find the return counter in a store, and know how to cut through red tape to get to the right person.
- To get from place to place quickly and efficiently, you need to know your city and be able to read a map.
- You need to like driving.

▨ Start-Up Costs

	Low	High
Business cards, letterhead, envelopes	$ 400	$ 600
Flyer	$ 200	$ 500
Late-model car or van	$2,500	$16,000
Pager or cellular phone	$ 100	$ 1,000
Totals	$3,200	$18,100

👍 Advantages

- This business is relatively recession resistant because you are working with an upscale clientele.
- It's gratifying to know that you are saving people time and making their lives easier.
- You're not confined to an office; you're outdoors, moving around and doing lots of different things.
- There may be variety in the type of errands you do.

👎 Disadvantages

- This business will not work in all communities. It works best in places where life seems hectic and complicated. It won't work, for example, where there is a mom-and-pop store handy on every corner or where parking is so limited that you'll spend your earnings on parking fees.
- Because you are limited to the number of errands you can run in a day, the key to earning a significant income is in having others working for you.

- If you do have employees, however, it means you'll have to bill clients, which can cause cash-flow problems. So you have to stagger your billing in order to have money coming in every day.
- The work can be wearing day after day; both on you and your motor vehicle.

💲 Pricing

Hourly rates range from $10 to $25 per hour. Some services require a 2-hour minimum.

🔲 Potential Earnings

TYPICAL ANNUAL GROSS REVENUES:
- *Working by yourself:* $26,250, based on working 7 hours a day, 5 days a week, 50 weeks a year, at $15 an hour.
- *With two employees* who will pay all their own expenses and receive 50 percent of the revenue: $52,000.

OVERHEAD: Moderate (20 to 40 percent).

🔳 Best Ways to Get Business

- Directly soliciting business from particular groups—for example, patrons of a charity, small bakeries, or gift-wrapping services.
- Backing up your contacts with this group with direct mail. Get a mailing list from charity rosters or membership directories.
- Taking out advertising in the program booklets at charity events to attract the interest of wealthy patrons.
- Delivering flyers to homes in select neighborhoods.
- Placing classified advertising in local and community newspapers.
- Networking with groups who could use your service.
- Getting publicity about your business in newspapers and magazines.
- Requesting establishments your clients use—for example, dry cleaners, shoe shops, and so forth—to allow you to post a card or flyer.
- Yellow pages advertising under Delivery Service, Messenger Service, and/or Shopping Service.

➕ Related Businesses

Additional businesses you could branch into are:
- concierge service
- messenger service (regulated by state utility commissions in some states)
- firewood delivery service
- publicity escort service for authors, celebrities, and corporate spokespeople.

🔋 First Steps

The key to establishing this business is finding a major long-term client to keep you busy several days a week while you start building your clientele. Such a client might be a business that you will do pickup and deliveries for.

■ ■ ■ ■

EXECUTIVE SEARCH

Matchmaking is an old profession that in the world of employment has become known as the search business, or *headhunting.* Companies turn to executive-search firms to match them up with top-notch personnel. Unlike an employment agency, however, which usually charges a fee to the people the agency places in jobs, executive recruiters are paid by the employer to find qualified people to fill positions for management, professional, and technical jobs. And unlike employment agencies, which are heavily regulated by state laws, recruiters are free of licensing requirements.

Because the overwhelming amount of work is done by telephone, executive searchers can work from anywhere. Of the 28,000 recruitment firms, an estimated 25 percent operate from home. Most of these home-based firms are one-or-two-person offices. Some states do prohibit recruiters from meeting with clients or candidates in their homes, but all other aspects can easily be done from home.

In fact, Paul Hawkinson, editor of the *Fordyce Letter,* a newsletter for the recruitment industry, found he was more successful after he moved his executive-search firm to his home. He says, "I was running a 40-employee operation from two floors of office space. Our billings were excellent, but my accountant told me that everyone was making money except *me.* I fired everyone, closed the offices, and moved to my house. My blood pressure went down, my happiness quotient soared, and I finally started putting some money into *my* pocket.

Anthony Burns, a consultant and trainer in the executive-search industry, says the opportunities in this field are excellent because it's one of the fastest-growing service industries in the world. In the '90s, the executive-search industry is going in two directions: toward companies with 6-to-15-person offices, which make heavy use of technology to work with large numbers of searches; and toward small firms with a specialized niche. Successful home-based recruiters are highly specialized by industry and type of personnel they place.

Bill Vick of Plano, Texas, a highly successful home-based recruiter, takes a middle road. He makes use of computer technology and psychological profiling to find executives for the microcomputer industry. Vick says, "My business is in my mind, in the information and knowledge I have and my ability to apply what I know. My office has only electronic walls. With a personal computer and fax machine I can use as an external printer, I can conduct business from anywhere, anyplace, and anytime."

About this business Vick observes, "The easiest thing is finding people to fill the jobs, but the most important thing is finding the clients. By this measure recruiters should be paid for finding clients, not people. But the opposite is true."

☑ Knowledge and Skills You Need to Have

■ Home-based recruiters must have knowledge of the kind of people needed in the specialized field in which they work: accountants, engineers, CEOs, and so forth.

■ This is literally a people business. Recruiters must be good at meeting people, developing relationships, judging character, assessing needs, and establishing trust.

■ Most successful recruiters have a sales personality. They are at ease with selling.

■ Recruiters must be patient yet tenacious. You must have high self-esteem and strong self-confidence to deal effectively with rejection. You'll hear 20 *nos* for every *yes* when you are looking for clients.

■ Home-based recruiters don't have the camaraderie of working with other recruiters to keep them motivated to work hard without a guaranteed return; therefore they must be self-motivated to keep themselves going.

■ Recruiters need to have the ability and desire to read and synthesize large amounts of diverse information. For example, you should be able to read through three to five magazines a day to keep up with trends and changes in the field you're working in.

🐾 Start-Up Costs

	Low	High
Computer with hard disk	$1,000	$2,500
Inkjet or laser printer	$ 500	$1,600
Modem	$ 100	$ 250
Database, word-processing, and communications software	$ 700	$1,000
Fax	$ 300	$ 600
Telephone headset	$ 40	$ 70
Office furniture, especially an ergonomic chair	$ 600	$ 800
Business cards, letterhead, envelopes	$ 200	$ 600
Brochure	$ 100	$2,000
Totals	$3,540	$9,420

🔥 Advantages

■ Start-up costs are low.

■ Bringing a candidate and an employer together can be very satisfying. With a good placement, the future of both parties is enhanced from the match. A company can turn around because of a placement you've made.

- The income can be high, as fees are usually substantial.
- This business provides a great deal of flexibility. By using a computer, your office is totally portable. You can take a month to travel in Europe and your business doesn't have to stop.

Disadvantages

- This is a high-risk business. You get paid only when you find the right person. If you miss out on finding someone, you have no income.
- The competition is stiff.
- The work has a relative lack of prestige.
- The business is stressful; there are big wins and big losses.
- Most of the work consists of making phone calls, and only highly motivated people can keep at it without colleagues and coworkers around for support.

Pricing

Recruiters charge 20 to 40 percent of the first year's earnings of someone they place in a position, with 30 percent the norm for the industry. However, according to Paul Hawkinson, editor of the authoritative *Fordyce Letter,* most home-based recruiters charge 20 percent, thereby competing on price with larger office-based competitors who have higher overhead.

Most recruiters work on a contingency fee basis. In other words, they get paid only when they locate a suitable candidate. Though the trend is toward contingent searches, some recruiters work on a retainer. With a retainer they receive 30 percent of the fee upon acceptance of search; 30 percent at 30 days; and 30 percent at 60 days. The closure rate on such searches is about half.

Potential Earnings

TYPICAL ANNUAL GROSS REVENUES: $122,000 (the industry average in 1990, according to a survey of 8,000 consultants conducted by the *Fordyce Letter.*) According to Hawkinson, "home-based self-employed recruiters do a higher gross for lower fees with higher net earnings." Most recruiters complete 15 searches a year.

OVERHEAD: Low (20 percent or less), with expenses basically telephone and computers.

Best Ways to Get Business

- Calling companies that have repeatedly advertised for a particular position in trade and professional publications. Carefully script your telephone calls, and use the same script over and over.
- Going to trade shows to make and renew contacts.
- Sending a newsletter to prospective and existing clients.
- Speaking about recruitment issues to professional and trade associations.
- Mailing postcards advertising your business to prospective companies.

First Steps

Don't start out cold in this business. Go to work for an existing search firm, where you can be trained in the industry, and decide whether this is a business you will enjoy and can succeed at. Spend a year or two learning the ropes. The turnover rate in the industry is high. Only two in ten stay with it after the first year, one in ten after two years.

Where to Turn for Information and Help

BOOKS

The Placement Strategy Handbook, by Paul Hawkinson and Jeff Allen, Search Research Institute, Box 31011, St. Louis, MO 63131; (314) 965-3883. They also publish *Placement Management,* by the same authors.

ORGANIZATIONS

Association of Executive Search Consultants, 151 Railroad Avenue, Greenwich, CT 06830; (203) 661-6010.

National Association of Executive Recruiters, 222 South Westmonte Drive, Suite 110, Box 2156, Altamonte Springs, FL 32715-2156; (407) 774-7880.

National Association of Personnel Consultants, 3133 Mt. Vernon Avenue, Alexandria, VA 22305; (703) 684-0180.

National Personnel Associates, 150 Fountain, N.E., Grand Rapids, MI 49503; (800) 826-4372. A member-owned cooperative that is similar to a real-estate multiple-listing service. Members list searches and can assist one another in locating candidates.

Executive Recruiter News, Jim Kennedy, Templeton Road, Fitzwilliam, NH 03447; (603) 585-9221. Trends and statistics, with emphasis on retained recruiters.

The Fordyce Letter, Box 31011, St. Louis, MO 63131.

■ ■ ■ ■

EXPORT AGENT

As the U.S. trade deficit has caused the dollar to drop dramatically against world currencies, the United States has become a relatively low-cost place to manufacture goods. This is dramatized by Japanese companies opening factories here with the intention of making goods to be exported. It follows that small U.S. manufacturers can profitably sell what they make abroad, and an increasing number are doing so.

However, to succeed in exporting, a company needs someone who can oversee export sales and establish relationships with foreign import agents who have the necessary business and political contacts. And it's this need that creates business opportunities for the export agent.

Manufacturing continues to be an important part of the U.S. economy, accounting for about one-fifth of all economic activity. Change is taking place in this segment of the economy, however, as manufacturing shifts from large manufacturers to small ones. In the most recent period studied by the Small Business Administration, 1976 to 1986, small manufacturing firms added 1.4 million jobs while large manufacturers eliminated 100,000 jobs. Small manufacturers are likely to need an export agent if they wish to take their products abroad.

According to John Jagoe, author of the *Export Sales and Marketing Manual,* "Success in this field, more than in most fields, depends on your own performance. There are tremendous opportunities for Americans."

☑ Knowledge and Skills You Need to Have

- You need an understanding of the business basics of locating suppliers, profits and margins, and credits and risks.
- You must have a knowledge of government regulations and forms for exporting.
- You need to be persistent in making contacts by telephone, letters, and announcements. You also have to be patient with the various steps in the process of exporting.
- You need the ability and willingness to do research in the library and on the phone.

- Good communications skills are a must. You are talking with people from other cultures and must explain the exporting process to manufacturers.
- The ability to maintain your composure and not be easily rattled by hassles in dealing with language barriers and red tape is necessary.

🐷 Start-Up Costs

	Low	High
Computer with hard disk	$1,000	$ 2,500
Inkjet or laser printer	$ 500	$ 1,600
Database, contact-management, word-processing, form-generation, and spreadsheet software	$1,200	$ 1,200
Fax	$ 500	$ 1,500
Desk, file cabinets, and especially an ergonomic chair	$ 600	$ 800
Business cards, letterhead, envelopes	$1,000	$ 1,000
Typeset introductory letters and brochure	$ 500	$ 1,500
Local trade-association dues	$ 75	$ 200
Publications	$ 50	$ 150
Total	$5,425	$10,450

📖 Advantages

- This is a growth area of the economy.
- This business has opportunities for international travel.
- You can develop loyal long-term relationships with businesspeople in other countries that lead to other opportunities, based on your providing good service.

🔧 Disadvantages

- Because international business transactions take longer, much patience is required.
- There are many hassles because of the complicated nature of international transactions. Murphy's Law often applies.
- Time differentials may stretch your normal working day.

💲 Pricing

- Commissions range from 2 to 3 percent for high-volume consumer items to 5 to 15 percent for costly proprietary items, such as software.
- With experience and a track record of success, it becomes possible to obtain retainers. To encourage getting a retainer, offer to deduct up to 50 percent of the retainer from your commission.

▣ Potential Earnings

TYPICAL ANNUAL GROSS REVENUES: $60,000 to $100,000 within three years from start-up.

OVERHEAD: High (more than 40 percent). Overhead is high because exporters make frequent use of outside professional services, especially lawyers to examine documents. A 24-hour answering service is preferable to an answering machine because calls must be taken at all hours of the day and night. Telephone costs can run from $300 to $500 a month. At this volume, however, you can expect to qualify for discounts on your long-distance service. Travel costs are high, but you should get your suppliers to share in the travel costs. Seminars to keep up on the field and to network can run $50 a month or more; entertainment, $100 a month and up.

▣ Best Ways to Get Business

- Making direct contacts with U.S. manufacturers by phone and fax.
- Speaking and offering seminars at meetings, trade shows, and conferences.
- Writing articles for publications read by your desired clientele.
- Networking and personal contacts in organizations, such as trade and business associations, particularly in industries or fields in which you have experience.

▣ First Steps

- Read and attend seminars on export procedures.
- Identify businesses and/or industries on which you wish to concentrate and learn about countries where their products would be well received.
- Make use of the free advice offered by experts with the state and federal government.
- Start contacting U.S. companies you'd like to represent.

▢ Where to Turn for Information and Help

MANUALS AND REFERENCES

Export Sales and Marketing Manual, by John R. Jagoe, Export USA Publications, 4141 Parklawn Avenue South, Suite 110, Box 35422, Minneapolis, MN 55435; (800) 876-0624. Very complete, usable information and forms. Updated quarterly; $295.

Thomas Register, Thomas Publishing Company, One Penn Plaza, New York, NY 10119; (800) 222-7900, ext. 200. Available both in print in libraries and as an on-line database (on CompuServe). Provides the names and addresses of manufacturers and can be used as a prospect list.

Trade Shows and Professional Exhibits Directory, Gale Research Company, Book Tower, Detroit, MI 48226; (313) 961-2242. Annual; $70.

Tradeshow Week Data Book, Tradeshow Week, 12233 West Olympic Boulevard, Suite 236, Los Angeles, CA 90064; (800) 521-8110. Cost: $265. An international edition is available for $175 from R. R. Bowker, Order Department, Box 762, New York, NY 10114.

GOVERNMENT RESOURCES

The Small Business Administration offers personal assistance through its Small Business Development Centers and Service Core of Retired Executives (SCORE), located throughout the country which offer free advice. In addition, the SBA's Office of International Trade Assistance, Office of Procurement Assistance, and Office of Minority Business Opportunities provide information and programs that may be helpful. To locate the SBA offices with these services nearest you, write to the SBA, Small Business Development Centers Headquarters, 1129 20th Street, N.W., #410, Washington, DC 20036.

U.S. Department of Commerce, 14th Street and Constitution Avenue, Washington, DC 20230. The department's experts in Washington and district offices throughout the United States have firsthand knowledge of overseas markets. They offer information on oversees trade opportunities, customs, regulations and procedures, market potential, and so forth. They have an export-advice hot line: (800) 343-4300; ask for operator 940. For more information call the U.S. and Foreign Commercial Service of the International Trade Administration at (202) 377-5777. And for information on licensing requirements and export-control regulations and policies, contact the exporter assistance staff of the Office of Export Licensing at (202) 377-4811. The Department of Commerce also offers seminars on exporting. Contact the export seminar staff at (202) 377-8731.

Most state governments have international trade offices to help companies within their state become successful exporters.

ORGANIZATIONS

For the names and addresses of local trade associations throughout the United States, contact the Federation of International Trade Associations, 1851 Alexander Bell Drive, Reston, VA 22091; (702) 391-6100.

MAGAZINES AND NEWSLETTERS

Business America—The Magazine of International Trade, Superintendent of Documents, U.S. Government Printing Office, Washington, DC 20402; (202) 783-3238. A biweekly published by the U.S. Department of Commerce.

Coble International, 1420 Steeple Chase Drive, Dover, PA 17315; (717) 292-5763. A newsletter that lists 750 to 1,000 export leads, with contact information.

Export Today, Trade Communications, 785 15th Street, N.W., Washington, DC 20005; (202) 737-1060.

■ ■ ■ ■

FACIALIST

Facialists help their clients take care of their skin. They work to slow down the natural aging process, avert wrinkles and skin problems, and keep the face looking as young and healthy as possible. Care of the skin is an ongoing process, so satisfied clients can become regular customers. Because skin needs taking care of between facials, facialists can sell their clients skin-care products as well.

The beauty business is a perennial one. People want to look and feel their best all year long in good economic times as well as bad. This is especially true now that the baby-boom generation is aging. By the year 2000, over half the population will be over 35 years of age. As people age, they spend more money, more frequently, on skin care. In fact, skin-care products will grow at the rate of better than 7 percent a year through 1995. Businesses that can provide service to help people preserve their appearance and health are doing well. This means the services of facialists will be increasingly in demand by both men and women.

All occupations for which people need to present themselves at their best are in the market for facialists. Executives, performers, service personnel, professional speakers, and airline attendants are just a few of the groups of people for whom appearance is an important element.

☑ Knowledge and Skills You Need to Have

- Becoming a facialist requires training to become a cosmetician, and most states license facialists as cosmeticians.
- This business requires that you have a nurturing nature and genuinely enjoy pampering people.
- You need to feel completely comfortable touching and having close physical contact with your clients.
- An outgoing personality is helpful if your business also involves product sales.

🐷 Start-Up Costs

	Low	High
Training	$2,000	$ 2,500
Table for clients	$ 800	$ 2,500
Steamer	$1,000	$ 2,000
Sterilizer	$ 600	$ 600
Towels and miscellaneous equipment	$ 200	$ 400
Specialized equipment	$2,000	$ 4,000
Brochure with rate card	$ 200	$ 600
Business cards, letterhead, envelopes	$ 400	$ 600
Total*	$7,200	$13,200

*These figures do not include remodeling or decorating costs for transforming a room in your home into a treatment area.

👍 Advantages

- The market will expand as more people want to stay looking young.
- The work is neither stressful nor physically demanding.
- Income potential is very good.
- You can see clients at the hours of your choosing.
- You can build a steady repeat clientele.

👎 Disadvantages

- This business requires having a separate room in your home, which must be decorated, equipped, and dedicated for use as a salon.
- Clients will be coming through your home unless you have a separate entrance to your treatment room.
- Zoning may be an issue because many zoning codes do not permit a continual stream of clients and customers coming to a home business.

💲 Pricing

Facialists charge by appointment. A basic facial runs between $35 and $60, with $40 to $45 being average. Additional services increase this amount. A regular customer will come monthly, yielding an annual income per regular customer of $420 to $720.

🅒 Potential Earnings

TYPICAL ANNUAL GROSS REVENUES: $50,000, based on 5 clients a day, 5 days a week, at $40 per session. About 6 appointments a day is the maximum. Earnings may be increased by selling products and teaching classes and seminars.
OVERHEAD: Low (approximately 20 percent).

◘ Best Ways to Get Business

- Personal contacts and informal networking.
- Networking in organizations, such as leads clubs.
- Passing out catalogues through friends.
- Creating a newsletter to send to past and prospective clients.
- Doing direct mail featuring special prices or offering complimentary facials.
- Giving your clients complimentary gift certificates to give to their friends.
- Holding an open house at which you provide information about your services.

FRANCHISES

Alloette Cosmetics, 234 Lancaster Avenue, Malvern, PA 19355; (215) 644-8200. Alloette is reported to be the only cosmetics franchise you don't need a storefront to operate. They've been in business since 1978, and they have 100 franchises. As an Alloette franchisee, you recruit and train beauty consultants, who sell skin-care products through home shows. The franchise fee is $80,000, part of which can be financed by Alloette. Although this fee is higher than that for most home-based franchises, the profits to be made in the beauty business are great.

A low-cost alternative is to become an Avon or Mary Kay distributor. For more information contact: **Avon Products,** 9 West 57th Street, New York, NY 10019; (212) 546-6015. Also **Mary Kay Cosmetics,** 8787 Stemmons Freeway, Dallas, TX 75247; (214) 630-8787.

◖ First Steps

First you must complete your training. Training as a cosmetician can be obtained at private cosmetology schools or community colleges. You'll find cosmetology schools listed in the yellow pages, or you can write the association of cosmetology schools listed below for schools nearest you. The formal training program is usually less than six months in length and leads to certification. Then, if your state requires it, you need to obtain your license. Look in the telephone book for your state's information number and call to find out which state agency will have the licensing information you need.

Once you are trained, and, if necessary, licensed, you must set up a room in your home as your salon and begin marketing your services. This is an ideal business for offering an initial complimentary session. So, in addition to the marketing methods mentioned above, to get your business under way offer to do a session for people you know who are in a position to pay for your service if they like the experience. While doing this demonstration, educate them about their skin and tell them why regular professional care is important. Talk with them about *their* skin in particular and, using a mirror, show them the benefits they could enjoy if they had regular facials.

▯ Where to Turn for Information and Help

MAGAZINES

Dermascope, 4447 McKinney Avenue, Dallas, TX 75205; (214) 526-0760. Bimonthly.

Skin, Inc, Allured Publishing Corporation, 2100 Manchester, Building C, Suite 1600, Wheaton, IL 60189; (708) 653-2155. Bimonthly.

ORGANIZATIONS

International Association of Aestheticians, 3606 Prescott, Suite D, Dallas, TX 75219; (214) 526-0760.

National Association of Accredited Cosmetology Schools, 1990 M Street, N.W., Washington, DC 20036; (202) 775-0311.

■ ■ ■ ■

GIFT BASKET BUSINESS

If you're good at handicrafts and also want to find a way to earn a living using your creativity and design skills, a gift basket business may be your ideal choice. In this frenzied world, most people have little time to shop for gifts. So what could be better than a gift that seems to be personally customized and yet takes no time to select, wrap, and deliver? Gift baskets are just such a gift. And as Camille Anderson, who operates a part-time gift basket service, points out, gift baskets last longer than flowers and candy.

It's no wonder gift baskets continue to grow in popularity as a way for a business to say thank you to a client or for an individual to send a gift for Christmas, Easter, Valentine's Day, Mother's Day, Father's Day, birthdays, graduations, weddings, anniversaries, baby showers, and so forth.

A gift basket can be filled with traditional gourmet foods, wines, and kitchen items, or it can be a specialty basket containing hobby interests, sports items, or almost anything. Baskets can be customized to all kinds of clients and interests—car dealers, politicians, realtors, parents with children at camp, chocolate lovers, and so on. One company we know of, Earth Basket, owned by Susan Fasberg, specializes in gift baskets for people who are environmentally conscious. By finding out about the personalities and interests of the people you're preparing baskets for, you can also personalize them to include items they would especially enjoy.

Some people create gift baskets to serve specific markets, such as hospital patients. Boredom Baskets/Boxes makes baskets consisting of individually wrapped packages. The baskets contain directions that a new package is to be opened each day, and the packages contain both silly and useful gifts, such as decks of old-maid cards, puzzles, and travel toothbrushes. Romance can be packaged, too, in the form of baskets filled with items like champagne splits and glasses; audiotapes and CDs with romantic music; and fragrant soaps, sponges, and bath mitts that might be used in a shared bathing experience.

With enough ingenuity and some marketing savvy you can develop a profitable part- or full-time business with a following of grateful customers who appreciate the compliments they get when their easy-to-give personalized gift baskets arrive.

The most profitable markets are corporate buyers, followed by individuals. Gift baskets can be sold directly to businesses through personal contact, by mail, or by placing them in retail stores like hospital gift shops, nail salons, boutiques, and health-food stores. Other regular customers might include wedding planners, resort hotels, real-estate agents, meeting planners, and contest operators.

☑ Knowledge and Skills You Need to Have

- Although you do not need any particular background, you do need to have an artistic sense and the ability to design baskets that are visually appealing.
- You need to know how and where to purchase supplies at a cost-effective price.
- You must be able to communicate effectively with customers and have sufficient enthusiasm and personality to sell your product.
- You need to be able to effectively manage your time so that you can make the most of peak seasons.
- Being good at organizing is essential, because an order for 100 baskets can take up a lot of space. And since a big order can result from just one telephone call, you need to be able to organize your work space effectively so your materials won't take over your home.

▧ Start-Up Costs

	Low	High
Initial inventory of baskets, excelsior, food, and other items	$ 500	$5,000
Hot-glue gun	$ 5	$ 20
Shrink-wrap machine	$ 80	$ 200
Business cards, letterhead, envelopes, invoices	$ 600	$ 800
Desk, chair, assembly tables	$ 600	$ 800
Computer and inkjet printer	—	$ 1,500*
Two-color flyer or brochure (sales go up with color)	$ 100	$ 2,000
Organizational dues for networking	$ 250	$ 250
Professional portfolio of photographs of your baskets to show to prospective customers	$ 100	$ 500
Total	$2,235	$11,070

*Although a computer will be helpful for this business, it is not essential when starting up, therefore, we have included a basic computer in the high-end estimate only.

🖎 Advantages

- This is a business in which you can earn a living by using your creative expression.
- People like to get gifts, so delivering them is a pleasant experience.
- You can easily start this business on a part-time basis.

🖅 Disadvantages

- This business can take over your home, with shredded paper and inventory everywhere.
- You may have to work around-the-clock during holidays and other peak periods to market, make, and deliver your baskets. You may even be so busy at holidays that you miss out on celebrating them yourself with your family.
- Business tends to be seasonal and can be slow during nonholiday times unless you are creative in lining up other types of business.
- You will do better at this business if you have at least one other person working with you.
- You will be competing with larger mail-order gift basket companies.

💲 Pricing

Baskets are priced anywhere from $10 to $300, with most priced between $35 and $50. Factors that enter into pricing are the products in the basket, the time the basket takes to assemble, and the uniqueness and artistic quality of the design. Most businesses give quantity discounts for corporate customers or other large orders.

🖳 Potential Earnings

Simply designed baskets can be assembled at 8 per hour, while more complex baskets can be assembled at the rate of 3 to 4 an hour. Simple designs need not be the least expensive ones.

Selling 25 baskets a week, 50 weeks a year at $40 a basket, will produce $50,000 in gross sales. However, during the days before holidays a one-person business with some temporary help from family or neighbors can produce $2,000 a day. One order of 100 baskets can produce $3,000 to $4,000. The cost of the baskets and its components should be about 25 percent of what you charge, but if you buy in small quantities and receive only small discounts, it can run as much as 50 percent of your sales price.

OVERHEAD: Moderate (20 to 40 percent). Overhead does not include direct costs of baskets and their contents.

Best Ways to Get Business

- Calling on corporate and organizational buyers, showing your portfolio, and leaving sample baskets for decision-makers.
- Obtaining publicity in local and national publications about your unique baskets.
- Networking and personal contacts in organizations, such as trade and business associations and church groups, and periodically providing a gift basket for a door prize at their meetings.
- Talking about and displaying your baskets at home parties and open houses, and then taking orders (like they do at Tupperware parties), and giving a gift basket to the hostess.
- Giving your flyers or brochures to reps exhibiting at gift shows, who can place your baskets with retailers.
- Exhibiting at craft fairs and home shows.
- Using direct mail with your own mailing list of people who have contacted you as a result of your publicity and exhibits at shows.
- Speaking to groups about gift giving.
- Donating baskets to nonprofit organizations for their fund-raisers in exchange for an acknowledgment in their printed materials and an announcement from the podium during the event.
- Having an 800 number to use with your publicity and direct mail.

First Steps

1. If you have no experience in design, take a course in floral design through your community college or a university extension program.
2. Take a short course in starting a gift basket business at an adult-education program like the Learning Annex.
3. Attend craft, gift, and novelty trade shows, looking for product ideas and suppliers.
4. Locate sources of supplies at trade shows and through wholesalers found in the yellow pages. Using local suppliers will reduce or eliminate shipping costs.
5. Talk with people in the gift basket business in the area.
6. Obtain a MasterCard and Visa merchant account. (See *Working from Home* for tips on obtaining a merchant account.)
7. Plan to have people available to come in and help you with assembling baskets for large orders. Assembly of less complex baskets can be kept out of your home at a reasonable cost by using the services of sheltered workshops employing the handicapped.
8. Order and keep sufficient materials and supplies on hand that you can get quantity discounts. Make sure the materials you use are easy to store.

Do not buy merchandise that will go out of date (like a calendar), spoil, or get stale. Susan Fasberg recommends that if an item is available in either a round or square shape, you should always choose the square one because it will be easier to store.

▣ Where to Turn for Information and Help

Books

Gift Baskets: How to Build a Profitable Specialty Gift Basket Business Working From Home, Camille Anderson and Don L. Price, 230 South Catalina #404, Redondo Beach, CA 90277.

The How-to's of the Gift Basket Business, Carol Starr, Bags 'N Baskets, 8045 Antoine, Box 147, Houston, TX 77088. Cost: $12.95.

Magazines

Gift Basket Service Business Guide, Entrepreneur Magazine, 2392 Morse Avenue, Box 19787, Irvine, CA 92713; (800) 421-2300; in California (800) 352-7449. You can also order an instructional video and computer software template for spreadsheets through *Entrepreneur* magazine.

■ ■ ■ ■

GROWER OF SPECIALTY FOODS

If you enjoy gardening, you may be able to cultivate your hobby into a full-time home-based livelihood without owning the acres of land typical of today's corporate farm or even the traditional family farm. Backyards, basements, or a lot of just a few acres is all you need to grow herbs, sprouts, mushrooms, edible flowers, and specialty vegetables in urban and suburban areas.

In fact, urban farming is becoming an important part of agriculture in America. Charles Walters, Jr., publisher of *Acres USA* magazine, says, "The only bright future in agriculture is to get a few acres, grow the product, and be near where the people are." Walters advises, "Find yourself a couple of hundred customers and make yourself a living."

Over the past 30 years Americans have developed a robust appetite for exotic and organically grown foods, and they are making vegetables and fruits a larger portion of the food they eat. As a result, gourmet shops, restaurants, upscale grocery stores, and health-food stores are eager to offer specialty foods. And the public is seeking out specially grown foods at swap meets, produce stands, and farmers' markets.

The popularity of farmers' markets has been a particular boon to vest-pocket farmers. In Southern California, for example, there's one farmers' market, and sometimes two or three, on any day of the week. There, people growing the perfect lettuce or tomato can charge near-store prices as people line up to buy.

Often this business begins with a desire to get closer to nature and return to a simpler life. It's attracting *green-minded* people like David and Susan Mountain, who have turned their love of mushrooms into a business: growing exotic mushrooms. David and Susan, like so many of these new farmers, have sought out a lifestyle very different from the one they knew when they held office jobs. They predict a bright future for small farming. Leslie Straus, owner of Sprout Time, who began growing sprouts with buckets in the back of her house, would agree. She found that with a large backyard, she could net $100,000 a year.

☑ Knowledge and Skills You Need to Have

- Tenacity and persistence are the bottom line in this business. No one is an "A" student the first year. You must be willing to learn what you need to do to grow crops of sufficient quality and quantity to make a living. A love for food or for growing things is essential to keep you motivated through the learning process.

- You need to have a sensitivity to the marketplace, to what people want to eat, what they find appealing, who's buying what, and when they're buying.

- Good bookkeeping skills are important because you need to know what it costs you to grow what produce.

◳ Start-Up Costs

Land. How much land you need to earn a full-time living depends on what kind of crops you have, the time your crops need for maturity, and crop rotation. If you don't have a yard, if you have zoning problems, or if you outgrow your backyard, find out if your city will rent low-cost land. For example, the Department of Water and Power of the city of Los Angeles rents plots of land. Or you can lease land from someone who has a large yard.

A vehicle to service accounts. You should be able to get a used truck or van for around $4,000; new vans cost around $16,000.

Setting up your business. Desk and furniture and a low-cost computer should run around $1,000. Business cards and stationery cost around $100 to $400.

⬚ Advantages

- This business provides the freedom to live an alternative lifestyle and still be in or close to cities.

- It provides the opportunity to experience a connectedness with the earth through growing living things.

- It's a way to express an environmental consciousness while earning one's living.

- This is a business you can start part-time in your backyard or basement.

⏚ Disadvantages

- Your livelihood is vulnerable to the weather and the seasons. After all, farming is the occupation that gave rise to the saying *Feast or famine*. If you live in a colder climate, your profits may be too seasonal for a full-time income.
- The popularity of growing particular *in* crops may result in heavy competition, and what's *in* may soon be *out*.
- Land near cities can be so expensive that it can be difficult to make a profit. Dr. Booker T. Whatley, Tuskegee University plant geneticist and agronomist, says that a farm needs to be within 40 miles of an urban center with a population of 50,000 or more, reachable on a hard-surface road.
- Growing crops is hard, dirty, physically uncomfortable work.
- Within cities, if your property is not zoned to allow agricultural use, you may have problems with zoning officials.

💲 Pricing

A rule of thumb is to set the retail price for what you sell at four times the cost of growing it. In addition, Richard Alan Miller, author and a leading consultant in this field, advises, "Add value before it leaves the farm." Adding value to your products prior to sale—for example, washing, cutting up, and mixing varieties of lettuce, or processing basil for pesto sauce—will multiply the price you can charge.

▣ Potential Earnings

TYPICAL ANNUAL GROSS REVENUES: $10,000 to $12,000 an acre for herbs, flowers, and spices.
OVERHEAD: Moderate (20 to 40 percent).

▣ Best Ways to Get Business

- Offering a unique product where you have an edge in the market. As Richard Alan Miller says, "Instead of growing basil, grow Thai basil."
- Selling directly to the public at farmers' markets and swap meets.
- Selling directly to local restaurants or exporters.
- Charging people to harvest their own food, if your land is located near a well-traveled roadway. Dr. Booker T. Whatley suggests charging 60 percent of supermarket prices. You need to have an attractive sign that will encourage people to stop.

⚒ First Steps

1. Check your zoning to be sure your property can be used for growing food.
2. Find an untapped market in your area and begin experimenting with growing a crop in your own garden.
3. Agricultural universities may not provide classes needed for very small farms, but you can learn about farming by taking workshops listed on bulletin boards of food cooperatives and reading about what will grow in your area and the best ways to grow it.
4. Decide whether you're going to grow organically or nonorganically and whether you are going to become a commercial producer selling to food stores or a quality producer selling to upscale restaurants or directly to the public at farmers' markets.
5. Do a feasibility study with a small crop the first year—on two acres of land, if possible.

▯ Where to Turn for Information and Help

BOOKS

How to Make $100,000 Farming 25 Acres, by Booker T. Whatley and the Editors of *The New Farm.* Emmaus, PA: Rodale Press, 1987. Rodale publishes a variety of books on farming; write for a catalogue: Rodale Press, 33 East Minor Street, Emmaus, PA 18098.

Knott's Handbook for Vegetable Growers, by O. A. Lorenz and D. N. Maynard. New York: John Wiley and Sons, 1988.

The Mushroom Cultivator, by Paul Stamets and J. S. Chilton. Olympia, WA: Agarikon Press, 1983.

Native Plants of Commercial Importance, by Richard Alan Miller. Oak, Inc., 1305 Vista Drive, Grants Pass, OR 97527. Oak Inc. also offers technical reports and farm plans. Call (503) 476-5588.

The Potential of Herbs as a Cash Crop, by Richard Alan Miller, Kansas City, MO: Acres USA, 1985.

ORGANIZATIONS

National Association for the Specialty Food Trade, 1270 Avenue of the Americas, New York, NY; (212) 586-7313.

Also check local farming organizations such as organic federations.

MAGAZINES AND NEWSLETTERS

Acres USA, Voice of Eco-Agriculture, 1008 East 60th Terrace, Kansas City, MO 64133.

Organic Gardening, Rodale Publishing Company, 33 East Minor Street, Emmaus, PA 18098.

The Herb Market Report, Oak, Inc., 1305 Vista Drive, Grants Pass, OR 97527.

The Herb Quarterly, Box 275, Newfane, VT 05345.

Business of Herbs, Box 559 Q, Madison, VA 22727.

Organic Food Matters, the *Journal of Sustainable Agriculture, Committee for Sustainable Agriculture, Box 1300, Colfax, CA 95713; (916) 346-2777.*

■ ■ ■ ■

HOME INSPECTOR

If you have a background or interest in construction or a related field, you can put on a white collar and become a home inspector. Home inspection began as real-estate prices skyrocketed in the 1970s. Buyers became wary of paying princely prices yet not knowing whether the roof would leak or the furnace would go out the night they moved in (as happened to us with the first home we bought).

In the 1980s many lending institutions began to require home inspections as a condition to making mortgage loans. Additionally, laws were passed in California, Florida, and Texas that called for or resulted in home inspections. The California law, for example, requires that sellers disclose any problems with their homes before sale. As a result, to protect themselves some sellers started calling inspectors, too. So having a home inspected is growing in popularity across the nation for both buyers and sellers. Ninety percent of home inspections are still done for buyers, however.

The role of the inspector is to take an objective look at a home and help his or her clients avoid costly surprises as they undertake what may well be the biggest purchase of their lives. The inspector typically spends two to three hours visually examining all aspects of a home, including the roof, foundation, and attic; insulation; walkways; heating and air conditioning; and plumbing and electrical systems. The inspector tells the buyers about the condition of the home, pointing out problems, such as signs of water damage, that may not be obvious to an untrained eye.

Following the inspection, the inspector prepares a written report. If defects are found, the buyer may choose to accept them and obtain a larger mortgage to fix the problems or renegotiate to have the seller correct the problems.

When working for a seller, the information provided by the home inspector helps the homeowners come up with a realistic price for their home based on its actual condition. After living in a home for fifteen years, owners may overlook problems to which they have become accustomed to but which lower the value of the home. Or, on the plus side, they may not have recognized features or special qualities in their home that the inspector notices.

Home inspectors have no vested interest in any particular work being done on the house. The professional code of ethics of the American Society of Home Inspectors (ASHI) prevents inspectors from doing the repairs they believe to be needed or from offering to do them. If the inspector is still in the construction business, he or she could be seen as drumming up business as a contractor.

Jules Falcone, spokesman for ASHI, says, "This business is a *comer.* The projected growth for this field is terrific." Home inspection is already a $216-million industry, and the number of inspectors listed in the yellow pages has quadrupled over the last five years. Falcone also points out that home inspectors are in heavy demand in areas of the country where there's an awareness of the value of home inspection. The demand is less in communities where there is no law or awareness of it, especially in rural areas. While some 4 million homes are bought and sold each year, only 25 to 30 percent of them are professionally inspected at this time.

At present only California, Texas, and Florida have laws that require home inspections. But more careful lending practices by savings and loans and by banks may result in home inspections becoming as common as appraisals and termite inspections. And the federal government may soon require home inspections as a condition for obtaining FHA and VA mortgage loans. So industry experts predict that home inspection will grow significantly during the '90s when, they say, as many as 90 percent of all homes sold will be inspected.

☑ Knowledge and Skills You Need to Have

- You need to have a background in or an understanding of construction to evaluate the structural soundness of a home and its strengths and weaknesses—from wiring to plumbing, from heating and air conditioning to roofing and building materials. You should also be familiar with the construction of swimming pools, decks, and spas and the operations of built-in appliances.

- You need to be familiar with the building codes in your state and local community.

- Inspectors need to have an inquisitive mind and enjoy solving puzzles. While most of the work is routine, you must figure out the causes for cracks, water stains, leaks, and so forth. And you can't have a fear of heights, because you will need to go up on roofs.

- You will be working face-to-face with clients and need to have good people skills and verbal abilities to point out maintenance problems and explain how simple maintenance can prevent big problems.

- You must be able to write clear, accurate, legible reports. As these reports will be vital documents in real-estate sales, careful attention to detail and accuracy are essential to prevent lawsuits.

- You must have errors-and-omissions insurance to cover your liability for oversights and mistakes.

✿ Start-Up Costs

	Low	High
Computer with hard disk	$1,000	$2,500
Printer	$ 300	$1,600
Word-processing software	$ 150	$ 150
Specialized software for home inspectors	——	$ 650
Office furniture	$ 600	$ 800
Business cards, letterhead, envelopes	$ 200	$ 600
Association membership	$ 250	$ 250
Tools such as screwdrivers, flashlights, ladder, electrical tracer, circuit tester, volt meter, moisture meter, and gas-leak detector	$ 200	$ 700
Errors-and-omissions insurance	$2,000	$2,000
Totals	$4,700	$9,250

In addition, brochures and promotional materials are available from the ASHI. (See below.)

📖 Advantages

- Inspectors are in demand in today's real-estate market, where people want value for their money.
- The income potential is good and the field is growing.
- The work is varied and much of it is done outdoors.
- Licensing may be right around the corner, which will put you in on the ground floor of a new profession. Licensing increases demand and stature and limits competition, and usually when licensing is introduced people already practicing in the field are automatically licensed. Texas is already licensing inspectors.

🔧 Disadvantages

- The buying or selling of a house is often an emotional issue, so you are often working with people whose nerves are on edge.
- Sometimes people have unrealistic expectations of what an inspection means and think that once a home has been inspected, it's okay.
- Some realtors regard home inspectors as a threat, fearing they'll lose the commission. But with realtors increasingly required to disclose defects, they are beginning to see that inspections are to their benefit.
- How much business you have is tied to the ups and downs of the real-estate market.

💲 Pricing

Fees for home inspections range from $150 to $400, depending on location and whether the report is a check-off form prepared and delivered at the site or a narrative report prepared upon the inspector's return to the office. In smaller and rural areas, fees will be at the low end; narrative reports, containing more explanation and detail, command higher fees than site-generated reports.

🔲 Potential Earnings

TYPICAL ANNUAL GROSS REVENUES: $48,000, based on a 1988 ASHI survey. However, a self-employed home inspector conducting 400 inspections a year at $200 each will gross $80,000. Inspectors can conduct 2 to 3 inspections a day, although 3 inspections a day is crowding it. In an active real-estate market, home inspectors who establish a referral network earn in excess of $100,000 a year.

OVERHEAD: Low (20 percent or less).

🔲 Best Ways to Get Business

- Getting referrals from realtors, corporate relocation departments, attorneys, and mortgage lenders. Call on these professionals directly or make contacts by networking at business, trade, and professional organizations. Jules Falcone estimates that "60 percent of a new inspector's business will need to come from real-estate agent referrals."
- Giving lectures in real-estate offices on topics like how to not let inspection kill your deal.
- Exhibiting at state and local home shows. Local ASHI chapters sometimes buy booth spaces in which members can participate.
- Getting publicity in real-estate sections of the newspaper and then using reprints in your promotional and sales materials to establish credibility.
- Listing in the yellow pages.

🔲 Franchises

AmeriSpec Home Inspection Service, 1855 West Katella Avenue, Suite 330, Orange CA 92667; (800) 426-2270. Their training program teaches people how to conduct home inspections, write a report, and get business. A background in related fields like construction, real estate, escrow, and property management is helpful, but not required. The franchise fee is $15,900 to $21,900.

The Building Inspector of America, 684 Main Street, Wakefield, MA 01880; (800) 321-4677. Provides training for doing residential and commercial property inspections. The franchise fee is $15,000 to $20,000.

HouseMaster of America, 421 West Union Avenue, Bound Brook, NJ 08805; (800) 526-3939. Does not require you to know or learn how to do home inspections yourself because they provide the training for inspectors you hire. The franchise fee is $17,000 to $35,000, depending on the size of the territory.

🔧 First Steps

If you have no background in construction or real estate, Lawrence Hoyt, president of the ASHI, recommends spending a day with a local inspector to see what his or her day is like. If you like what you see, you can gain the training, credentials, contacts, and experience you need by apprenticing with an established free-lance inspector. You can locate inspectors through the yellow pages or through ASHI local chapters.

You can also learn about the field by attending local chapter meetings of the ASHI. The ASHI publishes a manual and offers training, educational workshops, and training institutes.

Some community colleges are now offering courses in building inspections with the guidance of the association. Home-study courses are also available for $250. Such courses are advertised in the *ASHI Technical Journal.* You can also learn the field by affiliating with one of the franchises listed above.

Whichever route you take, it is wise to gain experience doing inspections under someone else before you start to do it on your own. We also suggest talking with people in real estate to find out their opinions of home inspection in your community and to determine if the market is saturated.

📕 Where to Turn for Information and Help

BOOKS

The following books are written for consumers, not professionals, but provide insight into the basics of home inspection.

The Complete Book of Home Inspection, by Norman Becker. New York: McGraw Hill, 1980.

The Complete Home Inspection Kit, by William Ventolo, Jr. Chicago: Longman Financial Services Publishing, 1990.

How to Buy a House, Condo or Coop, by Michael Thomsett and the Editors of Consumer Reports Books, New York: Consumer Reports Books, 1990.

COURSES

A Training Manual for Home Inspectors, American Society of Home Inspectors, 3299 K Street, N.W., 7th Floor, Washington, DC 20007; (202) 842-3096. Home-study course; $450.

Other courses on establishing a home-inspection business and/or technical courses are offered by HomePro (703/761-1400), Home-Tech (800/638-8292), and PITI (309/983-9371).

ORGANIZATIONS

American Society of Home Inspectors, 3299 K Street, N.W., 7th Floor, Washington, DC 20007; (202) 842-3096. The ASHI provides its members with pamphlets to be used as handouts, conducts regular seminars, and publishes the *ASHI Technical Journal.*

■ ■ ■ ■

IMAGE CONSULTANT

People have used clothing to communicate who they are and their status throughout the ages, but it was not until the 1970s that a popular consciousness developed that how one looks and presents oneself has a direct effect on career, love-life, and self-esteem. John Molloy, in his classic book *Dress for Success,* portrayed wardrobing as a science, and today more and more people subscribe to the idea that you can shape your image through your choice of clothing, hairstyle, and even gestures and speech. This interest in appearance has created the image consultant.

Image consulting has grown from being virtually unknown 15 years ago to a $130-million-a-year industry in 1990. In the 1970s, image consultants were hired primarily by wealthy women, but in the 1980s, image consultants' clients grew to include many professionals, corporate executives, and even corporations themselves. In the nineties image consultants will undoubtedly expand still further and will include among their clients a growing number of self-employed people who must market themselves effectively to prosper.

Through videotapes, computer-aided imaging, and other audio-visual aides, image consultants help their clients use clothing, makeup, hairstyle, speech, and body stance to create a desired effect. The goal, according to Jacqueline Thompson, who does research on the industry and publishes the *Directory of Personal Image Consultants,* is to help clients insure that their visible image matches their inner talents and aspirations.

In addition to helping clients with the components of their image, some consultants audit their clients' closets and then go shopping with clients. Some actually do their clients' shopping for them. In this case, they may call themselves personal shoppers, which has become an image-consulting specialty in itself. Some even go through clients' closets showing them how to make the most of what they have and throwing out the rest.

Today's clients are both men and women. They may come to the consultant having realized that they are being repeatedly passed over for a desired promotion in favor of more-attractive-looking candidates. Or they may be looking for a job and want to make the best possible impression. Or they may simply be people who want to be sure they're presenting themselves in the best possible light. Single or newly divorced men and women also come to image consultants wanting to create a more appealing image.

Sometimes the client's look simply needs updating, according to Brenda

York, who has done image consulting since 1976 and offers a training program to become an image consultant. In the 1990s, for example, the hard-driving power look of the 80s has been replaced by a "kinder and gentler" look. A more up-to-date look may be as simple as replacing harsh black-rimmed glasses and dark suits with a less intimidating, more approachable look. At other times, the consultant needs to help the client enhance his or her desirable features and play down or camouflage less appealing ones through choice of color, use of accessories, or type of tailoring.

In addition to working with individual clients, an image consultant may work with an entire organization, assisting all the executives, sales personnel, or customer-service representatives in looking and presenting themselves at their best. One image consultant, Bobbi Gee, actually helps companies decide on the corporate image they wish to project and then assists them in projecting that image throughout the organization.

Corporate image consultants are concerned with both the company's visual image and its customer and public relations. Some consultants also specialize in preparing corporate representatives for public appearances.

About 50 percent of the image consultants who belong to the Association of Image Consultants International work with the visual aspects of image such as clothing style and selection. Another 30 percent work primarily with the verbal aspects of image, offering speech coaching and presentation-skills training.

Other aspects of this business that are emerging in the '90s, especially in the corporate market, include focusing on nonverbal communication skills, etiquette, aromacology, and cross-cultural communications. As Americans must deal more with people of other cultures, cross-cultural communications and etiquette will be popular topics for seminars and corporate training. The consultant may work with clients one-on-one, taking them out to social or business events, or may offer in-house training classes.

The 1990-91 edition of the *Directory of Personal Image Consultants* lists 364 image-consulting firms. Jacqueline Thompson says that number has remained stable over the past five years. However, Faith Feldman, whose image firm is called Options with Faith, believes that number will grow because the market for this business has just begun to be tapped. "Many people still don't know what image consulting is," she says. "Just wait until we're as well known as interior decorators!"

✅ Knowledge and Skills You Need to Have

- The type of background you need depends on what aspects of the field you will be consulting in. Typical backgrounds of image consultants include experience in education, fashion, clothing, cosmetics, broadcasting, communications, speech, acting, and modeling. Jennifer Maxwell Morris, president of Look Consulting International, advises, "Don't be scared away if you don't have a professional creative background as long as you have an innate sense and love of creativity and style."

- You need to have a nurturing personality. A good image consultant doesn't dictate or impose a verbal or visual persona on somebody. Whereas initially image consultants were prone to follow formulas and believed there were sets of rules for how to dress for success, today the profession stresses bringing out an individual's strengths within the boundaries of what the culture expects and values.
- You need to be a good communicator, drawing out your clients' needs and personalities. You must provide feedback and suggestions in a tactful and caring way.
- Image consultants need to be skillful at presenting themselves. Essentially you have to be a walking, talking, breathing example of what you teach. You need to have excellent speaking and teaching skills, because this is how you get business.
- If you specialize in fashion or color, you need to be visually oriented.
- You must keep abreast of fashion trends in business.

▣ Start-Up Costs

Fashion/Visual Specialization

	Low	High
Training	$ 500	$ 3,500
Reference books on style, color, etc.	$ 100	$ 200
Set of color swatches for advising on use of color	$ 200	$ 200
Business cards, letterhead, envelopes	$ 200	$ 600
Portfolio of before-and-after photographs	$ 200	$ 500
Media kit with articles by and about you, and testimonial letters	$ 50	$ 100
Price list of services	$ 50	$ 100
Personal wardrobe with 2 or 3 complete outfits	$1,500	$ 5,000
Polaroid camera	$ 80	$ 200
Organizational dues	$ 250	$ 250
Total	$3,130	$10,650

Verbal/Speaking Specialization

	Low	High
Computer with hard disk	$1,000	$ 2,500
Laser printer	$ 650	$ 1,600
Word-processing, presentation-graphics, and desktop-publishing software for visual aids and workshop materials	$ 650	$ 1,000
Business cards, letterhead, envelopes	$ 200	$ 600
Brochure	$ 100	$ 2,000
Camcorder and monitor	$1,000	$ 2,500
Organizational dues	$ 250	$ 250
Total	$3,850	$10,450

🖒 Advantages

- People are interested in and curious about their image, making this an easy topic to talk to people about.
- There is plenty of opportunity to use your creativity in providing a valued service.
- The work can be very rewarding. Sometimes even small changes can dramatically improve the lives of your clients, and you'll hear about the sales records, promotions, and new jobs they've attained with your help. Image consultants also get credit for weddings.
- The business is well suited to raising a family because you don't work during holidays and traditional vacation times.
- If you are working with wardrobes, you can often get clothing free or at a discount from retail chains.

🖓 Disadvantages

- Because many people are not yet familiar with the benefits of image consulting, you must educate them before you can sell your service.
- Advertising doesn't work. You have to demonstrate your skills and build a relationship with people before they will hire you. Some people may initially think your work is superficial or insignificant.
- Multilevel organizations selling cosmetics have diluted this young profession by casting their sales representatives as image consultants.
- Clients may be easily offended or resistant to your feedback and suggestions.
- If your clients are individuals you will probably need to sell products or teach seminars in addition to providing private consultations in order to earn a sufficient full-time income.
- This industry is sensitive to the economy because hiring an image consultant is a discretionary purchase.

💲 Pricing

Image consultants provide their services through private consultation, in group workshops, or in corporate seminars. A tabulation of fees shown in the listing of the 1990-91 edition of *Directory of Personal Image Consultants* indicates that for consultants specializing in speech, communication, and presentation skills, *hourly fees* ranged from $50 to $350, with the most typical fees between $75 and $150 an hour. *Daily seminar fees* ranged from $750 to $4,450, with the most typical fees between $1,000 and $3,300 a day. *Per-person workshop fees* ranged from $395 to $975, with an average fee of $845.

For consultants specializing in wardrobe and color analysis, *hourly fees* ranged from $15 to $150, with the most common fee charged being $100 an hour, particularly in California. For shopping, closet audits, and related tasks, the average was $70 an hour. *Daily seminar fees* ranged from $500 to $2,500, with the most popular fees ranging from $1,000 to $1,500 a day. *Per-person workshop fees* ranged from $25 to $250, with $70 the average.

Some consultants receive annual retainers from corporations for regularly working with their executives and sales staffs. A consultant might receive $2,500 a year to work with a certain number of employees each month.

Potential Earnings

TYPICAL ANNUAL GROSS REVENUES: $86,000 for consultants specializing in speech, communication, and presentation skills, based on the equivalent of 2 training days per week at $1,000 a day, 43 weeks a year. For consultants specializing in wardrobe and color analysis, estimated annual gross revenues are $39,000, based on 1 1-day workshop a month at $1,000 (11 months a year) and 5 private 2-hour consultations a week at $75 per hour (48 weeks per year).

Wardrobe and color consultants commonly increase their earnings by selling scarves, accessory items, jewelry, cosmetics, books, and tapes. Consultants conducting corporate training programs, particularly those teaching speech and presentation skills, can earn six-figure incomes.

OVERHEAD: Low (20 percent or less).

Best Ways to Get Business

- Word of mouth is especially important in this business. You will want to get many clients who have lots of contacts and can tell others about how much you helped them. Therefore, you may want to do complimentary sessions with key individuals to get started.

- Potential clients may need a period of time to get to know you before they hire you. Therefore, networking and making personal contacts by participating in organizations and professional and business associations, particularly in industries or field in which you have experience, can be valuable.

- Give free speeches and seminars on image and use these as an opportunity to show off the dramatic results you can achieve; show slides or videotapes of your clients before and after. (Be sure you have obtained their written permission).

First Steps

1. Many private training programs designed to teach you how to be an image consultant are listed in the *Directory of Personal Image Consultants*. Their fees range from several hundred to several thousand dollars. Contact the programs that interest you for more information. There are also many books on the various aspects of image consulting, some of which are listed below.

2. Brenda York recommends that image consultants who want to work with individuals begin their business as a sideline. Often clients prefer evening and weekend sessions anyway, and by starting part-time you can gain some experience and build a clientele before leaving your job.

3. If you wish to work within a corporate setting, target a particular industry and concentrate on marketing to that industry. Any industry in which the appearance of the personnel plays an important role is a good candidate—for example, hotels, entertainment facilities, health-care industries, and retail stores. Contact their human-resource directors to discuss your doing a two-to-three hour introductory seminar for their personnel. You can identify human-resource directors through the local-chapter directory of the American Society of Training and Development. You can also find human resources personnel simply by reading want ads in the newspapers. Contact these individuals personally. Direct mail alone will rarely be effective. You might contact public-relations firms about working with their clients for media appearances.

4. Whatever market you select, get as much training in marketing yourself as you can. Develop your own presentation skills and get yourself a wardrobe of two or three outfits that show off your talents to the maximum.

▢ Where to Turn for Information and Help

BOOKS

If you cannot find these books in your bookstore, these and other books related to this field are available from Image Industry Publications, 10 Bay Street Landing 7F, Staten Island, NY 10301.

The Directory of Image Consultants, compiled by Jacqueline Thompson, Image Industry Publications, published biannually.

Do's and Taboos around the World, edited by Roger E. Axtell. New York: Wiley, 1985.

Flatter Your Figure, by Jan Larkey. Englewood Cliffs, NJ: Prentice Hall, 1991.

Image Consulting: The New Career, by Joan Timberlake. Washington, DC: Acropolis Books, 1983.

Image Impact: The Aspiring Woman's Personal Packaging Program, edited by Jacqueline Thompson, Image Industry Publications, 10 Bay Street Landing 7F, Staten Island, NY 10301. Written by 19 of the industry's pioneers.

The Language of Color, by Dorothee L. Mella. New York: Warner Books, 1988.

Say It Right: How to Talk in Any Social or Business Situation, by Lillian Glass. New York: Putnam Publishing Group, 1991.

You Are the Message: Secrets of the Master Communicators, by Roger Ailes with Jon Kraushar. Homewood, IL: Dow Jones-Irwin, 1988.

ORGANIZATIONS

Association of Image Consultants International, 509 Madison Avenue, Suite 1400, New York, NY 10022; (212) 877-2366.

Image Industry Council, 1255 Post Street, San Francisco, CA 94109; (415) 775-3145.

MAGAZINES AND NEWSLETTERS

Image Networker, Box 5051, Lake Wylie, SC 29710; (803) 831-8800.

■ ■ ■ ■

INDOOR ENVIRONMENTAL TESTER

The 1980s saw the environmental movement turn indoors with the realization that our homes and offices are assaulting us with a variety of pollutants that are making us sick. A number of indoor environmental experts have told us that today everyone is environmentally sick and that most people are just so conditioned to it that they don't recognize it. They point out, for example, that even a common product like shoe polish contains benzene, a carcinogen, and that most people don't know this.

This new awareness of indoor pollution has spawned a variety of new businesses through which people can turn their personal commitment to improving the environment into concrete services from which they can earn a living. The most promising of the many environmental businesses we considered is testing the indoor environment for unhealthy conditions and working with homeowners and business operators to make any changes necessary to solve environmental problems the testing identifies. Testing services are growing as awareness of the dangers of indoor pollution spreads. Allergists, for example, are now sending patients they once sent to psychiatrists to physicians who specialize in environmental problems and to environmental testers instead.

It used to be that only environmentally sensitive individuals with serious allergies were willing to spend money for environmental services and products. But today, as awareness of environmental sensitivities spreads, a growing number of people are willing to invest discretionary dollars to have their homes tested on a regular basis. Cancer patients especially want to reduce all influences in their homes that might suppress their immune response, and a growing number of seemingly healthy people are investing in improving the quality of their living environment.

Environmental testers test for a variety of things:

■ indoor air pollution created by mold spoors, dust, bacteria, formaldehyde, and toxic gases such as carbon monoxide, carbon dioxide, and sulfur dioxide

- electromagnetic radiation from high-voltage transmission lines, home electrical wiring, meters, appliances, electric blankets, water beds, video display terminals, and other office equipment
- lead found in paint, dishware, lead solder, and crystal
- geomagnetic influences such as magnetic grid crossings around a bed area
- toxic substances in carpet fibers, dyed fabrics, cosmetics, food, pesticides, and so forth
- asbestos used in insulation

(The testers we interviewed do not test, however, for radon, because radon levels fluctuate and testing needs to be done over six months. They advise people to buy an inexpensive canister for testing radon, which homeowners themselves can monitor over a period of months.)

Joe Riley's environmental-testing business, Healthwaves, took off immediately when he and his wife, a Ph.D. in neurophysiology, began specializing in testing for electromagnetic problems. With Joe's background in marketing, they were able to earn $1,000 a week right away. Knowing the potential of publicity, he combined free exposure through public relations with referrals from the people he served to launch his business quickly. He identifies the problems, but he does no electrical modifications himself. Instead he works with and directs electricians selected by his clients.

Not everyone in this new field achieves such immediate success, however. For other testers like Gene Burke, building his service was a slower though ultimately successful proposition. Gene, who calls his business the Environ Doctor—Home and Office Detect Detox, is a certified naturopath. His interest in this field arose from his own experience in recovering from environmental illnesses, and he describes what he does as "acting like the canary with a tool kit in a coal mine." Burke also draws from *feng shui*, the Chinese art of placement, in making recommendations to reduce harmful geomagnetic influences.

Joe Riley and Gene Burke use specialized testing equipment, but have also gained the ability to use their own sensitivity to see and sniff out health problems.

Audrey Hoodkiss also came into this field because of her own environmental illness. She had been an interior designer when she developed a chemical sensitivity. She now works with architects, designers, and contractors to locate attractive yet environmentally safe building and decorating materials. She also works directly with medical patients who need to redecorate to create a healthier environment. Jim Nigra worked as a taxi driver to support himself while he started what has become a successful business as an environmental-equipment broker. He sells everything over the phone, from environmentally safe shoe polish to pollution-busting vacuum cleaners.

These are just a few examples of this emerging environmental business, ripe for creative development. They and other related businesses in various stages of being defined could develop into some of the fastest-growing opportunities of the nineties.

☑ Knowledge and Skills You Need to Have

- Environmental testing requires the ability to synthesize vast amounts of information, because new research on environmental and health issues is surfacing weekly. New problems, remedies, and resources, new nontoxic and low-toxic materials, and new shielding mechanisms are becoming known, requiring some understanding of chemistry and toxicology, although you can learn this quickly.
- This work demands an intense interest in health and a willingness to be self-taught, since there are few courses in this area.
- Interpersonal skills are required to advise people who are living with extreme difficulty because of serious sensitivities or illnesses. You also need to be able to recognize the emotional needs of hypochondriacs and psychosomatics and not let them become dependent on you.
- Intuition and the ability to be highly sensitive to your own bodily reactions is helpful. (However, you don't want to use your own body to sense for electromagnetic problems; use meters.)

⬛ Start-Up Costs

	Low	High
Computer	$1,000	$ 2,500
Word-processing software	$ 100	$ 250
Printer	$ 300	$ 1,600
Professional-quality electrical equipment to measure electrical interference and various test sampling kits to measure toxic substances	$8,000	$ 9,000
Totals	$9,400	$13,350

⬛ Advantages

- This is a challenging and stimulating field that will certainly grow.
- It provides the environmentally conscious with the opportunity to do meaningful work.
- Helping people feel better and get well can be highly rewarding and fulfilling.

⬛ Disadvantages

- Because you work in *sick* buildings, you expose yourself to hazardous pollution.

- The clientele is predominantly people who are environmentally ill and cancer patients, so the work can be emotionally draining. You must guard against absorbing the emotional pain of the people you serve.
- This work is viewed by many as controversial, particularly the electromagnetic aspect. You may feel that you have to justify what you're doing to some people.
- You need to acquire a lot of technical knowledge.

💲 Pricing

Environmental testers sometimes charge by the hour and sometimes by the job, especially for people on fixed incomes. Hourly rates range from $60 to $100, with $65 and $75 the most typical. Representative by-the-job rates are $125 for an electromagnetic check for senior citizens, and $525 for a 3,500 square-foot home.

💾 Potential Earnings

TYPICAL ANNUAL GROSS REVENUES: $65,000, based on billing 20 hours a week, 50 weeks a year, at $65 an hour. An experienced tester can complete electromagnetic checks in 1 hour. Full home checks may take 3 to 10 hours.

OVERHEAD: Low (20 percent or less).

📇 Best Ways to Get Business

- Developing relationships with doctors and dentists who will refer patients with possible environmentally caused complaints. Some doctors will subcontract with a tester and include the testing service as part of a patient's total health-care program, in which case the tester's findings are reported directly to the doctor, who will relate them to the patient.
- Getting listed in health and environmental-resource guides.
- Getting referrals from environmental-resource groups, and city planning departments.
- Listing in the yellow pages under Environment and Ecological Services and listings related to hazardous-waste disposal.
- Making contacts at environmental conferences, symposiums, and trade shows.
- Speaking and conducting seminars on indoor pollution.
- Writing articles for magazines and newspapers.
- Obtaining publicity about your work.

➕ Related Businesses

Other possible environmentally-related businesses include:
- selling, installing, and servicing water-filtration systems

- consulting on recycling programs, waste reduction, and using recycled industrial materials for new products
- recycling toner cartridges for laser printers and copiers

🔖 First Steps

1. Become an expert. This is a fast-changing field. So develop a broad and eclectic understanding of what's going on in building biology (a term popular in Europe), indoor ecology, and suspected health problems.
2. Contact recognized organizations and authorities in the field.
3. Start conducting environmental audits for family and friends, and encourage referrals.

📙 Where to Turn for Information and Help

BOOKS

Cross Currents: The Promise of Electromedicine, the Perils of Electropollution, by Robert O. Becker. Los Angeles: Jeremy P. Tarcher, 1990.

Currents of Death: Power Lines, Computer Terminals, and the Attempt to Cover Up Their Threat to Your Health, by Paul Brodeur. New York: Simon and Schuster, 1989.

Ecopreneuring: The Green Guide to Small Business Opportunities from the Environmental Revolution, by Steven J. Bennett. New York: John Wiley and Sons, 1991.

Electromagnetic Man, by Cyril Smith and Simon Best. New York: St. Martin's Press, 1989.

Interior Design with Feng Shui, by Sara Rossbach. New York: Dutton, 1987.

The Naturally House Book: Creating a Healthy, Harmonious and Ecologically Sound Home Environment, by David Pearson. New York: Simon and Schuster, 1989.

Nontoxic, Natural, and Earthwise: How To Protect Yourself and Your Family from Harmful Products and Live in Harmony with the Earth, by Debra Lynn Dadd. Los Angeles: Jeremy P. Tarcher, 1990.

MAGAZINES AND NEWSLETTERS

Delicate Balance, 1100 Rural Avenue, Voorhees, New Jersey, 08043; (609) 429-5358.

The Earthwise Consumer, Box 279, Forest Knolls, CA 94933, (800) 488-3233.

Environ: A Magazine for Ecologic Living and Health, Wary Canary Press, Box 2204, Fort Collins, CO 80522, (303) 224-0083.

In Business: The Magazine for Environmental Entrepreneuring, JG Press, 419 State Avenue, Second Floor, Emmaus, PA 18049.

The Reactor, Box 575, Corte Madera, CA 94925; (415) 924-5141.

National Association of Environmental Professionals, Box 15210, Alexandria, VA 22309; (703) 660-2364.

National Electromagnetic Field Testing Association, 628-B Library Place, Evanston, IL 60201; (708) 475-3696.

■ ■ ■ ■

INFORMATION SEARCH AND RETRIEVAL SERVICE

With the sheer quantity of information in the world doubling every seven years, our society is drowning in information. Finding the particular information we need when we need it is increasingly a challenge. In the past 10 years, the information broker or information professional has stepped in to meet this challenge. And over that time information search and retrieval has become a $13-billion industry that is growing by 12 to 14 percent a year.

Like private investigators, information brokers track down and locate the specific information their clients need. Acting as specialized research librarians, they search computer databases and libraries as well as conducting interviews for their clients. Typical clients include businesses that are seeking information about introducing possible new products, expanding into new markets, or wanting to know more about their competitors. Other clients are professionals whose work requires that they become what information-industry pioneer Sue Rugge calls *instant experts*, clients such as lawyers preparing for a trial, advertising agencies developing an ad campaign, marketing and public-relations firms preparing a proposal, or private investigators and management consultants working on a particular project.

Some information professionals do their work primarily through interviewing and library searches. Others perform most of their work from home, searching on-line computer databases using a computer and modem. Some information, such as news wires and new-product announcements, is available intact only on-line, but only a small percentage of trade publications are available on-line, and therefore they must be searched for manually at libraries, using directories and indexes.

Increasingly, information brokers specialize in the type of information they research, such as law, technology, medicine or even particular branches of medicine. There are more than 4,000 databases available, and no one can become efficient at more than several dozen. Specializing also allows information professionals to concentrate their marketing efforts for maximum effectiveness.

☑ Knowledge and Skills You Need to Have

- To do this business well, you must have a love for information and details.

- Because this is a new field, you need to have the ability to sell intangible services that people may not be familiar with.
- Creativity is required to track down information; you have to think of various possibilities for how to locate the data you need. Then you need the critical ability to distinguish what is important to your client from all the other information that's available.
- Continuing to search for information even when you're told it cannot be found requires persistence and perseverance.
- For on-line searching, you must know how to use expensive on-line databases efficiently and have the poise and confidence to avoid becoming overly cost conscious with each passing moment you spend searching.

💠 Start-Up Costs

	Low	High
Personal computer with a modem	$1,100	$2,700
Communications and word-processing software	$ 100	$ 350
Printer	$ 300	$1,600
Office furniture, especially an ergonomic chair	$ 600	$ 800
Business cards, letterhead, envelopes	$ 400	$ 600
Brochure	$ 100	$1,000
Organizational dues	$ 250	$ 250
Training and documentation for on-line services	$1,000	$2,500
Totals	$3,850	$9,800

👍 Advantages

- This business involves interesting and varied work that results in constant learning.
- It offers an opportunity to be creative and to provide valuable information to clients.
- The field is growing and provides ample opportunity for newcomers who are able to market information effectively.

👎 Disadvantages

- Obtaining clients can be difficult because many people are as yet unaware of this business and don't understand its benefits for them.
- You may not be able to fulfill client requests on time and within budget.

💲 Pricing

Information brokers charge by the hour or by the job. Expenses are additional and are either billed at cost or marked up by 15 to 20 percent. Hourly rates range between $35 and $100. Pricing by the job involves estimating how many hours the job will take, and allowing for unexpected difficulties in finding information.

Potential Earnings

TYPICAL ANNUAL GROSS REVENUES: $17,500 to $75,000. The low-end estimate is based on billing 500 hours a year (10 hours a week) at $35 per hour. The high end is based on billing 1,000 a year (20 hours a week) at $75 per hour.

OVERHEAD: Moderate (between 20 and 40 percent).

Best Ways to Get Business

- Networking and personal contacts in organizations, such as trade and business associations, particularly in industries or fields in which you have experience.
- Speaking and offering seminars on information at meetings and trade shows.
- Writing articles.
- Collaborating with other information brokers to do specialized work and overload.
- Getting media publicity about you.
- Advertising in trade journals if you are in a specialty field.

First Steps

Sue Rugge believes finding a special niche is the first step in starting this business. She advises, "Specialization is necessary. I think it is essential to penetrate a market. You must have visibility. Pick a market that has a trade association with local and annual meetings. Go to the meetings, speak to the group, write articles for their publications. Word of mouth is our most powerful marketing tool, but it takes a lot longer to get it going if you are trying to work in many different markets. When you can cluster your clients in a group that speaks to each other, word of mouth goes faster."

Where to Turn for Information and Help

BOOKS

Find It Fast: How to Uncover Expert Information on Any Subject, by Robert Berkman. New York: Harper and Row, 1987.

How to Look It Up Online, by Alfred Glossbrenner. New York: St. Martin's Press, 1987.

Information for Sale: How to Start and Operate Your Own Data Research Service, by John Everett and Elizabeth Powell Crowe, Tab Books, Blue Ridge Summit, PA 17294; (800) 822-8138.

Reporter's Handbook: And Investigator's Guide to Documents and Techniques, by John Ullmann and Steve Honeyman. New York: St. Martin's Press, 1983.

Directory of Online Databases. Los Angeles: Cuadra/Elsevier. Annual.

ON-LINE DATABASE SERVICES

Dialog Information Services, 3460 Hillview Avenue, Palo Alto, CA 94304; (800) 227-1927; in California, (800) 982-5838. The largest of the database services, offering hundreds of databases. Dialog also offers Knowledge Index, a lower-cost subset of Dialog, for use in off-peak hours, but contractually limits its use commercially.

Dow Jones News/Retrieval, Dow Jones and Company, Box 300, Princeton, NJ 08540; (800) 257-5114 or (609) 452-2000. Primarily financial information.

Mead Data Central, Box 933, Dayton OH 45401; (800) 227-4908 or (513) 859-1611. Offers Nexis, a full-text database service, and Lexis, a legal database service.

Newsnet, 945 Haverford Road, Bryn Mawr, PA 19010; (800) 345-1301 or (215) 527-8030. Full-text retrieval of over 100 printed newsletters.

ORGANIZATIONS

Association of Independent Information Professionals, 38 Bunker Hill Drive, Huntington, NY 11743.

National Federation of Abstracting and Information Services, 1429 Walnut Street, Philadelphia, PA 19102; (215) 563-2406.

Society of Competitor Intelligence Professionals, 818 18th Street, N.W., Suite 225, Washington, DC 20006; (202) 223-5885. Newsletter and semiannual meetings. Membership costs $100 a year.

Special Libraries Association, 1700 18th Street, N.W., Washington, DC 20009; (202) 234-4700.

COURSES

Dialog Information Services, 3460 Hillview Avenue, Palo Alto, CA 94304. Dialog offers a variety of courses in using databases.

Newsnet, 945 Haverford Road, Bryn Mawr, PA 19010

MAGAZINES AND NEWSLETTERS

Database and Laserdisk Professional, Online, 11 Tannery Lane, Weston, CT 06883; (800) 248-8466.

Information Today and *LINK-UP,* Learned Information, 143 Old Marlton Pike, Medford, NY 08055.

How to Make Money Doing Research with Your Computer, by Sue Rugge, Here's How, Box 5172, Santa Monica, CA 90409.

■ ■ ■ ■

MAILING-LIST SERVICE

A mailing-list service is one of the easiest businesses to start from home with a computer and can grow into a substantial business. As a mailing-list service, you can earn money in various ways, including:

- creating and maintaining mailing lists for your customers
- producing your own mailing lists that are stored on your computer and then renting names
- selling monthly updated reports of your lists
- marketing, supporting, and teaching mailing-list software

Creating mailing lists for customers involves using the customer's existing records, such as their invoices or client files, to create a mailing list for them. This is a valuable service for many small businesses because it's well accepted that it's easier to get more business from an existing customer than to find a new one. Often, however, small businesses don't have the time or resources to do regular mailings to their own customers and therefore miss out on this readily available source of additional business. In addition to creating mailing lists for customers, you may also do their mailings for them and update their lists.

Compiling and selling your own mailing lists is another way to make money as a mailing-list service. While you cannot think of competing with large mailing-list companies that sell thousands of names in any one of thousands of categories, you can create lists that are tailored to your local community or to a very specialized market. For example, you might create a list of new businesses or residents in your community, or a list of sole-practitioner chiropractors in your city. Often you may obtain the names for such lists from public records, such as records of new business licenses. You can sell your list as a printed report that gives names, addresses, and phone numbers, as a set of mailing labels ready for use, or as both a report and a set of labels.

Selling monthly updates of the lists you compile can be another important source of revenue. You can add value to your monthly reports by phoning new businesses to verify phone numbers and by obtaining additional information, such as contact names, titles, whether it's a male- or female-owned business, whether it's minority owned, dollar sales volume if they've established a track record, and whether it's a new or relocated business, as well as the size of the business based on the number of employees.

These reports can be issued every month and can be sold as six-month or twelve-month subscriptions, payment for which you can collect in advance. You can also sell software and training to customers who want to keep up their own mailing list. You can train their personnel in how to use the software and make the most of their mailing list.

✔ Knowledge and Skills You Need to Have

- You need typing skills; the more accurate and speedy you are, the more you can earn.
- You need to be able to use a computer and mailing-list software.
- You need to be able to do detail work accurately.
- You need to be responsible about meeting deadlines.

⬛ Start-Up Costs

	Low	High
Personal computer with a large hard disk	$1,400	$2,500
Printer	$ 300	$1,600
Database or special mailing-list software that will allow you to store more than names and addresses and will provide sorting capabilities	$ 40	$ 500
Office furniture, especially an ergonomic chair	$ 600	$ 800
Business cards, letterhead, envelopes, pricelist	$ 200	$ 600
Total	$2,540	$6,000

⬛ Advantages

- Mailing-list services are relatively easy to start and sell.
- They can be operated on a part-time or full-time basis or even as an adjunct to another business such as bookkeeping, word processing, or even a translation service.

⬛ Disadvantages

- Requires precise attention to detail.
- The work is routine and uninspiring.
- Unless you take necessary precautions, you risk developing repetitive-motion injuries as a result of constant keyboarding.

💲 Pricing

For entering the names into a mailing list, services can charge from 5 to 7 cents per line of input. Thus, a 3-line entry consisting of name, street address, and city/state/zip would be 15 cents; a four-line entry, which adds a title, would be 20 cents. If other variables are entered, like a phone number, each extra entry is 5 to 7 cents each.

For printing out labels, services can charge 6 to 8 cents per label (including the label stock); envelopes run 10 to 12 cents per envelope printed. Envelopes that can be fed through an auto feeder are priced lower than those that must be hand fed. You may also offer special services, such as pick up and delivery and rush service, at additional charges, both to increase your revenue and to gain a competitive edge.

Alternatively, you can charge an annual fee, such as $1 per name per year, to enter, correct, update, and print lists a specified number of times per year.

🖸 Potential Earnings

TYPICAL ANNUAL GROSS REVENUES: $10,000 to $75,000, based on reports of people in the business. Earnings may be increased by adding additional services, such as pickup and delivery, quick turnaround time, printing labels at 600 dots per inch, or printing labels in a variety of font types.

OVERHEAD: Low (under 20 percent).

🖭 Best Ways to Get Business

- Directly approaching personnel of locally owned stores to ask how they handle their mailing list. In stores that ask customers to fill out cards or to sign guest books, ask what they do with the names they get.
- Spreading the word through personal contact to reach small businesses, organizations, and churches.
- Networking in organizations, such as chambers of commerce and leads clubs.
- Sending direct mail to businesses that advertise in the yellow pages and in newspapers, and following up the mailing with personal phone calls.
- Advertising in the yellow pages.

🖹 First Steps

- Learn how to use mailing-list software.
- Determine what service you are going to offer.
- Work on acquiring customers.

🗋 Where to Turn for Information and Help

Franklin Estimating Systems (801) 486-5954 publishes a catalogue that contains prices covering mailing-list data entry.

ORGANIZATIONS

Direct Marketing Association, 11 West 42nd Street, New York, NY 10036 (212) 489-4929. Many publications. Annual meeting.

AUDIOTAPES

How to Make Money in the Mailing List Business, by Katie Allegato, Here's How, Box 5172, Santa Monica, CA 90409.

■ ■ ■ ■

MAIL-ORDER BUSINESS

The idea of opening your mailbox to find it stuffed with checks intrigues upwards of 8 million people a year. Even though a small percentage of these people actually try a mail-order business, and perhaps as few as one person in 25 succeeds, the fact that you probably know someone or know about someone who's making money this way makes the idea all the more attractive.

In a mail-order business, instead of selling products face-to-face or by phone, you sell products by placing advertisements, usually classified ads, in publications or by doing advertising using a catalogue or another form of direct mail. You then fill the orders that come in from these ads. While the cost of getting into a mail-order business is rising, someone who is selling products that cannot be found elsewhere or that are otherwise difficult or time-consuming to find can establish a profitable mail-order business from home.

Certainly there is ample evidence that people are using the mail to shop. According to *Time* magazine, 63.7 billion pieces of third-class mail were delivered nationwide during 1989, and 92 million Americans responded to one of these direct-mail offers. This represents a 60 percent increase in mail orders over the six preceding years. And it's no wonder so many people are shopping by mail. Americans today are simply too busy to go shopping, while by using a catalogue they can shop anytime and anyplace.

Although the average American household receives about 43 pounds of junk mail each year, a well-done specialty catalogue can stand out from the rest. David Starkman, who with his wife, Susan Pinsky, publishes the 3D Real Photography direct-mail catalogue, claims that "often a mail-order catalog can actually do a better job of providing information about a product than having it stocked in a store where the clerks have little knowledge about your product."

Starkman also finds that selling by mail is more recession proof than selling through retail stores. You don't need to rely on whether someone goes into a store to get your products. You can generate your own business by sending information about your products directly to your customers. Also, you don't need to keep an inventory of products on hand. And by using the database capability of a personal computer, you can track who is buying from you and build a select list of repeat buyers and those who have made recent orders.

All sorts of products are being sold successfully by mail, including books, toys, artwork, makeup, foods, recipes, novelties, instructional materials, and career or financial information. The best mail-order products however, are ones that:

- you own and completely control, preferably manufacture, or at least can obtain from more than one supplier
- are not readily available in local stores
- are unique and attractive, lightweight and easy to mail, requiring no special packaging, sturdy rather than fragile
- can be offered for a substantial mark-up
- require little inventory
- are consumable or part of a complete line that provides an ample base for repeat orders
- have no breakable mechanical parts to be returned

Herman Holtz, author of *Mail Order Magic*, points out that specialized, brief how-to reports or folios of a few thousand words each are an example of the ideal kind of mail-order product that meets these criteria. Books are also ideal because they don't break and are rarely returned.

☑ Knowledge and Skills You Need to Have

- You have to be able to research the market and find out what's already available. You don't want to try to sell something someone else has done better and cheaper.
- You will need to become skilled at marketing, advertising, and selecting or designing your product.
- Direct mail requires creating a strong ad, direct-mail piece, or catalogue, which involves being able to write, photograph, lay out, and paste-up material about your products. If you don't have these skills, you will need to acquire them or hire others to do them for you while you learn what works. It's a fallacy to think, however, that you must have a glossy catalogue of full-color pictures. Attractive, clear, well-designed materials that present a lot of information about your products in an interesting way work best.
- You must be able to wear a lot of hats and be willing to do routine, menial tasks, like filling requests and shipping orders.

⬛ Start-Up Costs*

	Low	High
Computer with hard disk	$1,000	$ 2,500
Copier for incoming orders	——	$ 900
Fax for orders	——	$ 400
Printer	$ 300	$ 1,600
Word-processing and mailing-list, or preferably mail-order software	$ 500	$ 1,950
Initial test using direct mail or print advertising	$1,000	$ 8,000**
Office furniture, especially an ergonomic chair	$ 600	$ 800
Credit-card terminal	$ 125	$ 1,000***
Answering machine or voicemail (not a service, because you must be able to get the exact message, and no service can answer the technical questions callers will have)	$ 125	$ 400
Business cards, letterhead, envelopes	$ 200	$ 600
Total	$3,850	$18,150

Other additional items you may wish to get later include a shrink-wrap system with a heat seal for packaging your products for $400 to $500, and a postage meter, which you rent for about $30 a month.

   *Costs of purchasing mailing lists are not included. They vary widely depending on the list you're renting.

  **The $8,000 figure is based on producing 25,000 copies of a catalogue using a web press with three spot colors.

***Your sales will increase by approximately 50 percent if you offer charge cards, particularly MasterCard and Visa. To offer these cards, obtain a merchant account from a bank or through membership in a chamber of commerce or business association. The terminal for getting credit-card approvals will cost $125 to $225. However, banks will rarely issue merchant accounts to new home-based mail-order businesses, so you may have to go through one of the companies that act as a broker between you and banks. These companies make a hunk of their profit by charging from $700 to $1,000 for a terminal.

⬛ Advantages

- Since there are no fixed hours, a mail-order business can be started on a part-time basis while you are still employed. Many people begin mail-order businesses by working 10 or fewer hours a week.
- Unlike retail sales,
  - you don't have the overhead of monthly rent for a store
  - you can specialize in products that wouldn't sell enough to support a shop

- you have more control over people seeing your product because you can take your product to the customer instead of depending on your customer to come to you
  - direct mail is not dependent on weather
■ Unlike a service business that involves selling your time, with a flourishing mail-order business your income doesn't stop because you take time off.

⚡ Disadvantages

■ To make money, you've got to find the right products, and sell them for a price people will pay, with the right promotions, to the right customers—which is a challenge.
■ You are tied to the business; filling orders day in and day out can be tiresome. Mail comes in six days a week; you can't turn it off. All you can do is wish for a slow week.
■ Taking extended vacations is difficult.
■ Since you are doing your business by mail, you may have limited face-to-face contact with people (not a disadvantage for some people).

💲 Pricing

While the general rule of thumb in mail order is to sell products for at least three to four times your in-the-mail cost of the products, you need to find the pricing level for your particular type of products. If your products are unique (which is desirable) and you therefore have nothing to compare them with, try out prices on a preliminary basis with as many people as you can who you think would be buyers of your product. (Two or three is not enough). Such a trial will help you establish the first prices to test in your ads, direct mail, or catalogue.

🇨 Potential Earnings

TYPICAL ANNUAL GROSS REVENUES: Depends entirely on the product line, but the upside potential is greater than for most salaried jobs.

OVERHEAD: High (more than 40 percent) because of advertising costs.

📭 Best Ways to Get Business

■ Getting publicity, but this requires that you have unique products. Send press releases with a full-color photograph announcing your products to new-products editors of publications targeted to your customers. From the inquiries and orders you receive you can build your own mailing list.
■ Mailing a direct-mail piece or catalogue to your own list; people on your list know you and/or have already bought from you.

- Advertising in magazines targeted to your customers. In this way you can get orders and develop your own list. Small classified ads can be cost-effective.

- You can rent or trade mailing lists. Look for lists that have names of people who are like your customers.

🖐 First Steps

Getting started in the mail-order business is a three-step process:

1. Create or select your products.
2. Develop or rent a mailing list or, alternatively, identify publications in which to advertise.
3. Produce and distribute your catalogue, direct-mail piece, or advertisement.

Although no specific background is required for mail order, before taking these three steps, take courses and seminars and read books on mail order, copywriting, and so forth, from knowledgeable individuals who have a successful track record in the mail-order business. Otherwise you will spend unnecessary time and money finding out what will work and what will not. Courses on mail order are available through community colleges and adult-education programs in most communities.

Once you have an understanding of the basic principles involved in mail order, your first step, as we have said, is to select the product or products you will sell. Then you must decide upon where and how you will advertise them. Most people find that this involves some experimentation. To test a product, however, you also must learn as much as you can about writing ad copy or designing mail-order pieces that sell.

We also advise collecting effective mail-order pieces you receive in the mail and clipping ads that grab your attention. Analyze what makes them effective. To find out firsthand how the mail-order business works, spend some time and money reading and answering other people's mail-order ads.

The best months for mail order are January, February, March, April, October, and November; the worst are May, June, July, August, and December. You will want to select a good month to test your mail-order product. Offering a guarantee of total satisfaction has been found time and again to be important. Provided you have a reasonable product, you can expect less than a 1 percent return for products priced under $50 or above $100, and under 5 percent for products priced between $50 and $100.

📖 Where to Turn for Information and Help

BOOKS

Building a Mail Order Business: A Complete Manual for Success, by William A. Cohen. New York: Wiley, 1985.

The Dartnell Direct Mail and Mail Order Handbook, by Richard S. Hodgson. Chicago: Darnell Corporation, 1980.

How to Create Successful Catalogs, NTC Publishing Group, 4255 West Touhy Avenue, Lincolnwood, IL 60646; (800) 323-4900.

How to Start and Operate a Mail-Order Business, by Julian L. Simon. New York: McGraw-Hill, 1987.

Mail Order Magic: Sure Fire Techniques to Expand Any Business by Direct Mail, by Herman Holtz. New York: McGraw-Hill, 1983.

Successful Direct Marketing Methods, by Bob Stone. Lincolnwood, IL: NTC Business Books, 1988.

MAGAZINES AND NEWSLETTERS

Mail Order Messenger, Box 17131, Memphis, TN 38187-0131.

Mail Profits, Carson Services, Box 4785, Lincoln, NE 68504; (402) 467-4230.

TRADE ASSOCIATIONS

Direct Marketing Association, 11 West 42nd Street, New York, NY 10036; (212) 768-7277. Offers courses on direct-mail advertising.

SOFTWARE

The Mail Order Wizard, the Haven Corporation, 802 Madison Street, Evanston, IL 60202; (800) 782-8278. Organizes and automates the order-entry, inventory-tracking, and accounting aspects of running a mail-order business.

SUPPLIERS

A number of companies will help you get started in a mail-order business. They usually import and warehouse merchandise of all kinds (figurines, jewelry, watches, handbags, and so forth) and provide you with catalogues of this merchandise along with circulars, order forms, envelopes, and other sales materials, and with instruction manuals for how you can sell these items through the mail. They will ship the merchandise directly to you or drop-ship it to your customers.

Of course, these items may or may not meet the criteria identified above, and by selecting items yourself you might be able to get better prices and will have more control over the products, from selection to advertising and pricing. The advantage to working with one of these companies is that they supply you with all the materials you need, and some guidance as well. The companies most frequently recommended by members of the Working from Home Forum on CompuServe are:

- **Specialty Merchandising Corporation,** 9401 De Soto Avenue, Chatsworth, CA 91311
- **The Mellinger Company,** 6100 Variel, Woodland Hills, CA 91367

Unlike Specialty Merchandising Corporation, Mellinger does not import items and then sell them to you, preferring that you deal directly with the suppliers rather than with middle-men and thus increasing your profit margin. They provide you with names of foreign suppliers and provide books, manuals, tapes, and seminars to teach you the ins and outs of making your own deals. They do have a small number of items they will sell you to get started.

■ ■ ■ ■

MANAGEMENT CONSULTANT

Professional consulting is the fastest-growing segment of the information industry, increasing by 16 to 18 percent a year. There are some 450,000 professional consultants of one kind or another in the United States. And while many jokes have been made about consultants, in actuality there is a strong demand for their services, and most are well paid. In fact, consultants' billings go up 22 percent annually and the Department of Labor projects the number of management consultants will grow by 46,000, a 35% growth rate between 1988 and 2000.

According to Jim Kennedy of Kennedy Publications, which publishes books and reports about the consulting industry, American corporations make a much greater use of consultants than do companies in other leading nations. Howard Shenson, known as "the consultant's consultant," says there are four reasons for the tremendous growth in this profession:

1. The principal resource today is technical knowhow. Consultants are the high priests of the information revolution. They possess the knowledge that drives our economic system.

2. As information proliferates, it is increasingly difficult for typical managers to maintain state-of-the-art knowledge in all the areas that they must be able to call on. In many areas, they must rely instead on the expertise of specialists.

3. Corporations are finding that the most productive way to get the specialized knowledge they need is to make use of outside experts. Hiring consultants not only saves the costs of hiring high-priced experts full-time; it also provides a company with a greater breadth of experience and a wider variety of contacts than its in-house employees have. In fact, as corporations scale back personnel, consultants are increasingly being paid to implement projects as well as provide guidance and expertise.

4. Consulting provides a lifestyle that people want. People want more control over their work. They want greater variety, more challenge, more respect. They want to be their own boss without a significant capital investment—and consulting fills this bill.

There are many types of consultants. In his newsletter *The Professional Consultant*, Shenson lists 57 different specialties ranging from accounting and broadcasting to telecommunications and traffic. The largest group of consultants, however, are management consultants (which includes marketing and financial consulting), followed by computer consultants, technical consultants (which includes engineering, scientific, and high-technology consulting), health-care consultants, and training/education consultants. Several of these specialties are treated individually in this book, including computer and training consulting as well as public-relations, professional-practice, and image and wedding consulting. Here we will address management consulting.

☑ Knowledge and Skills You Need to Have

- You must have expertise of some kind that others need and that is not common knowledge or in ready supply. For example, as yellow-pages advertising has become more complex, Barry Maher has been able to establish himself as a yellow pages consultant, helping businesses make the most cost-effective placement decisions for their yellow pages advertising. Tom Drucker and Marsha Seligson specialize in consulting with managers on building worker morale and incentive. David Gardner and Grace Beatty consult with human-resource development departments on how to reduce employee stress.

- The level of expertise you need to be a consultant in your area of specialization depends on the clients you're serving. Consultants must be outstanding in their field if they're going to work with sophisticated clients. People with more modest skills, on the other hand, must package themselves well and can serve a less sophisticated clientele. For example, Howard Shenson tells about a man we'll call George who when he first started out as a direct-mail marketing consultant didn't know much more about direct mail than most corporate marketing managers, but his clients knew less. Over the years he's learned a great deal, and now he consults for marketing managers who know more than he did when he began as a consultant.

- You need to enjoy problem solving, creating order from chaos, planning, and strategizing.

- Consultants need to have people skills in order to understand clients' needs and problems and to communicate what they understand.

- You have to be willing to take risks. Howard Shenson's research shows that many, although not all, successful consultants rank high in entrepreneurial spirit.

- You must be marketing oriented and able to sell yourself. You have to know how to demonstrate to people that you can be of advantage to them. It is more a facilitative or educational process than a traditional sales strategy.

⬛ Start-Up Costs

	Low	High
Computer with hard disk	$1,000	$2,500
Inkjet or laser printer	$ 500	$1,600
Word-processing software	$ 100	$ 250
Relational database software	——	$ 450
Voicemail (preferable to an answering machine)	$ 300	$ 300
Office furniture, especially an ergonomic chair	$ 600	$ 800
Business cards, letterhead, envelopes	$ 200	$ 600
Brochure or other promotional material	$ 100	$2,000
Organizational dues	$ 250	$ 250
Totals	$3,050	$8,750

⬛ Advantages

- You receive maximum pay for what you know and can do.
- The work offers a variety of experiences and contacts.
- It can be very satisfying for you to see your ideas and strategies implemented and to get positive feedback when they are working.
- Consulting stimulates your creativity. Most consultants are problem solvers. They have a different way of looking at situations than the client and can therefore respond with innovative solutions.

⬛ Disadvantages

- The work can be lonely and solitary.
- The results of your work may not be known until far into the future.
- Consultants want to sell their knowledge and advice; clients want to buy benefits. Until you can demonstrate to the client how he or she is going to see tangible results as a result of your work, you won't be successful in marketing.

⬛ Pricing

Consultants can charge by the hour, by the day, or by the job. According to a study* of professional fees, the national average in 1991 for all types of consulting was $1,102 per day. In major markets the average was $1,218 per day; in small markets, $899 per day. The median daily fee for the 10 percent of professionals reporting the highest billing rate was $1,994 per day; for the bottom 10 percent $486 per day. The average charge for large clients was $1,173 per day; for small clients, $891 per day.

⬛ Potential Earnings

Typical Annual Gross Revenues: $110,200, based on billing 100 days a year at the national average rate of $1,102 per day.

OVERHEAD: Moderate (20 to 40 percent).

*Based on the 1991 "Economic Status of the Consulting, Training and Advisory Professions" survey, published annually in *The Professional Consultant* newsletter (listed below).

Best Ways to Get Business

- Networking and personal contacts in organizations, such as trade and business associations, particularly in industries or fields in which you have experience.
- Writing articles and books about your specialty for target audiences.
- Speaking at trade, professional, and civic organizations.
- Using an informational brochure featuring the key information your clients need to know about your specialty. Advertise this free brochure in classified ads or mention in the articles you write that you will send one to anyone who requests it.

First Steps

- Learn to market consulting services. There are many books on this subject; some are listed below.
- Define a target market. You can't be all things to all people. You can be several things to several people. Know your clients' expectations.
- Make a commitment to be successful. If you are successful in other areas of life, you can be successful in consulting if you make the commitment. Better yet, follow Howard Shenson's advice and obligate yourself financially by taking some risk. Buy a car with $300 monthly payments. Put yourself under financial pressure so you need to come up with income and can't goof off.
- Write an article for a regional business magazine. Write it strategically to set yourself apart from others in the field.
- Make a list of everyone in the local area that you know personally who would be a good prospective client or who is in a position to refer clients to you. Don't stop until you have at least 20 people. Send a letter to each of these people saying that you've gone into business for yourself as a consultant and want to take him or her to lunch. Let the person know in the letter that you would like to ask several questions about his or her most pressing issues. Then call to set up a time. Most will accept the invitation for lunch. Talk about what you do. You should be able to pick up two or three clients this way.

☐ Where to Turn for Information and Help

BOOKS

Complete Guide to Consulting Success, by Howard L. Shenson. Enterprise Publishing, Inc., 725 Market Street, Wilmington, DE 19801; (302) 654-0110. 1991.

Consulting to Management, by Larry E. Greiner and Robert O. Metzger. Engelwood Cliffs, NJ: Prentice Hall, 1983.

Contract and Fee Setting Guide for Consultants and Professionals, Howard L. Shenson, 20750 Ventura Boulevard, Woodland Hills, CA 91364; (818) 703-6295. Also available is Shenson's *How to Develop a Profitable Consulting Practice.*

How to Be a Successful Consultant in Your Own Field, by Hubert Bermont. Rocklin, CA: Prima Publishing, 1989.

How to Succeed as an Independent Consultant, by Herman Holtz. New York: Wiley, 1988.

Shenson on Consulting, by Howard L. Shenson. New York: Wiley, 1990.

DIRECTORY

Consultant and Consulting Organization Directory, Gale Research, 835 Penobscott Building, Detroit, MI 48226. This directory accepts free listings and is available at virtually all reference libraries.

ORGANIZATIONS

There are 25 to 30 associations for consultants. Join one that relates to your specialty. One of the chief benefits of such a trade organization is meaningful certification.

Institute of Management Consultants, 19 West 44th Street, Suite 810-811, New York, NY 10036; (212) 921-2885.

MAGAZINES AND NEWSLETTERS

The Professional Consultant, Howard L. Shenson, 20750 Ventura Boulevard, Woodland Hills, CA 91364; (818) 703-6295. Shenson has a full line of books, tapes, and computer software. Write for a free catalogue.

SOFTWARE

Rate-setter evaluates what you should charge and *ClientBase* keeps track of client data so you can market to them effectively. Order from Howard L. Shenson, 20750 Ventura Boulevard, Woodland Hills, CA 91364; (818) 703-6295.

■ ■ ■ ■
MEDICAL BILLING SERVICE

Billing and invoicing are the lifeblood of non-cash-and-carry businesses. Many small businesses and professionals need help getting their billing done quickly and accurately, but none more so than medical offices. Changes in the health-care delivery system over the past few years have made doing medical billing one of the most desirable and accessible home-based businesses of the '90s.

The job of the medical biller is to maintain records and process claims for payment from medical and private insurance carriers for hospitals, clinics, physicians, and individual patients. At one time this role was done by office staff. But today most of a doctor's income comes from billing third-party insurance companies, Medicaid, and Medicare. As a result, the process of getting paid is increasingly cumbersome for today's physicians.

In September 1990, a federal law went into effect requiring doctors to submit claims for Medicare reimbursements on behalf of their patients. In having to take over this task, which was previously done by the patients themselves, doctors more than ever need efficient billing procedures. Because doctors can be fined in some instances for misfiling claims, they are becoming more dependent on competent claims processing. As a result they are turning to outside billing services that specialize in doing the job well and can do it for less than it would cost the doctor to hire full-time in-house staff to do the work.

In many cities, services tend to specialize by focusing on particular medical specializations, such as anesthesiology and psychiatry, or particular types of claims, such as worker's compensation.

☑ Knowledge and Skills You Need to Have

- Medical billers must be organized and have the ability to be accurate and precise in handling details.
- Medical billing requires that you know the rules and regulations for making insurance claims, and the billing procedures for Medicaid and Medicare. You also need to know diagnostic coding systems and have an understanding of medical diagnostic procedures.
- You should know how to advise and educate clients on what they must do to meet standards established by the government and insurance companies for payment.
- Good communication skills on the telephone are important. Medical billers must make many phone calls to government and insurance officials to get information crucial to a doctor's claim. You must often be persuasive, advocating your clients' interests. Private insurance companies require even more diplomacy than the government. And because the government or an insurance company often pays only part of the bill and the remainder must be billed and collected from the patient, you also need to have the ability to collect money from patients.

⬛ Start-Up Costs

	Low	High
Computer with hard disk	$1,000	$ 2,500
Printer	$ 300	$ 1,600
Electric typewriter	$ 150	$ 250
Medical-billing software with electronic billing capability	$1,100	$10,000
Office furniture, especially an ergonomic chair	$ 600	$ 800
Copier	$ 400	$ 1,000
Business cards, letterhead, envelopes	$ 400	$ 600
Flyer or brochure	$ 100	$ 2,000
Total	$4,050	$18,750

⬛ Advantages

- The work can be interesting because of its variety and problem-solving nature.
- Lots of business is available.
- There is an element of excitement in being able to use your wit and skill to collect money.

⬛ Disadvantages

- Dealing with and collecting money from difficult or reluctant patients can be very draining.
- Private insurance companies are increasingly difficult to collect from.
- Doctors are having to work harder and see larger numbers of people each day in order to maintain their earnings; therefore, you are often working with highly stressed individuals.
- Unless you take necessary precautions, you risk developing repetitive-motion injuries as a result of constant keyboarding.

⬛ Pricing

Medical billing services are priced in a wide variety of ways:

- By the hour. Hourly fees range from $10 to $25, plus sometimes a percentage of collections.
- Flat fee per claim, ranging from $5 to $100. Higher amounts are justified for worker's-compensation cases.
- By the number of patients. An example of such an approach would be charging $300 for the first 50 claims and $250 for each subsequent claim.
- A straight percentage of the amount of money collected. Percentages may range from 3 to 8 percent for only filing a claim to 50 percent for dealing with problem collections.

▣ Potential Earnings

TYPICAL ANNUAL GROSS REVENUES: $20,000 to $50,000, based on billing a 40-hour week at $10 to $25 per hour.

OVERHEAD: Low (less than 20 percent).

▣ Best Ways to Get Business

- Calling on doctor's offices and hospitals where doctors practice, and circulating a brochure or flyer.
- Responding to classified ads placed by medical offices seeking billing personnel.
- A direct-mail letter appealing to doctors who are having problems with billing and collections, followed up by a personal telephone call.
- Working full- or part-time in a hospital and getting to know physicians who need billing services.

▣ First Steps

If you do not have experience in the medical field, you could begin by taking relevant community-college courses. You might begin by working or temping in medical facilities as a receptionist, clerk, or typist to learn the procedures and practices. To learn how to file Medicare claims, contact the insurance company in your area with the contract to process Medicare claims and find out when classes in filing Medicare claims are offered; these classes are usually free. Also learn to use billing software. (Also see "Where to Turn for Information and Help" for *Medical Transcription Service*.)

▣ Where to Turn for Information and Help

GOVERNMENT RESOURCES

Free booklets on how to file claims are available from Medicare and Medicaid. Free training programs are conducted by government and insurance companies. Training in regional occupational programs is also available. (See also "Where to Turn for Information and Help" for *Medical Claims Processing Service*.)

■ ■ ■ ■

MEDICAL-CLAIMS PROCESSING SERVICE

Although insurance companies pay out $50 billion in individual health-insurance claims each year, submitting and collecting these claims is increasingly complex. This can be a hardship for individuals, where a delay in getting a claim processed can mean having to come up with thousands of dollars to cover hospital or medical bills while waiting for payment from the insurance company.

Many hospitals and doctors have turned the task of filing claims over to the patient, and instead of dealing with the hassles and red tape of filing themselves, growing numbers of people are turning to claims processing services to file their medical claims for them, much as they take their taxes to a tax preparer. The claims processor fills out and submits claims to the appropriate medical and dental insurance companies to make sure his or her clients get paid the benefits they're due.

Ricky Horne, who operates a successful medical-claims processing service in California, says "First of all, I sell peace of mind. Even if the doctor's office is filing the claim, people want to make sure their claims are being taken care of properly." Like Ricky, medical-claims processors find they can serve several kinds of clients:

1. People who simply don't want to file their own claims. These are the same people who turn to professionals to have their taxes done or to draw up a will. They include busy individuals who are perplexed by the medical billing process, as well as dual-career couples and single parents who simply don't have the time to handle the paperwork. Also, some people turn to a processing service because filing insurance claims reminds them of their illness.

2. Individuals who are referred by their employer. Some small companies (5 to 10 employees) don't have a personnel office to help employees with medical claims, so they refer their clients to a claims processor. In addition, some employees of large corporations seek out help when they have had an illness they don't want their companies to know about.

3. Individuals with an illness or disability that leaves them incapable of filling out their own claims. In this case referrals will come from doctors and hospital business offices.

4. Senior citizens who have Medicare and Medicare Supplement. As of September 1, 1990, physicians were required to file Medicare claims for their patients. But many seniors have policies that supplement Medicare. The American Association of Retired People has 10 such policies alone. Blue Cross, CNA, B'nai Brith, Golden Rule, and United America also offer such policies.

This is a growing business limited only by the fact that, unlike tax preparation, many clients do not know about it. Even if the United States adopts national health insurance, there will still be private insurance policies, just as there are in England. So the need for this service will continue.

A claims processing business can also be expanded to include bill-paying and bookkeeping services, and sometimes doctors' offices will ask you to do their insurance billing as well.

☑ Knowledge and Skills You Need to Have

■ You need a knowledge of medical terminology, insurance policies, and Medicare policies and procedures.

- You need to be compulsively organized, because this business demands that you be highly precise and accurate.
- You must be facile and comfortable working with numbers.
- You must have the ability to analyze policies and the client's situation.
- You should have good people skills and the ability to gain and keep people's confidence.

Start-Up Costs

	Low	High
Computer	$1,000	$2,500
Spreadsheet and time-and-billing software such as *Timeslips III*	$ 500	$ 650
Inkjet or laser printer	$ 500	$1,600
Photocopier	$ 400	$1,500
Office furniture, especially an ergonomic chair	$ 600	$ 800
Business cards, letterhead, envelopes	$ 200	$ 600
Brochure	$1,000	$2,000
Totals	$4,200	$9,650

Advantages

- This is a feel-good service. You're doing good for people, making their lives easier.
- The overhead is low.
- This business can easily be started on a part-time basis.

Disadvantages

- There is a great deal to learn.
- Many people who could use such a service are unfamiliar with it.
- Since you must educate your customers about the service before you can sell them on it, starting this business takes more time.

Pricing

Hourly rates range from $25 to $60 with an average of $40.

Potential Earnings

TYPICAL ANNUAL GROSS REVENUES: $60,000, based on billing 30 hours a week at $40 an hour.

OVERHEAD: Low (20 percent or less).

Best Ways to Get Business

- Directly contacting hospital social workers and the people responsible for billing and insurance in doctors' offices. Leave brochures.
- Networking in organizations and making personal contacts.
- Speaking to senior-citizen groups in affluent areas.
- Sending out direct mail to people over 65 in selected affluent zip codes, with a brochure explaining the service.

First Steps

1. Take a course in medical terminology at a community college.
2. Learn how to file Medicare claims. Contact the insurance company in your area with the contract to process Medicare claims and find out when classes in filing Medicare claims are offered; the classes are usually free.
3. Do insurance claims for friends and family for free. Learn what the problems are. Learn about policies and what doing claims is like. Study the policies.

Where to Turn for Information and Help

COURSES

Insurance companies offer classes on filing claims for the personnel of doctors' offices. Call major insurance providers in your community and tell them about your business and that you would like to attend such classes.

MANUALS

Medical Claims Processing Business Guide, *Entrepreneur* magazine, 2392 Morse Avenue, Box 19787, Irvine, CA 92713; (800) 421-2300; in California, (800) 352-7449. Guide for starting a medical-claims processing business. Includes claim forms and insurance-company policy procedures. *Entrepreneur* also offers a software template for use with major spreadsheets.

■ ■ ■ ■

MEDICAL TRANSCRIPTION SERVICE

Medical transcriptionists produce typed reports and documents from audiotapes that doctors have dictated regarding their medical cases. Having a medical transcript produced quickly is vital to health-care providers' cash flow because many insurance companies are requiring transcribed reports before they will pay doctors or hospitals. Transcribed copy also provides health-care providers the necessary documentation for review of a patient's history and care and provides legal evidence of patient care and data for research and statistical purposes.

Increasingly hospitals and doctors in private practice are contracting out their medical transcription work. In part, this is because there is a shortage of transcriptionists. According to the American Association for Medical Transcription (AAMT), this job is in demand throughout the country and in some communities the demand is critical. Still another factor is computer technology. As Pat Forbis, director of Member Services of the AAMT, observes, "the technology that took us out of our homes is taking us back into our homes. Today if a transcriptionist has a modem and the proper interfaces, he or she can hook directly into hospital digital dictation equipment using the phone lines."

In addition, research shows that home-based transcriptionists are more productive than transcriptionists working in hospitals and offices. A study by the University of Wisconsin Hospital and Clinics found that the statistics "consistently showed that what would take six to eight hours to produce in the office would take three to four hours to do at home."

Independent transcriptionists tend to either take overload work from hospitals or work with doctors in private practice. Transcriptionists doing work for hospitals must know about all fields of medical practice, while a transcriptionist working for physicians may concentrate on only one or several medical specialties, such as orthopedics, neurology, or surgery. Transcriptionists can also seek work from agencies which may either treat them as subcontractors or as employees. Some of these agencies will let you work from home.

Vicki Fite, founder of Southwest Medical Transcription, says, "Marketing this business is easy when you have a high-quality product. Doctors are very particular, and rightly so, about the material transcribed. The one thing that can really hurt you in this field is if you put out an inferior product. If you make a bad mistake you can count on losing about five accounts from that one source."

Services that can increase your competitiveness include offering pickup and delivery, seven-day-a-week service, same-day service, and a phone-in dictation system. Home-based medical transcriptionists can gain a competitive edge by offering remote printing or downloading into medical facilities' computer systems. This is a plus because turnaround time of transcription is a primary concern to health-care providers. So if a transcriptionist is able to provide a less-than-24-hour turnaround and not compromise quality, it is an advantage. Additionally, 24-hour or second-and-third-shift coverage is a plus.

☑ Knowledge and Skills You Need to Have

- As a medical transcriptionist, you need to have the discipline to sit in front of a computer and concentrate throughout the day, with earphones linking you to transcribing equipment.
- You need excellent listening skills and good eye, hand, and auditory coordination. You also need to be able to understand diverse accents and dialects.

- You must be able to type quickly and accurately using word-processing, dictation, and transcription equipment.
- In addition to having keyboard speed, you also must be able to transcribe quickly, because the faster you can transcribe, the more you earn. The medical transcriptionist rarely does work verbatim. One of your major functions is editing.
- You need to understand medical diagnostic procedures and terminology and spell them accurately (anatomy and physiology, clinical medicine, surgery, diagnostic tests, radiology, pathology, pharmacology, and whatever medical specialties you work with).
- You need to enjoy doing accurate, precise work.
- A love for language is helpful because often you must become a *word detective*, interpreting how terms are being used.

Start-Up Costs

	Low	High
Computer	$1,000	$2,500
Printer (may not be necessary if you are using a modem)	$ 300	$1,600
Transcriber or appropriate transcribing unit with conversion capability to different sizes of tapes	$ 450	$ 450
Word-processing software compatible with your client base	$ 250	$ 250
Office furniture, especially an ergonomic chair and a bookcase	$ 700	$ 800
Business cards, letterhead, envelopes	$ 200	$ 600
Reference books (medical-transcription style guide, medical dictionary, drug reference, multiple word books to address various medical specialties)	$ 100	$ 200
Total	$3,000	$6,400

Advantages

- This is a rapidly growing field, with more work than there are trained transcriptionists.
- The medical field can be interesting.
- The work is steady and recession-resistant.

Disadvantages

- You must be highly self-disciplined and focused while you work. The work demands total involvement both physically and mentally. Every distraction creates a slowdown in productivity and possibly even quality.
- The demand for increasingly fast turnaround times creates time pressures and at least occasionally the need to work nights and weekends.

- Not everyone is temperamentally suited to being plugged into a pair of headphones hour after hour, day after day.
- Unless you take necessary precautions, you risk developing repetitive motion injuries as a result of keyboarding.

$ Pricing

AAMT recommends that transcriptionists charge by the character, but some charge by the line or by the page, and with the adoption of computers, some are now charging by the byte. If you are charging by something other than the character, it is important to define what is meant by *word, line,* or *page*, because definitions vary from transcriptionist to transcriptionist and client to client.

Charges range from 7 cents to 14 cents per line (remember that what constitutes a *line* varies from transcriptionist to transcriptionist) or $2 to $5 a page. Sometimes transcriptionists charge $15 to $30 an hour for doctors who are difficult to understand, particularly those with heavy accents. Turnaround time also influences pricing; you can charge more for second-and-third-shift, 24-hour, or weekend coverage.

▣ Potential Earnings

TYPICAL ANNUAL GROSS REVENUES: $30,000 to $60,000, based on billing 2,000 hours a year (40 hours a week) and charging from $15 to $30 an hour.
OVERHEAD: Moderate (20 to 40%).

▣ Best Ways to Get Business

- Directly soliciting work from doctors, hospitals, or attorneys with medical disability cases (can include malpractice cases).
- Responding to classified ads for medical transcriptionists, proposing to do the work at home.
- Advertising in the publications of the medical societies to which doctors belong in your community.
- Taking overload or referral business from other transcriptionists.

▣ First Steps

If you already know this field, you might begin by contacting the directors of hospital departments where transcribing is done, such as medical-records offices, radiology offices, and emergency rooms.

If you don't have experience in the medical field, the AAMT has developed a list of competencies, skills, abilities, and performance standards that should be achieved and will provide information regarding recommended courses upon request. (See listing that follows.) Students are encouraged to evaluate educational programs based on the length of the program, whether actual physician voices and dictation are included on practice tapes, and what types of reports and how wide a variety of specialties, voices, and accents are covered. Some community colleges offer relevant courses.

Where to Turn for Information and Help

BOOKS

Medical Transcription Guide: Do's and Don'ts, Fordney and Diel. Philadelphia: W. B. Saunders, 1989.

ORGANIZATIONS

American Association for Medical Transcription, Box 576187, 3460 Oakdale Road, Suite M, Modesto, CA 95357; (209) 551-0883. The association publishes a bimonthly journal, holds an annual meeting, produces educational products, and sponsors local chapters, and state and regional associations. The association also offers a voluntary certification program. Successfully passing the examination for certification entitles one to the title of certified medical transcriptionist (CMT).

HOME STUDY COURSES

At Home Professions, 12383 Lewis Street, Suite 103, Garden Grove, CA 92640; (714) 971-0916. Offers a 22-week study-at-home course, completion of which provides you with the knowledge and expertise you need to do medical transcription.

■ ■ ■ ■

NOTE READER/SCOPIST

Court reporters spend five to eight hours a day in courtrooms or in lawyers' offices taking down testimony on a stenograph, which is a machine for writing words phonetically—that is, according to how they sound instead of the way they're spelled. Older machines simply typed characters on a narrow strip of paper. Newer machines also record the characters on a floppy disk or on tape. The result is called stenotype.

Before court reporters are paid, however, they must convert the stenotype into a fully written transcript. However, because court reporters get paid only for producing finished pages and not for the time they spend transcribing them, they make more money if they hire someone to get the testimony into final form while they record testimony in courtrooms and depositions.

As a result of this economic reality, court reporters hire what are called note readers or scopists. The note reader/scopist may prepare the transcript for the court reporter directly from the court reporter's stenotype notes or may edit what is automatically transcribed by a computer from the floppy disks or tapes created by the court reporter. Editing is necessary, even when a computer is used, because the software does only a preliminary job of translating the stenotype, and the scopist has to correct errors in the text such as the spelling of street names and so forth.

Note readers/scopists are hired either directly by self-employed court reporters or by court-reporting agencies. In either case they may do their work from home. Note readers/scopists are widely used and readily accepted in most parts of the country. However, in areas where scopists have not yet been used, court reporters must be educated as to the scopist's ability to produce quality work and to enable the court reporter to earn more money.

☑ Knowledge and Skills You Need to Have

- Note readers/scopists must be able to understand stenotype.
- Quick, accurate keyboarding skills are essential—the faster you transcribe, the more you earn.
- You must be good at spelling and grammar and have an intuitive ability to know what a word is when the court reporter has erred.
- You need to be familiar with medical terminology used in legal cases.

♣ Start-Up Costs

	Low	High
IBM-compatible computer	$1,000	$2,500
Printer	$ 300	$1,600
Word-processing software	$ 250	——
Computer-aided transcription software*	——	$2,000
Office furniture, especially an ergonomic chair	$ 600	$ 800
Business cards, letterhead, envelopes	$ 200	$ 600
Reference books, including a medical dictionary, area telephone books, a map book with street names, and a directory with the names of area physicians	$ 100	$ 125
Answering machine	$ 75	$ 125
Totals	$2,525	$7,750

*There are about 20 different brands of this software that are not compatible with one another. So a court reporter using one system can work only with a scopist who has matching software. The only important consideration in choosing software is to buy the type that is compatible with court reporters in the area in which it is likely you will be working.

▣ Advantages

- The hours are flexible. You have the freedom to come and go.
- People in this field report that they enjoy reading testimony reflecting the dramas of people's lives and that they learn from testimony by experts in many fields.

- Work is done in one's home.
- There is little or no pressure.

Disadvantages

- Some people are not intellectually stimulated by working with other people's words.
- In some areas, court reporters aren't aware of the value and capability of note reader/scopists. In some areas, the courts use other technologies like facial masks into which court reporters speak the words they hear in court. However, these court reporters may still use legal transcriptionists, who transcribe their recordings.
- The job can cause eyestrain and repetitive-motion injuries from long hours of keyboarding if precautions are not taken to prevent them.

Pricing

Using computer-aided transcription software, the per-page rate ranges from 50 cents to $1. A scopist will produce from 25 to 30 pages an hour.

Potential Earnings

TYPICAL ANNUAL GROSS REVENUES: $18,750 to $45,000, based on working 6 hours a day, 5 days a week, 50 weeks a year, and producing 25 to 30 pages an hour and thereby earning $12.50 to $30 per hour.

OVERHEAD: Low (20 percent or less).

Best Ways to Get Business

- Directly contacting court reporters and court-reporting agencies in your area with an introductory letter, followed by a phone call. You can obtain names of court reporters through the yellow pages, from a list available through your state's court-reporter association, or from the membership directory of the National Court Reporters Association (see listing below).
- Posting notices on the bulletin boards of court-reporting agencies.

First Steps

1. Check the community in which you live to determine the market for note readers/scopists.
2. Learn how to read stenotype. This can be learned through some community colleges, court-reporting schools, or an at-home study course, (see listing below).

3. Get your keyboarding speed up to at least 70 words per minute. You can increase your typing speed by using a software program like *Mavis Beacon Teaches Typing*, which costs as little as $30 and can help you increase your typing speed within a few weeks.

4. Establish a relationship with one or two court reporters or a court-reporting agency.

Where to Turn for Information and Help

ORGANIZATIONS

National Court Reporters Association, 8224 Old Courthouse Road, Vienna, VA 22182; (703) 556-6272.

COURSES

At Home Professions, 12383 Lewis Street, Suite 103, Garden Grove, CA 92640; (714) 971-0916. Offers a 16-week study-at-home course, that provides you with the knowledge and expertise you need to be a note reader/scopist.

■ ■ ■ ■

PARALEGAL

If you find being a part of the fastest-growing occupation in the country appealing, becoming a paralegal or legal assistant may be for you. The Bureau of Labor Statistics projects that paralegals, including all types of legal assistants, will have grown by 75 percent from 1988 until the year 2000, representing an increase of 62,000 paralegals. According to Marge Dover, executive director of the National Association of Legal Assistants, the number of self-employed free-lance or independent paralegals is growing at the same pace.

One reason for this growth is that consumers are pushing for increasing use of paralegals as a way to make legal assistance more affordable, just as the use of nurse practitioners is growing as a way of reducing medical costs. Although at present paralegals must work under the direct supervision of an attorney, they may be called on to do anything an attorney does with the exception of signing documents, making court appearances in contested proceedings, and giving legal advice to clients.

They assist in doing such things as summarizing testimony, doing statistical research, searching public records, coordinating evidence for trial, and key-wording documents for retrieval. On very large cases, they can also help with case management, which includes everything from creating and accumulating exhibits for trial to scheduling witnesses, communicating with clients, and digesting depositions.

Clients include law firms and corporate legal offices, which do not want to hire a person full-time to do such tasks. But by using a freelance paralegal they can have the trained person they need without the obligation of permanent employment. And whereas an attorney might charge $175 an hour to do these tasks, a paralegal's fee of $45 to $85 an hour helps keep costs down.

Paralegals are not licensed in any state, and there are multiple routes to becoming a paralegal. Some are hired without prior experience by law firms, corporate law departments, insurance companies, bank trust departments, and government offices. As many as half of all current paralegals have entered the field by first being legal secretaries. Increasingly, the route to becoming a paralegal is to complete an educational program, which may range from a 15-week course to a full master's-degree program.

In some states, like New York, paralegals perform primarily clerical duties. In others, like California, free-lancers have become specialists, preparing particular types of motions, offering computerized litigation support using specialized software, and serving as expert consultants. By specializing, paralegals may know more about a certain subject or activity than the attorneys they work for, who may have only infrequent experience in that area.

According to Fran Chernowksi, who owns her own firm, Litigation Resources and Consulting, and who is a cofounder and vice president of the California Association of Freelance Paralegals, most paralegals do specialize—in corporate law, litigation, family law, probate law, real-estate law and so forth.

☑ Knowledge and Skills You Need to Have

- Paralegals need to know how to:
  - locate and interview witnesses
  - do research for statistical and documentary evidence
  - do legal research
  - draft legal documents including pleadings and motions
  - summarize depositions, interrogatories, and testimony
- As a paralegal you should develop some specialty such as bankruptcy, probate, real estate, family law, and so forth.
- Paralegals have to know the practical logistics of managing a legal case (where to go, when to get there, and so forth), not legal theory.
- You need to be proficient at using the specialized computer software designed for accomplishing legal tasks.
- You need to be self-confident, assertive, able to take criticism, and comfortable with ambiguity.
- You must know your area of expertise well and yet also know how to ask people for help and how to find information.

💠 Start-Up Costs

	Low	High
IBM-compatible computer with minimum 40-megabyte hard disk	$1,000	$2,500
Inkjet or laser printer	$ 500	$1,600
Word Perfect for word-processing; *TimeSlips III* for keeping track of billable time	$ 450	$ 450
Typewriter for typing court forms	$ 150	$ 400
Office furniture, especially an ergonomic chair	$ 600	$ 800
Business cards, letterhead, envelopes	$ 200	$ 600
Organizational dues	$· 200	$ 200
Law books, particularly form books and court rules; local codes, depending on what you're doing; books for legal secretaries and paralegals	$ 300	$ 500
Subscriptions to legal periodicals	$ 100	$ 300
Two- and three-hole paper punches	$ 100	$ 140
Totals	$3,600	$7,490

👍 Advantages

- There is a strong consumer movement to license paralegals, so by getting involved now will put you on the ground floor of a new profession. Licensing a profession increases its stature and thereby its fees while limiting competition. And usually those who are already practicing when licensing is instituted are automatically licensed.

- The field is in a state of growth and flux, so there are few limitations, and the paralegal role is constantly being redefined and enlarged. Your career can move quickly if you are good.

- The work offers plenty of opportunity for variety and to exercise responsibility.

- You feel like a professional working with other intelligent professionals.

👎 Disadvantages

- Work is affected by the economic ups and downs of the legal profession, so it may be sporadic.

- Law demands perfection and attention to detail. A small mistake or oversight can have major consequences. There is always the stress and uncertainty of wondering if you are doing it right.

- Paralegals often work under time pressures.

- Working with attorneys can be difficult because they are not accustomed to providing recognition or giving instruction.

- There may be a lengthy lead time in building a clientele, so it's wise to have your living expenses covered for six months.

- Clients do not necessarily develop loyalty to particular paralegals; many will hire whoever charges less.
- The New Jersey Supreme Court has decided that doing free-lance paralegal work constitutes performing the unauthorized practice of law, ruling out New Jersey as a place to be a freelance paralegal.

💲 Pricing

Fees vary widely from city to city, ranging from $15 to $100 per hour according to special expertise, years of experience, quality of education, and the acceptance of paralegals by the legal community. The median range is $25 to $40 per hour. The highest rates are in Los Angeles, Houston, and Dallas, according to leaders in the field.

The low end of the scale is for trial preparation, which includes organizing and date-stamping documents for trial; the rates for research and drafting pleadings and motions are higher.

🖫 Potential Earnings

TYPICAL ANNUAL GROSS REVENUES: $31,250 to $50,000, based on working 25 hours per week (1,000 hour per year) at $25 to $40 dollars per hour. However many paralegals who work closer to 35 hours a week for higher hourly rates earn over $100,000 a year.

OVERHEAD: Moderate (20 to 40 percent).

🗈 Best Ways to Get Business

- Directly soliciting attorneys and law firms.
- Networking with attorneys and other paralegals at legal functions.
- Writing articles for legal newspapers and paralegal magazines.
- Speaking to paralegal organizations and organizations for attorneys.
- Sending direct-mail brochures and letters to potential firms.

🏃 First Steps

- If you don't have a legal background or if you need additional training, complete a paralegal training program. Which program you take will depend on your prior education. If you have a bachelor's degree, go to a program that awards a certificate, not to a program that includes academic education. The better training programs orient paralegals toward a specialization.
- Take advantage of placement services at paralegal schools, or gain experience by apprenticing with a law firm or corporation.

- Plan to spend two years in such a position, during which time you can make contacts, gain experience, and develop a specialization that will place you in demand.
- When you go out on your own, select a slogan of some sort for your business that differentiates you from other paralegals.

▢ Where to Turn for Information and Help

COURSES

The American Association for Paralegal Education publishes a directory of schools teaching paralegal education. The association's address is Box 40244, Overland Park, KS 66204; (913) 381-4458.

The United States Department of Agriculture Graduate School offers reasonably priced correspondence programs in paralegal studies. Contact Correspondence Programs, South Agriculture Building, 14th Street and Independence Avenue, S.W., Room 1114, Washington DC 20250; (202) 447-7123.

ORGANIZATIONS

National Association of Legal Assistants, 1601 South Main, Suite 300, Tulsa, OK 74119; (918) 587-6828.

National Federation of Paralegal Associations, 104 Wilmot Road, Suite 201, Deerfield, IL 60015; (708) 940-8800.

MAGAZINES AND NEWSLETTERS

California Paralegal, Box 6960, Los Osos, CA 93412.

Legal Assistant Today, James Publishing, 3520 Cadillac Avenue, Suite 3, Costa Mesa, CA 92626.

Legal Professional, 6060 North Central Expressway, Suite 670, Dallas, TX 75206; (800) 225-8347.

■ ■ ■ ■

PRIVATE INVESTIGATOR

Most television private detectives are shown with downtown offices. So it may come as a surprise that a large number of private investigators work from their homes. Added to that is the fact that the field of private investigation is changing and growing. Hallmark Systems, a company that studies the private security industry, projects that the number of private investigators will grow by 2 percent a year through the year 2000.

In the past, private investigators have been kept busy working for attorneys on criminal and civil cases, tracking down white-collar crime for corporations, locating missing persons, and doing insurance investigations. However, today's private investigators, according to Ralph Thomas, director of the National Association of Investigative Specialists, are specializing in particular types of investigation.

For example, some private investigators are using personal-computer technology to search public records and consumer information for business intelligence investigations and premarital and preemployment screening. With the use of computers and other new modes of communication, private investigators will increasingly become home-based.

Private investigators are required to be licensed in most states, with Alabama, Colorado, Idaho, Kansas, Mississippi, Missouri, Oregon, South Dakota, Washington, and Wyoming being exceptions. However, some municipalities in states that do not require a license do require private investigators to register with the city or the police department. The requirements for licensing vary and usually involve some sort of experience in investigative work, which may even be met by working in a collection agency.

Contrary to the TV image created by characters like Rockford, Spencer, and Mike Hammer, being a private investigator is not necessarily a dangerous business. Most private investigators don't carry a gun, and according to Bob Taylor, an investigator from East Brunswick, New Jersey, who has been in the business for 25 years, weapons are unnecessary. "Unlike on television, the mainstay of private detective work today is not the private client. It's lawyers, insurance companies, and businesspeople," says Taylor.

In fact, you may create a profitable business providing only one or a few of the specialized services private investigators can offer. For example, you can build a business doing background screening and reference checking of prospective employees or prospective tenants; verifying credit; or doing *skip tracing*—that is, finding difficult-to-locate people. In many states, however, providing a specialized service does not relieve you of becoming licensed as a private investigator.

☑ Knowledge and Skills You Need to Have

- While no formal training is required, a few years' experience in some type of investigative work, such as claims adjusting, collections, police work, or even investigative journalism is required by most states for licensing.

- People skills are important, including the ability to *read* people, develop rapport, manage conversations, and persuade people to give you information. As Bob Taylor says, "You have to be more of a communicator than a Joe Friday."

- Tenacity and creativity are necessary for gathering information that is sometimes difficult to find.

- You have to be able to write an investigate report.

⬛ Start-Up Costs

	Low	High
Computer and modem	$1,000	$2,500
Printer	$ 300	$1,600
Fax	$ 400	$ 800
Word-processing and communications software	$ 350	$ 350
Desk, chair, filing cabinet	$ 600	$ 800
Business cards, letterhead, envelopes	$ 200	$ 600
Tape recorder for interviewing	$ 50	$ 200
Total	$2,900	$6,850

⬛ Advantages

- Private investigators enjoy prestige and a glamorous image.
- Private investigators enjoy the challenge of fitting together bits of information for a variety of cases.

⬛ Disadvantages

- It takes at least two years to establish a clientele.
- Hours are typically long and you're often required to work weekends and evenings.
- Private investigators have difficulty making firm time commitments because of the unpredictable demands of some cases. If you're on a stakeout, for example, you need to stay with the person under surveillance until you get the information needed.

⬛ Pricing

Hourly fees for private investigators range from $25 to $125, with $40 to $70 typical in metropolitan areas.

⬛ Potential Earnings

TYPICAL ANNUAL GROSS REVENUES: $50,000, based on billing 1,000 hours a year at $50 an hour. Private investigators bill additionally for many expenses associated with investigations.

OVERHEAD: Moderate (20 to 40 percent).

⬛ Best Ways to Get Business

- Directly soliciting trial lawyers and their office managers, insurance companies, and corporate personnel departments.
- Yellow-pages advertising if seeking private clients for collections and marital work (which accounts for only 25 percent of private investigators' work today.)

- Direct mail, such as introductory letters and newsletters, followed up by phone calls.
- Speaking at meetings.
- Presenting seminars on specialized topics such as debugging.

First Steps

- If you do not have the experience to qualify for a license, the best way to get into this field is to apprentice with a private investigator.
- Obtain a license where needed.

Where to Turn for Information and Help

BOOKS

Business Intelligence Investigations, by Ralph Thomas. Austin, TX: Thomas Publications, 1991.

Check It Out: The Ultimate Guide to Background Investigations, by Edmund G. Pankau. Austin, TX: Thomas Publications, 1991.

How to Find Anyone Anywhere, by Ralph Thomas. Austin, TX: Thomas Publications, 1991.

How to Investigate by Computer: 1990, by Ralph Thomas with Leroy Cook. Thomas Publications: Austin, TX, 1990.

Legal Investigation Training Manual, by Ralph Thomas. Thomas Publications: Austin, TX, 1991.

Techniques of Legal Investigations, by Anthony M. Golec. Springfield, IL: Charles C. Thomas, 1985. Cost: $53.25.

MAGAZINES AND NEWSLETTERS

P.I. Magazine, 755 Bronx, Toledo, OH 43609.

ORGANIZATIONS

National Association of Investigative Specialists, Box 33244, Austin, TX 78764; (512) 832-0355. Publishes and distributes many books and manuals.

National Association of Legal Investigators, 2801 Fleur Drive, Des Moines, IA 50321.

■ ■ ■ ■

PROFESSIONAL ORGANIZER

The professional organizer has emerged as the knight in shining armor of the information age. Our lives today are oversaturated with an ever increasing flow of information. Our mailboxes are stuffed with mail, and most people have more belongings than previous generations, as evidenced by the fact that older homes never have enough storage space. Yet most Americans feel they have less time than ever to manage and organize all the added *stuff* in their lives. The professional organizer steps into our homes and offices to help us take control and put our lives in operating order.

Professional organizers help us organize everything from paper flow to patient flow, from desktops to filing cabinets, from bookshelves and closets to computer files. Says editor turned organizer Harriet Schechter, "As an organizer, instead of editing words, I edit other people's time and space."

Although this profession is barely five years old, it has doubled every year since 1985 and its practitioners already specialize in five principal categories:

1. Space planning—setting up and laying out a home or office so people can get the maximum and most efficient use of the space they have, taking into consideration such things as lighting, traffic patterns, noise, and comfort needs.

2. Time management—assisting clients to set goals, develop action steps, define priorities, and schedule and delegate tasks and activities.

3. Paper management—helping people know how to respond to and what to do with incoming materials and setting up filing and retrieval systems so people can find things when they need them.

4. Clutter control—restoring a sense of order and preventing the further accumulation of clutter.

5. Closet/storage design—designing and organizing closet and storage space.

Some organizers work only in residential settings; other work exclusively in offices, serving organizations such as banks, hospitals, schools, professional practices, and other business enterprises. Some organizers develop a particularly narrow specialty like packing and moving, or paying bills and putting finances in order.

Schechter, whose company is called the Miracle Worker Organizing Service, says an organizer's clients are not necessarily disorganized people. "Often they are quite the opposite," she says, "but are overwhelmed with too many projects and a reluctance to delegate." Everyone who feels he or she could benefit from being more organized is a potential customer. But first that person must decide he or she wants the service, and then must be willing to pay for it. At this time only a small percentage of those who need the service are willing to pay. It's not uncommon for a potential client to wait three years before deciding to call for help.

Harriet Schechter believes this business is almost like a calling. "Good organizers have an overwhelming need to bring order to the world," she says. "They get satisfaction from helping people organize their lives." Susan Silver, organizer and author of *Organized to Be the Best*, finds that "this is a very creative business. It provides many creative outlets to express your abilities. As an organizer, you can be an author, seminar leader, trainer, or hands-on consultant."

Silver believes that metropolitan areas provide the best opportunities for organizers because hiring an organizer is not yet viewed as a necessity. As such it's a business that could be vulnerable to recession. On the other hand, Silver says, "In tough times we have to find better ways to do more with less." So with creative marketing, this service can be positioned as a cost saver—a way to trim off fat and compensate for downsizing.

☑ Knowledge and Skills You Need to Have

There is no particular training or background required to be an organizer. The following skills are important, however, in order to do it successfully.

- You need to be organized yourself, although not necessarily perfectly. Once people find out you're an organizer, they look at you through a microscope, looking for any problem. So you need to be able to be on time, deliver on your commitments, and locate information that you need when you need it without stress.

- You must be flexible enough to work with individual needs and quirks; you cannot have a cookie-cutter mentality that imposes one regimen on all.

- You should have a knowledge of various systems, products, furniture, supplies, and accessories for organizing a home or office. Dee Behrman, who specializes in working with medical, dental, and legal offices, believes that "a broad-based product knowledge is essential so you can offer your clients a range of options and customize a system for their particular needs." In working with four medical offices, for example, she found that each one wanted to use a different type of chart.

- Although many organizers are not computer literate yet, we believe that a sound knowledge of computer hardware, software, and other high-tech equipment to streamline an office or household will soon be a must for any organizer to remain competitive.

- You must be able to analyze your clients' needs and develop clear plans for how to make order out of their chaos. You must feel challenged instead of stressed by disorder.

- You need to be able to listen and advise tactfully. Telling people what to do doesn't work. You need to be able to understand your clients sufficiently to figure out what will work for them within their budget range.

- You must be willing to admit you don't have all the answers and to keep your mind open to new ideas and new ways of doing things.

- You must be compassionate toward, not judgmental of, your clients. As Harriet Schechter says, "You must have a poker face when you see people's disorder. Some people are insane over a small pile of papers; others seem unperturbed by huge mountains of paper."

🐖 Start-Up Costs

	Low	High
Computer	$1,000	$2,500
Printer	$ 300	$1,600
Word-processing software	$ 100	$ 250
Time-management software	$ 50	$ 275
Form-design software	——	$ 200
Office furniture	$ 600	$ 800
Business cards, letterhead, envelopes	$ 200	$ 600
Brochure or press kit	$ 250	$1,000
Organizational dues	$ 250	$ 250
Totals	$2,750	$7,475

📖 Advantages

- This is still a new field, new enough that competition will not be a problem.
- The need for organizers will grow as the amount of information we must process continues to grow and our lives continue to become more complex.
- Your clients can see dramatic results of your work quickly.
- There is ample opportunity to use your creativity.
- There are many different facets of what you can do as an organizer, so you need not get bored from doing the same thing over and over again.
- This is an evolving business, so if you like to grow, this business matches that need.

🔖 Disadvantages

- Since this is a new field, many people still don't know what an organizer is. Some confuse it with *union organizer* or *community organizer*. So you often must educate before you can sell.
- Some clients are not very well organized (that's why they need you), so sometimes you're working with people who reschedule a lot, can't find their checkbook, forget their appointments, and so forth.
- This work demands a lot of time and energy to get under way, and it may take considerable time before you'll be able to make a full-time income.
- You won't have much repeat business unless you have clients who hire you on a retainer or you are an on-site consultant to a larger company, so you will have to continually look for new clients.

💲 Pricing

Organizers can charge in one of three ways:

Fixed fee. Fixed fees are charged for discrete organizational tasks like organizing a work space or setting up a filing system. For example, Jeffrey

Mayer of Chicago charges $1,000 to organize an executive's desk. An organizer might also charge a fixed fee to do an introductory training program, a needs assessment, a workshop, and a follow-up session. For example, Susan Silver sells such packages to corporations. Fees for such programs will vary with their length and the level of personnel with whom you are working. You can charge more to train executives than you can to train secretaries.

Hourly rate. Fees range from $25 to $125 depending on your location, experience, and expertise. Residential and garage organizers will tend to be at the lower end of the scale; corporate organizers charge more.

Retainer. Organizers contract to work with a company for a certain period of time each month. Retainers may range from several hundred to several thousand dollars a month.

▣ Potential Earnings

TYPICAL ANNUAL GROSS REVENUES: $40,000, based on billing 800 hours a year (16 hours per week) at $50 an hour.
OVERHEAD: Low (20 percent or less).

▨ Best Ways to Get Business

- Teaching workshops and classes for community colleges and adult education programs, and speaking before community and business organizations.
- Networking in organizations, such as trade and business associations, as well as with professionals who work in industries related to this field, like business consultants, interior designers, and architects, who can refer clients to you.
- Personal contact with people you meet.
- Yellow-pages advertising under Organizing Services or Personal Services.
- Publicity through news releases and writing articles.
- Listing in the directory of the National Association of Professional Organizers.
- Writing a newsletter, with organizing tips, for past and potential clients.
- Developing cross-referrals with other types of professional organizers.

▦ Franchises

Priority Management Systems, 500 108th Avenue NE, Suite 1740, Bellevue, WA 98004; (800) 221-9031. Sets you up in business as a trainer for middle- and upper-level managers on topics such as priority setting, project planning, and time management. Management experience is required. In business since 1984. The minimum fee is $29,500.

Closet organizers design and install storage systems that make the most of every square inch of space and keep a full closet neat and tidy. You can design and build such systems yourself, or you can become a distributor for a closet organizing company such as:

Closet Classics, 3311 Laminations Drive, Holland, MI 49424; (616) 399-3311.

Closet World, 42B Cherry Hill Drive, Danvers, MA 01923; (800) 334-3392.

First Steps

- Read books on organizing and identify a specialty or focus for the type of organizing you will do and which industries you want to work with.
- To practice your craft, volunteer to work for friends, charity, or nonprofit organizations that will give you letters of recommendation. Susan Silver's advice is to "get as good as you can as fast as you can."
- Begin speaking and offering workshops on your specialty and start networking, since these will be your primary ways to get business.

Where to Turn for Information and Help

BOOKS

How to Be Organized in Spite of Yourself, by Sunny Schlenger and Roberta Roesch. New York: Signet, 1990.

How to Get Organized When You Don't Have the Time, by Stephanie Culp. Cincinnati: Writer's Digest, 1986. Also available: *How to Conquer Clutter*, by Stephanie Culp.

Organized to Be the Best, by Susan Silver. Los Angeles: Adam Hall, 1991.

ORGANIZATIONS

National Association of Professional Organizers, 1163 Shermer Road, Northbrooke, IL 60062; (708) 272-0135. Newsletter, conferences, local chapters, and a directory for media and consumers.

NEWSLETTERS

These newsletters are for people who have problems with clutter. Many organizers read them, however, because they provide insight into their clients' problems.

Messies Anonymous Newsletter, 5025 Southwest 114th Avenue, Miami, FL 33165; (305) 271-8404.

Packrat Support and Information Newsletter, 12662 Hoover Avenue, Garden Grove, CA 92641; (714) 894-8223.

MANUALS

Harriet Schechter's How to Become a Professional Organizer Resource Packet, 3368 Governor Drive, Suite F-199, San Diego, CA 92122.

■ ■ ■ ■

PROFESSIONAL PRACTICE CONSULTANT

Being a businessperson and a practicing professional are quite different roles, each with its own set of required skills. An increasing number of dentists, doctors, chiropractors, osteopaths, podiatrists, psychotherapists, and other professionals are recognizing this difference and are turning to business consultants for advice and even to actually have them manage the business side of their professional practices.

Full-service private practice consultants help professionals do virtually any aspect of running their offices. They will handle payroll, hire and fire personnel, train personnel, handle collections, do billing, manage the facility (if the client owns a building), oversee investments, and select computer hardware and software. They may also help with patient scheduling.

Some practice consultants are generalists, working with a variety of professions, although about 75 percent of the clients for this business are physicians, dentists and other professionals in the medical field. Others are highly specialized—working, for example, only with anesthesiologists or dentists. Their clients include solo practitioners as well as group practices, and sometimes even hospital administrators may use their services. Although a consultant may run the entire business for a client, most are not stationed in the office.

The demand for private practice consultants has exploded in the past five years. As the practice of medicine becomes both more sophisticated and more competitive, doctors need to spend more time keeping up with their field. At the same time they are feeling greater pressure to market and administer their practice as a business. In fact, some consultants specialize in marketing the professional, although 75 percent of their work is still in practice management.

Gray Tuttle, past president of the Society of Professional Business Consultants, estimates that despite recent growth in this field only 5 percent of the need has been met to date. There are 450,000 doctors in private practice, and as Tuttle says, "today most doctors are facing an earnings squeeze. There is plenty of opportunity for the practice consultant."

Charles Wold, author of *Managing Your Medical Practice*, told us that 15 years ago doctors weren't particularly interested in hiring consultants. Ten years ago they began hiring consultants to make things easier. Today he finds physicians facing an increasingly hostile business environment. "There's not enough money coming in to tolerate mistakes," he says. "They have to be better managed in order to survive."

☑ Knowledge and Skills You Need to Have

There is no formal training for this business, but several skills are needed:

- You must be able to manage a doctor's practice, which means you need to have either experience or education in office management in the medical field. Successful consultants have primarily come from two backgrounds. Some began as staff in a professional's office and learned the business from the ground up. Others are CPAs or MBAs who saw the need and decided to specialize in this field.

- In addition to being competent in handling professional business practices, you must have confidence and high self-esteem in order to communicate that you know your stuff when talking with the professionals, office staff, and government agencies you will be dealing with.

- You need to be able to manage your time effectively in order to balance running your own business with running the businesses of multiple clients.

- You need common sense and an organized mind to deal effectively with patient-care issues and office systems.

🐄 Start-Up Costs

	Low	High
Computer with hard disk	$1,000	$2,500
Printer	$ 300	$1,600
Spreadsheet, word-processing, and accounting software	$ 950	$1,200
Fax	$ 400	$ 800
Telephone headset (you spend a lot of time on the telephone going over facts, figures, schedules)	$ 40	$ 70
Office furniture, especially an ergonomic chair	$ 600	$ 800
Business cards, letterhead, envelopes	$ 200	$ 600
Brochure	$ 100	$2,000
Organizational dues	$ 250	$ 250
Totals	$3,840	$9,820

📑 Advantages

- This business is recession-resistant because doctors need help running their practice as a business even more acutely in tough times.

- This is an excellent opportunity to use any management skills you may have developed during your career.

- You are working in one of the most highly educated sectors of our society.

- The work involves handling a variety of problems, which means you are always learning to deal with new things. As Gray Tuttle says, "There's no boredom in this business. You can learn as much as you care to."

- This service is in demand, and people will value and appreciate your work.

- Practice-management consultants may have clients throughout the country, which is a plus if you love to travel.

- This business is easy to set up. All you need is a phone and some office equipment. Your clients will not usually come to your office.

Disadvantages

- All the doctors you work with will view you as *theirs*, so there will be competition for your time.
- Often you will be working on someone else's schedule because your clients will want to see you at their convenience.
- The work can be stressful because many unexpected demands arise.
- Being a personal service, you are limited in your earnings by how much time you can bill, unless you hire employees.

Pricing

Private practice consultants charge in two ways:

By the hour.   Rates range from $60 to $300.

On monthly retainers.   Rates range from a few hundred dollars (which purchases several hours) to thousands of dollars a month.

Potential Earnings

In 1990, doctors earned $155,000 on the average. Practice-management consultants can equal the earnings of their affluent clients. Some consultants bill up to sixty hours a week.

TYPICAL ANNUAL GROSS REVENUES: $90,000 to $187,500 or more, based on 30 0billable hours a week at from $60 to $125 per hour.

OVERHEAD: Moderate (20 to 40 percent).

Best Ways to Get Business

- Having contacts in the field prior to starting the business. Network with those contacts and build new contacts through professional and civic associations.
- Positioning yourself to get referrals from your doctor clients. Professional organizations will also make referrals.
- Offering workshops on practice-management issues for professional organizations.
- Writing columns with tips and guidance about practice management for business and professional journals.
- Serving on fund-raising committees in organizations that have doctors as members.

Franchises

Professional Management Group, Box 1130, Battle Creek, MI 49016; (800) 888-1932. Provides bread-and-butter business services for professionals. They seek people who have some accounting, business, or financial background, and who are familiar with some aspects of the health-care field. They offer preceptor (observer) and mentor (apprentice) arrangements, new-consultant workshops, and continuing education. The fee is approximately $25,000 and the franchise provides geographical exclusivity.

First Steps

■ Take educational programs on professional-management topics from institutes and professional associations.

■ Work for an established firm that does professional practice consulting—in effect, apprenticing.

Where to Turn for Information and Help

BOOKS

Encyclopedia of Practice and Financial Management, by Lawrence Farber. Oradell, NJ: Medical Economic Books, 1985.

Managing Your Medical Practice, by Charles R. Wold. New York: Matthew Bender. Looseleaf; updated annually; Cost: $100.

Medical Practice Management, by Horace Cotton. Oradell, NJ: Medical Economic Books, 1985.

Medical Practice Management Desk Book, by Charles H. Walsh and Morton Walker. Englewood Cliffs, NJ: Prentice-Hall, 1982.

Practice Management for Physicians, by Donald L. Donohugh. Orlando, FL: W. B. Saunders, 1986.

ORGANIZATIONS

Society of Medical-Dental Management Consultants, 6215 Larson Street, Kansas City, MO 64133; (800) 826-2264.

Society of Professional Business Consultants, 600 South Federal Street, Chicago, IL 60605; (312) 922-6222.

MAGAZINES AND NEWSLETTERS

The Consultant, Society of Professional Business Consultants, 600 South Federal Street, Chicago, IL 60605; (312) 922-6222.

Dental Management, Edgel Communications, 7500 Old Oak Boulevard, Cleveland, OH 44130; (216) 249-8100.

Medical Economics, Medical Economics Company, Box 1010, Oradel, NJ 07649; (201) 262-3030.

Physicians Management, Edgel Communications, 7500 Old Oak Boulevard, Cleveland, OH 44130; (216) 249-8100.

■ ■ ■ ■

PUBLIC RELATIONS SPECIALIST

Public-relations specialists help establish a high profile for their clients. This is important, because, in today's information age, visibility is power. They obtain publicity for their clients in magazines and newspapers, and on radio and television. They produce written materials such as newsletters, news releases, annual reports, speeches, and brochures that call attention to their clients.

The Bureau of Labor Statistics projects a 40 percent growth in public relations specialists through the year 2000, and there are several reasons we have included this business on our list of best businesses for the '90s. First, the demand for public relations is growing. PR, as it is often called, is increasingly recognized as a cost-effective solution for marketing a business. In fact, Daniel J. Edelman, founder of Edelman Public Relations Worldwide, says PR is actually more efficient than advertising under four circumstances:

- when introducing a revolutionary, breakthrough product
- for small companies with little budget for advertising
- when TV is not an option, as with some products that can't be advertised or do not fit well with television
- when public opinion is negative and has to be turned around quickly

Secondly, corporations and organizations of all sizes are cutting back on their in-house PR staff. As a result, more and more companies are contracting out their public-relations work.

Lastly, with today's personal computers, faxes, modems, and other modern technology, a PR specialist working independently at home can produce the same quality of work once reserved for large, high-budget agencies. Information available from on-line databases, coupled with the capabilities of desktop publishing and electronic communications, enables the PR specialist to create and send written materials and artwork to and from virtually anywhere instantaneously.

Clients for a home-based PR agency might include businesses, nonprofit organizations, public agencies, and individuals, particularly authors and practicing professionals. PR professionals may find a particular niche by specializing, for example, in annual reports, employee communications, newsletters, copywriting, or media or investor relations. Some work only with certain types of clients such as authors, restaurants, environmentally conscious companies, and so forth.

To provide a snapshot of what a public relations specialist does we asked

Ron Solberg of the Doron Alliance, who operates the PR and Marketing Forum on CompuServe, to describe a typical day in the life of a home-based PR firm. Here's what he told us:

"The day might begin by running out for a breakfast meeting with a client or prospective client. Then after returning home, you might draft a news release for a client, spend some time updating your media list, and then go out again for a luncheon meeting with another client to develop visuals for a presentation. Following lunch, you might prepare a summary of activities for a client, follow up on some correspondence, talk to a reporter, research a database for some specific information you need, and begin formatting a newsletter for another client. After supper you might return to your office to finish the newsletter before you close the door on work. Throughout the day, of course, you would also be getting calls from suppliers, clients, and people you're working with."

✔ Knowledge and Skills You Need to Have

- PR specialists need strong communication skills. You have to be able to write well to attract attention and interest with the materials you prepare for your clients. You must have good telephone skills because much of your contact with clients, reporters, and editors will be on the phone.

- You must be pleasant, persistent, positive, and persuasive in your communication.

- You must be creative and colorful to provide clients with a new angle that will capture the interest of their market and the media. You must follow current trends, news, interests, needs, and likes and dislikes by keeping up with the latest in sports, entertainment, business, and world events.

- Free-lance PR specialists must be able to come up with stimulating ideas on their own since they don't have other staff with whom they can discuss ideas.

- You need to be able to organize abstract ideas or technical jargon into tangible, meaningful material for publications, speeches, newsletters, ad copy, and so forth.

- A PR specialist must have a lot of energy. PR projects are referred to as campaigns. There are deadlines, and there is little down time to regroup and recharge emotionally and physically.

- You must have or gain knowledge of the media that your clients want to reach and establish relationships with the editors and producers who will make publicity decisions. You need to know the deadlines they operate under, their focus or theme, the types of guests, features, or articles they like to run, and so forth, so you will know how to talk with them about your clients.

🐘 Start-Up Costs

	Low	High
Computer with hard disk	$1,000	$ 2,500
Laser printer	$ 650	$ 2,500
Modem	$ 100	$ 500
Fax machine	$ 400	$ 1,500
Word-processing, communication, mailing-list, grammar-checker, and time-and-expenses software	$ 650	$ 850
Telephone headset (can increase phone productivity by one-third)	$ 40	$ 70
Office furniture, especially an ergonomic chair	$ 600	$ 800
Business cards, letterhead, envelopes	$ 600	$ 1,000
Brochure or press kit	$ 200	$ 2,000
Organizational dues	$ 250	$ 250
Two phone lines for business, with call forwarding and conferencing features	(part of overhead)	
Totals	$4,490	$11,970

PR firms can barter for many of these costs and thereby reduce start-up expenses.

🖐 Advantages

- This business can be exciting and vastly stimulating. It provides enjoyable and interesting experiences.
- You are not limited to doing any particular thing at any given time. Throughout the day you can move from one kind of activity to another and build an interesting day for yourself.
- Public relations is perceived as prestigious.

👎 Disadvantages

- Public relations is a competitive field. Many people who were unable to find a job in a corporation after college start out doing public relations on their own, working from home. Through internships during school, they have had some experience and will work at cut-rate prices, which may bring down the price others can charge.
- You must prove your value over and over again with your clients. You're only as good as your last job. There is always the pressure of how many stories you can place and what response you will get from a news release.
- The work can be stressful because of deadlines, time pressures, and the fact that often you do not control the end result for your client, which may lie in the hands of editors and producers who have their own priorities, whims, and preferences.

- PR is sensitive to the economy. Some businesses pull back on PR if times are tough, even though such times are ideal for doing more PR.
- This business has a slow start-up. You can expect two years of taking out less than you're putting in.
- Prospecting never ends. You always need to have business lined up after your current projects come to a close. The average client relationship lasts only 9 months.

💲 Pricing

Fees range from $200 to $1,500 per day. The national average for public-relations consultants is $850 per day. PR professionals serving large corporations average $1,000 per day while those working for smaller companies average $600 per day. The highest rates for PR professionals are for those who provide consulting services; they charge as much as $200 per hour.

🔲 Potential Earnings

As reported in the June 1990 issue of *Public Relations Journal,* the median annual earnings after business expenses and before income taxes for solo practitioners was $39,803, with 37 percent earning over $45,000. Billing 20 hours a week should be a minimum goal; 30 billable hours is realistic.

OVERHEAD: Low (20 percent or less).

🗂 Best Ways to Get Business

- Networking and personal contacts in organizations, such as trade and business associations, particularly in industries or fields in which you have experience.
- Speeches for community groups promoting the benefits of public relations.
- Volunteer work for nonprofit organizations.
- Telemarketing, particularly if you can barter with a professional to do it for you.
- Publishing a newsletter for former and prospective clients.
- Identifying potential PR opportunities for companies by reading electronic news services and then contacting by phone companies to whom the information you've gleaned is pertinent.

👆 First Steps

Many colleges and universities have certificate programs in public relations that can provide you with an understanding of the field and a credential without your having to earn a four-year degree. Another way to get experience is to work part-time assisting an established free-lancer, doing it for free if necessary.

If you already have some background in the field, begin by contacting 25 people you know and asking their opinion about your going into this business. Talk with people who might become clients themselves or refer clients to you.

🔲 Where to Turn for Information and Help

BOOKS

Effective Public Relations, by Scott M. Cutlipp et al. Englewood Cliffs, NJ: Prentice-Hall, 1985.

Lesly's Public Relations Handbook, by Philip Lesly. Englewood Cliffs, NJ: Prentice-Hall, 1983.

DIRECTORIES

O'Dwyer's Directory of Public Relations Firms, 271 Madison Avenue, New York, NY 10016.

Bacon's Publicity Checker, Bacon Publishing Company, 332 South Michigan Avenue, Suite 1020, Chicago, IL 60604.

Business Periodicals Index. H. W. Wilson Company, 950 University Avenue, Bronx, NY 10452. Annual.

Gale Directory of Publications and Broadcast Media, Gale Research, Book Tower, Detroit, MI 48226. Annual.

Gebbie Press All-in-One Directory, Gebbie Press, Box 1000, New Paltz, NY 12561. Annual.

ORGANIZATIONS

Public Relations Society of America, 33 Irving Place, New York, NY 10003; (212) 995-2230.

International Association of Business Communicators, 870 Market Street, Suite 940, San Francisco, CA 94102; (415) 433-3400.

PR and Marketing Forum, CompuServe Information Service.

MAGAZINES AND NEWSLETTERS

PR Reporter, Box 600, Exeter, NH 03833. Weekly newsletter of PR, public affairs, and communications.

Public Relations Journal, 33 Irving Place, New York, NY 10003; (212) 995-2230.

Public Relations News, 127 East 80th Street, New York, NY 10021; (212) 879-7090.

■ ■ ■ ■

REAL-ESTATE APPRAISER

Real-estate appraisers estimate the value of residential and commercial property. People need to have real estate appraised prior to sale of the property, when getting insurance, in the event of a loss, at the time of bankruptcy, during a divorce, and at various other times.

The real-estate appraisal industry is undergoing a fundamental transformation in the '90s. The good news is that a growing demand for appraisers means opportunity and incomes for appraising will rise. The bad news is that failed real-estate loans made by banks and savings and loans during the '80s have spurred Congress to pass the Financial Institutions Reform, Recover, and Enforcement Act, which requires all states to license or certify real-estate appraisers—without grandfathering the 250,000 appraisers now working. This means that even appraisers who have been working for years have to complete formal course work and pass an examination to work in this field (although in some states it appears that someone who has been a realtor and has valued property may be able to get at least partial credit for this experience toward a license or certificate).

This is in sharp contrast to the situation in the past, when, according to Dan Greenlaw, a Connecticut appraiser who works from his home, all you had to do to call yourself an appraiser was hang out a shingle and fill out a form. As Greenlaw says, at that time the training program to become an appraiser "was to simply go around for a day or two with another appraiser." Now, however, appraisers must take formal course work and have two years of work experience to qualify for a license.

Despite these changes, however, appraising is an excellent business opportunity. According to Ken Twichell of the National Association of Real Estate Appraisers, 65 percent of those 25,000 members are self-employed and 43 percent of whose members work from home, "Many of the existing appraisers are in their sixties, and they don't want to take the course work and tests now necessary to qualify to do the work they've been doing for decades. So they're retiring, and nobody is coming out of college wanting to be an appraiser. We're going to have a shortage of appraisers from 1991 onward."

Greenlaw believes that these changes mean appraising is becoming a full-fledged profession, with an income commensurate with a professional status. And much of the work, he projects, will be done from home.

In addition to doing appraisals for lending agencies when a loan is being made, appraisers also work with attorneys, making appraisals when a property is going through foreclosure, during divorce settlements, or for probate and bankruptcy estate administration. Appraisals may also be needed to insure property.

Real estate is not the only field in which appraisers are needed. Personal collections, jewelry, art, and other valuables need appraising, too. So if you have gained knowledge about a particular type of valuable property from a hobby or past jobs, you can establish yourself as an expert and make good money by providing appraisal services.

☑ Knowledge and Skills You Need to Have

- You will need to obtain a license proving you have knowledge of the regulations, procedures, and practices of appraising. (See the "First Steps" section below for details.)
- You will need to have a working knowledge of values for the type of property you appraise and know what characteristics constitute value.
- Contacts with lawyers, bankers, insurance agents, and others who are able to refer business to you are important.
- You need to have good communication skills in order to market yourself, to answer questions when asked to justify your appraisals, and to break news to people whose livelihood depends on a transaction.

🐷 Start-Up Costs

	Low	High
Course work for license	$ 975	$1,250
Personal computer	$1,000	$2,500
Printer	$ 300	$1,600
Word-processing and form-making software	$ 300	$1,350
Business cards, letterhead, envelopes	$ 200	$ 600
Organizational dues	$ 250	$ 250
Camera	$ 80	$ 200
Still video camera incorporated into software and used with a color laser printer	——	$5,000
Total	$3,105	$12,750

👍 Advantages

- This is not a desk job. You're outside much of the time instead of sitting in an office.
- Computers and modems mean you spend even less time in clients' offices.
- Overhead and risk are low in comparison to other businesses in the real-estate and development field.
- The work offers a wide variety of activities.
- Your clients become regular customers.

👎 Disadvantages

- Your hours are a bit erratic. Job requirements may necessitate that you attend evening meetings or do your work at the property owners' convenience.
- Appraisers are being sued and held legally responsible for losses of savings and loans and banks.
- The new licensing process is time consuming.

$ Pricing

The typical appraisal fee on a residence is $225.

▣ Potential Earnings

TYPICAL ANNUAL GROSS REVENUES: $56,000 for residential appraising, based on completing 5 appraisals a week at $225 each. Commercial appraisers, who must have more qualifications, earn over $100,000 per year.

OVERHEAD: Low (under 20%).

▣ Best Ways to Get Business

- Personal contact with mortgage companies and banks to get on approved lists of appraisers.
- Networking in organizations such as mortgage bankers' associations and mortgage brokers' associations.

▣ First Steps

The first step is to get licensed. Course work entails 75 hours of actual classroom time to appraise residential property and 150 hours to appraise commercial property. Each 15 hours of training costs from $195 to $250. In order to get the required experience, you must then work for a licensed appraiser for two years, splitting the fees you earn for your appraisals.

You can take the necessary course work in local real-estate schools, from community colleges, or from one of the 30 appraisal organizations in the United States (three of which are listed below).

▣ Where to Turn for Information and Help

BOOKS

Appraising Residences and Income Properties, by Henry S. Harrison. New Haven, CT: H2 Company, 1989.

ORGANIZATIONS

The first three organizations listed here offer courses.

Appraisal Institute, 430 North Michigan Avenue, Chicago, IL 60611; (312) 329-8559. With 39,000 members, this is the largest appraisal organization. Members are mostly commercial real-estate appraisers.

Appraisers Association of America, 60 East 42nd Street, New York, NY 10165. (212) 867-9775. This is an association for appraisers of personal property other than real estate.

National Association of Independent Fee Appraisers, 75-1 Murdoch Avenue, St. Louis, MO 63119; (314) 781-6688.

National Association of Real Estate Appraisers, 8383 East Evans Road, Scottsdale, AZ 85260; (602) 948-8000. This group has a residential orientation.

■■■■

RESUME WRITING SERVICE

People change jobs and careers many times over the course of their working lifetimes, and with an increasing number of companies being downsized, merged, or acquired, there are lots of resumes to be written. But many job seekers don't have the time or the ability to create an effective resume. They need professional help to create clean, sharp-looking and concise documents that will make a good impression on a prospective employer. This need has brought about a growing industry—resume writing.

A resume service does not simply type up someone's resume in an attractive form. Resume writers work with their clients to develop and write their resumes and then organize the information into an attractive, professional-looking document. The resume writer begins by interviewing clients about their background, skills, accomplishments, strengths, and weaknesses and how and to whom they want to present themselves. The writer then organizes this information into a concise and attractive format that highlights the clients' most noteworthy accomplishments and skills. Clients are given a number of copies of their completed resume, usually 5 to 25, as part of the basic service.

Some resume services provide additional assistance. They may write the cover letter, some design the letterhead so the cover letter, resume, and accompanying documents can be presented as a matched set; they may also do mass mailings of the letter, resume, and materials to prospective employers.

Resume services serve two primary groups of clients: university students, and people in the business and professional community. The first group includes seniors getting ready to graduate, sophomores and juniors seeking internships, and older students returning to the work force after going back to school. Business and professional clients include those seeking an opportunity to advance their careers as well as those who have been victims of mergers, purges, downsizings, or are otherwise in need of a job. Another possible source of business is physically handicapped people, referred to you by your state department of rehabilitation, who are in need of resumes.

Steve Burt, who runs a resume service in Gainesville, Florida, deals exclusively with resume development. Half or more of his clients are university students. He says, "I am not a typing service. My clients usually come to me with nothing in hand but perhaps an old resume. Sometimes they don't know what type of work they want to pursue, and I may find something in their background that suggests a direction for their job search."

Burt sees a growing need for his services. He finds that the writing skills of college students have declined over the seven years he's been in business. He advises, however, that "to succeed in this business you can't do the standard cookie-cutter eight-dollar resume. You've got to separate yourself from others and offer a high-quality service."

☑ Knowledge and Skills You Need to Have

You do not need to have a background in personnel or employment counseling to help a client develop an effective resume. You can become an expert on resumes by reading the vast amount of material written on this subject, a representative list of which appears at the end of this section. You do need the following skills and abilities:

- Strong writing skills and the ability to organize information logically and concisely are an absolute necessity. You also need a good command of the English language, including punctuation, spelling, and grammar.

- The ability to interview clients is important. You need to be able to make them feel comfortable and to draw out key information about their skills and experience.

- At the same time you need to be able to think like the personnel directors who will read the resumes, and be able to anticipate the questions they will ask so you can cover them in the resumes you prepare.

- You must live within 20 minutes of a college or university or of business establishments so your clientele can conveniently meet with you. Preferably you will live near both a college or university and business establishments.

- Most importantly, you must enjoy this type of work. You need to be able to show a personal interest in every client's resume and believe everyone has some valuable skills and experience that can be highlighted.

◆ Start-Up Costs

	Low	High
Computer with hard disk	$1,000	$2,500
Laser printer	$ 900	$1,600
Word-processing, grammar-checking, and database software	$ 550	$ 850
Copy machine (you can use a laser printer as a copier initially)	——	$1,000
Office furniture, especially an ergonomic chair	$ 600	$ 800
Business cards, letterhead, envelopes	$ 200	$ 600
Brochure or price list	$ 100	$ 500
Answering machine or answering service	——	$ 100
Because you're seeing people in your home, your office needs to convey a professional image. It's best if you can have a separate entrance to your office. And if you don't already have them, you'll need:		
Two identical comfortable chairs	$ 600	$1,000
End tables or coffee table	$ 100	$ 500
Appropriate artwork	$ 50	$ 500
Totals	$4,100	$9,950

▣ Advantages

- You get the satisfaction of knowing you're helping others succeed. Steve Burt says, "It's great to hear people call with a job and say, "I know the reason is because of the resume you wrote for me."
- The business can grow as large as you want it to.
- You meet people with a variety of interesting backgrounds.
- Resume writing can be an added service to other businesses like word processing, career counseling, or a specialized temporary service.

▣ Disadvantages

- People sometimes confuse you with a typing service. You have to make it clear that you write and develop resumes.
- If you have an academic market, work can be seasonal and can come all at once, creating pressures around the time of career expos and graduation.
- People may call you at any time of day or night.

▣ Pricing

Following are typical prices for developing and writing resumes.

- One-page student resumes: $25 to $75, with an average price of $50.
- One-page resume for middle managers: $25 to $100, with an average of $65.
- Two-page resume for engineers: $25 to $125, with an average of $90.
- Two-page executive resume: $25 to $200, with an average of $100; full curriculum vitae can command prices of over $300.

▣ Potential Earnings

TYPICAL ANNUAL GROSS REVENUES: $39,000, based on preparing 12 resumes a week, 50 weeks a year, at $65 per resume.

A typical resume takes 2 hours to complete. This includes interviewing, writing, and meeting with the client to turn over the completed resume and collect the fee. Keep in mind, however, that the resume business is seasonal, with the busiest months being January, February, March, and May and the least busy months being July, November and December. During busy times, Steve Burt has taken as many as 23 appointments a day!

Frank Fox, executive director of the Professional Association of Resume Writers, points out that the resume business soars with recession and high unemployment. During off-seasons, resume writers may offer workshops. And although some also provide word-processing services, Steve Burt believes that to command top dollar as a resume writer, it is important to distinguish yourself from a word-processing or secretarial service. To distinguish himself from less professional resume services, Burt has joined the Better Business Bureau.

▣ Best Ways to Get Business

The most successful methods for getting business, according to the results of the Professional Association of Resume Writers, 1990 membership study, are:

- Yellow-pages advertising.
- Classified ads under "Employment, Professional" section in college or university newspapers and in newspapers read by businesspeople and professionals.
- Networking in professional, trade, and civic organizations and referral groups.
- Direct mail to graduating students, attendees at job fairs, and so forth.
  - Postcards and letters describing your service. Steve Burt finds that people hold onto these for two years.
  - Renting a mailing list from a college or university and sending a pamphlet to seniors just before school starts in September and January.
  - Keeping a database of your resumes for one year and, prior to the end of the year, sending out a mailer to clients, suggesting they may want to update their resume or have you write a new cover letter.
- Referrals from print shops, radio spots, and job fairs.
- Giving workshops, seminars, and speeches on how to write a resume.

Other methods that work well include:

- Offering to pay a cash referral fee to existing clients who refer new clients to you.
- Developing reciprocal referral arrangements from employment agencies that don't offer resume writing service. These agencies like for their clients to have good-quality resumes. You may also be able to get referrals from desktop-publishing or word-processing firms that type and lay out resumes but don't write and develop them.
- Placing notices on bulletin boards at colleges, print shops, large companies, and so forth.

▣ First Steps

If your writing skills need polishing, take a writing course. Concentrate on developing your vocabulary; it's your ammunition. Your toughest client to get is the first one. You have to be prepared to answer the questions *What makes you think you could write my resume?* and *Why are you better?* Develop samples so people can see what an excellent job you do. Do your first resume for free if necessary.

▣ Where to Turn for Information and Help

BOOKS

Go to your local library and/or bookstore and read everything you can find about resume writing in order to familiarize yourself with many approaches so you can develop the right resume for each individual. Compare examples in books; some may actually be poorly done. Here are some books recommended by resume writers.

High Impact Resumes and Letters: How to Communicate Your Qualifications to Employers, by Ronald L. Krannich and William J. Banis. Manassas, VA: Impact, 1988.

Power Resumes, by Ron Tepper. New York: John Wiley and Sons, 1989.

Resumes That Get Jobs, by Jean Reed. New York: Arco, 1990.

MANUALS

A Resume Writer's Guide to Asking Effective Questions, Professional Association of Resume Writers, 3637 4th Street North, Suite 330, St. Petersburg, FL 33704.

ORGANIZATIONS

Professional Association of Resume Writers, 3637 Fourth Street North, Suite 330, St. Petersburg, FL 33704; (800) 822-7279. This organization provides a newsletter, professional membership identification including name and logo to use in advertising layouts, and a toll-free consultant line.

SOFTWARE

Software is available but too restrictive for professional use except perhaps in writing a college student's resume. Software such as *ResumExpert* and *The Resume Kit* for the Macintosh can be helpful in organizing simple resumes. *The Resume Kit* is also available for DOS computers.

■ ■ ■ ■

SECURITY CONSULTANT

One way of taking action on crime reports we're bombarded with by the media is a career in the security field. Because security considerations are becoming an increasingly routine part of everything from building design to organizational policy, the private security field is growing. Hallcrest Systems predicts that security consulting will be one of the major growth areas of the security industry during the nineties.

Security consultants provide advice on security policies and procedures. They evaluate the physical design of buildings and spaces, assess telephone security, and make recommendations on security equipment. Security policies involve such business matters as employee selection and preventing both internal and external theft, as well as assuring the security of company information.

Security consultants may or may not be private investigators. In any case, these fields may overlap. For example, security consultants may conduct background investigations on personnel and pre-employment screenings for their clients—services private investigators also provide.

Nate Lenow is certified as a security consultant and licensed as a private investigator. He points out that security consultants have typically served banks, large corporations, and universities. As a security consultant, he focuses on small businesses and specializes in restaurants. As a certified consultant, he recommends but does not sell equipment, such as alarm and video-monitoring systems. When we talked with him he had just finished saving a client several thousand dollars by buying equipment at Sears and installing it himself. Robert Gardner specializes in working with architects and developers during the design phase of construction.

Unlike private investigators, security consultants are not licensed. Professional recognition in the field is achieved by passing a rigorous examination given by the American Society for Industrial Security.

☑ Knowledge and Skills You Need to Have

- Several universities now grant degrees in security administration; however, experience with the crime-prevention unit of a police department, serving as a military policeman, or doing survey work for a private security service will provide the necessary knowledge and experience.
- You need the ability to analyze situations.
- You need to know how to read blueprints.
- You must know how to use equipment like closed-circuit TV.

🐘 Start-Up Costs

	Low	High
Computer and modem	$1,000	$2,500
Printer	$ 300	$1,600
Word-processing software	$ 100	$ 350
Office furniture	$ 600	$ 800
Brochure	$ 100	$2,000
Business cards, letterhead, envelopes	$ 200	$ 600
Tools	$ 100	$ 200
Camera	$ 100	$ 200
Organizational dues	$ 250	$ 250
Totals	$2,750	$8,500

📖 Advantages

- Security consultants command professional respect and provide valued services.
- New technologies introduced into security work make the field challenging and interesting.

ⓘ Disadvantages

- It takes at least two years to establish a clientele.
- To succeed as a security consultant, you've got to be good at it.
- People summon you only when they have a problem.

Ⓢ Pricing

Security consultants' fees range from $75 to $150 per hour.

ⓔ Potential Earnings

TYPICAL ANNUAL GROSS REVENUES: $75,000, based on billing 1,000 hours a year at $75 an hour.

OVERHEAD: Moderate: (20 to 40 percent).

ⓘ Best Ways to Get Business

- Getting articles you've written published.
- Getting publicity about your work.
- Direct mail followed up with telephone calls.
- Yellow-pages advertising.
- Advertising in publications read by your prospective clients.
- Speaking at seminars, meetings, and trade shows.
- Networking and personal contacts in organizations, such as trade and business associations, particularly in industries or fields in which you have experience.
- Getting listed in bar-association directories of expert witnesses.

ⓘ First Steps

- If you do not have the experience to qualify you as a security consultant, the best way to obtain the necessary knowledge and experience is to take a job in which you conduct surveys of new client premises for a private security service.
- Become certified by the American Society for Industrial Security.

ⓘ Where to Turn for Information and Help

BOOKS

Security Consulting, by Charles A. Sennewald. Boston: Butterworths, 1989.

ORGANIZATIONS

American Society for Industrial Security, 1655 North Fort Myer, Suite 1200, Arlington, VA 22209; (703) 522-5800. Offers certification.

International Security Review, Queensway House, 2 Queensway, Redhill, Surrey RH1 1QS, England.

Security Magazine, Box 5080, Des Plaines, IL 60018.

Security Management, American Society for Industrial Security, 1655 North Fort Myer Drive, Suite 1200, Arlington, VA 22209; (703) 522-5800.

■ ■ ■ ■

TECHNICAL WRITER

It's been calculated that after adjusting for inflation, free-lance writers in nontechnical fields are earning less today than they were in 1970. But if you have the ability to communicate technical information in an understandable way, you can earn up to $800 a day. In fact, the growing need for technical writing is undoubtedly one reason the Bureau of Labor Statistics projects a 34 percent increase in the number of professional writers between now and the year 2000.

Whenever a new product involving technology is introduced, information in the form of brochures, manuals, reference cards, instructional materials, reviews, and media releases needs to be developed that will communicate to those who will be involved with the technology: the buyers of the product; the users, who may be different from the buyers; the people who install the product, and those who repair it; and, of course, the people who sell and promote it. Each of these audiences creates a need for a different type of information.

Therefore, technical writing has four distinct markets:

1. writing articles for trade magazines
2. writing publicity materials, such as press releases and feature articles, for manufacturing and service companies that need editorial coverage in business and consumer publications
3. writing and editing technical books and instructional materials
4. translating technical information about new products and processes into user manuals and instruction booklets that can be read and understood by the people who will use them

Writers for technical magazines are in demand, and the demand for writing instructional materials is also growing because companies today are often using outside writers to create their instruction manuals, documentation, training materials, and technical information. "This form of technical writing is about helping people *do* something, not simply *know* something, says Michael Greer, cofounder of the I.D. Network, a highly successful Los Angeles instructional design firm.

☑ Knowledge and Skills You Need to Have

- Technical writers must have good writing skills.
- You need to have the ability to understand and translate technical information into terms that are clean and understandable to nontechnical readers.
- You must have a background in or be able to learn about high-technology products in order to understand what must be communicated and at the same time have an appreciation for the needs of people who may have little knowledge, experience, or patience with technology.

☐ Start-Up Costs

	Low	High
Computer	$1,000	$2,500
Printer	$ 300	$1,600
Word-processing software	$ 100	$ 250
Office furniture, especially an ergonomic chair	$ 600	$ 800
Business cards, letterhead, envelopes	$ 200	$ 600
Total	$2,200	$5,750

☐ Advantages

- You can set your own hours and work wherever you want.
- An increasingly technological world provides a favorable market for this type of work.
- Making technically difficult things understandable to people can be very rewarding.

☐ Disadvantages

- Technical writing is hard work because you are dealing with information that is difficult to communicate, especially because you may not have a background in what you're writing about.
- Sometimes the pressures of working under tight deadlines can be stressful.
- If someone is interested in doing more creative and imaginative forms of writing, technical writing can seem restrictive.

☐ Pricing

A recent survey by the Society for Technical Communication found that among self-employed technical writers, 6 percent charged under $20 per hour; 22 percent charged from $20 to $29; 40 percent charged from $30 to $39; 18 percent charged from $40 to $49; 7 percent charged from $50 to $60; and 4 percent charged over $60. The 1991 edition of *Writer's Market* reports that technical-writing fees range from $35 to $75 per hour, or $35 per manuscript page.

Writing articles for trade magazines can pay $400 to $500 per article. Technical writing on instructional design projects pays from $250 to $800 per day.

Potential Earnings

TYPICAL ANNUAL GROSS REVENUES: $30,000 to $67,500, based on billing 1,000 hours per year (20 hours per week) at $30 an hour at the low end and billing 1,500 hours per year (30 hours a week) at $45 per hour at the high end.

OVERHEAD: Low (under 20 percent).

Best Ways to Get Business

- Networking and personal contacts in trade associations and computer user groups, and at trade shows where prospective clients exhibit.
- Assignments from previous employers.
- Responding to ads for writers.
- Placing ads in publications read by prospective clients.
- Finding work through job shops that place temporary technical personnel, including technical writers.
- Joining a writers' organization and using its job-referral service.
- Directly soliciting work from the companies you want to write for, stressing the advantages of using free-lance writers for peak-work-load situations. Michael Greer got 40 percent of his business this way.

First Steps

While writers for trade publications are in demand, sending the standard query letter proposing an idea for an article to such magazines is not apt to result in a writing assignment because the editorial calendars for trade journals, unlike those of popular magazines, are usually set as much as a year in advance. Your goal should be to become one of a trade publication's cadre of free-lancers.

Where to Turn for Information and Help

BOOKS

Instructional Design Principles and Applications, by Leslie J. Briggs et al. Englewood Cliffs, NJ: Educational Technology Publications, 1977.

Literary Market Place with Names and Numbers. New York: R.R. Bowker Company. Published annually. Cost: $115.

Writer's Market: Where and How to Sell What You Write, Cincinnati, OH: Writer's Digest Books. Published annually.

ORGANIZATIONS

The following organizations are composed of either purchasers of technical writing or people in the field of technical writing.

American Society of Engineering Education, 11 Dupont Circle, N.W., Suite 200, Washington, DC 20036; (202) 293-7090.

American Society for Training and Development, 1630 Duke Street, Alexandria, VA 22313; (703) 683-8100. Publishes a journal and a catalogue of resources. Its special-interest groups are of particular interest to technical writers.

Institute for Electrical and Electronics Engineers, 345 East 47th Street, New York, NY 10017; (212) 705-7900.

International Association of Business Communicators, 1 Hallidie Plaza, Suite 600, San Francisco, CA 94102; (415) 433-3400.

National Society for Performance and Instruction, 1300 L Street, N.W., Suite 1250, Washington, DC 20005; (202) 408-7969.

Society for Technical Communication, 901 North Stuart Street, Suite 304, Arlington, VA 22203; (703) 522-4114. The society has local chapters, some of which have an employment referral service or resume bank.

Writers Guild of America West, 8955 Beverly Boulevard, West Hollywood, CA 90048; (213) 550-1000. **Writers Guild of America East,** 555 West 57th Street, New York, NY 10019; (212) 245-6180. Publishes the *Directory of Informational Program Writers.*

MAGAZINES AND NEWSLETTERS

Sources of information about what various publications are doing and who is coming out with what new products:

Adweek, Network A/S/M Communications, 49 East 21st Street, New York, NY 10010; (212) 529-5500.

Magazine Week, Lighthouse Communications, 233 West Central Street, Natick, MA 01760; (508) 650-1000.

Publishing News, 6 River Bend Center, 911 Hope Street, Box 4949, Stamford, CT 06907.

Washington Journalism Review, 4716 Pontiac Street, Suite 310, College Park, MD 20740; (301) 513-0001.

United States Department of Agriculture Graduate School offers reasonably priced courses in English and writing skills. Write for a catalogue: Graduate School, USDA, South Agriculture Building, 14th Street and Independence Avenue, S.W., Washington, DC 20250. Or call to speak with a course counselor at (202) 447-5885.

■ ■ ■ ■

TEMPORARY HELP SERVICE

When you think of a temporary help service, you probably think of the traditional temp agency that provides secretarial, administrative, and clerical personnel. These services are the third-fastest-growing sectors of our economy, with an annual growth rate of over 10 percent a year. It would be difficult, however, for a home-based business to compete head-to-head with traditional temp services, which are staffed with many employees who test, train, and place hundreds of temporary personnel in a single day. Home-based businesses can, however, compete successfully as *specialized* temporary services.

Specialized temporary services are the fastest-growing part of the temporary help industry. In some fields they are referred to as *registries*. No doubt their growth is in response to the frustration employers experience when they call a regular temporary help agency but cannot get workers with a specialized skill. A specialized temporary service is able to send them just the type of specialist they need, and save them the cost and time of looking for someone, training new personnel, and paying employee benefits.

A temporary agency can specialize in providing any type of personnel, including:

attorneys	librarians
association executives	marketing specialists
assemblers	medical-records personnel
bookkeepers	medical secretaries
convention help	nurses
court reporters	paralegals
data-processing personnel	pharmacists
hospital social workers	printing pressmen
legal secretaries	short-order cooks

You need not limit yourself to this list of known specialty services if another field you know of uses temporary workers in your market.

A specialized temporary service works like any other temp service. The specialty service first recruits its pool of specialists. Then when clients need them, the specialists are put on the service's payroll. The service pays all the taxes and benefits and then bills the client companies that have used the temporary help at a rate that covers costs and profits. By using a personal computer, specialized temporary services can be operated from home and outperform the traditional larger services, because whereas the latter compete primarily on price, specialized temporary services can compete on the quality of the specialized personnel they are able to send out.

Judith A. Wunderlich, for example, who operates the Wunderlich Graphic Agency from her suburban Chicago home, specializes in finding free-lance workers in the graphic-arts field such as photographers, copy editors, proofreaders, designers of all types, desktop publishers, typesetters, copywriters, keyliners, and illustrators. She has built a successful business, earning over $50,000 a year her first year in business while being a full-time mother and working less than 30 hours a week.

Wunderlich locates her specialists by running classified ads. Once a specialist contacts the service, he or she becomes part of her database. As with most services, many of these specialists are self-employed individuals, using temp work to tide them over while they start up their own businesses. They do not want to become permanent employees.

When a company requests a particular type of specialist, Wunderlich simply turns to her database to locate the person whose qualifications meet their need. She points out, however, that the database should include each specialist's complete employment history so that no one will be sent out to a company from which they have been laid off; complete information in a database helps avoid any such problems.

✔ Knowledge and Skills You Need To Have

- You need to have a knowledge of and contacts in the field you're specializing in, so stick to what you know. Nurses, for example, operate the best temporary nurses registries.

- You need to know how to use a computer and database software.

- You should know something about the routines and forms a temporary service uses, such as time sheets and contracts.

- You need to be organized and adept at record-keeping because you need to keep track of which specialists you have sent out, for how much time, and at what price. This is a task you can accomplish more easily with special software.

🐾 Start-Up Costs

	Low	High
Computer with hard disk	$1,000	$ 2,500
Printer	$ 300	$ 1,600
Software: database, word-processing, payroll, scheduling, and accounting with a payroll module (unless you use an outside payroll service)*	$ 900	$ 2,100
Telephone headset	$ 40	$ 70
Office furniture, especially an ergonomic chair	$ 600	$ 800
Business cards, letterhead, envelopes	$ 200	$ 600
Brochure	$ 100	$ 2,000
Organizational dues	$ 250	$ 250
Forms, time cards and contracts	——	$ 50
Attorney fee for consultation on employment laws, taxation, and potential liability	$ 150	$ 500
Liability insurance to protect you from lawsuits arising from acts of your employees	$ 600	$ 600
Working capital	$5,000	$20,000
Totals	$9,140	$31,070

*Specialized software for temp services that has a database with payroll and accounting capabilities costs $10,000, but is not necessary for a small service.

📖 Advantages

- Most of your work is done on the phone, so this is a home business that allows you to do most of your work *at* home.
- This business provides high earnings relative to the time and energy involved.
- There are no materials and no inventory. The business can almost run itself.
- You're not doing the work, the temps are; so your income is not limited by the number of hours you can work.
- There's a strong need for this service.
- It can be a 52-week-a-year business because even holidays and vacation times can be busy.
- Temporary help services do better than most businesses during recessions.

📖 Disadvantages

- Cash flow is the challenge of this business because you must pay the specialists at least every other week, but there is a delay between the time you must pay them and when you will be paid. Therefore you need to make certain not to rely too heavily on only one client. Some services offer a 2 percent discount for payment within a specified number of days.

■ Unless you are willing to grow very slowly, you need to have a nest egg of about $20,000 to cover operating expenses. This may mean taking out a loan.

■ You need to keep up with the changing tax, worker's-compensation, and employment laws. These changes affect your responsibilities to the specialists you employ.

■ You have a potential liability for employee misconduct; therefore, you need insurance to cover yourself. It may be wise to incorporate as well, although incorporation increases your cost of doing business and involves additional red tape.

■ You may need to bond employees, depending on the type of temps you provide.

💲 Pricing

You mark up the going salary for specialists by 40 to 50 percent depending upon availability and skill level. The more skilled the specialist, the higher the pay rate. To stay in touch with the going rates for full-time employees in your field, keep current with trade publications and the latest information published by the Bureau of Labor Statistics.

📠 Potential Earnings

TYPICAL ANNUAL GROSS REVENUES: Income will vary depending on the value of the specialists you are placing and how many specialists you place each week. Based on 10 people working 15 hours a week at $21 an hour 52 weeks a year, and after deducting payroll costs and the employer share of payroll taxes, you will have $69,628, from which you will deduct other business costs.

OVERHEAD: Moderate (20 to 40 percent)

📇 Best Ways to Get Business

■ Sending out direct mail in the form of a letter, postcard, or brochure (depending on what your competition is doing). This works well because there is such a need for this service that customers will save mailers for years.

■ Networking in business and trade associations in your field.

■ Publishing a newsletter for past, current, and potential clients.

■ Publicity about your special business.

🖳 First Steps

Ideally, you would start in a field you know well. If you've worked in the medical field, for example, you could select a medical specialty. Or if you've worked in a bank you could set up a bank-related service. If, however, you aren't in a field that lends itself to a temporary service, you can bring in experts to help you learn the ins and outs of the field.

For example, Linda Morse and Dorothea Green had no experience in the escrow field when they started Escrow Overload. To make up for their lack of knowledge, they hired escrow experts to help them develop tests and criteria for interviewing specialists for their database. Again when they expanded into Lender's Overload, they had never been loan officers, so they brought in loan processors to help them choose good personnel. Morse also suggests that going to one national convention of the National Association of Temporary Services will provide quite an education.

You can begin building your database of specialists by taking out classified ads in trade and professional publications in your specialty. There is little cost involved in building your database prior to opening your business. Another way of attracting personnel as you grow is to give referral bonuses to temps of yours who refer others to you. Once you have a strong pool of specialists, send out a direct-mail piece to employers who would have frequent needs for them.

🖳 Where to Turn for Information and Help

ORGANIZATIONS

National Association of Temporary Services, 119 South Saint Asaph Street, Alexandria, VA 22314; (703) 549-6287. Your employees are eligible to join a group insurance plan through this organization, which also publishes the *National Association of Temporary Services Research Reference Kit,* which is helpful in writing business plans for obtaining loans.

MANUALS

The Temporary Help Manual, National Association of Secretarial Services, 3637 Fourth Street North, Suite 330, St. Petersburg, FL 33704; (813) 823-3646. Although written for secretarial services, this manual outlines how to get started as an independent in the temporary help field.

Temporary-Help Service Business Guide, *Entrepreneur* magazine, 2392 Morse Avenue, Box 19787, Irvine, CA 92713; (800) 352-7449. Cost: $69.50.

■ ■ ■ ■

TRANSCRIPT DIGESTING SERVICE

Providing that you have the ability to write clearly, this is a business that takes a minimal amount of time to learn, costs little to start, and has the potential for earning good money. As a transcript digester, also called a *deposition digester*, you become part of the lucrative and intriguing field of law, transcribing statements taken under oath from parties involved in legal proceedings.

Lawyers don't like to be surprised in the courtroom when someone takes the stand. Discovering what people are going to say before they appear at a trial plays an important role in the American legal system. So prior to a trial, lawyers take testimony in what is called a deposition. Depositions are recorded by a court reporter, and then the entire testimony is transcribed into a document that the lawyers study carefully before the trial. As you can imagine, the transcripts are quite long, so to save time for the lawyers (many of whom now charge up to $400 an hour), transcript digesters identify relevant points and summarize the transcript. Each page of testimony is reduced to a paragraph. Depositions are also carefully indexed for the lawyers.

Digesters also digest trial transcripts during the course of a trial. An attorney may need an expedited transcript of a previous day's proceedings to prepare for cross-examination. In lengthy trials, which can last for months, digests of prior testimony are essential. Digests are also used in making appeals.

Sometimes digests are prepared by trained paralegals. In fact, digesting transcripts is part of paralegal training, but a digest can also be done by someone who has the ability to analyze and write succinctly. As digester Mary Helm points out, "good writing skills are more important in this business than legal knowledge. The writing needs to flow so the transcripts don't have to be read two or three times."

Today more and more law firms are using outside services. In the two years since Helm and her husband started their home-based digesting company, their business has expanded beyond the two of them to two full-time and eight part-time employees.

A digester's clients range from the solo practitioner to firms with 100 or more lawyers. Each firm has its own reasons for using independent digesters. The lawyer in solo practice may be buried in motions by a large firm and need outside help. Large law firms realize the economic advantage of using outside services instead of a licensed attorney, who would bill at $90 an hour.

☑ Knowledge and Skills You Need to Have

- As a deposition digester, you must be familiar with legal terminology and procedures so you can read and understand what is said in transcripts and condense it without changing the meaning.

- You must be able to read and type quickly. The faster you read and type, the higher your earnings.

- You must also be able to write concisely. The digester's role is not to decide whether testimony is relevant, but to know how to condense it skillfully.

- Prior expertise in a field can be helpful in understanding whatever terminology might be involved in a trial.

- You must prepare your digests on a computer using word-processing software (some law firms require that you use *Word Perfect*). You should also know how to use a modem to transmit your completed digests.

■ Start-Up Costs

	Low	High
Computer with hard disk	$1,000	$2,500
Ink-jet or laser printer	$ 500	$1,600
Modem	$ 100	$ 500
Word-processing, database, and communications software	$ 550	$ 700
Desk and ergonomic chair	$ 600	$ 800
Business cards, letterhead, envelopes	$ 400	$ 600
Brochure	$ 100	$2,000
Totals	$3,250	$8,700

■ Advantages

- Transcript digesting pays better than such similar businesses as word processing and being a note reader/scopist.
- You can learn what you need to know to do this business in as little as six days.
- The work is interesting and challenging.
- You learn useful information that you won't come across anywhere else.

■ Disadvantages

- The work is isolating. You are at your computer many hours each day.
- Because you are at the keyboard so long, you can suffer from computer-related disability. It's important to use an ergonomic chair, a keyboard pillow with wrist rests, and a glare screen. Also, you should get up frequently and walk around.

■ Pricing

Novice transcriptionists receive 80 cents per page. Experienced digesters get $2.50 to $4 per page. You'll earn substantially less when working through an agency, and agencies expect a digester to produce at least 10 pages per hour. Ten to 20 pages per hour is typical for digesters in an 8-hour day.

■ Potential Earnings

TYPICAL ANNUAL GROSS REVENUES: $38,000 to $100,000.

OVERHEAD: Low (20 percent or less).

■ Best Ways to Get Business

- Making personal contacts with people in law firms.
- Offering to digest one 50-to-100-page deposition for free.

- Looking for classified ads from law firms seeking digesters.
- Using display ads in legal publications as a long-term investment to build your name recognition.
- Directly soliciting law firms by phone and making an appointment to talk with them about your services. You can use a salesperson to set up appointments for you, but this person must know the business.
- Listing with agencies that will refer work to you.

⚡ First Steps

If you have no experience, find a college extension program that teaches transcription. Paralegal programs also have courses in deposition digesting and writing skills. Or you can teach yourself using the tutorials listed below. Once you have mastered the skill, to gain experience you might consider working for an agency at first, before marketing yourself directly to law firms. You can locate deposition digesting agencies in your community through ads in local legal publications.

🗇 Where to Turn for Information and Help

TUTORIALS

The **Working from Home Forum** on CompuServe Information Service offers files covering the basics of digesting transcripts, a sample deposition, and sample summaries in various formats. This material is available in Library 3.

Mary Helm's Transcript Digesting Manual, Hillside Digesting Service, Box 3911, Tustin, CA 92681. Complete with *WordPerfect* macro commands on disk.

■ ■ ■ ■

WEDDING CONSULTANT

Marriage has taken on a new importance in the '90s, and today's weddings are getting more expensive. Brides and grooms are older; often they both have careers. It's more than likely that they are paying for their own wedding than that their parents are covering the bill. Many of today's brides and grooms are children of divorce or are returning to the altar for a second or third marriage; they want their marriages to last.

It's not that today's couples aren't cost conscious, but they are creating a fantasy and they want it to be perfect. A big wedding makes a psychological statement. It says, "We're taking this marriage seriously." It's almost as if the bigger and fancier the wedding, the more of a commitment it represents and therefore the greater the chances the marriage will last. Gerard Monaghan, president of the Association of Bridal Consultants, says, "Some brides have been designing their wedding since they were two and a half years old." The result is that weddings have become big business.

Brides and grooms and their families spend $33 billion a year to create the wedding day of their dreams. The informal family wedding of the past few decades has been replaced by the elaborate, formal wedding. In fact, today's weddings are more like productions, with the average wedding costing from $5,000 to $6,000, and some going as high as $200,000. Today's weddings usually involve a formal wedding gown and veil for the bride, a tuxedo for the groom, several bridesmaids and groomsmen, ushers, floral arrangements, invitations, special napkins, cake and table decorations, beverages, music, seating for 100 to 200 people, a photographer, a videotaping service, a wedding makeup artist, a catered reception or sit-down meal, and of course a dream honeymoon.

Producing this one-day event is a considerable task, and one for which most couples are not well prepared. Growing up in the more informal '60s and '70s of blue jeans and beer, most young couples today have little or no experience with how to create an elegant, formal occasion. And since the bride and her mother probably both work, they seldom have the time to produce such an event.

That's where the wedding consultant comes in. Also called *bridal consultants, wedding planners* or *wedding coordinators,* wedding consultants play the role for the bride and groom that a contractor plays in building a dream home or that a director plays in the making of a movie. The wedding consultant works with the bride and groom and their families to help the couple articulate what they want, establish a wedding budget, and create their dreams within it. The wedding is an event that needs to be planned and produced. The consultant coordinates the production of the wedding, from finding and renting the facilities to negotiating contracts and overseeing the many elements and personnel involved, such as florists, photographers, videographers, caterers, travel agents, musicians, and disc jockeys.

Despite the uncertainties of the economy, Monaghan says the wedding consulting business is just hitting its stride. "Ten years ago there was no list of wedding consultants," he says. "Now there are 10,000 wedding consultants listed in the yellow pages coast to coast." Weddings have become a thriving industry. And although Monaghan acknowledges that the number of weddings will drop as the baby boomers pass the peak marrying age, he predicts that the amount spent on each wedding will continue to grow, thus keeping the dollars spent on weddings constant. Since wedding consultants typically work with at least $10,000 weddings, the upward drift of wedding spending should keep consultants busy.

☑ Knowledge and Skills You Need to Have

- Wedding consultants need to be gregarious, enjoy pressure, and be able to keep their wits about them when all around them is in turmoil. They must be able to take the unexpected in stride and calm the nerves of those around them.

- This is a people business, so communication skills are a must. The wedding consultant must be an expert at helping all those involved handle the tensions and emotions of situations where feelings about every little detail run deep. For example, Monaghan points out that "one of the unspoken functions of the wedding consultant is to serve as a buffer between brides and mothers." Therefore, knowledge of human behavior and psychology is helpful.

- Wedding consultants must be creative negotiators. They must develop solutions and negotiate prices with suppliers so that a wedding costing $10,000 seems like a wedding costing thousands more, thus justifying their fee.

- Wedding consultants need to be effective arbitrators to help the bride and groom reach decisions on such things as the guest list, music, and facility harmoniously—so there is a wedding.

- Wedding consultants must keep up with and be knowledgeable about fashion, food, music, and wedding styles.

- Wedding consultants must have basic business and financial-management skills and organizational ability, not only to run their own business but also to oversee the wedding budget.

- A good wedding consultant is both creative and practical—creative enough to talk about the nuances of wedding gowns or make a VFW hall look like a palace, but practical enough to make sure everything gets ordered and delivered on time.

- You need contacts with high-quality, reliable wedding services: photographers, printers, florists, hotels, bakeries, makeup artists, jewelers, caterers, travel agents, musicians, and disc jockeys.

◼ Start-Up Costs

	Low	High
Computer with hard disk	——	$ 1,000
Printer	$ 300	$ 1,600
Word-processing, database software	$ 100	$ 350
Telephone headset	$ 40	$ 70
Office furniture, especially an ergonomic chair	$ 600	$ 800
Wardrobe*	$ 500	$ 5,000
Business cards, letterhead, envelopes	$ 200	$ 600
Brochure	$ 200	$ 2,000
Organizational dues	$ 150	$ 250
Totals	$2,090	$11,670

*Wedding consulting is a glamor business, so you need to have a wardrobe, makeup, and hairstyling in accord with the image of your clientele. You need three types of outfits: (1) business suits for meeting with suppliers; (2) more casual yet attractive clothing for meeting with bride and bridal party; (3) more formal attire appropriate for attending the wedding.

📑 Advantages

- This is a glamorous, exciting, challenging business, and the work calls upon you to be creative.
- You are dealing with clients at one of the happiest times in their lives, so your work is fun.
- There is great satisfaction in creating a dream event that may live for a lifetime in a couple's memory and serve as an anchor for the marriage.
- You can branch out to plan other types of events, particularly in smaller communities, where there may not be enough weddings for a full-time business.

📑 Disadvantages

- The business can be very competitive and your profit margins small.
- The work is on weekends.
- The work is seasonal. May, June, and July are very busy, but the winter months are slow, and although you're planning during the slow months, you can attend only so many weddings during the busy months.
- You are coordinating many elements over which you have no control.
- Because weddings are planned six months to a year in advance, it may be at least that long before you receive a fee. Payment arrangements should be spelled out in a letter of agreement signed by the consultant and the couple.

💲 Pricing

Wedding consultants may charge a flat rate, a per diem rate, or an hourly rate for their services. Flat fees may be from 10 to 15 percent of the wedding budget; because the average wedding involving a consultant costs $15,000, a typical fee may run from $1,500 to about $2,000. Per diem rates range from $300 to $600. Hourly rates range from $50 to $75. Consultants may also derive income, with the consent of their clients, by obtaining referral commissions from wedding suppliers.

🖥 Potential Earnings

TYPICAL ANNUAL GROSS REVENUES: $37,500, based on 25 weddings a year at $1,500 per wedding. There are approximately 40 *marrying weeks* during the year, according to Gerald Monaghan. A full-time consultant can service 50 weddings a year.

OVERHEAD: Low (20 percent or less).

▣ Best Ways to Get Business

- Calling on, networking with, and cross-referencing to others providing wedding services: photographers, printers, florists, hotel and banquet-hall managers, bakeries, makeup artists, jewelers, caterers, travel agents, musicians, and disc jockeys.
- Exhibiting at bridal shows (although purchasing a booth is expensive).
- Advertising in specialty wedding publications or guides.
- Building visibility by advertising regularly in wedding supplements in local newspapers.
- Listing in the yellow pages.
- Getting repeat business by doing parties and other events like anniversaries for your clients, their family, and their friends.
- Using direct mail to recipients of wedding planning guides, and sending out newsletters to prospective and past clients.
- Offering free consultation for couples, advising them of what will be involved in planning their wedding. Use this time to establish a trusting relationship and to gather information for a written proposal you can submit to them after the meeting.

▣ First Steps

- To gain some experience before you begin working on your own, work for free on a couple of weddings with an established consultant. The Association of Bridal Consultants (listed below) will provide names and addresses of members in your area.
- Establish a network of suppliers on whom you can rely. Attend bridal shows to get to know the trends.
- Organize weddings for friends and relatives for free, to build a portfolio of your work. Be sure to get pictures from the photographer.

▣ Where to Turn for Information and Help

TRADE ASSOCIATIONS

Association of Bridal Consultants, 200 Chestnutland Road, New Milford, CT 06776; (203) 355-0464. Membership is composed of all types of professionals working in the wedding industry. Bi-monthly newsletter, professional development program, nationwide advertising, bridal and media referrals.

BOOKS

The Bride: A Celebration, by Barbara Tober. New York: H. N. Abrams, 1984.

Complete Wedding Planner, by Edith Gilbert. Hollywood, FL: Fell Publishers, 1989.

Planning a Wedding to Remember, by Beverly Clark. Los Angeles: Wilshire Books, 1989.

Weddings, by Emily Post. New York: Simon and Schuster, 1975.

MAGAZINES

Bride's, Conde Nast, 350 Madison Avenue, New York, NY 10017; (212) 880-8800.

Modern Bride, Cahners Publishing/American Baby, 475 Park Avenue, New York, NY 10016; (212) 503-5300.

MANUALS

Wedding Planning Business Guide, *Entrepreneur* magazine, 2392 Morse Avenue, Box 19787, Irvine, CA 92712; (800) 421-2300.

■ ■ ■ ■

WEDDING MAKEUP ARTIST

Doing makeup for brides and bridal parties is an exciting and glamorous business. A wedding makeup artist provides on-location makeup services for brides and their attendants to make sure they look naturally beautiful for the ceremony, the photo sessions, and the video camera, which is used for taping the majority of today's weddings.

In recent years the wedding industry has undergone some changes that have led to the popularity of wedding makeup artists. The 1980s witnessed a rebirth of the large and lavish formal wedding and the birth of a wedding industry that includes wedding consultants, videographers, disc jockeys, makeup artists, and, of course, caterers and photographers. Most of these businesses are usually operated from home.

Even for modest weddings, in this increasingly media- and image-conscious decade, wedding makeup artists are in demand. Sally Van Swearingen, a pioneer specializing in wedding makeup, says that weddings will always be in. And on that special day, every bride wants to look her most beautiful.

But for today's bride, looking great has become an increasingly complex matter. Makeup that might look natural and vibrant in person can look washed out on film or video. Extra makeup to make their features stand out for film and video, however, can make the bride and her bridal party look too made up in person. That's where the wedding makeup artist comes in. He or she is a specialist who understands how to make the bride and bridal party find the right balance to meet all the makeup demands of the wedding day.

The wedding makeup artist works with all kind of clients, from young brides who are getting married for the first time to older brides who are remarrying. Van Swearingen has even worked with brides over 60 years old.

Two sessions are required in working with the bride. The first session, before the wedding, provides a time to find out about the plans for the wedding (the color scheme, number of people involved, and so forth,) and to show the bride the various possibilities. Then on the day of the wedding, the makeup artist arrives at the wedding site very early, before the photos are done, does the makeup for the entire bridal party, and puts on the bride's headpiece. At this point, the makeup artist may either leave or stay on hand to touch up the makeup at various times during the festivities.

After the wedding, of course, you want the bride to continue as your client. So you can offer products and special makeup sessions as a way to stay in touch with your clients.

☑ Knowledge and Skills You Need To Have

- In some states you need to obtain a license as a cosmetician or cosmetologist in order to be a makeup artist. Cosmeticians are also called estheticians.
- You need to know makeup techniques for the camera, which demands specialized highlighting if the makeup is to look natural under various lighting conditions.
- Makeup artists need to have good interpersonal communication skills and be sensitive to the bride and her needs. You need to be empathetic and able to handle the range of emotions and ego issues that may arise for a bride under the pressure of her wedding.
- You need to have a basic knowledge of fashion and makeup trends.

▣ Start-Up Costs

In addition to having a car or other means of transportation to get to and from wedding sites, you will have the following expenses in starting this business:

	Low	High
Makeup equipment and supplies	$ 500	$1,000
Portfolio of photographs of your work*	——	$1,000
Director's chair	$ 100	$ 100
Business cards, letterhead, envelopes, price lists	250	$ 650
Legal fees to develop a contract for use in bookings**.	——	$ 250
Totals	$ 850	$3,000

*Sometimes you can do makeup for photographers in exchange for getting free samples of photos for your portfolio.

**Even if you develop the contract yourself, use a standard contract from a form book or software package, or borrow a contract from another artist, it's still a good idea to have an attorney review the contract.

▣ Advantages

- Wedding makeup artists are well paid for their time. The pay is better than what a studio makeup artist receives.

- Normally you are working around happy people at a very exciting and positive time in their lives.
- Your work begets more work. Doing a good job for your clients can be one of your best means of marketing, because they will refer their friends to you.
- Because weddings are usually on weekends, this business is easy to start on a part-time basis while you are still employed.

ⓘ Disadvantages

- There is no built-in repeat business. You must be clever at creating ways for your clients to continue seeing you for their makeup needs after the wedding or you will have to be constantly recruiting new clients.
- Although a wedding is a positive celebration, it can also be stressful, because there are many people involved, and expectations are high for everything to be perfect. Also, people can become temperamental and emotional under such circumstances.
- Being a bridal makeup artist *types* you. Your portfolio has bridal pictures and not much of anything else should you also want to do work for ad agencies, films, or television.
- The majority of your work is on weekends.

ⓢ Pricing

Makeup fees range from $75 to $200 for the bride, and from $25 to $50 for each other member of the wedding party. Additional fees can be charged for traveling to the site and for staying throughout the ceremony for touch-ups.

ⓒ Potential Earnings

TYPICAL ANNUAL GROSS REVENUES: $22,000 to $52,000, based on doing 175 weddings a year for a bride and 2 members of the wedding party. Weddings are almost always on a Saturday or Sunday, and you can work a maximum of 2 to 3 weddings a day.

OVERHEAD: Moderate (20 to 40 percent).

ⓘ Best Ways to Get Business

- Exhibiting at bridal trade shows; showing your photographs, and doing makeovers in your booth.
- Advertising in local bridal magazines, with coupons included.
- Paying a fee to wedding consultants for their referrals.
- Holding a mixer for people in the wedding business—consultants, photographers, caterers, florists, and so forth.

- Getting publicity about your service in the print media, and on radio or TV. Because this is a glamor business that lends itself to photos and demonstrations, it's ideal for the media.
- Networking in organizations and at events for women, and in business organizations where other professionals involved in wedding services gather.

🖉 First Steps

Begin by finding out if your state requires that you get a cosmetician's or cosmetologist's license in order to become a makeup artist. If so, obtain the training you need for such a license from a cosmetology or beauty school. The cost of this schooling can range from $150 to $1,000; some schools have scholarships available. The training to be a cosmetician can be completed on a full-time basis in nine weeks. Becoming a cosmetologist requires more training because you also are trained to work with hair.

Learning special techniques for camera makeup and working with different skin tones in different types of lighting requires creativity and experience. The best way to get this experience is by working with another makeup artist as an assistant. Because weddings are on weekends, you can gain this experience while you are still employed. You can also practice on willing friends and relatives until you get your technique perfected.

Once you are getting good results, develop a portfolio of photos showing off your work and then start promoting yourself as a bridal specialist, using the avenues for getting business described above.

🗍 Where to Turn for Information and Help

BOOKS

Diane Von Furstenberg's Book of Beauty, by Diane Von Furstenberg. New York: Simon and Schuster, 1976.

How to Be a Photogenic Bride, by Sally Van Swearingen and Valerie Smith, 16250 Ventura Boulevard, Suite 215, Encino, CA 91436.

Instant Beauty, by Pablo. New York: Simon and Schuster, 1978.

MAGAZINES

Bride's, Conde-Nast, 350 Madison Avenue, New York, NY 10017; (212) 880-8800.

Modern Bride, Cahners Publishing/American Baby, 475 Park Avenue, New York, NY 10016; (212) 503-5300.

Vogue, Conde-Nast, 360 Madison Avenue, New York, NY 10017; (212) 880-8800.

ORGANIZATIONS

Association of Bridal Consultants, 200 Chestnutland Road, New Milford, CT 06776; (203) 355-0464.

National Association of Accredited Cosmetology Schools, 1990 M Street N.W., Washington, DC 20036; (202) 775-0311.

National Association of Aestheticians, 4447 McKinney Avenue, Dallas, TX 75205 (214) 526-0760.

■ ■ ■ ■

WORD PROCESSING SERVICE

Word processing services provide typing and secretarial services to companies that need to rely on outside services to do their word processing. The demand for outside word processing is growing. Cheryl Myers, who operates a word processing service in suburban Chicago, has found that "the demand for outside services is coming from small-to-medium-sized companies that do not wish to invest the time or dollars in in-house systems and personnel. Using an outside service and paying only for the work produced is extremely cost effective. Also, more and more companies are cutting their administrative costs by allowing their reps to work out of their homes; these reps need secretarial services, and the cost is covered on their expense accounts."

While word processing services are common today and competition can be fierce, specializing your business for particular markets is a way to carve out a niche for yourself. Examples of word processing specialities include law, medicine, small businesses, academia, script writing, and work bid out by local governmental bodies. Some specialties, such as transcribing legal and medical materials, pay better than others like serving academic and student markets. The key to success in this business is the quality of your work and your ability to provide quick turnaround. To be additionally competitive, you may want to offer pickup and delivery.

☑ Knowledge and Skills You Need to Have

- You must have fast and accurate typing skills. You should be able to type at least 65 words a minute, and the faster you type, the more you can earn.
- This business calls for a customer-oriented service attitude.
- You need to have the desire and ability to pay attention to details.

⬛ Start-Up Costs

	Low	High
Macintosh or IBM-compatible computer with hard disk	$1,500	$ 4,000
Laser printer	$1,600	$ 2,500
Word-processing software	$ 250	$ 500
Office furniture, especially an ergonomic chair	$ 600	$ 800
Copy machine	$ 400	$ 1,200
Business cards, letterhead, envelopes	$ 400	$ 600
Direct-mail advertising	$ 500	$ 2,500
Organizational dues	$ 250	$ 250
Total	$5,500	$12,350

⬛ Advantages

- The material you type can be interesting.
- There is good income potential.
- You have the opportunity to earn additional income by providing other secretarial services such as editing, mailing-list management, and desktop publishing.

⬛ Disadvantages

- The field is growing increasingly competitive.
- Your income is limited by your speed and the number of hours in a day.
- You are often working under the pressure of tight deadlines.
- Unless you take necessary precautions, you risk developing repetitive-motion injuries as a result of constant keyboarding.

⬛ Pricing

By the hour, $15 to $30; by the page, $2 to $7.50; by character count, $1 per 1,000 characters. You can also charge by the job, using standards for estimating established by the National Association of Secretarial Services.

Consider charging by the hour for handwritten or highly edited originals, or materials that include statistical charts, tables, and complex documents. Charge by the page if, because of interruptions, such as from young children, you would not be able to accurately keep track of your time.

⬛ Potential Earnings

TYPICAL ANNUAL GROSS REVENUES: $22,500 to $45,000, based on billing 30 hours a week at $15 to $30 an hour for 50 weeks a year.

OVERHEAD: Moderate (20 to 40 percent; because yellow pages advertising under multiple headings can be expensive).

▶ Best Ways to Get Business

- Advertising and promotional efforts focused within a 5 to 10 mile radius (no more than a 20-minute drive).
- Notices or flyers with tear-off phone numbers on bulletin boards in copy and print shops, banks, supermarkets, libraries, and at college and universities, particularly on bulletin boards seen by graduate students.
- Networking in organizations, such as chambers of commerce.
- Direct mail in the form of postcards or four-by-six cards with lists and prices of services to new businesses. Names and addresses of potential businesses can be found in city business journals. Follow up mailings with phone calls.
- Advertising in the yellow pages under Secretarial, Typing, and Word Processing headings. A recent National Association of Secretarial Services membership survey showed that services spent an average of $2,534 on yellow pages advertising during 1990. Eighty-two percent of those responding ranked yellow-pages advertising as an important part of their marketing efforts.
- Following up on help-wanted ads to find companies that have overload work.
- Contacting other word-processing services for their overload or work in which you specialize.
- Advertising in university newsletters and church, club, chamber-of-commerce, and other business bulletins.

🛈 First Steps

- To increase your typing speed you can use a software program like *Mavis Beacon Teaches Typing,* which costs as little as $30 and can help you increase your typing speed within just a few weeks.
- To get this business started, specialize in serving a particular field or industry. Consider contacting successful established word-processing services about doing overload.

🛈 Where to Turn for Information and Help

BOOKS

Word Processing Profits at Home, by Peggy Glenn. Huntington, Beach, CA: Aames-Allen Publishing, 1989.

ORGANIZATIONS

National Association of Secretarial Services, 3637 4th Street North, Suite 330, St Petersburg, FL 33704; (800) 237-1462 or (813) 823-3546. Publishes a monthly newsletter and a variety of manuals on topics like pricing, sales and promotion, and the how-tos of expanding into other related services.

COURSES

Word Processing, NRI, School of Home-based Businesses, McGraw-Hill Continuing Education Center, 4401 Connecticut Avenue N.W., Washington, DC 20008. This home-study program includes a computer system and software and provides training for starting a word-processing business. No computer experience required. A free brochure is available.

MANUALS

Starting a Successful Secretarial Service, by Frank Fox, National Association of Secretarial Services, 3637 4th Street North, Suite 330, St. Petersburg, FL 33704; (800) 237-1462 or (813) 823-3546. A 100-page blueprint for starting a secretarial service.

SOFTWARE

NASS/ESN Industry Productions Standards of Software, National Association of Secretarial Services, 3637 4th Street North, Suite 330, St. Petersburg, FL 33704; (800) 237-1462 or (813) 823-3546. Guidelines for bidding and for pricing services (also available in print form). Members using these standards report that they increase billings 25 to 50 percent for the same amount of work with no price increase.

PART II
....

The Rest of the Best

■■■■

DISC JOCKEY SERVICE

If you love music and are willing to learn to get an audience dancing, you can earn your living as a free-lance or private disc jockey. Private disc jockeys provide professional sound at conferences, parties, weddings, and special events in homes, clubs, churches, hotels, public halls, schools, and companies for far less than the cost of live musicians.

As a disc jockey, you select and supply the music and the equipment to play it on. You usually also need to provide some patter to entertain the audience and encourage everyone to dance. Essential equipment includes two high-quality compact-disc players, a cassette deck (to play tapes handed to you by people in the audience and as backup for the CD players), and, if you intend to use records, a professional turntable. You will also need a mixing console, a power amplifier and speakers with clear output, and a cordless microphone for your patter. You can add strobe lights and other special effects to enhance your presentation.

You will need something to haul your equipment in—a truck, van, or trailer—and something to carry it into the location—a hand truck, dolly, or rolling cart. Be prepared for stairs. You should also have some sort of backup for your equipment, but in some cases you will be able to get loaner gear from the stores where you purchased your own or you may be able to rent unused equipment from other disc jockey companies. Better than relying on backup, however, is to store and transport equipment in protective cases; by being careful with it, it should last for years with little downtime.

The most crucial part of your equipment is your disc collection. You will probably start out combining new releases with what you already own. Used-CD stores are a good source. And you may need to fill out your collection from used- or rare-record stores. Or better yet, simply order the golden-oldies recordings advertised on late-night cable TV.

To get this business started, begin by contacting restaurants, catering halls, booking agents, mall managers, sororities and fraternities, college student-affairs offices, fraternal organizations, private clubs, and private party services. If you have no experience, contact other disc jockey services about working for them while you learn the business. The best way to strut your stuff is to make a videotape of yourself in action to show to prospective clients.

Also, create a clever business card and, if possible, a flyer to leave with contacts and to send to individuals if they call. Jeff Greene, who operates Party Time DJ's from his home, has 20 operating systems and 24 disk jockeys working for him. He says, "Remember, you are in an artsy and personal business. You want to get people to look at you, and your graphic image will play a part in that happening. Black-and-white business cards won't get much attention in comparison to a colorful card and a clever logo and type font."

Start-up costs will run between $500 and $2,000 for the basic equipment at rock-bottom prices (probably used; check the classified ads in your local paper for good buys) and a few thousand business cards and simple flyers. To keep costs down, use your business card or flyer as the artwork for any advertising you do.

Private disc jockeys charge $50 per hour and up depending on experience, draw, location, and type of show, so you can earn several hundred dollars per night. Some events and bars or restaurants may net you less money but can get you good exposure, so make sure they include your name in their advertising and that you can hand out flyers.

Work can be seasonal, with especially heavy bookings during the Christmas holidays, spring prom season, May and June (weddings), and early fall (parties). There are lots of events in between, but you will have to develop your reputation in order to get the word-of-mouth referrals you will need.

■ ■ ■ ■

EDITORIAL SERVICE AND PROOFREADING

Writers, publishers, first-time authors, business offices, law firms, software houses, and other organizations all need professional help readying documents for publication or use. Many of them hire free-lance editors and proofreaders for these tasks.

Depending on your skills and experience, one of two types of proofreading services or two types of editing services may suit you. Content proofreaders read word-for-word against the original to check for typos, misspellings, and so forth. They earn anywhere from $10 to $20 an hour depending on the field and area of the country. Design proofreaders, in addition to proofing content, check the proof for design specifications, typographical correctness, kerning, improper or excessive hyphenation, and so on once copy has been typeset. They earn between $15 and $25 an hour. Copy editors rewrite text, suggest style changes, check for proper grammar and clarity, make corrections, and proofread content. They usually earn from $15 to $30 an hour. And finally, developmental editors help authors develop or completely rework ideas and assist throughout the creation of the manuscript. They may charge from $6,000 to $9,000 per manuscript, and their hourly rates range from $15 to $50 or more.

Start-up costs are nominal—business cards, letterhead, and colored pencils. However, what is essential is some contact or credibility in the industry to which you want to market your services. The first step is to identify what types of clients you want to work with: authors, book or magazine publishers, public-relations firms, corporate communications offices, and so on. Then begin making contacts, and get a yellow-pages listing under Editorial Services. As you develop your portfolio, contact literary agents in your area for referrals to authors and publishers.

Unless you are a published author yourself, or highly respected in a particular field, do not expect to be hired as a developmental editor. These editors usually come from the ranks of the very experienced. But if you are, then make it known to agent, editor, and publisher alike that you are available. Personal contacts will be your best marketing tool. Leave your business card and follow up with a thank-you letter. Then keep in touch on a regular (not constant) basis—about every other month—so that you remain foremost in their minds. Once you are established, most of your clientele will come from referrals from previous clients and from these contacts.

■ ■ ■ ■

FITNESS TRAINER

How would you like to have all the time you want to exercise and work out? And get paid for it, too? You can, because the more Americans do work that binds them to desks and telephones, the more they become involved in exercise and fitness. Of course, a regular stream of scientific evidence continues to pour in that being physically fit increases mental and physical health, keeps us looking more attractive, and may even extend our lives, an increasing concern for the now graying baby-boom population. This has made fitness a big business. While you cannot operate a gym at home, you can establish a successful business as a personal trainer.

Personal trainers design workout routines for individuals or small groups and guide clients through their workouts two or three times a week either at the client's home or at a gym. Some trainers also teach classes like yoga or aerobics, either in their own home or at facilities they rent. Others specialize in fitness training for children or pregnant women.

Depending on their reputation and locale, personal trainers charge from $50 to $125 per session. Therefore, billing 20 hours a week (which can mean working with as few as 7 clients) at $75 per hour for 50 weeks per year can produce an income of $75,000 a year.

Start-up costs are low as you don't need to purchase any workout equipment yourself. In fact, some trainers sell equipment to their clients. You will, of course, need to look physically fit yourself, and it helps in getting business to be able to talk as well as demonstrate what you do before groups of people at meetings.

If you use a gym to work out with your clients, you will need to maintain a membership. You also need business cards, a letterhead, and well-done flyers or simple brochures. You must have a sound knowledge of fitness principles, exercise, and workout routines. Most successful personal trainers have evolved their own method of training. A solid understanding of nutrition is also helpful.

The best routes to building a client base are through personal contacts, giving seminars and presentations on fitness, exhibiting at health shows, and doing demonstrations. Having photos of people you have worked with before and after is effective. Publicity is also valuable.

One of the most challenging aspects of this business is keeping your clients motivated to continue working out. Although it may go unstated, this is a large part of why they hire you. So in addition to knowing how to design effective workout routines, you must be able to encourage, inspire, and motivate your clients to continue with you, even when they don't see immediate results.

A book that begins with a wonderful quote from Winston Churchill ("Those whose work and play are one are fortune's favorite children")is *For Fun and Profit: Self-Employment Opportunities in Recreation, Sports and Travel,* by Crawford Lindsey (Live Oak Publications, Box 2193, Boulder, CO 80306). Kinderdance International, (Box 510881, Melbourne Beach, FL 32951; 800/666-1595) offers a franchise for teaching dance and motor-development skills to pre-school-age children.

■ ■ ■ ■

HAULING SERVICE

Getting rid of things is not a new problem, but it can be a major one. Every time you move, you discover things that don't work, don't fit, or that you simply don't want. And not only when you move. What do you do with the old refrigerator or range when you buy a new one? Or that ratty-looking sofa that your mother insisted you take? Or the debris from the last remodeling project you finally got finished? Or the broken chair? Or the rusted fender in the garage? Or the old fence, the garden debris, the falling-down shed that finally fell down? Unless you have a truck, you have to call someone to haul this stuff away, because most garbage services won't touch it.

That leaves a wide-open opportunity for a hauling service. And what you get paid by the hour or the load is not all the income you can earn. One person's junk is another person's treasure. People get rid of old things like oil paintings, antiques, and rare books; new things like presents they don't want and leftover construction materials; and reusable things of all sorts. You can keep, donate to charities, or sell items of value. The possibilities for selling things is almost limitless—through the classified ads, at flea markets or garage sales, or to anyone who can use what you've got. Because you've got a truck, you can deliver, too.

All you need is a pickup truck or van, preferably one that's equipped with a hydraulic lift gate, and tarps, blankets, rope, and some toting equipment such as a hand truck and a four-wheel dolly.

Your other primary need is to identify places to take the materials you haul away. You must make preliminary inquiries with companies that accept these materials. Scrap-metal companies may or may not take old appliances. Dumps may not accept certain types of furniture. Landfills usually won't take garden debris, but organic gardeners or farmers may. Secondhand shops may not want old mattresses or appliances that don't work. You will find that most of these places will pay you for the materials they accept. If you also charge the consumer or business for hauling away the waste, you will be able to keep your rates competitive enough to make it worth your while on both ends.

Some states require a special license to move other people's stuff, so check this out, as well as dumping regulations in your area. Unless you are close to a state line and your business will take you across that line, you will not be bound by Interstate Commerce Commission regulations.

To promote your business, you should leave stacks of business cards and well-done flyers or simple brochures with realtors, contractors, apartment rental services, condominium management offices, appliance stores, furniture stores, garden-supply stores and nurseries, and senior-citizen clubs. Since consumers usually start out by calling scrap-metal companies, secondhand stores, and interstate movers (for whom their job may be too small), you should be sure these businesses are aware of you. Keep in touch with them regularly so they will refer clients to you. Going to auctions can also be a good source of business. Let the auction personnel know you're there, and by having a sign painted on your truck or using a removable magnetic sign, people will notice you. Often other moving jobs or other kinds of handy work will develop from a satisfied customer. Classified or small display ads in your local paper and yellow-pages ads are important ways of getting business. We met someone once who claimed he got all the business he needed from the yellow pages because of the name of his company—Grunt N' Dump. For further imformation, refer to *How to Earn $15 to $50 an Hour and More with a Pickup Truck or Van,* by Don Lilly (Glendale, AZ: Darian Books, 1989).

■ ■ ■ ■

IN-HOME HEALTH CARE

A new way of controlling rising medical costs is to place patients in the homes of caretakers instead of in hospitals. Mentor, a Boston-based health-care company, has taken the lead with this new approach. Mentor contracts with independent in-home care providers, which they call *medical technicians* or *mentors,* to care for people under the supervision of health professionals. Over nine out of ten patients are people between the ages of six and eighteen who either are too ill for outpatient treatment or require custodial care but are not necessarily so ill as to require hospitalization. The types of problems such patients have include emotional problems, developmental disabilities, head injuries, and substance-abuse problems.

Mentors take only one patient into their homes at a time. The care provider helps prepare patients for a successful transition back to their own home as soon as possible. In the case of an emotionally disturbed patient, the mentor provides praise and other rewards for positive behavior and controls, as necessary, out-of-control behaviors by the patient.

No particular background is needed to become a mentor, although mentors must have no criminal record. Mentor provides all necessary training. The company looks for compassionate, caring individuals who have good communication skills and an interest in helping people. Life experience with caregiving is helpful, as is having a knowledge of substance abuse. All types of people are doing this work—singles, empty nesters, parents with children. What is required to get started as a mentor is a spare bedroom, because that's where the patient lives, and a car for taking the patient to outpatient medical facilities.

Mentors are paid as independent contractors and can expect to earn somewhere in the range of $50 to $60 for each day a patient is in their home, which is comparable to the pay of a mental-health technician on a hospital staff.

This is a brand-new, burgeoning field. As of this writing Mentor provides service in 13 states (New Jersey, Pennsylvania, Maryland, Illinois, Connecticut, Rhode Island, Texas, Georgia, North Carolina, South Carolina, Ohio, New York, Maine, and Washington, DC.) It is the only company of its kind, but with the cost of inpatient care skyrocketing, we predict that more and more companies will leap in to take up the slack. For more information, call Mentor at (800) 669-6368 or (617) 951-0071.

If you have a background in medicine, psychiatry, or psychology, you might consider starting a company of your own. Study the pattern created by Mentor carefully, and work with public health officials, insurance companies, employee-assistance programs, preferred-provider organizationss, and health-maintenance organizations, which will be your sources of business.

■ ■ ■ ■

INTERIOR DECORATOR

Americans plan to redecorate and or remodel their homes at an unprecedented rate in the '90s. A recent survey for *Home* magazine indicates that 46 percent of Americans plan to redecorate or remodel in the next five years, compared with 35 percent who did so in the past five years. The high price of buying a home is causing people to improve what they have rather than moving up the housing ladder as their parents did.

This means lots of work for interior decorators because, according to a Louis Harris survey, almost one out of every seven Americans gets help from a professional home decorator. These numbers translate into 5 million clients for professional decorators in the residential market alone.

What does it take to be an interior decorator? It takes someone with a sense of color and balance or proportion, a positive attitude toward change (because a decorator needs to keep up with what's fashionable,) and the ability to communicate through graphic presentations.

Decorators are now able to use computers in working with clients. With computer-aided design software, such as *Archicad* for Macintosh computers, it's possible to devise and present design solutions to clients with three-dimensional realism.

Decorators charge for their services in several ways. Some charge a flat fee for design work. Others charge by the hour, at rates ranging from $35 to $125. Still others add a service charge of approximately 20 percent to items they buy for clients, such as furniture, fabric, and floor coverings. Still others charge their clients the retail price of items they are able to purchase at wholesale, keeping the difference as their fee. Thus, the client gets the decorator's service at a price no greater than he or she would have paid for the products retail. To avoid misunderstandings, it's important to formalize a client relationship with a contract or a letter of agreement.

Decorating Den is a franchise available in the decorating field. A franchisee drives a van loaded with samples to a customer's home or office and allows busy customers to order directly from him or her. The profit of the Decorating Den franchisee comes from selling items at retail that you buy at wholesale. Decorating Den can be contacted at 7910 Woodmont Avenue, Suite 200, Bethesda, MD 20814; (301) 652-6393.

The largest professional association is the American Society of Interior Designers, (608 Massachusetts Avenue, N.E., Washington, DC 20002; 202/546-3480). Its membership is limited to interior designers who have completed a degree program or have many years of experience. Interior designers are required to have a working knowledge of building and fire-safety codes, and tend to work more frequently with business and industrial clients (contract work) than with residential ones. The society has several classes of members, including professional members who have obtained a four-year college degree in interior design and/or have acquired sufficient years of experience to pass a three-day examination to become certified as interior designers. While being an interior *decorator* does not require a special license or training, 13 states now require licensing of interior *designers*. Magazines read by professionals in the field include *Interior Design,* (249 West 17th Street, New York, NY 10011) and *Interiors,* (Box 2154, Radnor, PA 19089).

■ ■ ■ ■

LEAK DETECTION SERVICE

Imagine being able to offer a service that can save a building owner from replacing a $100,000 roof by making a $1,200 repair! That is exactly what the new field of leak detection can do. Leak detectors may specialize in finding roof leaks, or they may go after water leaks behind walls, under concrete foundations, or in swimming-pool, spa and reservoir structures, fountains, and all kinds of piping systems—drain, waste, sewer, and so on. To detect leaks, inspectors use inert gases, radio signals, ultrasonic listening devices, thermographs to detect moisture, and even nuclear instruments.

Probably no one leak-detection company has all types of equipment or detects all varieties of leaks. For example, Elsie and Ted McConnel have built a thriving home-based business detecting roof leaks using a nuclear instrument called a Datamax, which they saw exhibited at a trade show they attended because they were managing an apartment building. The newest leak-detection devices are nondestructive and use special instrumentation to detect hydrogen contained in moisture. The reading from the instrument is then put into a computer, which produces a roof graph showing the condition of the roof. Clients then use the graph in a process that leads to a precise repair.

Because of new building-code requirements in many areas of the country, inspections for leaks are necessary prior to any roof repair. And in areas where buildings are especially susceptible to moisture damage, such inspections can become a part of regular building maintenance on an annual or biannual basis.

Roof-leak detection is just one of many specialized leak-detection businesses. In drought-stricken areas, detecting leaks in swimming pools, spas, and fountains keeps companies busy 60 to 70 hours a week. A primary advantage to the pool owner is that these newer processes do not require the pool or fountain to be drained for inspection, which both conserves water and saves time and money.

No specific experience is required to do this business, but good hearing and a mechanical aptitude are helpful. A franchise is available in this field from American Leak Detection. This company provides the necessary training for a franchise fee of $40,000, which covers both training and equipment. Almost nine out of ten of their franchisees operate from their homes. For further information, contact American Leak Detection at Box 1701, 1750 East Arenas, Suite 7, Palm Springs, CA 92262; or call (800) 755-6697 or (619) 320-9991.

Prices for residential leak inspections range from $175 to $275 and go into the thousands for industrial work. Earnings from leak detection are quite good, with businesses typically showing earnings of over $50,000 a year; earnings of more than $100,000 are not unusual.

■ ■ ■ ■

MANUFACTURERS' AGENT

Many salespeople find being a manufacturers' agent or manufacturers' representative to be the graduate level of selling, offering potentially higher earnings and freedom from the company politics of being an employee. A manufacturers' agent or rep needs to be a self-starter, as he or she represents the products of two or more manufacturers on a commission basis. (By representing only one manufacturer you risk not qualifying for valuable self-employment tax deductions while at the same time not receiving company fringe benefits.) Many companies have their own cadre of salespeople, but there are even more small-to-medium-sized manufacturers who utilize the services of independent agents to sell for them as an alternative to or in addition to their own salespeople. The types of products represented by agents range from abrasives to zithers, sold either to wholesalers or large retail stores, and may also include raw materials, machines, electronic equipment, or parts needed by companies for the production of finished products.

What you need to get started is a car, an answering machine, an answering service or voicemail, and enough cash to cover your expenses until you begin producing commissions. Today a car phone, a fax, and a laptop computer become important next acquisitions.

The first step is to find products you want to represent. The best agents know as much about their products as an employee of the manufacturer would know, so select products you feel you can do the best job selling. In *Agency Sales,* the monthly magazine of the Manufacturers' Agents National Association, the largest trade association of manufacturers' agents, are pages of ads from companies seeking manufacturers' agents and agents seeking product lines.

Since you will be working on straight commission, there is little risk to the manufacturer other than sending you some samples, so you will probably find most to be eager takers. If you prefer to specialize in a particular area, you can take on a series of complementary products, such as computer chips from one manufacturer and the boards on which they can be used from another. Do not, however, take on competing products or products from manufacturers who compete directly. If you want to represent only a portion of a manufacturer's product line or even a single product, feel free to make that request.

Commission rates will vary with the particular industry. Many manufacturers will want you to agree to their standard commission rate for salespeople. However, keep in mind that as an independent rep you will be paying your own expenses. Therefore, the agreed-upon rate must be high enough to take those expenses into consideration. In industries where the standard rate is 5 percent, you will probably want to request 15 to 20 percent, at least for the first order filled. Since expenses drop with each successive sale until they reach an average flat amount, you might be willing to accept as little as 10 percent on succeeding sales. For other industry standards, you will need to adjust your rates accordingly. Most commission-based salespeople are paid on a monthly schedule.

By keeping careful track of your expenses (every mile driven, telephone call made, lunch on the road, repair, photocopy, stamp, tank of gas), you will be able to determine whether a product is profitable for you. All details regarding your role and compensation should be worked out carefully in an agreement letter or contract between you and the manufacturer.

A key resource in this field is the Manufacturers' Agents' National Association, which offers, in addition to *Agency Sales* magazine, a bibliography, educational seminars, specimen contracts, a national directory, and trade missions to other countries. You can contact the association at Box 3467, Laguna Hills, CA 92654; (714) 859-4040.

■ ■ ■ ■

MEETING PLANNER

If you rate high in resourcefulness and organizational skills, enjoy working with people, can handle stress, and have an eye for detail, you may find a career in a *happy* business—professional meeting planning. Meeting planners plan events, from small private parties to major conventions.

Planners who work with well-to-do clients planning birthdays and special holiday parties are sometimes called party planners. A new specialty is prom consulting. Party planners may be paid either by a flat fee (around $250), an hourly rate (which is appropriate if the client requires a lot of handholding), or a percentage of the budget for the event. In all cases, out-of-pocket expenses are charged to the client. Party planners handle everything from selecting the location to purchasing flowers, decorations, food, and entertainment.

Meeting or event planners work with corporations, associations, and nonprofit organizations to plan conventions, fund-raising events, special banquets, hospitality events, sales meetings, shareholder meetings, and so forth. When planning events of this scale, you will need to be skillful at negotiating contracts, budgeting, making housing arrangements, acquiring speakers, arranging exhibits, taking care of safety precautions, making special provisions, handling VIPs, and arranging for transportation, registration, information presentation, and everything else necessary to the success of an event. Like party planners, meeting planners charge either an hourly rate, a flat fee, or a percentage of the budget. Your income can range from $25,000 to over $100,000 a year.

Personal contacts are the best way of getting business in this field. Shari Johnson, who specializes in business entertainment, got her first major client as a result of a breakfast meeting of a networking organization. Other meeting planners can be a source of subcontract or overload work. You can meet other planners at local chapter meetings of Meeting Planners International (1950 Stemmons Freeway, Dallas, TX 75207; 214/746-5224).

Banquet and catering managers of hotels can be important sources of referrals. You may also volunteer to plan a charity or civic event as a way to demonstrate your capabilities, make key contacts, and get referrals, but be careful of giving away too much time or advice. To learn about upcoming conventions, you can subscribe to calendars published by city convention bureaus. You can then contact appropriate organizations and companies by mail and phone.

The perks of a successful meeting-planning business, besides the financial rewards, include the fact that you get to participate in every one of the events, from hot-dogs-and-beer bashes to champagne-and-caviar events aboard yachts. The main drawback is that you also have to be prepared for crises. You have to be ready for the unexpected—torrential rains during an outdoor wedding, a blizzard that closes an airport, a hotel that fouls up its reservation schedule, a caterer that had you on the calendar for next week instead of today, programs that have not been delivered, and dozens of other little wrinkles sure to make you age quickly.

A specialty for some corporate meeting planners is developing incentive programs and contests. Such programs have become a popular way for companies to boost sales, enhance productivity, or improve safety records. In keeping with the trend for companies to downsize staff, they often contract out with specialists to provide the format and techniques for these events, and this provides an ideal area of specialization for some meeting planners with expertise in sales promotion or office or plant management.

For further information about starting this business, *Entrepreneur* magazine sells an *Event Planning Business Guide,* (2392 Morse Avenue, Box 19787, Irvine, CA 92713; 800/421-2300; in California, 800/352-7449).

■ ■ ■ ■

NEWSLETTER PUBLISHER

Chances are very good that you find several newsletters each week in your mail. You subscribe to some newsletters, while others are sent to you by organizations to which you belong or companies wanting your business. Sometimes the distinction between newsletters, magazines, and newspapers gets blurry, but a newsletter is usually considered to be a publication that is one to eight pages in length, with a format no larger than 8½ by 11, that is not available on newsstands.

Today there are over 19,500 subscription, membership, and free newsletters, bulletins, and similar serial publications—and more are appearing every day. That represents an opportunity for a home-based newsletter publisher. There are three primary ways you can make money publishing newsletters:

You can publish your own special-interest newsletter.   In this case you earn your income from subscriptions and/or advertising. To publish a successful newsletter, you need to select an identifiable group of people who are motivated to pay for information that you can provide and that they could not easily obtain elsewhere. Such a special-interest newsletter might provide information for sufferers of rare diseases and their families; describe business developments in another nation; track an emerging field or technology; or discuss financial transactions of an industry. Another possibility is to write about an everyday item. For example, Seena Sharp of Sharp Information Research discovered in a recent research project that there was no publication at all for the earring industry, since jewelry publications do not cover this market.

For a newsletter to be profitable, annual subscriptions should cost no less than $50 a year, and depending on the sophistication and availability of information, newsletters may carry subscription prices of $500 or more. Additional sources of income include renting your list of subscribers as a mailing list, using the newsletter to sell products that you either produce or buy from others, and using the newsletter to let people know about your availability for speaking and consulting engagements.

Newsletters are not necessarily mailed anymore, but may be sent by fax or published on-line, accessible by computer.

For print newsletters, if you are already equipped with a computer, high-resolution laser printer, desktop-publishing and design or clip-art software, your start-up costs can be as low as several hundred dollars, which includes sending free sample issues along with a reply card on which subscribers can place a charge-card number for ordering. A more direct but expensive approach is to mail out 5,000 to 20,000 copies of your first issue along with your order form and reply envelope. Be sure to boldly label the newsletter SAMPLE COPY.

You can produce newsletters for other people.   Companies, churches, clubs, charities, accountants, and real-estate agents are all potential newsletter users. Whether their purpose is to communicate with employees or members, or used to promote products to past, present, and potential customers, newsletters are more apt to get people's attention than most forms of direct mail. In this case your client pays you a flat fee or an hourly rate to develop his or her newsletter, usually on a periodic basis (monthly, quarterly).

Standard rates for writing in-house company newsletters range from $20 to $60 per hour or from $200 to $500 for 2 to 4 pages to $500 to $1,000 for 4 to 8 pages. Rates for writing for retail stores range from $175 to $300 for a 4-page publication. Small associations pay from $15 to $25 per hour for writing projects; large associations pay up to $85 per hour.

If you have the necessary computer hardware and software and, of course, the skill to use them, you can offer complete production services. Your tasks would include layout, paste-up, and preparation for printing, in addition to writing and editing the material. You might also handle contracting with a printer and maintaining the mailing list for the distribution of the newsletter. Providing photographs for the newsletter is a good way of adding to your revenue. Each of these services should be priced separately, even when you charge the client a flat fee per issue.

You can write a standard monthly newsletter usable by the same type of client. The newsletter appears to be that of a particular client, such as a dentist or an environmental consultant, because the first page is customized to have a message from the client plus any other custom touches he or she may wish to add. Professionals and small companies who don't have the time, staff, or budget to produce their own newsletter but for whom newsletters are a good marketing tool are candidates for using a newsletter service.

To find out what newsletters already exist in your fields of expertise, check *Newsletters in Print* (Gale Research), the *Newsletter Yearbook Directory* (Klein Publications), the "Newsletters" volume of *Standard Rate and Data Service,* the *Oxbridge Directory of Newsletters* (Oxbridge Communications), and *Ulrich's International Periodicals Directory* (R.R. Bowker). At least one of these volumes will be available in most libraries.

For help in starting a newsletter business, you can refer to the book *Publishing Newsletters,* by Howard Penn Hudson, (New York: Scribner's, 1988) and the audiotape program *How to Publish a Profitable Newsletter,* (Here's How, Box 5172, Santa Monica, CA 90409). The Newsletter Association (1401 Wilson Boulevard, Suite 207, Arlington, VA 22209; 703/527-2338) conducts research on the newsletter industry, offers seminars, monitors legislation, and represents the newsletter industry before federal agencies.

■■■■

900-NUMBER AUDIOTEXT SERVICE

It's hard to turn on late-night television without seeing a commercial for a 900-number service. And several times a week the newspapers contain stories of state attorney generals investigating or clamping down on 900-number rip-offs or children running up big telephone charges listening to joke lines.

But like the Phoenix emerging from the ashes, audiotext is emerging from the swamp of its origins by providing useful, entertaining, and profitable information to people in an easy-to-access manner. Recognizing the profitability of audiotext, major corporations including ABC, AT&T, Dow Jones, NBC, Revlon, the *Wall Street Journal,* and *USA Today* are allowing 900 numbers to add to their bottom lines. One service we use regularly is Business Infoline (900/896-0000) which is the audio equivalent of over 5,000 of the nation's yellow pages and can be used to locate a company anywhere in the United States or to check on whether someone is using a business name you're considering. Other popular topics are insurance information, humor lines, pet lines, tax tips, lines listing prices such as those for automobiles, and businesses offered for sale.

To get into the 900-number business, you don't need to worry about technology or expensive equipment. Service bureaus and brokers sometimes lease lines for only a few hundred dollars in start-up fees, and sometimes even for no start-up cost at all. Such services make their money by sharing in the profits of your success.

Since technology is no longer a roadblock, the two key ingredients to a successful 900 service are finding a topic people will pay for, and finding a way to let people know about it. To have a successful 900-number business, you need:

1. a topic that either has mass appeal or services a targeted population of customers
2. unique information or uniquely packaged information
3. exclusivity of your way of marketing, such as having a flyer advertising your 900 service inserted into mailings shipped by a mail-order company with a catalogue related to your subject
4. offering the information at a price people are willing to pay

Effective advertising is the key to getting callers. Because of the murky beginnings of the 900 industry, print and electronic media shy away from positive editorial coverage of 900 numbers. To keep the cost of advertising down, you may be able to negotiate a split in the revenue produced by your 900 number in exchange for television and radio advertising, billboards, or inclusion in all kinds of direct mail (card decks, catalogues, as an insert). While you usually have to pay for classified ads, these can often be purchased in bulk through classified-ad brokers.

In addition to a growing number of free seminars advertised in newspapers at which you can learn about this business and purchase tapes and manuals on how to start one, there are several magazines serving this industry: *Info Text*, (34700 Coast Highway, Suite 309, Capistrano Beach, CA 92624), and *The Fourth Media Journal*, (13402 North Scottsdale Road, Scottsdale, AZ 85254).

■ ■ ■ ■

PET SITTING

Americans are nuts about their pets. Consider the fact that pets are apparently more popular than children, at least according the number of U.S. households that contain pets—43 percent, versus 38 percent with children. Furthermore, American homes hold almost as many pets as people. Three out of ten households have at least one dog, and just over two of ten households have one or more cats. As popular as dogs and cats are (52 million to 58 million dogs and 49 million to 60 million cats), fish are even more numerous (78 million).

Because pet owners travel just like other people, pet-sitting services are gaining customers. Pet sitters feed and care for pets, homes, and plants. Sheldon Belinkoff, who with his wife, Janet, operates both a pet-sitting service with over 20 sitters and a pet-transportation service, advises, "To really make money at pet sitting, you must be around seven days a week and be prepared to give up your time. It's a seven-day-a-week business.

If pet sitting appeals to you, there are three ways you can approach it. Some sitters make daily stops at a customer's home to feed and visit with the pets as well as water the plants. Other sitters actually live in the home while the residents are away. Still other sitters open up their homes to clients' pets. Another alternative is to operate your pet-sitting business as an agency or referral service matching sitters to clients.

Whether you choose to do the pet sitting yourself or develop an agency, your primary market will be people who travel regularly or for extended periods of time. And though travelers can usually rely on friends or relatives, your service can also offer them an alternative. New residents to a community, who do not yet have family or community ties should especially welcome your service.

The income potential of a pet-sitting business depends on whether you do the sitting yourself or act as an agent in procuring sitters. As a full-time visiting sitter, you charge $5 to $20 per daily visit depending on the specific duties you agree to. Unless your travel area is very small, you will be able to cover 8 to 12 clients a day (based on a half-hour visit plus travel time). On the average, you would earn about $120 a day, less your travel expenses. At this level of activity, you should net between $450 and $550 per week, or about $2,100 a month.

If you choose to act as an agency, you have several alternative ways to charge. You may take a commission of 10 to 20 percent for each visit by a staffer; you may evenly split an overnight charge with the sitter; or you may charge a flat fee to the client alone or to both the client and the sitter.

Classified ads in local newspapers and a yellow-pages listing play an important part in getting business. You also can develop referral relationships with travel agents, cleaning services, veterinarians, the local humane society—anyone pet owners would call or talk to about finding someone to look after their pet. You can provide them with business cards and attractive flyers to give to their customers. Travel agents might include your card or brochure with tickets they send out. Posting notices on bulletin boards may produce clients, too.

Patti Moran, a pet sitter in Pinnacle, North Carolina, has written a book, *Pet Sitting for Profit,* and has produced an audiotape on starting a pet-sitting service. Write to her at New Beginnings, Box 540, High Bridge Road, Pinnacle, NC 27043. Bill and Ann Locke, of Katz-Kastle Kitty Sitter Service, offer a Sitting for Kitty Supplementary Income System for $99, consisting of a manual, forms and consultation (Box 10255, Rochester, NY 14610).

Franchises are also available at fees ranging from $2,000 to $8,500. These include: Pets Are Inn, (12 South Sixth Street, Suite 950, Minneapolis, MN 55402; 800/248-PETS); Critter Care, (1825 Darren Drive, Baton Rouge, LA 70816; 504/273-3356); and Pet Nanny of American, (1000 Long Boulevard, #9, Lansing, MI 48911; 517/694-4400).

■ ■ ■ ■

REFERRAL SERVICE

Have you ever had something break and not know who to call to fix it? Sure, the yellow pages have listings, but how can you know who's good and who's a rip-off? Most city people don't know, and who has time to do research? That's where a referral service can help. You've probably seen ads on television for services offering referrals to doctors or dentists. This idea can be applied to almost any area of need and interest: appliance repair, art events, auto repair, baby sitters, caterers, child care, contractors and tradespeople, hair dressers, house sitters, landlords, musicians, party locations, pet sitters, plumbers, printers, real-estate agents, restaurants, roommates, shopping information, special events, therapists, travel and tourist information, tutors, wedding services, even friendship.

Referral services may be set up to receive their income in one of several ways. Probably the most common is for the service to charge the business or professional a fee, with the service free to the consumers. The business might pay the fee monthly or annually, or pay a commission on each referral. Services that offer roommate matching, friendship matching, or house/pet/baby sitting often charge both parties equally. An on-line referral service is another possibility, with users paying on a per-use basis or buying an annual subscription good for a certain amount of research time.

The key to a successful referral service is the quality of the research you do in order to screen the businesses and professionals you send people to. Your credibility depends on people being able to trust the accuracy of your information and the reliability of those to whom you refer them. Therefore, you must gather enough information so that either you can refer with confidence or the consumer can make an informed decision. Some referral services specializing in professional services, such as dentistry or therapy, use a review board to pass on professionals to be served. You'll also need to drop vendors from your referral list who don't meet your standards or about whom you get complaints that are not solved to the customer's satisfaction.

All you need to start a referral service is a business telephone line and well-organized information. This database type of service needs a computer and database software that allows vendors to be listed by the criteria the consumer requests. You'll also need business cards and brochures or flyers suited to the type of vendor you specialize in making referrals to. You'll need a more expensively produced brochure for professionals than you will for tradespeople. If you're able to use flyers, you may be able to distribute them to potential users of your service as well. For example, let's suppose you are starting a home-repair referral service. Leave flyers with hardware stores, and post them on grocery-store bulletin boards, on church bulletin boards, on car windshields, and in mall or boutique parking lots.

If you can afford to do so, advertise on the radio and television (it can be cheaper than you think!), in a *Pennysaver*-type newspaper, and/or in the local newspaper. Such advertising will not only attract calls, but also make it easier to sell your services to vendors, since they know you are making an investment to reach people who want to use them. You can also write articles for local publications on choosing the right repair person.

Franchises in this field are offered by Family Friend Management, (895 Mount Vernon Highway, N.W., Atlanta, GA 30327; 404/255-2848), Homewatch, (2865 South Colorado Boulevard, Denver, CO 80222; 303/758-7290), and the National Tenant Network, (Box 1664, Lake Grove, OR 97035; 800/228-0989), which offers computerized tenant-screening services for landlords.

▪ ▪ ▪ ▪

REPAIR SERVICE

Despite the fact that America is said to be a disposable society, most of us prefer to keep what we have if we can keep it in working order. We don't want to dispose of a computer or a VCR that falters after the warranty expires. We don't want to take the washing machine to the dump just because it breaks down. We don't want to throw out our favorite chair just because it has a rip in the upholstery. But we simply don't know how, nor do we usually have the time, to fix the things that break down, rip, or tear. That's why there are literally dozens of business possibilities for repair services. In fact, the number of people doing computer and office machine repair work is expected to grow by 44,000 by the year 2000, which represents a 35 percent growth from 1988.

Repair services run the gamut from the jack-of-all-trades handyman who does small home repairs and remodeling to specialists who repair vinyl, woodwork, windshields, telephones, clocks and watches, home appliances, and— the fastest-growing area—computers and other high-tech products, such as laser and ink-jet printers, fax machines, copiers, and scanners.

A repair business can be started on a part-time basis. Each item has its own potential market as a repair business. A specialist in repairing old watches and clocks, for example, has a natural market in antique shops and their customers. A vinyl repair service mends rips, tears, and color damage to diner seats, automobiles, movie-theater seats, and furniture in sports locations, hospitals, offices, hotels, government agencies, and homes.

Specialized equipment is needed for each type of repair service, but other than the cost of necessary equipment, the start-up costs for a repair business are modest: business cards, well-done flyers or simple brochures stating what you do, and forms for quotes or proposals. Rates vary greatly, ranging from $15 to $100 an hour, depending on what you repair and your location. One formula used by a California firm that calls itself the PC Doctor is to charge a one-hour minimum at $80 an hour. The work is done on-site whenever possible. Parts, which are usually power supplies and disc drives, of course, are additional.

Consider what you have for repairing, and, if necessary, what training you'll need and where that's available—community colleges, trade schools, home study courses. If you are concentrating on small jobs, which is what clients usually have the most difficulty finding people to do, keep your travel area as localized as possible to reduce the amount of nonbillable time you spend driving.

Repair work can come from either the front door or the back door. *Front door* refers to repairs for customers who contact you. The work may be done either on the customers' premises or on your premises. *Back door* refers to work that is brought into a retailer's or a repair shop but that the retailer or shop subcontracts out; the outside repairer then does the work on his or her own premises.

To get front-door work, you can do any of the following.

- Distribute well-done flyers or simple brochures in your neighborhood. For office equipment repairs, focus particularly on small offices, schools, and businesses.
- Post flyers with tear-off phone numbers at bus stops and on kiosks and bulletin boards.
- For office products, like computers, that have user groups, circulate or post flyers at meetings.
- Run classified and small display ads in neighborhood publications and local business journals, which reach potential customers at a reasonable cost.
- Advertise in the yellow pages.

To get back-door work, contact retailers and repair shops directly.

Resources to help getting into a repair business include:

Vinyl

The Vinylman Company, 13453 Pumice Street, Norwalk, CA 90650; (213) 921-9993. Not only provides you with materials to set up a vinyl-repair inventory, but also offers courses all over the country to train new business owners in the basics of vinyl recoloring and repair.

Upholstery

The Foley-Belshaw Institute, 6301 Equitable Road, Box 593, Kansas City, MO (800) 821-3475. Offers an at-home study course in upholstery repair; $699.

A. Weldon Kent Enterprises, 2641 Esplanade, Redondo Beach, CA 95926. Publishes a book that teaches the art of upholstery.

SMALL ENGINES

McGraw-Hill's NRI Schools, 4401 Connecticut Avenue, N.W., Washington, DC 20008. Offers a course in small-engine repair for $1,495 that includes a small engine and generator.

WINDSHIELDS

GlasWeld, 63065 Sherman Road, Bend, OR (800) 321-2597. Offers start-up kits for $299 to $2,995.

HOME REPAIRS

Handyman House Calls, 640 Northland Road, #33, Forest Park, OH 45240; (513) 825-3863. A franchise that provides handymen to do home maintenance and repair. Their fee is $6,250.

COMPUTER REPAIRS

Computer Repair Service Business Guide, *Entrepreneur* magazine, 2392 Morse Avenue, Box 19787, Irvine, CA 92713; (800) 421-2300; in California, (800) 352-7449. Cost: $69.95.

McGraw Hill's NRI Schools. 4401 Connecticut Avenue, N.W., Washington, DC 20008. Offers a course in microcomputers and microprocessors for $2,495 that includes a computer and diagnostic hardware and software.

■ ■ ■ ■

RESTORATION SERVICE

Consumers today no longer simply cover stained hardwood floors with linoleum; they want the floors sanded, stained, and finished to bring out the old luster, sometimes with modern protections. They don't throw out old rugs and carpets; they want them repaired and restored. They prefer the old enameled iron or porcelain plumbing fixtures to the new plastic variety, and they want someone to refurbish the old finishes. They don't take the old dining table to the dump; they want it carefully hand stripped, and they want the damage repaired and the wood and carvings restored to their original beauty. They sometimes even want to have the furniture stripped and then do the rest themselves. They don't want to rip out and replace old tile work. They want to see cracks and glazing repaired and refinished. They don't tear down old houses; they want to match the detailing that remains and restore old homes to their original appearance.

Both appreciation for what's old and the cost of what's new are making restoring architectural features, plumbing fixtures, floors, and antiques into lucrative businesses that can be started on the side and built into full-time businesses. Each specialty provides a natural market for the skilled craftsperson or someone wishing to develop a skill.

Like many repair businesses, these are based on getting a deposit from the customer to cover parts and materials. It's also important to provide the customer with a written proposal and to get a signed contract so both you and the customer know precisely what work will be done and for what price.

In addition to working with residential clients, you can also work with commercial ones, such as antique shops and interior designers. A business or an apartment or hotel owner can save thousands of dollars by restoring floors, bathrooms, tile, or even quantities of damaged furniture rather than replacing them.

To reach residential customers, you can rely on yellow-pages ads; flyers posted on bulletin boards and kiosks, and in antique shops, hardware stores, and lumber yards; radio advertising; and tear-off pads. It is far easier to reach commercial clients. You can contact them with letters, brochures, and personal selling. Sometimes a single commercial client can become an ongoing source of business, keeping you busy part of each week.

In either case, in addition to a yellow-pages ad, you will want to get as much publicity about your service as possible. Publicity will give you credibility with both consumers and businesses. Your publicity campaign might involve writing articles for the local newspaper or regional magazine on such subjects as how to decide if something is worth restoring, the various types of restoration methods available (including the pros and cons of each, or the ways to prolong the life of wood, tile, enamel, floors, or whatever else your specialty might be. You can also send news releases to the home-improvement or antiques editor of your local newspaper that focus on a particularly unusual item or location that you have restored.

Start-up costs for a restoration business depend entirely on the particular type of restoration service you wish to perform and can range from around $100 (to purchase strippers, rags, steel wool, and sandpaper) for small projects (more if you want a small compressor for cleaning crevices) to as much as $17,500 for some restoration franchises. In fact, there are a number of restoration franchises that provide training, tools, and materials for a turnkey business:

Floors. Hardwood Floor Restoration, 2270 Pope Road, Douglasville, GA 30135; (404) 739-6946.

Tile. Ameribrite Systems, 170-180 East Hillsboro Boulevard, Deerfield Beach, FL 33441; (305) 481-2929; Perma-Brite, 88 Pierson Lane, Box 369, Windsor, CT 06095; (203) 683-1957; Perma-Glaze, 1200 North El Dorado Place, Suite A110, Tucson, AZ 85715; (602) 722-9718 or (800) 332-7397.

Baths. Bathcrest, 2425 South Progress Drive, Salt Lake City, UT 84119, (800) 826-6790; Worldwide Refinishing Systems, 508 Lake Air Drive, Waco, TX 76710; (817) 776-4701.

Carpets. Langenwalter Carpet Dye Concept, 4410 East La Palma, Anaheim, CA 92807; (800) 422-4370.

Fixtures. Worldwide Refinishing Systems, 508 Lake Air Drive, Waco, TX 76710; (817) 776-4701.

■ ■ ■ ■

REUNION PLANNER

The 1990s will see more 20-, 25-, and 30-year high-school and college reunions than any other decade in history. Besides perhaps reviving styles of the '60s and '70s, why is this important? Because reunions provide the basis for a happy kind of service business. In the past, reunions were arranged by people who had more time than today's two-career and single-parent households, so today the staging of reunions is often turned over to paid planners.

The job of a reunion planner is to locate missing class members, mail invitations, take reservations, hire the band or disc jockey, arrange for food, make name tags with yearbook pictures on them, and otherwise coordinate all aspects of the actual reunion. In addition to high-school and college graduating classes, other groups that have reunions include military units, former dormitory residents, and families.

What primarily differentiates reunion planners from party or event planners is their ability to locate long-lost class members. The focus of the party is the people, not the event. So it is a highly specialized undertaking, and even the criteria for selecting locations, food, and decorations are different from those associated with other kinds of parties.

Locating classmates involves making telephone calls; searching computer databases; contacting college record keepers, alumni associations, and previous employers; searching telephone directories, birth and marriage records, and voter registration lists; tracking through friends, neighbors, and associates; and even using special tracking companies such as Re-Unite of Florida.

The size of this research task is one of the reasons reunion planners start their work a year or more in advance of a reunion.

According to Judy and Shell Norris, founders of Class Reunions, the first reunion planning business in the country, this work is seasonal, with the season running from April through Thanksgiving. Judy and Shell plan approximately 100 reunions per year from their home and employ over 20 home-based researchers and six other people.

Reunion planners take their fee from the money paid by each attendee—the more people who show up, the higher the income per reunion. Thus reunion committees do not risk any money, and reunion planners are rewarded for their success in getting large turnouts.

To get started, begin with smaller reunions. Once established, you can set minimums, such as a class having at least 300 members to get a better return on your time. Annual income from reunion planning can range from something you do part-time to six figures.

To get an idea of how many reunions are being held in your area, just count the number of high schools. Each year there are likely to be as many as eight reunions per high school: 5-year, 10-year, 15-year, 20-year, 25-year, 30-year, 40-year, and 50-year.

To get started, you need business cards, stationery, a brochure, and a computer with database and desktop-publishing software. Much of your business will depend on networking, to make contact with reunion committees. Start with your own high school, or your spouse's, or your children's. Make contact with hotels, printers, display companies (for decorations), florists, caterers, public-address-system providers, booking agents, photographers, name-badge suppliers, restaurants, and any other service that might be useful in planning a reunion.

Training to become a reunion planner, and further information, can be obtained from Shell and Judy Norris, (Box 844, Skokie, IL 60076; 708/677-4949). The Norrises are also a way to contact the National Association of Reunion Planners, open to qualified planners.

■ ■ ■ ■

RUBBER STAMP BUSINESS

This business surprised us, but people are making good money making and selling rubber stamps. People love them, and buy them through mail order, at arts-and-crafts shows, and in specialty stores. People are known to sell as much as $2,000 to $5,000 worth of rubber stamps a day at arts-and-crafts shows.

People adorn envelopes and stationery with rubber-stamp impressions of animals, moons, stars, clouds, people, rockets, spaceships, and an endless variety of designs. Using an embossing powder, raised impressions can be created. Metallic and glow-in-the-dark inks humble the customary red and blue stamp pads available in office-supply stores. Special inks enable stamps to be used on fabrics, glossy wrapping papers, foil, and mylar. You can also use rubber stamping techniques to make badges, buttons, and magnets to be sold as gift items by using a Badge-a-Minit system (Badge-a-Minit, 348 North 30th Road, Lasalle, IL 61301; about $50).

It is not difficult to make your own rubber stamps, and you can use free public-domain clip art, which offers an almost unending supply of subjects. If you like to create your own designs, rubber stamps can be the vehicle for you to be a commercially successful artist, with thousands of people enjoying your creations.

New technology has made making rubber stamps easier. Instead of using hot-metal type, matrix boards, and a vulcanizer to melt rubber, nowadays you can produce stamps quickly and easily with a personal computer and laser printer used in conjunction with a photopolymer system ($2,800). The principal source for equipment and supplies is Stewart-Superior (1800 Larchmont Avenue, Chicago, IL 60613; 800/621-1205 or 312/935-6025).

This mini-industry has a newsletter, *Rubber Stamp Madness* (RSM Enterprises, Box 6585, 420 South Geneva Street, Ithaca, NY 14851), listing conventions and equipment manufacturers.

If you make your own stamps, you can sell them at about six times your cost at retail and three times at wholesale; if you resell other people's stamps, you can expect to double your money. Bobby Boschan, who is a partner in Stamps, Stamps, Stamps, in Los Angeles, says many manufacturers sell both retail and wholesale.

■ ■ ■ ■

SIGN MAKER

Can you imagine a city or town without signs? Probably not, because signs are everywhere—not just street signs, but signs on storefronts, buildings, and short and tall posts, in front of homes and farms, scattered through parks and zoos, and generally in most places we look. These signs tell us more than the name of the business or individual occupying a building; they give us more than a direction or an instruction. A good sign not only conveys basic information about who or what is located there, but also communicates something about the occupants and what they do.

Ken Berry got the idea for a sign-making business when visiting a friend who published a magazine for people selling their own homes. Ken's friend was overwhelmed with work, so Ken answered the phone for him and discovered people were asking where they could get a good real-estate sign. Ken went home and started making For Sale by Owner signs that he now sells through retail outlets such as hardware stores. Ken also makes customized signs for realtors, lumber companies, contractors, architects, roofing companies, boat brokers, and boat owners.

To make good signs, you need to have an eye for design. However signmaking is simpler now than it was in the past thanks to optical scanners, computer-aided design software, drawing software, and plotters that hold a knife that cuts pressure-sensitive films, which become the sign bases. The same process can be used for car detailing, awnings, and T-shirts, which can provide additional sources of income.

To sell your sign-making services, you need samples of signs you have made. In order to make signs for a type of business he's never made signs for, Ken Berry will make signs for one or two customers at near cost in order to have them for his portfolio. Ken points out that the customer, therefore, is "paying for your setup and the cost of your samples." Another idea is to create custom signs for worthy causes or highly trafficked locations that will get people talking about your work.

A natural source of customers is people who have signs that need replacing; it just takes observation and shoe leather to find them. Ken Berry says, "The trick is being willing to make sales calls. People will procrastinate making a sign, so you need to go to them. Then you need to show them enough samples that they're making a choice—not deciding yes or no.

Real-estate brokers are a good source of referrals as well as of information on what people are paying for signs and whether they're happy with the quality of the signs they have. Another source of customers is new businesses, which you can find in the listings of new businesses in your city's daily or weekly business journal.

The price for just one or two signs can run from $30 to $50, but if a customer buys 50 signs, the price can come down to about $3 each. For that kind of quantity, you'll need to use a printing press. If you bring the ink and screen to a printer, so the printer is supplying only the press and labor, you should be able to find printers who will print at a reasonable price. Printing on plastic is almost as economic as printing on cardboard, and your customers will be happier. If you get your own printing press, which you may be able to find used for $6,000 to $7,000, you'll need enough space both for the press and for drying racks for the signs. Sign making can easily be started as a part-time venture and later developed into a full-time business.

■ ■ ■ ■

TAPE DUPLICATING SERVICE

A spare bedroom, attic, garage, or basement can be a suitable setting for an audio and video duplicating service. Such a service makes copies of audio and/or video tapes for customers such as businesses wanting employees or customers to receive taped information; motivational speakers and professionals wanting to sell tapes of their speeches and seminars; associations that want to sell copies of their workshops and meeting sessions; musicians wanting to produce their own recordings for sale or as dubs for auditions; individuals who want to have old beta-format tapes converted to VHS or eight millimeter; and people who want copies of their home movies.

You can start with only one type of duplication-and-conversion machine and grow to multiple machines for large orders and for converting from multiple formats. With some equipment you can also add titles, voice-overs, and graphics to videotapes. You should invest in the best professional equipment you can afford, preferably equipment that can be added to and upgraded with ease. Approximately $1,000 to $1,500 should cover your initial equipment costs and a stock of tapes. Buying used equipment can reduce your start-up costs.

Most major urban areas have a variety of equipment sellers and renters. Renting first, even though it is more costly than buying, allows you to become familiar with a particular type of equipment before you purchase it and gives you time to determine what direction your business will take.

A general working knowledge of audio and video equipment and formats is helpful. Also, a knowledge of electronic technology will be extremely useful, particularly if you don't have access to a technician. But more important is your knowledge of the market. If that market is already pretty well covered, you will need to specialize—to think up new wrinkles to the business that no one has covered.

However, there is one great caveat for any tape-duplicating service. Duplicating tapes that are protected by copyright is illegal. Doing so innocently can still result in a hefty fine and open you up to lawsuits. Selling illegally copied tapes can get you a hefty jail sentence as well. Therefore, you must be certain that the customer either owns the material outright or has bought, leased, or been granted the rights to the material to be duplicated.

You can charge by the hour for studio work and by the tape. We found pricing for duplicating audiotapes varies all the way from 75 cents to $3 each. Videotapes are copied at an hourly rate ranging from $5 to $10. You can expand into providing other services such as taping conferences and speaking events on-site and recording tapes for clients in your own studio; however, zoning may prevent you from having people record in your studio. Other events that you can tape include training sessions, seminars, intracompany video memos, and so forth. You might also consider a service that transfers 35-millimeter slides to videotape, makes 35-millimeter slides from videotape, or makes films for overhead projectors from 35-millimeter slides, videotape, or computer screens. You might even consider your own home recording studio for local musicians.

Each of these related activities requires additional equipment, of course, but they can be piggybacked onto your duplication service as a natural extension of what you are doing. One way of earning additional money is to contract with large taping facilities for jobs too large to do on your own equipment. In this way you can bid on big jobs, earning money as essentially a broker.

■ ■ ■ ■

TOUR OPERATOR

People spend more of their leisure time traveling than they do reading, watching sports, pursuing hobbies, and attending church and cultural events. And by addressing people's passion for travel, you earn a living while fulfilling your own love of travel. Although restrictions on airline ticketing may prevent your having a full travel agency in your home, you can associate with a company like Computerized Travel Services Network, which for $8,000 will sell you the opportunity to provide travel-agency services in your home, or you can organize and package tours from your home.

Probably because travel is so popular, multiple words describe the same thing: *tour operators* are the same as *trip packagers*, *travel organizers*, and *travel coordinators*.

Tour operators organize and conduct tours, charging participants a fee sufficient to cover their costs and make a profit. Tours best suited to a home business cater to highly specialized interests like fitness tours, spiritual tours, tours of English gardens, tours of the great vineyards, and so forth. Many of the most popular involve adventure, such as rock-climbing tours, kayaking tours, bicycle tours, river-rafting tours, and cross-country or downhill ski tours.

To succeed in the tour business, you must have a knowledge of unique places or experiences that you can share with others. For example, if you lead tours to Europe, you need to be fluent in one or more European languages and know the countryside and sites where you will be traveling. If you lead rock-climbing expeditions, you must be an expert climber and be familiar with the particular routes you will be covering.

If you are a tour operator, you must not only know uniquely pleasurable locations and excursions, but also be able to sell your tours and orchestrate the entire trip for all those who participate. You plan the tour, make the arrangements, and recruit the participants—and you can even lead the tour. There are considerable up-front costs involved in undertaking a tour (attractive brochures, direct mail, tour buses, and so forth), so you need to get nonrefundable, partial or full deposits to help cover these costs. You can set your fees at 40 percent above your costs. So if you package only 5 tours a year for 20 people each and charge $2,000 for the tour, your gross profit will be $80,000.

Success as a tour operator depends on three things. You must: (1) estimate your costs accurately and then keep them within that budget; (2) fill all the openings on your tour; and (3) plan and provide appealing, rewarding tours, because much of your future business will come from repeat customers. Usually this means finding a specialty or niche that you understand well. For example, Patricia and Ronald Douglas operate Northstar Tours for senior citizens. Another popular type of tour to package is wilderness trips for women over the age of 30 who are inexperienced with the outdoors. Other tour operators specialize in tours for families with children or side trips for business executives attending trade and professional conventions.

There is a National Tour Association (Box 3071, Lexington, KY 40596; 606/253-1036). If you're interested in acting as a travel agent, you can contact Computerized Travel Services Network at 4388 Civic Center Plaza, Suite 200, Scottsdale, AZ 85251; (800) 735-0541. A book on small-business opportunities in the travel industry is *For Fun and Profit: Self-Employment Opportunities in Recreation, Sports and Travel,* by Crawford Lindsey (Boulder, CO: Live Oak Publications, 1984).

APPENDIX

. . . .

Lists of Top-10 Best Businesses

Based on the kinds of characteristics people interested in a business that they can operate from home have told us are important to them, we have selected the businesses that possess those qualities to the greatest degree. In most instances, what the following lists describe is obvious. However, a word of explanation about several of the lists is in order.

In one we list what we've called *evergreen* businesses. An evergreen business does work that that is always in demand and may well always be. Working alone, one is not apt to get rich or famous at an evergreen. This is a trade-off, for others have trod the way to establish this businesses.

The businesses listed under *Easiest to Enter* are those we think take the least education or experience to enter.

BEST ALL AROUND

Bill Auditing Service
Cleaning Services
Mailing-List Service
Medical-Claims Processing Service
Medical Transcription Service
Note Reader/Scopist
Pet Sitting Service
Repair Services
Rubber Stamp Business
Temporary Help Service

EASIEST TO ENTER

Auto Detailing Service
Cleaning Services
Grower of Specialty Foods
Hauling Service
In-Home Health Care
Mailing-List Service
Manufacturers' Agent
Pet Sitting Service
Rubber Stamp Business
Tape Duplication Service

HIGHEST INCOME POTENTIAL

Bill Auditing Service
Business Broker
Business Plan Writer
Computer Tutor and Trainer
Desktop Video
Executive Search
Export Agent
Management Consultant
Professional Practice Consultant
Rubber Stamp Business

BEST-KEPT SECRETS

Association Management Service
Bill Auditing Service
Business Plan Writer
In-Home Health Care
Leak Detection Service
Medical-Claims Processing Service
Pet Sitting Service
Rubber Stamp Business
Tape Duplicating Service
Transcript Digesting Service

FASTEST-GROWING FIELDS

Cleaning Services
Computer Consultant/Computer Programmer
Executive Search
Management Consultant
Medical Transcription Service
Paralegal
Public Relations Specialist
Repair Services
Technical Writer
Temporary Help Service

HIGHEST DEMAND—EASIEST TO SELL

Bill Auditing Service
Cleaning Services
Home Inspector
Leak Detection Service
Medical Billing Service
Medical-Claims Processing Service
Medical Transcription Service
Note Reader/Scopist
Repair Services
Rubber Stamp Business

MOST RECESSION RESISTANT

Bill Auditing Service
Bookkeeping Service
Collection Agency
Medical Billing Service
Medical-Claims Processing Service
Medical Transcription Service
Note Reader/Scopist
Repair Services
Resume Writing Service
Temporary Help Service

LOWEST START-UP COSTS

Abstracting and Indexing Services
Cleaning Services
Day-Care Provider
Gift Basket Business
In-Home Health Care
Manufacturers' Agent
Pet Sitting Service
Technical Writer
Wedding Consultant
Wedding Makeup Artist

LOWEST STRESS

Auto Detailing Service
Facialist
Fitness Trainer
Grower of Specialty Foods
Mailing-List Service
Note Reader/Scopist
Pet Sitting Service
Pool Maintenance Service
Restoration Service
Rubber Stamp Business

EVERGREEN BUSINESSES

Bookkeeping Service
Cleaning Services
Collection Agency
Computer Programmer
Hauling Service
Mailing-List Service
Medical Transcription Service
Repair Services
Word Processing Service
Tax Preparation Service

UP AND COMING HOME BUSINESSES

900-Number Audiotext Service
Consultants of all types
Desktop Video
Home Inspector
Indoor Environmental Tester
Information Search and Retrieval Service
In-Home Health Care
Real-Estate Appraiser
Referral Service
Temporary Help Service

INDEX

■■■■■■■■■■■■■■■■■■■■■■■■

Do You Have Questions?

The authors of this book, Paul and Sarah Edwards, want to answer your questions. They can respond to you, usually within 24 hours, by leaving a message for them on the *Working From Home Forum* on CompuServe Information Service.

If you have a computer and access to CompuServe, simply type "GO WORK" at any "!" prompt; their ID is 76703,242. If you do not now have access to CompuServe, you can obtain a complimentary CompuServe membership and receive $15.00 of free connect time by calling 1-800-524-3388. Ask for Operator 395.

If you do not have a computer, you can write to Paul and Sarah in care of "Ask Paul & Sarah," *Home Office Computing* magazine, 730 Broadway, New York, NY 10003. Your question may be selected to be answered in their monthly column. However, they cannot respond to every letter.